THE LIFE OF
FREDERICK THE GREAT

THE LIFE OF
FREDERICK THE GREAT

By FRANCIS KUGLER

Comprehending a Complete History of the Silesian Campaign and The Thirty Years' War

WITH AN INTRODUCTION
By G. MERCER ADAM

WITH ILLUSTRATIONS

A. L. BURT COMPANY, ❧ ❧ ❧ ❧
❧ ❧ ❧ PUBLISHERS, NEW YORK

Copyright, 1902,
BY E. A. BRAINERD,

PREFACE.

FREDERICK THE GREAT—who in many cases served as the model for England's ablest foe, the Emperor Napoleon—was one of those monarchs whose lives form at once the most interesting and instructive episodes in the annals of history. Subject in childhood to the insane whims of a half-crazed father—the victim of unexampled parental tyranny—his very life in momentary danger from the sword which still dripped with the blood of his dearest friend, the period of his youth was rendered one of more than tragic interest. Arrived at manhood, we find him seated on a throne which totters beneath the repeated shocks of his countless foes; at once calculating and bold, he rushes to the field, dissipates the hosts of adversaries, and returns in triumph to his capital. From thenceforward his existence seems to oscillate between the laurel-wreath which was to deck his brow in the event of victory, and the poison-phial which was to terminate his existence, when, outnumbered and defeated, he wished to spare his country the cost of his ransom. A career so chequered must of itself prove interesting to the reader; but Frederick has other claims on the attention beyond his merits as a warrior. The originality of his views—the enlightened character of his policy—his talents as a legislator, statesman, and scholar, must render his reign the most interesting epoch in the history of Europe. Alike distinguished in the cabinet and the camp, the virtual

PREFACE.

founder of the present monarchy of Prussia, his name will descend to distant ages as the most uncompromising champion of his country's rights: time will but confirm his title to the flattering distinction which his countrymen have conferred in styling him THE GREAT.

CONTENTS.

BOOK I.—YOUTH.

	PAGE
CHAPTER I.	
BIRTH AND BAPTISM	1
CHAPTER II.	
INFANCY	6
CHAPTER III.	
BOYHOOD	13
CHAPTER IV.	
DISUNION BETWEEN FATHER AND SON	19
CHAPTER V.	
DISCORD BETWEEN FATHER AND SON	29
CHAPTER VI.	
ATTEMPT AT FLIGHT	39
CHAPTER VII.	
THE TRIAL	45
CHAPTER VIII.	
THE RECONCILIATION	57
CHAPTER IX.	
MARRIAGE	65
CHAPTER X.	
FIRST SIGHT OF ACTUAL WARFARE	72
CHAPTER XI.	
RESIDENCE IN RHEINSBERG	79
CHAPTER XII.	
DEATH OF THE FATHER	92

CONTENTS.

BOOK II.—GLORY.

	PAGE
CHAPTER XIII.	
FREDERICK'S ACCESSION	97
CHAPTER XIV.	
OPENING OF THE SILESIAN WAR	109
CHAPTER XV.	
CAMPAIGN OF THE YEAR 1741	120
CHAPTER XVI.	
CAMPAIGN OF THE YEAR 1742	134
CHAPTER XVII.	
TWO YEARS' PEACE	142
CHAPTER XVIII.	
OPENING OF THE SECOND SILESIAN WAR.—CAMPAIGN OF THE YEAR 1744	150
CHAPTER XIX.	
CAMPAIGN OF THE YEAR 1745	158
CHAPTER XX.	
CONCLUDING CAMPAIGN OF THE SECOND SILESIAN WAR	169
CHAPTER XXI.	
FREDERICK'S ADMINISTRATION UP TO THE SEVEN YEARS' WAR,	176
CHAPTER XXII.	
THE PHILOSOPHER OF SANS-SOUCI	191
CHAPTER XXIII.	
POLITICAL RELATIONS PREVIOUS TO THE SEVEN YEARS' WAR.	204

BOOK III.—HEROISM.

CHAPTER XXIV.	
FIRST CAMPAIGN OF THE SEVEN YEARS' WAR	212
CHAPTER XXV.	
OPENING OF THE CAMPAIGN OF 1757.—PRAGUE AND KOLLIN	223
CHAPTER XXVI.	
CONTINUATION OF THE CAMPAIGN OF 1757	236

CONTENTS.

CHAPTER XXVII.
CONTINUATION OF THE CAMPAIGN OF 1757.—ROSSBACH 241

CHAPTER XXVIII.
CONCLUSION OF THE CAMPAIGN OF 1757.— LEUTHEN 252

CHAPTER XXIX.
OPENING OF THE CAMPAIGN OF 1758.—THE EXPEDITION TO MORAVIA 264

CHAPTER XXX.
CONTINUATION OF THE CAMPAIGN OF 1758.—ZORNDORF 275

CHAPTER XXXI.
CONCLUSION OF THE CAMPAIGN OF 1758.—HOCHKIRCH 285

CHAPTER XXXII.
CAMPAIGN OF THE YEAR 1759.—CUNNERSDORF 302

CHAPTER XXXIII.
OPENING OF THE CAMPAIGN OF 1760.—DRESDEN AND LIEGNITZ, 322

CHAPTER XXXIV.
CONCLUSION OF THE CAMPAIGN OF 1760.—TORGAU 338

CHAPTER XXXV.
CAMPAIGN OF 1761.—THE CAMP AT BUNZELWITZ 350

CHAPTER XXXVI.
CONCLUSION OF THE CAMPAIGN OF 1761.—THE CAMP AT STREHLEN 359

CHAPTER XXXVII.
CAMPAIGN OF 1762. BURKERSDORF AND SCHWEIDNITZ.—PEACE, 367

BOOK IV.—OLD AGE.

CHAPTER XXXVIII.
ORDERING OF INTERNAL RELATIONS DURING PEACE 381

CHAPTER XXXIX.
FRIENDLY RELATIONS WITH RUSSIA AND AUSTRIA.—ACQUISITION OF WEST PRUSSIA 391

CONTENTS.

CHAPTER XL.
FREDERICK'S SOLICITUDE FOR GERMANY. — THE BAVARIAN WAR OF SUCCESSION.—THE PRINCES' LEAGUE............ 407

CHAPTER XLI.
FREDERICK'S INTERNAL ADMINISTRATION FROM THE PERIOD OF THE SEVEN YEARS' WAR................................ 417

CHAPTER XLII.
FREDERICK'S DOMESTIC LIFE IN OLD AGE.................... 428

CHAPTER XLIII.
FREDERICK'S DEATH... 442

FREDERICK'S LAST WILL AND TESTAMENT..................... 451

INTRODUCTORY NOTE.

ALMOST numberless are the instances of writers, as well as nations, who have come under the glamour of a great historic name. Mr. Kugler, in his able and vigorously written Life of Frederick the Second, styled "the Great," is himself an example of this, for his Memoir is a eulogy of the great Prussian soldier and his phenomenal military career, one of conquest and glory, without, as we think, giving due consideration to the crime his hero committed in invading and wresting Silesia—the loved inheritance of Maria Theresa—from Hapsburg dominion, in the interest of Prussian hegemony and ascendancy. The conduct of Frederick in his aggression on Austria in Silesia is, we know, palliated by some historians on the plea that Prussia had some early claim to the region; while they excuse his act on religious grounds, in that it was the spoliation of a Catholic by a Protestant power—a plea certainly flimsy enough when one remembers how little of a Christian was the cynical materialist Frederick, save in his toleration of all religions. Moreover, had he not given his adhesion to the provisions of the Pragmatic Sanction of Charles VI., which guaranteed, after the latter's death, the indivisibility of Austrian territories; and was not his act a defiance of international morality in the interest of his own ambition, while he put a reproach upon his gallantry by a cruel wrong done to a woman? The consequences were terrible, in that Frederick, taking advantage of the crisis that arose over the Austrian Succession set Europe aflame for years, and clouded the judgment of the world upon a cause by the bloody triumphs of battle. Aside, however, from the question of morals

INTRODUCTORY NOTE.

involved in a consideration of the origin of the conflict, Frederick's career from its outbreak, in 1740, to the close of the War of Austrian Succession, in 1748, and throughout its terrible aftermath, in the Seven Years' War, is a confirmation of the Prussian king's title to fame as a renowned warrior; while great also were his statesmanship and administrative qualities, and heroic his courage and determined will under disaster and defeat and the depressing circumstances in which he often found himself. These high qualities are flatteringly dwelt upon in the following pages by the patriotic historian and art-critic, Mr. Kugler, who finds in his world-famed royal countryman his ideal of his hero, whom he naturally reveres as the maker of Modern Germany, and in many respects justly eulogizes for his ever-memorable services to the Fatherland.

England's aid to Frederick, Mr. Kugler properly acknowledges, not only in that nation's early endeavor to mediate between Prussia and the Empress-Queen of Austria, and, when war was launched, by sending him troops and money subsidies; but also in the part she took against France on the continent and in wresting Canada from her Gallic foe in the New World. Helpful also to Prussia was England's struggle in India, in ending French dominion in the Far East, and in her successful efforts, as a maritime nation, to win supremacy on the sea. The influence of all this aid to Prussia obviously was substantial, and greatly helped Frederick when beleaguered by the combination of European Powers, with its disasters as well as victories; while, when the end came, it secured him in the occupation and retention of Silesia.

The annals of the Seven Years' War on the Continent, beginning with Federick's invasions of Saxony and Bohemia, are fully narrated by Mr. Kugler, with their vividly described accounts of sieges and long list of stubbornly contested battles, including Prussia's memorable victories over the French at Rossbach, over the Austrians at Leuthen, and over the Russians at Zorndorf. In these

INTRODUCTORY NOTE.

and other sanguinary fields Frederick proved his consummate skill as a strategist, tactician, and master of the art of war. With the campaign of 1762, after many darkenings and brightenings of Prussia's prospects, peace at last fell upon the several contestants; while all were exhausted in both men and money by the prolonged and bloody conflict. In the final result, Frederick's courage, constancy, and skill met with their reward; while a new era of consolidated power, with quickened progress and remarkable expanding forces, fell upon the newly-arisen Prussian Nation.

G. MERCER ADAM.

FREDERICK THE GREAT.

CHAPTER I.

BIRTH AND BAPTISM.

FREDERICK, on whom his contemporaries conferred the title of the Great—an honorary distinction which succeeding generations have concurred in adopting—was born on the 21st of January, 1712, in the royal palace at Berlin. His birth was naturally greeted with every demonstration of joy, for in him centred all the hopes of the royal family. Although at the time of his birth, his grandfather, King Frederick I., still occupied the Prussian throne, yet, as the father was an only child, and had already lost two sons in the first stages of infancy, there appeared but too good grounds for apprehending a failure of direct heirs, and the consequent passage of the crown to some collateral branch of the family. It is said that the glad tidings were conveyed to the ruling monarch just as the ceremonies of the dinner-table were about to commence; that he instantly arose from his seat, and hastened to offer his congratulations to the august patient on her safe delivery, and, in person, greet the future inheritor of his crown. The merry peals of the church-bells, and the thunder of the guns from the ramparts, soon spread the joyous intelligence throughout the capital. Numerous were the promotions and advancements in honor of the occasion, and the distribution of alms throughout the various poor-houses of the city tended to heighten the universal festivity of the day.

Frederick I. had inherited his dominions from his father, Frederick William, surnamed the Great Elector. To the Great Elector belongs the honor of having been the first, who, after the prostration of Germany's energies through the horrors of the Thirty Years' War, succeeded in vindicating the honor of the Teutonic name, and resisting the encroachments of France. His dominions, originally mere settlements of some Wendish tribes, were by him raised to such a degree of political power and importance, as could not fail of commanding respect. In short, he fought so successfully and governed so wisely, as to awaken the jealousy of the imperial court of Austria; it being but little in accordance with the views of his imperial majesty, then struggling for unlimited sovereignty over Germany, that any considerable share of power should fall into the hands of subordinate electoral princes. The bare idea of a new Wendish king starting up on the shores of the Baltic, was of itself sufficient to create uneasiness at Vienna.

Frederick had to the many measures of his father superadded one, which, though it has been at times derided as puerile, ultimately proved of incalculable importance, and evinced no ordinary degree of political foresight in its author. He erected his Duchy of East Prussia, (West Prussia had been already wrested by the Poles from its former masters,) which formed no part of the empire, into a monarchy, and placed the royal crown upon his own head on the 18th of January, 1701. In the accomplishment of this design he was continually thwarted by Austria; but the untiring perseverance with which he pursued his aim eventually triumphed over all obstacles. The real importance of this measure is attested by the dictum of Prince Eugene of Savoy—at once the greatest statesman and soldier that Austria could then boast—who pronounced "the ministers, by whose advice the emperor had been induced to recognize the independence of Prussia as a monarchy, deserving of death." And, in truth, the title of King and the ceremonials of royalty were, in that punctilious age, far from being mere empty forms, as Prussia was thereby placed in a position, as regarded the empire—the power of which was daily sinking —that could not fail of suggesting a struggle for independence. To the final success, however, of this struggle, a very considerable development of the resources of the Brandenburg-Prussian state was absolutely essential.

It was not accorded to the first monarch of this kingdom to complete the task he had begun. For the accomplishment of a design so vast, a combination of favorable external and internal relations was altogether indispensable. Frederick contented himself with giving to his crown that lustre which he deemed essential to the support of its dignity, and which, at the period we allude to, was in reality not without its value. He introduced dazzling ceremonials, and performed all their exactions with the most untiring assiduity. He celebrated the memorable events of his reign with a degree of pomp and magnificence that filled his neighbors with astonishment, and inspired the hearts of his subjects with feelings at once of admiration and awe. He at the same time displayed much mildness of character, and was really beloved by those he governed. Nor was he less anxious to impart a more elevated character to the externals of pageantry by a liberal patronage of science and art. Noble works of genius were called by him into being. Andreas Schlüter, who for many years enjoyed his patronage in Berlin, was an artist, such as the world has not for many years prior nor subsequently seen. To this monarch the Berlin Academy of Sciences is indebted for its existence; an institution of which Leibnitz, unquestionably the greatest philosopher of his age, was the soul, although it was found impossible to induce him to take up a permanent residence at Berlin. At the period to which we allude Berlin was universally known as the German Athens.

The birth of a future successor, especially under the circumstances above recorded, appeared to be an event by far too important not to form a fitting occasion for an unusual display of regal pomp and magnificence. The circumstance of the birth of the infant prince having occurred in the month of January, the same in which the coronation of his grandfather had taken place, was regarded as a highly favorable omen; and in order to lend additional importance to this coincidence, it was arranged that the baptismal rites should be administered within that month. Accordingly, on the 31st of January the christening took place, in the chapel attached to the royal palace, attended with extraordinary splendor. The distance from the chambers of the infant prince to the palace was lined with double files of Swiss and Life-Guards. The Margravine Albert, the king's sister-in-law, supported by her husband and the Margrave Louis, bore the royal infant in her arms. The latter wore on his head a small gold crown, and was arrayed in a robe of silver tissue, sparkling with brilliants, the train of which was borne by six countesses. The king and queen, together with the infant's father, and Prince Leopold of Anhalt-Dessau, the warrior so illustrious in the annals of Prussia, awaited within the chapel the arrival of the procession. The monarch stood beneath a gorgeous canopy embroidered with gold, the four supporters of which were borne by as many chamberlains, whilst each of the four tassels was held by a knight of the order of the Black Eagle. In front of the king stood a table, sustaining a costly baptismal font. The infant was then placed in the monarch's arms, and received, in honor of its grandfather, the name of Frederick. The numerous bells throughout the city now pealed out anew, seconded by the volleys of the artillery, whilst the ceremonies within the chapel proceeded amidst the most entrancing strains of sacred music. Brilliant fêtes at court closed the festivities of the joyous day.

Some months subsequent to the birth of the prince, during the summer of 1712, an American aloe was observed to blossom in the royal gardens of Köpeneck, near Berlin. This plant had stood there, without blossoming, for a period of forty years. Its stem was full thirty feet in height, and not less than 7277 of its blossoms had been counted. Crowds streamed from far and near to gaze at this giant-flower; and its surpassing grandeur formed the subjects of pamphlets and poems. It was regarded as symbolical of that splendor which Prussia was destined one day to attain; and this allegorical signification was amply wrought out in the form of mottoes and devices. The hopes which the birth of an heir had awakened, appeared to derive additional confirmation from this event. Nor was the fact of the plant itself decaying, whilst its flowery crown retained all its pristine beauty, left uninterpreted; this being held to forebode the speedy dissolution of the regnant monarch. Such an interpretation was, in truth, not very hazardous; for the king, whose constitution was from infancy feeble, had been for some time indisposed. And, indeed the birth of an heir was the last gleam of splendor that gladdened his career.

The following anniversary festival in honor of his birthday was the last occasion of his appearing in public. The disease under which he labored now assumed a very dangerous character, so much so, that on the 13th of February he summoned the various members of his household and family to his bedside, and there took a formal leave of them. On the 28th of February he expired, after having conferred his solemn blessing on the prince royal and his grandchildren, as they knelt beside his couch.

CHAPTER II.

INFANCY.

DURING the period immediately succeeding the accession of Frederick William I. to the throne, now rendered vacant by the death of his father, vast changes were introduced, as well in the government of Prussia, as in the household and domestic arrangements of the royal family. The character of Frederick William I. was diametrically opposed to that of his father. To him the strict formalities, in which he had been hitherto obliged to acquiesce, were burthensome, and the costly pomp of royal festivities absolutely odious. The higher walks of science and the amenities of refinement, for which his mother, the highly accomplished Charlotte Sophia, likewise deceased, had endeavored to inspire him with a love, were in his eyes alike worthless, nay, even regarded as injurious. Nature had formed his mind in a decidedly practical mould. His efforts were directed to replenish his exchequer, instead of permitting it to be drained by the lavish expenditure of an extravagant household, or the rapacious cupidity of court favorites; and, by arousing his subjects to the advantages of unremitting industry, he strove to advance the general prosperity of his kingdom. He determined that the authority and dignity of his crown should be no longer sustained by a brilliancy that dazzled, but by a numerous and well-disciplined army. That the festivities, which were to shed lustre on his career, should consist in displays of the arts of war. His indefatigable zeal and perseverance succeeded in introducing a degree

INFANCY.   7

of rapidity, uniformity, and precision in the execution of military manœuvres, hitherto wholly unknown. He was also particularly anxious that his regiments, especially the foremost ranks, should be distinguished for their personal beauty and lofty stature; nay, he actually went so far as to lavish sums for the attainment of these objects, wholly irreconcilable with his ordinary parsimony. This *penchant* not unfrequently involved him in strife and disputes with the neighboring States, arising out of his forcible abduction of recruits. Berlin, under his government, was no longer termed the German Athens, but the German Sparta.

His private life resembled that of an ordinary citizen, and his frugality—at a time when the corruption of manners at courts was absolutely frightful—is not undeserving of praise. Connubial fidelity occupied the first place in his esteem. It was his wish to bring up his family, which in time became numerous, according to his own strong devotional feelings. His efforts were from an early period directed to accustom them to a regular mode of life, the most implicit obedience and useful occupations, with a view to render them efficient members of society, at least, according to his ideas of efficiency. On the other hand, everything appertaining to science or the elegancies of life was strictly proscribed from his domestic circle. Beneath this rude exterior his heart was German, and he was ever ready to show justice to all who approached him frankly; but, a refractory spirit, or opposition to his well-meant ordinances found in him an inexorable judge; his natural violence of temper leading him, at times, to visit such disobedience with the most extreme rigor.

The early infancy of Frederick, now prince royal, was entrusted to the management of females, as it was impossible that the peculiar tenets and sentiments of the father could be inculcated at so tender an age. His mother, Queen Sophia Dorothea, daughter to the then King of Hanover, (afterwards under the title of George

I. King of England,) was eminent for the good qualities of her heart and by no means so inimical to learning as her spouse. She endeavored to implant her own kind feelings in the bosoms of her children; but she wanted, unhappily, that devoted love, which, in harmony with the will of her husband, might have proved most beneficial to her family.

Madame de Kamecke, one of the ladies-in-waiting on the queen, was the person selected to superintend the education of the prince. Madame de Rocouilles, who acted as under-governess, exerted, however, much more influence on his future destinies, and earned a much larger share of gratitude. The latter had tended the father in his infancy; and her noble and decided character, together with her devoted attachment to the interest of Prussia, recommended her so strongly, that it appeared but a proper act of gratitude to assign her this distinguished office. By birth a Frenchwoman, she belonged to that numerous class of reformers whom bigotry had expelled from France, much to the detriment of that country, and who had found a welcome reception in the Brandenburg States.

It can hardly be a matter of surprise that a Frenchwoman should, even at the court of Frederick William, have been entrusted with the education of children; inasmuch as the world was at that time completely under the influence of French literature, and a knowledge of the French tongue was altogether indispensable for the purpose of conversation in the higher circles of society. Besides, in consequence of all such emigrants as had brought with them any degree of eminence in the arts or sciences having selected Berlin for their place of residence, French was much more generally spoken in that city than elsewhere. Thus, the crown-prince received from his infancy particular instruction in the French language; a circumstance which exerted no inconsiderable influence on his after-life. The fidelity with which his instructress discharged her duty towards him, is amply attested by the permanent attachment which he displayed towards her to the close of her life.

On Frederick's attaining his fourth year a singular prophecy was uttered concerning him. There happened to be at that time several Swedish officers in Berlin, who had been made prisoners of war at the capture of Stralsund, on Christmas-day, 1715, during a war into which Frederick William had been forced by the continual encroachments of Charles XII. of Sweden, and which terminated in the cession of a part of Pomerania to Prussia. One of these officers named Croome, was reputed to possess the power of reading the future in the stars, and the lineaments of the human hand. The whole capital was full of his prophecies; and even the queen and the ladies of the court became anxious to have their future destinies revealed to them. Croome was accordingly summoned to the chambers of her majesty. He here examined the various hands offered for his inspection, and did, in reality, predict events which subsequently came to pass with marvellous exactitude. He announced to the queen, then pregnant, that she would in two months give birth to a daughter. To the eldest princess he foretold a series of delusive hopes, and a life embittered by many sorrows. To some of the ladies of the court he prophesied a speedy and ignominious dismissal. On the crown-prince being presented to him, he predicted many crosses during youth, but that he should in after years become an emperor, and one of the greatest sovereigns of Europe. With the exception of the title of emperor this prophecy has been completely fulfilled.

During infancy, and until his limbs had become steeled by military toils, the constitution of the prince was so delicate that fears were entertained for his life; the more so from the circumstance of two of his brothers having already died in infancy. This delicacy of frame, combined with a great keenness of susceptibility for external impressions, lent a sad and melancholy tone to his mind, and this circumstance increased still further the apprehensions which were already entertained regarding him. Proportionable care was therefore bestowed on his physical education. The weakness of his constitution seemed to seek support in his eldest sister, to whom he clung with the most tender attachment. She in turn, repaid this fondness by devoting her hours of recreation to his amusement. These feelings of strong reciprocal attachment remained unbroken up to the hour of the sister's death.

A scene which occurred in those early years has been preserved to posterity in an admirable painting by Pesne, at that time court-painter. The prince had received a present of a small drum, and the joy which he displayed in beating a march upon it was observed to contrast strongly with the ordinary stillness and gloom of his disposition. The queen had on one occasion given him permission to amuse himself in this way in her apartments, where his sister was likewise engaged with her toys. The latter, weary of the sound of the drum, begged him to amuse himself by drawing her coach, or playing with her flowers; whereupon the prince with much seriousness replied, though ever ready to accede to a wish on the part of his sister: "To beat the drum well is more useful than playing, and more pleasant than flowers." This reply appeared of so much importance to his mother, that she immediately sent for the king, to whom this evidence of a martial taste gave the highest satisfaction. It was arranged that the scene should be repeated in the presence of the painter, without the children being aware of the object, and by him transferred to canvas. He introduced a Moorish servant as appertaining to the attendance on the royal children.

The king passed much of his time amongst his family, and his fondness was evinced in his frequently taking part in their sports. On one of these occasions Forçade an old general, happening to enter the royal chamber without having been previously announced, found the king engaged in a game of ball with the prince. "Forçade," said

INFANCY. 11

the monarch, " you are yourself a father, and know that fathers must at times be children with their children,—play with and amuse them."

We have already taken occasion to remark, that the queen sought to imbue the minds of her children with her own charitable and benevolent feelings. She had made the prince her almoner at an early age. The needy who appealed to the well-known sympathy of her heart were admitted to her presence, there comforted, and their distresses relieved by presents from the hands of the prince royal. This virtuous habit was not without its influence on his subsequent character. He was as yet extremely young, when he gave a strong proof of how deeply the principles of benevolence inculcated by his mother had sunk into his heart. His parents had been, for some years after their marriage, in the habit of paying an annual visit to the queen's father in Hanover, and the prince royal generally accompanied them from the time of his attaining his third year. The king usually made a short stay at Tangermünde, for the purpose of discussing matters connected with the administration of affairs with the provincial officers of state. On these occasions a considerable crowd would assemble to catch a glimpse of the young prince. The queen used to give him permission to go out freely amongst the people. On one occasion he begged of one of the spectators to conduct him to a baker's shop, where he opened his little purse, and emptying the contents upon the counter, demanded to be supplied with rolls and biscuits to that amount. One portion of the eatables was carried by himself, and the remainder by a servant. On his return he turned to the crowd, and divided his spoil amongst them. His parents, who had been spectators of the affair from the windows of the government-house, commanded that a second supply should be procured, in order to lengthen the enjoyment he felt in the distribution. Up to the time of the prince's attaining his twelfth year, he annually repeated this distribution of alms at Tangermünde, and always laid by some portion of his pocket-money for this purpose previous to starting. The inhabitants of Tangermünde were in the habit of styling him, *par excellence*, **their** prince. On Frederick's subsequently ascending the throne, he is known to have asserted, that at Tangermünde alone he experienced the pleasure of seeing himself really beloved by his subjects, and received with tears of gratitude by both young and old.

CHAPTER III.

BOYHOOD.

MASTERS were provided for him at the commencement of his seventh year, when his education was taken out of the hands of his female instructors. In the room of his former governesses, Lieutenant-general Count Finkenstein and Colonel Kalkstein were entrusted with the superintendence of his education. The sons of both these eminent men, together with some junior branches of the royal family, were his playmates. For one of these, young Count Finkenstein, the youthful attachment which Frederick had in boyhood formed, ripened into permanent regard ; and this young man, whom Frederick subsequently made a cabinet-minister, long enjoyed his fullest confidence.

The king drew up certain instructions for both the tutors, as to the mode in which he wished the education of the young prince to be condncted. His chief aim was to inspire the boy with a lively spirit of Christian piety :—" He must," so ran the instructions, " be carefully informed of the omnipotence and being of the Almighty, so that he shall at all times feel a holy fear and veneration for the Deity ; this being the only means of setting bounds or limits to sovereign power, freed as it is from all the restraints of human laws and punishments." Next to this, veneration, respect, and esteem for his parents were to be inculcated, the king adding, however, the following fine expressions :—" But, in consideration that too great fear can be productive of nothing but servile love and slavish submission, let it be a paramount consideration with both the tutors, to instil into the mind of my son, not this slavish submission, but real love and confidence; and to impress upon him, that such love and confidence will ever meet with a cordial return from me." These "instructions" are replete with admonitions to virtuous conduct: pride, arrogance, and all the whisperings of flattery were to be carefully guarded against. Modesty, moderation, economy, order, as also steady and unremitting industry, were to be on all occasions most strenuously enforced. As regarded scientific attainments, the instructions confined themselves to the more practical branches. The prince was not to receive instruction in Latin, but to acquire a good style in both French and German composition. As regarded history, his attention was to be particularly directed to the events immediately connected with his own family and kingdom; and especially to all such facts as might be calculated to shed light on the annals and existing relations of Prussia. Particular attention was likewise to be paid to the physical education of the prince, so as to invigorate his frame, without, however, tasking his strength to excess. "Above all," such are the words of the instructions, "let both tutors exert themselves to the utmost to inspire him with a love of soldiery, and carefully impress upon his mind, that, as nothing can confer honor and fame upon a prince except the sword, the monarch who seeks not his sole satisfaction in it must ever appear a contemptible character in the eyes of the world."

His scientific education was conducted by a Frenchman, Duhan, who had fled from France in his youth, and had been met by the monarch in the trenches of Stralsund, in charge of a young count. Duhan exercised, unquestionably, a vast influence on the education and subsequent mode of thought of the prince royal, who was indebted to him for his knowledge of history and French literature. German literature was at that period at its lowest ebb; whilst the literature of France had already attained the zenith of its splendor Thus Frederick's mind drank in all its enthusiasm from French sources; the more so from the circumstance of conversation with his governess having rendered him more proficient in that than in his native tongue. For Duhan, likewise, Frederick continued to feel the strongest regard up to the hour of his death.

Instruction in Latin had been interdicted by the king, yet Frederick has himself often in after-life asserted, that he had had a Latin master in early years: but whether with the consent of his father or not does not appear. He would likewise relate, how the monarch, happening to enter his chamber as the master was explaining some passages from the celebrated law of the empire, known as the Golden Bull, and hearing some bad Latin expression, addressed the tutor: "What are you doing, you scoundrel, with my son?" "Explaining the Aurea Bulla to him, your majesty." The king raising his staff, chased the pedagogue from his presence with the threat: "I will Aurea Bulla you, you villain!" and the instruction in Latin ceased from that hour.

The monarch, averse as he was to all the more refined enjoyments, yet found pleasure in music—especially in that powerful style of which Händel was then the great master; it is even said that Händel was the monarch's favorite composer. The musical education of the prince was, therefore, not neglected. From the cathedral organist he received the elements of instruction on the harpsichord, but it would appear that this instruction was of a very technical character. When in after-life a natural taste for music sprang up in his bosom, he became a passionate performer on the flute. The religious instruction which was communicated to him seems to have been of a still more technical and superficial nature; the most sublime truths and the deepest mysteries of religion having been presented to him in such a shape as to be but little calculated to produce any very lasting impression. It may be likewise regarded as a serious error on the part of his father, that the latter was in the habit of compelling him to learn by rote the Psalms and portions of the catechism as a punishment. That which has been impressed upon the memory by threats and commands, can hardly be expected to take deep root in the heart.

Great pains were taken to inspire the prince during infancy with a martial spirit; he was not alone instructed in all the minutiæ of the service, but even the more extended branches of strategy. At the earliest period possible he was compelled to doff the dress of childhood, assume a military uniform, and submit to the tonsure, which had been about this period introduced into the Prussian army. This latter circumstance was a severe trial for the boy, who had hitherto worn his flaxen locks in wavy ringlets round his brow. It was, however, idle to oppose the will of the monarch. The court-barber was summoned to remove the hair from the sides of the boy's head. The child had to submit without a murmur, with the tears starting in his eyes. The barber, taking compassion on the child, commenced operations with so much ceremony, that the attention of the king, who superintended the operation in person, became engaged with other matters. Taking advantage of this propitious moment to comb the hair to the back, the barber cut off only as much as was absolutely necessary. For this act of clemency Frederick afterwards liberally rewarded the considerate barber.

In order to practise the prince in the details of the military service, the prince royal's cadet company was formed, in 1717, and afterwards increased to a battalion. The prince was then placed under the guidance of a young subaltern officer of this battalion, De Wrenzell. With this young officer, whose congeniality of tastes and partiality for the flute attracted him, the prince formed a lasting attachment. So great was the aptitude which the prince displayed for military tactics, that he was able to put his little army through their exercise, much to the satisfaction of his grandfather, King George I. of

England, on that monarch's visiting Berlin, and being confined to his room by gout.

The king took other means, likewise, to render warfare a subject of interest to the prince. He fitted up a spacious chamber in the palace as an armory, and had every species of weapon arranged within it. Here the crown-prince learned the use of the various weapons without labor. On his attaining his fourteenth year Frederick was promoted to be captain, at sixteen to be major, at seventeen to be lieutenant-colonel, and had to discharge the various duties of these different posts.

At the grand parades and general reviews all the members of the royal family, residing in Berlin, were required to attend, so that the prince could perceive, long before he himself took any active part in the manœuvres, the importance which his father attached to soldiery. He subsequently accompanied the king to the provincial reviews, and there derived ample information as to the administration of the provinces. The king's plan was to accustom him gradually to the discharge of his regal functions.

In short, his father left nothing untried in order to mould him to his own wishes and sentiments, and give him a relish for his own pleasures. Being an ardent lover of the chase he devoted the greater portion of his leisure to that sport. The prince was obliged to accompany him on those excursions. In the evening the king would collect around him a number of such men as enjoyed his special confidence, and in this assembly, which bore the name of the Smoking College, beer was drank and tobacco smoked, according to the Dutch fashion. The conversation was here carried on with the most perfect freedom from the restraints of court etiquette, and every possible topic discussed. At these meetings several lettered men were also present, whose duty it was to explain all matters mentioned in the newspapers; but who, at the same time, completely discharged the office of court-buffoons. The attendance of the young princes was likewise required; and they were not unfrequently compelled to go through their military exercises, under the command of some of the officers present for the amusement of their father and his guests. At a later period the crown-prince was formally installed as a member of this club.

CHAPTER IV.

DISUNION BETWEEN FATHER AND SON

UNDER a system of control, such as we have just described, Frederick grew on to manhood. His exterior displayed peculiar grace and elegance. In figure, slight and tall, his features noble and regularly formed, his every glance betrayed a fiery spirit; wit and fancy were at his command. But this spirit could little brook to travel any path but its own, and its wandering from that which the severity of his father had marked out, dissolved the bands of friendship between father and son.

It could hardly fail to have been a subject of annoyance to the father to find that the religious instruction which was to have confirmed the crown-prince in the principles of Christianity, had not been attended with any extraordinary success. Some months previous to the day appointed for his confirmation, it was announced by the tutors, that he had made but small progress in the doctrines of revealed religion. An increased amount of instruction from the lips of the venerable court-chaplain, Nollenius, sufficed, however, to remove this impediment, and on the 11th of April 1727, Frederick was in a condition to pass a public examination, make a full profession of faith, and receive the sacrament.

There were, however, a thousand other matters, of more or less importance, which tended to contrast strongly the characters of the father and son. The military predilections of the king, his unceasing and minute attention to the most trifling details of soldiery, were as little to the taste of the prince, as the rude amusements of the chase, or the dull uniformity of country-life at the hunting-palace of Wusterhausen. The tobacco and coarse jests of the Smoking College, the feats of the rope-dancers, and the musical performances in which his father took delight, were equally unattractive. The men by whom his father was surrounded were not always to his taste, and he naturally sought out companions of more congenial habits. He was grave as often as his father was gay; and even expressions derisive of men and things dear to his father would at times escape him. Chess, which he had been taught by Duhan, was his favorite game, whilst the father preferred toccadille. To him his flute afforded the highest gratification, but the softness of its tones was but little in harmony with the feelings of the monarch. He was still more attached to literary pursuits; the brilliancy of French poetry, but more especially that reckless game, which was just about this period opened by men of the first genius in France, against all antiquated institutions, possessed for him, who felt within himself a similar power and turn of mind, charms the most seductive. How little such pursuits were congenial to the taste of the king may be readily conjectured. At times, too, if the father were absent, the tight military uniform would be discarded for the loose fashionable robes of France, and the long locks which had been rescued from the hands of the barber might be seen falling in graceful curls around his arched forehead. This was of itself sufficient, when coming to the knowledge of the king, to excite his wrath; and thus many an unhappy hour was brought about. The father thought to succeed by severity, but thereby estranged the heart of his son the more. "Fred is a poet, and a fiddler," the father would often say in his anger, " and will spoil all my labor."

These disagreements were the more frequent and fatal as there was, unfortunately, no third person to interpose and mediate between them—one, who possessing the

DISUNION BETWEEN FATHER AND SON.   21

confidence of both father and son, might have healed their differences and brought about reconciliations. The mother might, from her position, have been of infinite service in this respect; but, unhappily, every act of hers tended but to widen the breach. The natural goodness of her heart was not sufficiently strong to induce her to sacrifice her own will to that of her lord. At an earlier period, too, conceiving that her children displayed more affection for their father than for herself, she felt her maternal pride wounded, and had even gone so far as to recommend some acts of disobedience. It is very possible that the first seeds of discord between the father and son may have been in this way sown.

Fraught with still worse consequences was a plan which she had formed, at first, certainly with the concurrence of her husband, but to which she obstinately adhered, despite the melancholy consequences arising out of its prosecution. This was a scheme to connect anew the family of her father with her own by means of a double matrimonial alliance, in the hope of seeing the crown of England one day resting on her eldest daughter's brow. According to this plan the princess Wilhelmine of Prussia was to be united in marriage with the then prince royal of England, and Frederick was to be betrothed to an English princess. This proposition had been long canvassed and had been approved of by the cabinets of both countries, and even, despite different delays occasioned by officious intermeddlers, the preliminaries had been already adjusted. Nay, the consequences appeared of such importance, that Frederick William saw himself induced to enter upon an alliance with England and France, which was intended to counterbalance a recent alliance concluded between Austria and Spain; notwithstanding that the Prussian monarch felt in his heart convinced that Germany's only hope of salvation lay in a union of its different constituent members. But the conclusion of this measure met with continual postponements on the part of England, and the warmth which had hitherto existed between the contracting parties began to subside. As ill luck would have it, some improper acts were, just about this period, committed by Prussian recruiting-officers on the Hanoverian frontiers; and this circumstance was little calculated to restore matters to their former friendly footing. In a short time Frederick William would listen to nothing on the subject of the marriage.

This alliance between Prussia and England had, however, awakened the jealousy of Austria. A subordinate prince of the empire, whose power had already become half independent, was likely thereby to attain so great a preponderance, that the supremacy over Germany, at which Austria then aimed, seemed endangered. The necessity of disengaging Prussia from this alliance, and of, if possible, blending it with Austria, was sufficiently obvious. To effect an object so desirable the imperial general, Count Seckendorff, was despatched to Berlin; and he succeeded in turning the coolness which had occurred between the courts of England and Prussia to so much advantage, that in October, 1726, an alliance was concluded between Prussia and Austria at Wusterhausen; which treaty was not, however, directed in any way against England. As a principal condition of this treaty, Frederick William stipulated for a recognition by the emperor of his claims to the inheritance of *Jülich* and *Berg;* and in consideration of this, he promised to recognize the pragmatic sanction—whereby the succession to the imperial crown was guaranteed to the emperor's daughter, in the event of a failure of heirs male. The emperor counterfeited acquiescence in the wishes of Frederick William, but had in reality so little desire to abet Prussia in the enlargement of her dominions, that he concluded, almost immediately after a treaty with the Pfalz families, who claimed an inheritance of those territories. By the employment of arts the most varied, he succeeded in amusing the King of Prussia for a series of years with barren hopes, and inspiring him with confidence in the honest and speedy fulfilment of the stipulations. So successful were

DISUNION BETWEEN FATHER AND SON. 23

the plans of Count Seckendorff, that Frederick William continued even warmly devoted to the interests of Austria; for such was the integrity of his own character, that he entered with his whole soul into every contract. Seckendorff had not neglected to win over to the interest of his master the services of general, afterwards field-marshal, De Grumbkow, at that time one of Frederick William's prime favorites. This man, in return for the lordly pension which he held from Austria, labored unceasingly to confirm the monarch in his delusions. The Prussian court was now divided into two factions, the English and the Austrians, each of which labored to the utmost for the attainment of its own ends. As regarded the queen, she felt little disposed to relinquish the idea she had once adopted: on the contrary, she neglected no opportunity of renewing the negotiations with England. Her efforts, as uncompromising as they were futile, so exasperated the monarch, that all domestic peace was at an end. Husband and wife watched each other's motions with the utmost jealousy; and their differences were still further fomented by the intermeddling of interested mischief-makers. The two eldest children were the principal sufferers in the strife between the parents: and the more so, as the mother had completely succeeded in winning them over to her own views. But this suffering in common had the effect of strengthening still further this strong reciprocal attachment. The estrangement of the father and son increased daily, and all prospect of anything like a cordial reconciliation wholly vanished. It was fated that other more important causes should conspire to widen the breach still further.

The violent temper of the monarch was not unfrequently attended with the most passionate outbursts; and these paroxysms would again subside into feelings of despondency and gloom, as is usually the case when the feelings have been overwrought. His religious tendency led him into all the consequences of bigotry and cant, and proved a regular plague to his family. He had summoned from

Halle the eminent theologian, Professor Franke; a man, who, as the founder of the Orphan Asylum in that town, deserves the name of a philanthropist; but professing so little liberality of principle, that his exertions had been mainly instrumental in procuring the expulsion from Halle of the distinguished scholar Wolff. Franke became the spokesman at the royal table, at which none but biblical subjects were now discussed. All recreations, especially music and hunting, (the latter of which had unquestionably degenerated into cruelty, and weighed oppressively on the small farmer,) were denounced as sinful. Every afternoon the king read a sermon to his family aloud; the chamberlain commenced a chant, in which all present were obliged to join. This mode of life had but few charms for the prince royal or his eldest sister. The solemn gravity which was natural to one section of the company was affected by the other, and must have, at times, led to singular scenes, and probably elicited some derisive remarks. Laughter could not be at all times restrained, despite every effort to suppress it; but such levities were repressed with all due severity, and such rebukes had to be received with the most studied humiliation. The monarch went so far in this hypochondriacal feeling as to entertain the idea of resigning the sceptre and government into the hands of the prince royal: he even began to draw up the necessary instructions. His wish was to secure for himself, and his wife and daughters, but a moderate provision, and to retire to Wusterhausen, there to devote his life to husbandry and prayer. The agricultural arrangements had been already made: one princess was to superintend the linen; a second, the provisions; a third to purchase the necessaries at market, and so on.

Numerous remonstrances had been used towards the king, in order to induce him to relinquish this whim; but they all proved for some time fruitless. The Austrian party, who must have been the greatest losers by the execution of such a project, eventually succeeded in draw-

DISUNION BETWEEN FATHER AND SON.

ing off the king's attention, by creating a diversion in his thoughts. He was persuaded to undertake a visit to the brilliant court of Dresden, it having been conceived that the best antidotes against melancholy were to be found there. Promises of considerable magnitude had been also held out to him, in the event of his succeeding in gaining over Augustus II., King of Poland and Electoral-prince of Saxony, to an alliance with Austria. He was thus at length prevailed upon, although strongly against his own inclination, to yield. An invitation was not slow in arriving from Augustus II., and Frederick William set out for Dresden in the middle of the month of January, 1728. The prince royal had not been included in the invitation, much to his annoyance at thus losing so favorable a chance of escape, at least for a time, from the dull monotony of his present existence. His sister, ever anxious to gratify his wishes, prevailed upon the Saxon ambassador to make arrangements that an invitation for the prince should be sent without loss of time.

In Dresden a new world opened upon Frederick. Of all the arrangements to which he had been hitherto accustomed at home—of that military severity—unceasing industry—parsimony in the conduct of the household—observance of the laws of morality—not a trace was here discernible. The existence of this court was passed in one unbroken round of revelry. Fête succeeded fête, and ingenuity was tortured to preclude satiety or disgust. Life was here adorned with all the adventitious aids of art, and everything capable of at all adding to the enjoyment of existence was to be found here. King Augustus, a man of refined parts, of a highly chivalrous spirit, and gigantic strength, had devoted his life to the worship of pleasure, and penetrated into all its mysteries. He was anxious that the few weeks during which his royal guests were about to sojourn with him should pass like the illusions of a dream. That for the support of his riotous enjoyments his subjects groaned beneath oppression—that the prosperity of his kingdom was reduced to the last stage of exhaustion—these were matters which he had no wish to obtrude upon the notice of the Prussian king.

The court of Augustus II. resembled a regular seraglio. Mistress succeeded mistress, and the number of his children it were difficult to calculate. Amongst his sons was Moritz, who became afterwards so distinguished in the annals of France, under the title of Marshal Saxe, and for whom Frederick formed a friendship which lasted to the marshal's death. Amongst his daughters was one bearing the title of Countess Orzelsha, particularly distinguished for her beauty. She was some years older than Frederick; her graceful figure, education, brilliant wit and humor made an irresistible impression upon his heart. She sometimes appeared in man's apparel, and this but tended to heighten her charms. Frederick found himself mastered by an irresistible passion, and his suit met with no rejection from the lovely countess.

In the meantime Frederick William had been completely cured of his hypochondria. The pleasures of the table and the sparkling tokay had done their duty, and it seemed as if a lasting friendship was in course of formation between the two kings. But the connubial fidelity which the Prussian monarch, in his citizen-like simplicity, preserved towards his queen, may have seemed strange enough to the Polish king. Curiosity prompted the latter to test the strength of this virtuous resolution, which in his eyes, appeared so singular. To this end he made the necessary dispositions. One evening, after they had partaken pretty freely of the sparkling tokay, they proceeded in dominos to a masked ball. King Augustus conversed with his guest, and conducted him from room to room, followed by the prince royal and some others. They at length arrived within a richly-furnished chamber, the decorations of which evinced the most refined taste. As the Prussian king was about to express his admiration of everything around him, a curtain was suddenly withdrawn, and an unlooked-for spectacle presented itself to the monarch's eyes. A nymph, slightly arrayed in loose robes, and masked, reclined on a couch; the brilliant tapers which filled the room revealing the most voluptuous form. Augustus, seemingly astonished, approached her with that easy gallantry by which he had already won so many female hearts. He entreated her to remove her mask; a proposition to which she signified her disinclination by a motion of her hand. Mentioning his rank, he gave expression to the hope, that she would not refuse this favor to the entreaties of two crowned heads. These words were of course a command, and a face of most exquisite beauty met their gaze. Augustus appeared completely enchanted, and gave utterance to his surprise, that such beauty and attractions should have so long escaped his notice. Frederick William, perceiving that his son was a spectator of the scene, hastily placed his hat before the youth's eyes, and commanded him to withdraw instantly. To this, however, the latter seemed but little inclined. Turning to Augustus, the King of Prussia dryly remarked: " She is very pretty ; " and immediately withdrew with his retinue from the chamber and ball. In his apartments he complained bitterly to his favorites of the ungracious conduct of the King of Poland, and much labor was necessary, in order to bring about a reconciliation between them. But the single glance which Frederick had obtained had fallen like a burning brand into his heart.

It is possible that the object of Augustus in preparing the above scene, was, in reality, by an offer of so much beauty, to draw Frederick off from the object of his own amours. For this purpose the young lady of the enchanted chamber may have been offered to Frederick's notice,—an offer which Frederick was not slow in accepting.

After having thus passed some weeks in Dresden, and obtained a promise of a visit from Augustus in return, Frederick William departed for his own capital. He here resumed his former mode of life. The prince royal fell into despondency, ate but little, and declined perceptibly in appearance; so that there seemed even symptoms of approaching consumption. The king entertained suspicions that the kind of life which the prince had been leading at Dresden was the cause of his present delicate state of health; but a medical investigation confirmed the apprehensions as to his tendency to consumption. The monarch had been advised to get the prince married as soon as possible, but he would not listen to any such counsels, and was of opinion that strict surveillance was amply sufficient to guard against all irregularities of conduct. It was at this period that Frederick composed his first poems, which were devoted to the charms of Orzelska. On the court of Dresden subsequently paying, in return, a visit to the court of Berlin, in the month of May following, and on Orzelska's appearing in the train, the prince became at once convalescent, and cured of his dejection. They contrived to arrange many private interviews. This visit, for which unusual preparations had been made, in order that Berlin might not be surpassed by Dresden in splendor, was of several weeks' duration.

CHAPTER V.

DISCORD BETWEEN FATHER AND SON.

In proportion as the feelings of independence which manhood awakens began to unfold themselves in the bosom of Frederick, the less inclination did he feel to submit to the dictates of his father's will, which was ever in opposition to his own; and the severity with which the father exacted the strict execution of his mandates, increasing in exactly the same ratio, scenes of a distressing nature had already begun to be of no rare occurrence. An alliance with an English princess had now for Frederick the additional charm of seeming to promise a greater measure of liberty. It was, therefore, with entire sincerity that he proffered his mother his fullest co-operation for the furtherance of her favorite scheme; he even went so far as to pen a letter himself to the court of England on the subject. But the relation between England and Prussia had in the meantime undergone very serious alterations. George I., whose death occurred in 1727, had been succeeded by his son, George II., between whom and Frederick William of Prussia there had always existed a strong feeling of dislike, which had even manifested itself in childhood. They were now carrying on a war of abusive epithets. The English monarch was in the habit of styling Frederick William "his well-beloved brother the Corporal," or "the Arch-Sand-shaker of the Holy Roman Empire;" (because the Prussian king, notwithstanding the very considerable military force at his disposal, had always displayed the most marked preference for the arbitration of the pen over that of the sword;) he was in turn styled by Frederick William, "his well-beloved brother the Mountebank;" or, still less wittily, "his brother Brown Cabbage." This ill-feeling between the monarchs was, of course, a matter of high gratification to the members of the Austrian party, who naturally neglected no opportunity of fomenting this ill-will. Nor were other causes of irritation wanting; the excesses and violent acts of the Prussian recruiting officers had been adopted and countenanced by the king; and this seemed all that was necessary to turn the scale, and convert the private feuds of the kings into open hostilities between the nations. In truth, every preparation was made for war, which had certainly broken out, were it not that some of the German princes, to whom the tranquillity of Germany was dear, interfered. All this contributed to render the subject of the matrimonial alliance more odious to Frederick William, and enkindle his resentment against all favorers of that scheme. The fact of the crown-prince having written to England coming to his knowledge, excited his utmost indignation. Fits of gout tending still further to inflame the natural irritability of his temper, his two eldest children had little lenity of treatment to expect at his hands.

The brother and sister sought to indemnify themselves for the harshness with which they were treated by the warmth of their mutual affection and co-operation. French literature formed their only resource. Amongst the works which they read together was Scarron's comic novel, the satirical portions of which they wrought into a drama, in which each member of the hated Austrian faction, the king not excepted, had his part assigned him. This production was shown to their mother; but she, instead of censuring this disrespectful conduct of the children towards their parent, was pleased with the talent for satire which its execution evinced.

During the summer of 1729, as the royal family were sojourning for some time at Wusterhausen, the violent

DISCORD BETWEEN FATHER AND SON. 31

hostility of the monarch towards his two eldest children became such, that they were banished altogether both from his and their mother's presence, except during meals. It was only by stealth, and when the monarch was engaged in his afternoon walk, that the mother ventured to enjoy the society of her two children; and even on these occasions sentinels were regularly posted to give warning of the king's approach, as no very mild treatment was to be expected in the event of the monarch's detecting any infringement of his commands. On one of these occasions, these piquets had discharged their duty so inefficiently, that on a sudden, and quite unexpectedly, the king's well-known footfall was heard in the corridor. As the queen's chamber presented no means of egress, there was little hope of safety, other than the concealment of the prince in a clothes-press, whilst his sister secreted herself under the queen's bed. The king, exhausted by the heat, seated himself in his chair, and continued to doze in that position for two weary hours, during which neither of the criminals dared to quit their uncomfortable prisons.

Similar infractions of the royal commandments led to similar scenes. Frederick had, during his stay in Dresden, made the acquaintance of Quantz, a distinguished performer on the flute, and was extremely anxious to avail himself of the instructions of this eminent virtuoso. The efforts of Frederick's mother, who was anxious for the cultivation of her son's musical taste, to win the services of Quantz for her household were unsuccessful, as King Augustus was not disposed to part with his favorite: permission was, however, obtained for Quantz to visit Berlin once a year, in order to instruct Frederick in the higher essentials of a finished performer. It is hardly necessary to observe that such visits were to remain a profound secret from the king. During one of these visits the prince and the musician were seated together in the most perfect composure; Frederick had exchanged his tight, suffocating, military uniform for a loose, comfortable dressing-gown of gold brocade, his stiff curls had been dispensed with, and his flowing hair confined in a bag. On a sudden the door of the chamber opened, and Lieutenant De Katte, a friend of Frederick's burst into the room, and announced that the king, whose presence was at that hour wholly unlooked for, was close at hand. The danger was imminent, and the dressing-gown of the prince, as well as the scarlet coat of the musician—scarlet being a color for which the king was known to cherish the most decided aversion—were not exactly calculated to allay the impending storm. Katte had just time to seize the box containing the notes and musical instruments in one hand, and grasping the *maestro* with the other, fly with him into a small adjacent recess, which served for lighting the stoves. Frederick had, likewise, scarcely time to slip on the uniform and hide the dressing-gown, when the king entered. The monarch felt evidently disposed to pass the chamber in review. That all was not right was sufficiently indicated by the presence of the hair-bag, an article which could in no way be brought into unison with the regulation of any known military costume. Subsequent investigations led the monarch to the discovery of certain shelves, which were screened from observation by the paper-hangings, and which had formed the depository for both books and dressing-gowns. The latter articles were immediately committed by the monarch to the flames, whilst the former were returned to the bookseller. Fortunately the lurking-place of our virtuoso escaped detection; but as long as the musician continued his secret visits, he took very particular care not to appear again within the precincts of Frederick William's palace in a scarlet coat.

Other matters were perhaps still more calculated, when coming to the ears of the king, to embitter him against Frederick. The visit to Dresden had been productive of the worst consequences to the purity of Frederick's mind. The licentious images which had there floated before his eyes, the pleasures which he had there tasted, left him no peace, and the cravings of nature, once felt, became imperious in their demands. For the heir to a throne, be his conduct ever so narrowly watched, the restraints of morality are of easy evasion, if the warning voice of conscience impose no check; aiding hands are never wanting to the high in station. The prince's first confidant was a Lieutenant De Keith, one of the royal pages, whose mild and sympathizing disposition induced him to view the distress of the prince with compassion, and whose position near the person of the monarch enabled him to give information of the feelings and intentions of the king, and thereby avert many unhappy scenes. In the prince's love-adventures, too, Keith rendered good service, as beseemed a royal page. The circumstance of both Frederick's tutors having been dismissed just at this period, left him still more exposed to the dictates of his passions. The father had been induced to take this latter step at the suggestion of Grumbkow, who, finding his Austrian views thwarted by the abilities of one of these tutors, Count Finkenstein, who had been indebted for his appointment to the interest of the queen, represented to the monarch how unseemly, now that Frederick had attained his present age, the continuance of such control had become. In the room of the tutors, two persons, Colonel De Rochow and Lieutenant De Keyserling were appointed companions; but the superintendence of the actions of the prince formed no part of their duty. The latter of these two, De Keyserling, afterwards became Frederick's most intimate friend; his lively imagination, gaiety of disposition, and cultivated taste endeared him to Frederick even from the first; but their intimacy never partook of that confidential character which subsisted between the prince and Keith.

This perpetual association of Frederick and Keith at length attracted the observation of the king, and was regarded by him with no favorable eye. Keith was shortly after dismissed to a regiment stationed at Wesel; but this separation availed but little. The prince was not long in finding a second, and far more dangerous associate, in Lieutenant De Katte. Katte's manners and address were engaging, though his exterior was anything but prepossessing; his shaggy, knitted brow, lending his physiognomy an even ominous aspect. Depraved in mind himself, he sought but to confirm Frederick in his vicious course. Nor did he want sufficient subtlety to enable him by plausible sophistries to gloss over such excesses: he had, by weaving together scraps of doctrines, which he but half comprehended, wrought out a system of fatalism, according to which, man, being without free will, and, consequently, without guilt, was the mere passive agent of predestined crimes. For doctrines such as these he found in Frederick a willing disciple. Nor did Katte possess even the necessary discretion for a post of so much danger: vain of the confidence which Frederick reposed in him, so far from taking any pains to hide it, he would even, at times, make a display of Frederick's letters, and much of their contents may have in this way reached the ears of the king.

The monarch had been for some time on the watch for an opportunity to inflict some serious punishment upon the prince. He had been already nowise sparing in the application of coarse epithets and harsh treatment. Frederick had been compelled to serve as an ensign for a long period. He had to hear, on public occasions, from the lips of the king the taunting expressions, "that had his (the king's) father treated him in the same way, he should have long since run away from him; but that such a step required more courage than Frederick could boast." Whenever the king met him in public, he invariably threatened him with his cane; and the prince had already assured his sister, that in the event of its coming to actual violence, he should be certainly compelled to seek safety in flight. Numerous and peremptory were the demands of the king that Frederick should resign the right of succession in favor of his brother, Augustus William, who was ten years younger, and had moulded himself completely to the wishes of his father, and for whom the monarch displayed on all occasions a preference the most marked. To such demands the prince replied, that he would sooner submit to have his head cut off than forego his good rights: he, however, after a time, declared his readiness to acquiesce in the proposed arrangement, on condition of his father's making a public declaration, that his exclusion from the throne was in consequence of his being an illegitimate son. To this condition the father could not possibly, as being at variance with his principles, assent.

To all the foregoing causes of disagreement we must still add one; namely, that the occupations and pleasures in which Frederick indulged rendered supplies of money, more or less considerable, necessary. The fund known as the prince royal's was large; but the sums over which Frederick had the virtual disposition were very insignificant. He found himself, accordingly, compelled to borrow money from strangers. It had come to the knowledge of the king that he had borrowed a sum of 7000 thalers, or about £1000, from Berlin merchants. Whereupon there appeared an edict, rendering a former one to the same effect more stringent, and forbidding any person, under severe penalties, and even on pain of death, to lend money to minors, but more especially to the prince royal or any of the junior branches of the royal family. The king paid the 7000 thalers, and the prince, on being questioned, admitted being further indebted to some small amount. The total of his debts was, in reality, somewhat more than double that, under the circumstances, very considerable sum.

The contracting of debts was, unquestionably, that which made the most unfavorable impression upon the father; and this it was which, when the thunder-cloud afterwards burst upon the head of Frederick, was singled out from the whole catalogue of his crimes as the blackest, and the one with which he was most repeatedly upbraided.

The impetuosity of the monarch's rage, which seemed at times to deprive him of reason, impelled him to commit acts of violence similar to the one which we are now about to detail. We cannot omit the present painful sketch, as it alone places what follows in its true light, and enables us to estimate the difficulty of the reconciliation afterwards effected. We give the occurrence as we find it detailed in the Memoirs of Frederick's eldest sister,—a source from which we have already borrowed many characteristic traits of Frederick's youth,—or rather, in Frederick's own words, as recorded by his sister: "They are daily preaching patience to me, (Frederick observes to his sister, in a stolen interview,) but no one knows how much I have to bear. I am daily beaten, treated as a slave, and debarred every amusement. Even the enjoyments of reading and music are denied me. I am not permitted to hold converse with anybody, and am surrounded on all sides with spies—unprovided with even sufficient clothing, still less with other necessaries. But that which has completely overpowered me is my father's recent treatment of me at Potsdam. The king summoned me, and on my entering, he seized me by the hair, flung me to the ground, and, after having beaten me with his fists, dragged me towards the window, and there, coiling the string of the curtain round my throat, pulled both ends with his utmost might. I had, fortunately, time to get upon my feet, and seize his arms; but as he tugged with both his hands I felt I was being strangled, and cried out for aid. A chamberlain rushed to my assistance, and rescued me by force out of the hands of the king. Say now, yourself, whether I have anything left but to fly. Katte and Keith are ready to follow me to the utmost limits of the world. I have the passports and orders for money all arranged, so that I run no risk. I shall fly to England; they will there receive me with open arms, and I shall have nothing to apprehend from the anger of my father. Of all this I have said nothing to the queen—that she, in the event of her being put upon her oath, may be able to swear that she knew nothing of the matter. As soon as the king sets out on his next journey outside his dominions, we will embrace the opportunity and start." His sister used her best efforts to dissuade him from his purpose, but renewed acts of ill-treatment confirmed him in his determination.

An opportunity offered shortly after, which seemed highly favorable to the execution of his design, inasmuch as the king undertook a journey to Saxony, attended by all the princes and several distinguished officers, in order to be present at a grand encampment, which Augustus had arranged at Mühlberg. The fantastic splendor with which the Prussian court was here received could but ill conceal the angry feelings of the Prussian king. The irascible temperament of the monarch derived fresh excitement from the suspicion that all the glittering pomp with which he was invested by the Polish king was in reality but a specious appearance, and planned solely with a view to lull him completely to rest, whilst Augustus was actively employed in pushing his claims to the contested inheritance of Jülick and Berg. The prince requested the cabinet-minister of Augustus to provide post-horses for two officers about to visit Leipzig incognito. The minister had his suspicions, and communicated them to his master; whereupon the Polish monarch, who was peculiarly anxious to avoid an open rupture with the king of Prussia, exacted from the prince a promise that he would make no attempt at escaping as long as the Prussian court sojourned in Saxony. Frederick was thus compelled to remain inactive, and await some more fitting opportunity. But his hesitation was fraught with danger, for he had, without being aware of it, allowed many unguarded expressions to escape him, and thereby put the king upon his guard. By renewed acts of severity, even in the Saxon camp, the king thought to coerce him; but such a line of conduct of course defeated its own object.

There appeared, in the meantime, a prospect of a

favorable change in Frederick's painful condition. We have already stated that the hostile relations between England and Prussia had been adjusted through the mediation of other German powers. The English court was at this time sincere in its professions, so much so that an ambassador extraordinary was despatched to Berlin to renew the negotiations as to the double matrimonial alliance, and bring it, if possible, to a speedy conclusion. But England was particularly anxious to assure itself of the personal feelings of the monarch, and to take him out of the hands of the Austrian faction. To this end the dismissal of Grumbkow, whose traitorous servility to Austria admitted of ample documentary proof, was insisted upon. The Austrian party naturally strained every nerve to work upon the monarch's weakness, and defeat this object, and their exertions were, unhappily, but too successful. The king made use of some unbecoming expressions whilst in conversation with the English ambassador, and the latter held it beneath his dignity to renew the negotiations. Thus this transient gleam of hope vanished; and the irritability of the Prussian monarch was still further inflamed. All that now remained for Frederick amidst such an accumulation of misfortunes was—flight.

CHAPTER VI.

ATTEMPT AT FLIGHT.

Not more than a few weeks had elapsed when a second opportunity for flight, and one seemingly more favorable than that offered by the encampment in Saxony, presented itself. The king had entered upon a tour through Southern Germany, and Frederick had been required to accompany him. The father having a knowledge of Frederick's designs, had been long in doubt whether it were safer to leave him behind or take him with him. He ultimately decided in favor of the latter, in order to have him perpetually under his own eye. As a measure of precaution, three officers of rank were charged to watch him narrowly; one of the three to sit continually beside him in the carriage. Frederick had, however, in concert with Katte,—although the latter had, at first, seriously endeavored to dissuade him,—formed his plans. He had written from the Saxon camp to the King of England, and sought the protection of the British court, but had received a reply, in which he was strongly cautioned against taking such a step. This had no effect upon his resolves; he still determined to fly through France to England. Katte received the custody of the prince's money, jewels, and papers. It was arranged that the moment he heard of the prince's departure he should start for England, and make the necessary dispositions for Frederick's reception there. To this end he was to apply for leave of absence, on pretence of going on the recruiting service. Keith had likewise notice of Frederick's intentions.

On the 18th July, 1730, the Prussian court left Berlin, and proceeded through Leipzig to Ansbach, where the king paid a visit to his second daughter, who had been married in the preceding year to the Margrave of Ansbach. Frederick made, even here, an attempt at escape. He repeatedly, and in pressing terms, solicited his brother-in-law to lend him one of his best horses, for the purpose, as he stated, of taking a ride. The favor was not granted, as information of Frederick's intentions had already reached Ansbach. Frederick here received a letter from Katte, advising him to postpone his flight, until after his arrival in Wesel, from whence he could escape the more readily to England through Holland. To this Frederick replied, that he could not postpone his departure much longer—that at Sinzheim, through which, according to their itinerary, they should pass, he would separate himself from the king's suite; that Katte should meet him at the Hague, under the assumed name of Count Alberville, and that, in the event of his being pursued, the monasteries on the road would afford him a safe asylum. In the haste in which this letter was penned, Frederick had forgotten to direct it to Berlin, and had merely superscribed it *via* Nurenberg. Owing to this omission, the luckless epistle fell into the hands of a cousin of Katte's of the same name, who resided in the latter city.

From Ansbach the king continued his journey through Augsburg to Ludwigsburg, where he paid a visit to the Duke of Wurtemberg. From thence he proceeded to Manheim. By this route he must have passed through Sinzheim, as stated by Frederick. It chanced, however, that the village of Steinfurth, a few miles distant from the town of Sinzheim, and not the town itself, was the place selected for passing the night. The king, whose habits were by no means of a luxurious character, selected some barns for the lodgment of himself and suite, preferring these airy quarters to the rather confined bedchambers of an inn. A barn had been assigned to the prince, and was shared by Colonel de Rochow and his

ATTEMPT AT FLIGHT.   41

attendant. Frederick now concerted his measures according to the circumstances. Taking advantage of the good-natured credulity of one of the king's pages—a brother of his friend Keith—he persuaded him that he had a love affair in the neighborhood—that he required horses, and begged of him to awaken him at the early hour of four o'clock on the following morning. It being market-day in the town the purchase of the horses was a matter of no great difficulty. The page obeyed the instructions with alacrity; but instead of awakening the prince, he mistook the bed, and awoke the valet. The latter had sufficient presence of mind to conceal his suspicions, and lay in bed observing all that passed. The prince sprang up, dressed himself hurriedly, not, however, in his uniform, but in a French dress and a red surtout, which he had privately got made during the journey. But no sooner had Frederick left the barn than the servant awoke Colonel de Rochow, and informed him of all he had observed. The colonel immediately summoned three officers of the king's household, and went with them in search of Frederick. They found him in the market-place leaning against a cart, awaiting the arrival of the page. His French dress confirmed their suspicions, and they ventured most respectfully to inquire the motive of his rising so early. Frederick, bursting with rage and disappointment, might have been, at that moment, capable of the most desperate resolves, had he been provided with arms. He returned an abrupt and sullen answer. Rochow informed him that the king had already arisen, and intended resuming his journey in less than half an hour; he advised him, therefore, to return with all possible dispatch, change his French dress, and thereby prevent the circumstance from coming to the ears of his father. Frederick refused, alleging that he intended to take a walk, and would return in sufficient time. Meanwhile the page arrived with the horses, and Frederick strove to mount one of them. This the officers prevented: he was compelled to return and put on his uniform, but not without the most desperate resistance on his part.

The king had been made aware of the circumstance, but dissembled all knowledge of it, in order to sound the plans of Frederick the more thoroughly. It was not until the *cortége* had left Manheim and reached Darmstadt, that the king sarcastically remarked to Frederick, how surprised he was to see him there, as he had supposed him to have been long since in Paris. The prince doggedly replied, " that were he so inclined, he might possibly have been there ere this."

But the catastrophe was much nearer at hand than could have been reasonably anticipated. Hardly had the king arrived at Frankfort on the Maine, from whence the royal route lay down the rivers Maine and Rhine, as far as Wesel, when he received from Katte's cousin an express, transmitting Frederick's letter, which, from its threatening contents, the latter had not conceived himself warranted in suppressing. The king, immediately on the receipt of the above, issued orders that Frederick should be confined in close custody on board one of the vessels which were to transport the royal train down the rivers. The following day the king came on board this vessel, and on seeing Frederick, became so completely overpowered by passion, that he fell upon and beat him so unmercifully with his cane as to make the blood stream down his face. Frederick, writhing with pain, exclaimed, "Never, till now, has a Brandenburg face been thus disgraced!" The officers present rescued him from the violence of his father, and prevailed upon the latter to permit him to continue the journey in a separate vessel. He was now treated as a state-prisoner; his papers and sword were demanded from him; he had, however, succeeded, by means of his attendant, in burning all his letters, which might otherwise have had the effect of compromising many.

Rarely has a tour on the Rhine's fair stream been attended with more melancholy circumstances. The visits,

ATTEMPT AT FLIGHT.

which were of necessity paid to the various spiritual princes in the neighborhood, were dispatched with as little ceremony as possible. Frederick's anxiety was not so much on his own account, as from a regard for those whom he had hurried along with him into destruction. Still he felt assured that Katte, who was already fully equipped for flight, would preserve sufficient presence of mind to provide for his own safety. Keith had received, ere the king had arrived in Wesel, a slip of paper, on which the prince had written, in pencilling, the words, "Save yourself—all is discovered." Keith lost no time: he instantly sprang on horseback, and reached the Dutch frontier in safety. Even at the Hague, when pursued by a Prussian officer whom Frederick William had dispatched to arrest him, he was so fortunate as to escape to England in a fishing-boat. From England he passed over to Portugal, into the service of which latter country he subsequently entered.

On arriving at Wesel Frederick was placed in confinement, and his chamber guarded by sentinels with fixed bayonets. On the day following, the commander of the fortress, Major von der Mosel, received orders to conduct the prince into the presence of the king. On Frederick's entrance his father inquired, in a threatening tone why he had sought to desert. "Because," replied the prince, "you have treated me not as a son but as a slave." "You are a faithless deserter," cried the king, "without heart or honor in your composition." "As much of both as yourself," replied the prince; "and I have done but that which you have a thousand times told me you would have done were you in my position!" These words infuriated the king to such a degree, that he drew his sword, and would certainly have run the prince through the body had it not been for the interference of General Mosel, who interposed himself, and exclaimed "Kill me, sire, but spare your son!" This bold conduct of the general made the king pause, and the former, taking advantage of the moment, succeeded in removing the prince to his chamber in safety. The other generals then prevailed upon the king to avoid coming in contact with the prince in future, and to entrust his custody to officers on whom he could rely. The king departed for Berlin a few days afterwards, leaving Frederick behind him in custody at Wesel.

The officers in charge of the prince had instructions to set out from Wesel with him somewhat later, and to transport him with all possible secrecy and dispatch to Mittenwalde; where he was to remain for the present. It was forbidden them to enter the Hanoverian territories during their progress, in order to avoid any attempt at a rescue through English agency. They were, likewise, to be extremely circumspect, and prevent his holding communication with any person whatsoever. Notwithstanding all these precautions, Frederick had nigh escaped in Wesel. The severity with which his father treated him was only equalled by the love which the people testified towards him, and his misfortunes had called forth perfect enthusiasm in his favor. Not a few would have even ventured their lives to purchase his freedom. He had been already provided with a rope-ladder, and the dress of a peasant girl; and in this disguise had descended, during the night, from his chamber-window, when a sentinel, whom he had not observed, challenged him. Nothing now remained but to surrender himself to his fate: he suffered himself to be removed from Wesel the following day, without offering any opposition. He made no further attempt at escape during the journey, although the Landgrave of Hessen-Cassel, and the Duke of Saxon-Gotha, would not have been disinclined to protect him from the violence of his father,—of this he was not, however, aware.

CHAPTER VII.

THE TRIAL.

KATTE had wholly neglected the necessary precautions for his own safety. Rumors of the arrest of the prince royal had already reached Berlin, and as Katte's connection with Frederick was but too well known, voices came from all sides whispering caution; but despite these repeated warnings, Katte lingered, complacently awaiting the completion of a French saddle, in the secret recesses of which he intended to conceal the papers, money, and jewels, which he proposed taking with him. At length he solicited—it was on the evening of the night on which the order for his arrest arrived—leave of absence from his commanding officer for the following day, ostensibly for the purpose of joining a hunting party. The execution of the order for arrest had been delayed until there was every reason to believe that he had effected his escape; but great was the surprise of every one, on the officers going at length to his lodgings, to find him but in the act of setting out. His fate was now decided; he had to surrender himself as their prisoner. To the queen he transmitted a sealed box, containing the papers and jewels of the prince royal.

The order for arrest had been accompanied by a letter from the king, directed to the mistress of the queen's household, requesting her to inform her majesty of the prince's attempt at desertion, and his subsequent imprisonment. The confusion and dismay which this intelligence spread through the royal family were still further increased by the receipt of the box from Katte, which they dared not venture to destroy, but which might contain not only much that was prejudicial to Frederick, but even to the queen herself, and more especially to the eldest daughter. An extensive correspondence had always been kept up between the several members of the family, without the knowledge of the father; and expressions had been used, particularly in relation to the project of the double alliance, in which the homage due to the king may have been at times lost sight of. It was finally resolved to remove the seals, force the lock, burn all papers of a dangerous character, and substitute others, of various dates and of a more harmless character, in their stead. The box was afterwards resealed with a crest as nearly resembling the former as it was possible to obtain.

On the 27th of August the king returned to Berlin. His first demand was for the box. On its production, such was his impatience to learn the contents, that he burst it open without examination, and took out the letters. It was his firm belief that the intended flight of the prince was the result of a regular plot, set on foot by England, and in which the queen and his eldest daughter were implicated. He even went the length of suspecting that ulterior views, beyond the mere matrimonial alliances, were entertained. His finding nothing in the box confirmatory of his suspicions, instead of tranquillizing him, had merely the effect of exasperating him the more, as he suspected some fraud had been practised upon him. His entire vengeance was now directed against his family, and against his eldest daughter in particular. He swore that he would have the prince royal executed, and that his eldest daughter should share the same fate. No one ventured to oppose him, except Madame de Kamecke, the mistress of the queen's household. She followed him to his chamber, and besought him to spare the feelings of the queen, and to regard the step Frederick had taken in its proper light, as the effect of youthful indiscretion. "It has been, as yet," said she, addressing him, "your pride to be a just and pious king, and for that God has blessed you; now you want to become a tyrant—beware of the wrath of God! Sacrifice your son to your fury, but be assured of the vengeance of Heaven. Call Peter the Great and Philip the Second to mind: they died without heirs, and their memory is regarded by men with horror!" These words seemed to make some impression upon the king; t was, however, but transient.

Katte had been, in the meantime, summoned and legally tried. The prisoner was greeted, on his arrival in the royal presence, with the most furious ill-treatment. Katte replied to the various questions put to him with composure: he admitted participation in the intended flight of the prince royal; that it had been the intention of the latter to seek protection in England from his father's displeasure; that he, Katte, had formed the medium of communication between Frederick and the English embassy: he declared that his plan had not been communicated to the princess Wilhelmine; and that, as regarded any undertaking hostile to the king's person, or in any way affecting him, such an idea had never been entertained. He then appealed to the letters of the prince royal. A second inspection of the latter led, of course, to nothing further of a criminatory character. But the suspicion that the more important papers had been destroyed still continuing to work upon the king's mind, the princess Wilhelmine was the victim of continual ill-treatment. At the conclusion of the trial, Katte was stripped of his uniform, and conducted to the chief guard-house, clad in a linen smock-frock. The other friends of the prince royal, and all such as seemed to sympathize with him, even although no participation in the present plot could be traced to them, were treated with the most extreme rigor; thus, for instance, his former tutor, Duhan, who now filled the office of a city councillor, was banished to Memel. The consternation which these acts excited became general, and every heart was filled with anxiety for the future fate of the prince royal.

Frederick had in the meantime arrived at Mittenwalde. He here underwent his first examination, on the 2d of September. The testimony given by Katte was laid before him, and he admitted its accuracy. To all further questions his answers were not over-explicit. In reply to General Grumbkow, who was present, and strove to damp his haughty self-reliance, he remarked, "that he hoped he was now indifferent to all that might befall him, and trusted his courage would exceed his misfortunes." Grumbkow thereupon informed him that he was, by order of the king, to be removed to Cüstrin, and that this fortress was to be his place of detention for the present. "Be it so," replied the prince; "I shall go thither. And if I am not to leave it until I make the request, I shall probably remain there some time."

The prince royal was on the following day conveyed to Cüstrin. An apartment was allotted him in the palace, the president of the chamber, De Münchow, having been obliged to give up one of his own rooms for the purpose. He was here, at the special command of the king, treated with great severity. His dress consisted of a coarse blue coat, without the star. Two wooden stools formed the furniture of his chamber. His food, which was very simple, was brought to him cut in small pieces, as neither knives nor forks were allowed to such prisoners as were confined in close arrest. The use of ink and paper was forbidden: his flute was likewise taken from him. He dare on no account leave his chamber. The door was guarded by sentinels, and opened but three times daily to admit food, and then in presence of two officers, and for but a very short time. These officers inspected the chamber daily, in order to see that no contrivances for escape were in preparation. As all conversation with the prince royal was strictly interdicted, no visitors were admitted.

Means were found, notwithstanding, to evade the severity of these regulations. The president of the chamber, De Münchow, who felt the liveliest sympathy in the sufferings of the prince, contrived to make an aperture in the ceiling of Frederick's chamber, through which he could communicate with him, offer him his services, and learn his wishes. Frederick complained of the wretched quality of the provisions, the mode in which they were served up, and the entire absence of all food for the mind. The president succeeded in supplying several of these wants. His youngest son, then eight years of age, was equipped in a wide, loose dress, worn by children, which he had years before laid aside ; and then, with his pockets filled with fruit and dainties of all kinds, he passed the guards, who could not refuse a child admission. A commode with secret drawers was subsequently introduced, and in this way the prince soon obtained knives, forks, pens, ink, and paper, books, letters, and in short, everything. The officers on duty examined the room with no severer scrutiny than their orders demanded.

Frederick felt, in the meantime, but little inclination to attribute the sad consequences of his father's displeasure to any fault of his own, or recognize the propriety of submitting with humility to his parent's will. He preserved, on the contrary, the most sullen demeanor towards such persons as were sent at different times by his father to communicate with him; and, in particular, toward the deputation which arrived in the middle of September for the purpose of examining him a second time. General Grumbkow, who formed one of this deputation also, went so far as to threaten him, that unless he laid aside his haughty demeanor, ways and means would be found to humble his pride. "I know not," replied the prince, "what may be your intentions towards me; but this I know, that you shall never induce me to cringe to you." The deputation laid the box of papers before him, with the question, whether he did not miss some of its original contents. The prince, perceiving that the most important documents were wanting, concluded they had been suppressed. He accordingly replied, that these were its entire contents. The deputation sought to exact an oath from him as to this fact; but this he declined, on the ground of his memory being, possibly, fallacious. The commissioners could not succeed in extracting any further admissions from him. Prospects of pardon were held out to him, in the event of his relinquishing his claims to the succession; but to this he likewise refused to accede. The king even intended to put Katte on the rack, but was restrained from the execution of his design by the interference of the family and friends of the latter, who filled high posts in the state.

The only charges against the prince royal or Katte consisted, as we see, in the attempt at flight, and the admissions and avowals of the latter. The king held this to be sufficient to warrant him in enforcing a most severe law. A court-martial was summoned to decide on their offence in a strictly military point of view. Frederick, in particular was to be tried as a common deserter, without reference to his rank. On the 25th of October, 1730, this tribunal assembled in Kopenick, and returned to Berlin on the 1st of November. Notwithstanding the king's positive directions, the tribunal would pronounce no sentence as to the prince royal; it declared itself incompetent to decide as to him. Katte, in consideration of his not having quitted his regiment, and the non-fulfilment of his evil designs, was ordered to be cashiered, and sentenced to hard labor for several years. But the king, highly displeased at the entire conduct of the court-martial, attributed its acts solely to the wish to ingratiate itself with the future monarch, whom he had now brought himself to regard as his natural enemy. His wrath was not to be appeased but by the blood of some victim. He accordingly declared, by virtue of his royal prerogative, Katte's crime to be treason, inasmuch as the latter, as an officer of the Guard-gens-d'armerie, was by oath especially attached to the person of the monarch, and had, notwithstanding, formed illegal connections with the ministers and ambassadors of foreign powers, for the purpose of aiding the desertion of the prince royal; this being to the injury of the king. For this crime he deserved, as the king thought, to be branded with burning irons, and then hung; but in consideration of his family, he should only be decapitated. On the promulgation of this sentence, Katte was to be informed, that it gave the king pain, but that it was better that he should die, than that justice should remain unexecuted. All supplications and intercessions proved of no avail. It was in vain that Katte's grandfather, the distinguished General Field-marshal Count Wartensleben, with tears in his eyes supplicated the monarch to spare the life of his grandchild, and afford him an opportunity for repentance. The king remained obdurate and unmoved, repeatedly appealing to the maxim, that it was better that one guilty man should suffer by the hands of justice, than that the kingdom or the world should perish.

Katte received his sentence with the greatest composure. In proportion as his former conduct had been frivolous, was his present bearing, during the few days granted him to prepare for death, becoming and grave. The sorrows which he had by his misconduct drawn down upon the heads of his parents and grandfather touched his heart to the quick: the letters in which he bade them farewell were filled with expressions of the most tender contrition. In a humble spirit he acknowledged that he had been plunged into all his misfortunes from his neglect of the Most High; but that even in this he recognized the love of his Heavenly Father, who had selected this means of conducting him to the paths of light. On the 4th of November he was led away to Cüstrin. This was done by command of the king, who wished to leave no means untried for subduing the heart of his son. The execution was to take place, in obedience to the express injunctions of the king, under the very eyes of the prince. The morning of the sixth of November was the day appointed. The prince was compelled to approach the window of his chamber, and on his seeing his friend in the centre of the awful procession, attended on either side by a clergyman, he called out from above: "Forgive me, dearest Katte!" "Death for a prince so beloved is sweet!" was the reply.

The procession then ascended the ramparts, and Katte, strengthened by the consolations of religion, received the fatal blow. Human nature could not sustain this shock; the prince royal was seized with fainting-fits. His very heart-strings seemed about to snap asunder.

Still the same sword which had fallen upon Katte hung suspended over Frederick. The continual threats of the king warranted the worst apprehensions. But in proportion as the excitement increased, which Frederick's imprisonment had everywhere throughout Europe awakened, the more repeated and urgent became the intercessions on his behalf. The king had already, in September, sent a circular to the different foreign courts, informing them, in general terms, of what had occurred, and signifying his intention of transmitting a more detailed account when the inquiry should have terminated. Thereupon there appeared various remonstrances from different courts, recommending lenity to the monarch. Austria, likewise, interfered, and with considerable earnestness,—now that the union between Prussia and England seemed completely dissolved, and little to be apprehended from the prince royal,—in the hope of attaching through its mediation the son as well as the father to its interests. Of still more weight with the king were the remonstrances of the most distinguished leaders of his army against so bloody a sentence. In reply to the objection that the king had not the power of inflicting the punishment of death upon an "Electoral Prince of Brandenburg," without a formal trial before the emperor and empire, the monarch declared that neither emperor nor empire should prevent him from punishing the "Prince Royal of Prussia," within his own realms, according to his own good pleasure. On hearing this, Major De Buddenbrock bared his breast in the king's presence, and heroically exclaimed: "If your majesty wants blood, then take mine; his you never shall have whilst I breathe!"

But if the voice of policy could not be wholly disregarded,—if the voice of honor still retained some hold of a soldier-monarch's heart—there was yet another voice, which had a much larger share than the two former in causing the king to relent. This voice proceeded from one of humble rank, but it conveyed the ardently-desired intelligence of his son's change of heart. Müller, the clergyman, who had prepared Katte for death, had been specially commissioned by the king to work upon the mind of Frederick, and, provided the latter seemed inclined to receive his religious instructions, to pass some time with him. The prince was, after the late blow, but too much in need of spiritual consolation. Müller was the bearer of a dear bequest from Katte; a series of written representations, in which the writer sought to guide his royal friend to the same pious feelings that had formed his own consolation in the hour of death. These representations consisted chiefly in the expression of Katte's belief, that his misfortunes were but the well-merited retribution of Heaven, and entreating the prince also to recognize the hand of God, and submit to his father's will; but, in particular, to renounce his belief in Fatalism. This last was the most important point, and the one to which the king wished the preacher to direct his particular exertions. For the prince, principally through Katte's instrumentality, had embraced the doctrine of Predestination, so rigidly enforced by the Calvinists; according to whom, each individual member of society was fore-doomed from eternity to weal or woe, and, therefore, sins involved no badness of the human heart. Frederick had in this way regarded all his former acts as the decrees of fate, over which he had no control. But his mind was now open to warmer impressions, and although he for a time strenuously combated the opinions of his adversary, the biblical lore of the latter eventually prevailed. He felt himself overpowered, and complained that his faculties were forsaking him. Summoning his energies at length, his first exclamation was: "I have, then, been the cause not alone of my own misfortunes, but of the death of my friend!" The minister confirmed this assertion; but, after allowing him for an instant to dwell upon the magnitude of his faults, directed his attention to the mercy of God, as being greater than all crimes. The prince then remarked, that though he might even succeed in obtaining the divine forgiveness, yet, so offensive had been his conduct towards the king, that he despaired of ever obtaining his father's pardon, and that the preacher had only been sent to him with the view of preparing him also for death. It was very difficult to remove these suspicions; and the prince was only restored to composure by a heartfelt prayer, which the preacher joined him in offering up. Frederick besought the latter to spend as much of his time with him as possible. Müller, thereupon, occupied a room near the prince's, from whence he was often summoned at an early hour in the morning to assist Frederick in his devotions. Frederick had on one occasion been presented with a religious work by his spiritual adviser; on the latter receiving it back, he found upon the cover the figure of a man, in a kneeling posture, with two swords crossed over his head, and underneath the words, "Lord, if I have but thee, I ask not after heaven nor earth; if my body and soul be afflicted, thou art still, O God, at all times the consolation of my heart and my portion."

The divine had been in the habit of transmitting to the king, from the time of Katte's execution, a daily return of the progress of the prince's conversion, and had suggested the danger of the monarch's withholding his clemency much longer, as there seemed grounds for apprehending that the continued melancholy under which the prince labored might affect his reason. The king lent a willing ear to the minister's suggestions. The latter was accordingly, on the 10th of November, authorized to communicate to the prince, that, " though the king could not grant him his entire forgiveness, still, he should be liberated from arrest, and only confined within the walls of the fortress, and should be employed as a counsellor in the Cüstrin chamber." This proof of the monarch's lenity so completely surprised Frederick, that he could not credit the announcement nor restrain his tears; nothing less than a perusal of the letter itself could assure him of its truth. The king at the same time stipulated that Frederick should, in the presence of a deputation specially appointed for the purpose, take a solemn oath to render, in future, to the commands of the king the most implicit obedience; and likewise took care that the attention of the prince should be particularly directed to the awful nature of an oath, and the risk he ran, in the event of his breaking it of being excluded from the succession, and of placing even his life in jeopardy. The prince declared his readiness to take the oath, but besought the king to submit it to him beforehand, to enable him to consider it the more fully, and give utterance to it with a purer conviction. The monarch acceded to his request. Whilst preparations were being made for the reception of the prince into the chamber, and until his future residence was in a state to receive him, he continued in prison, and pursued his religious meditations, aided by Müller. At length, on the 17th of November, the deputation, named by the king, arrived at Cüstrin. After the oath had been duly administered, Frederick received back his sword and order, and then proceeded to the church, where he partook of the sacraments. The court-preacher, in allusion to the fortunes of his noble auditor, selected as the text of his discourse the words of the psalm: "I must suffer; the right hand of God can change everything." Frederick then wrote a second letter to the king, declaring his entire submission, and once more soliciting forgiveness, and conveying the assurance that the acknowledgment of his errors arose not from the restraints which had been imposed, but from a sincere change of heart. The king had, however, but pardoned the son, not the lieutenant-colonel, nor was Frederick, as yet, granted permission to wear a uniform, his attire consisting of a simple light gray suit, with narrow silver facings: he therefore made a request to the king, through Müller, who had returned to Berlin, for permission, now that he had received back his sword, to wear a porte d'épée. On the request being signified to the monarch, the latter burst out into the joyous exclamation: "Is Frederick, then, after all, a soldier? well, that's good, at all events!"

CHAPTER VIII.

THE RECONCILIATION.

As soon as it became generally known that a reconciliation had taken place between the father and son, the joy with which the announcement was received became perfectly universal. The serious apprehensions for the fate of the prince, which had been so long entertained, served but to endear Frederick still more to the hearts of the people. The Austrian party had not been, however, remiss in representing the pardon as solely attributable to the exertions of the Austrian court. Seckendorff had even, without much difficulty, succeeded in inducing the king to state distinctly, in his answer to the mediative letter of the emperor, that the prince was solely indebted to the latter for his pardon, and expressing the hope that Frederick would ever feel grateful for the kind intercession of his imperial majesty. Frederick was likewise compelled to give utterance to the same feelings in a letter to the emperor. The oath and the employment at Cüstrin had been both suggested by Seckendorff; but, in a public circular which the king addressed to the several courts on the occasion, he ascribes his forgiveness to royal clemency and paternal lenity alone.

Frederick was provided at Cüstrin with a separate house, a small retinue of servants, and a very limited income. The utmost economy was necessary in the management of the latter, and returns of the expenditure were regularly made out.

In the sessions of the chamber, to which he was on the

21st of November first introduced, and on his entrance congratulated by the members of the council, the prince took part as a junior war and domain councillor, but without the privilege of voting. He received theoretical instruction in the various departments of finance and police, and also in agriculture and the management of the royal domains. In other respects his position was subject to many restrictions; he dare not leave the city; and books, particularly French works, and music were still interdicted.

President De Münchow strove hard, notwithstanding, to render the confinement at Cüstrin as agreeable to the prince as possible; nor were there wanting some pleasing social relations, which soon restored the prince to his natural hilarity and repose. Thus an attachment between Frederick and a widowed sister of De Münchow sprang up. As the latter was, towards the close of the year, about to pay a visit to her estates, Frederick, parodying his own fortunes, transmitted her a mimic cabinet order, protesting solemnly against her intended desertion, and testifying his high displeasure at so criminal a project. The ban regarding French books had been evaded, as we have seen, even within the walls of his narrow prison. The restrictions as to music had been still less regarded, for we find that Frederick was permitted to solicit from Major-general De Schwerin the assistance of Friedersdorff, a distinguished performer on the flute, to aid him in his musical performances. He had become acquainted with the latter several years previously, on his visiting Frankfort, where he had been honored by the students with a serenade, during which Friedersdorff's performance on the flute attracted his attention. Frederick appointed him, afterwards, his private chamberlain; and Friedersdorff enjoyed his esteem to the close of his life.

The prince had flattered himself with the hope that his unconditional and sincere submission to his father's will could not fail of regaining him the love of his parent; **but the mind of the king was by no means free from sus-**

picions, and the monarch feared that this compulsory submission was only the offspring of dissimulation, and that the heart of his son was incapable of love. As the winter had now gone by without Frederick receiving any one mark of the king's sympathy or regard, though he had mastered the various branches of instruction with a degree of talent and ability which filled his instructors with surprise; and as the sphere of his exertions remained as circumscribed as ever, a new storm of ill-feeling, arising from disappointment, threatened to burst forth. He had already reflected on the means of liberating himself—but not without the knowledge and consent of the king—from his irksome position. Conceiving the English project of alliance to be the mainspring of the king's distrust, he announced, in a confidential communication addressed to Grumbkow, his total abandonment of that scheme, and his readiness to form an alliance with the emperor's daughter, if such, as was said, were the wish of his father. He took much pains to prove how easy such a plan was of accomplishment, provided he were not compelled to change his religion, and declared his readiness to submit to the condition of renouncing the succession to the Prussian throne in favor of his younger brother, since the Austrian possessions, in default of heirs male, must pass to the daughter of the emperor. Grumbkow, conceiving this to be nothing but a stratagem in order to sound the father's sentiments, explained the entire impracticability of the scheme, and here the matter rested.

Grumbkow became, however, seriously anxious to effect a real reconciliation between father and son, with a view to promote the interests of Austria. The first proof of the father's favor was a present of religious books, accompanied by a letter of exhortation. This occurred in May; but several months elapsed ere the king could prevail upon himself to submit to an interview with Frederick. At length, on the 15th of August, 1731, he happened, during a tour, to visit Cüstrian. He stopped at the Government-House, and ordered Frederick to be sum-

moned to his presence. His son's exterior had undergone
such a complete change within the past year, that this
alone was sufficient to predispose him in his favor: the
French gaiety of his manner had disappeared, and been
succeeded by a manly gravity. On the prince's seeing
his father he threw himself at his feet. The king bade
him arise, and once more recapitulated, in an impressive
manner, his different transgressions; he then assured him
that nothing had given him such sincere pain, as the
want of confidence which his child betrayed towards him,
whose only aim in all he did was the advancement of
Frederick's interests. The latter conducted himself during this interview with so much propriety, and answered
the king's inquiries relative to the flight with so much
sincerity and candor, that the king affectionately assured
him of his forgiveness. As the monarch was about to
depart, Frederick conducted him to his carriage, whereupon the king embraced him in presence of the crowd,
remarking, that he now no longer doubted his sincerity,
and that arrangements should be made for his happiness
in future. Frederick testified the high delight he felt—a
feeling in which he was heartily joined by the numbers
who had crowded round the Government-House, in order
to be spectators of this important interview.

The immediate result of this reconciliation was the concession to Frederick of a greater measure of freedom than
he had hitherto enjoyed, although it was far from the
king's intention to liberate him at once from all control.
On the contrary, the king wisely resolved that Frederick
should derive as much solid information as possible from
his sojourn in Cüstrin. He was still obliged to attend
the sessions of the Chamber, but received a seat next the
president, together with the right of voting on all matters,
and his signature was attached to all documents already
signed by the president. He received orders likewise to
visit the royal domains in the neighborhood of Cüstrin,
and learn practically what he had hitherto studied theoretically. Provision was at the same time made for his

THE RECONCILIATION. 61

domestic comfort; his wardrobe was increased, and a carriage placed at his disposal.

Frederick devoted himself to his new duties with great zeal. During his visits to the different estates he took pains to gain information on all points connected with farming and husbandry; he forwarded an account of everything to the king, and exerted himself to discover plans for improving the revenues. He would propose, for instance, that one spot of land, which had been waste, should be tilled, that offices should be built on a second, or that premises which had fallen into decay should be repaired: such suggestions were always accompanied by an estimate of the probable expenses, calculated by himself. The king entered readily into these views, and by directing Frederick's attention to the relative advantages and disadvantages of such plans, stimulated him to further exertion. He had soon the satisfaction of receiving the most flattering accounts of Frederick's industry and information, from those to whose care he had committed him. Nor did Frederick neglect to consult the wishes of his father in matters of less moment. Although feeling no inclination for the chase, he sent in accounts of the state of the game in the different districts; described such strange animals as he chanced to meet with; and gave particulars of the number of boars he had killed, and the like. In his letters the allusions to military affairs were frequent, and, doubtless, not without a motive, for the highest token of the king's approbation was still withheld —a military uniform. However, Frederick's conduct became, by the advice of prudent friends, daily more and more in unison with the wishes of his father; and in this latter respect Grumbkow's conduct was highly commendable.

In Berlin, too, the situation of the royal family had considerably improved, and began to wear a more peaceful aspect. The princess Wilhelmine had consented, notwithstanding that her mother had by no means relinquished her project of the double alliance, to give her hand to the Prince of Baireuth—one of three suitors proposed by her father, who, although wholly unknown to her, had been selected by herself, from her aversion to the other two, whom she both knew and hated. Nor had she afterwards any reason to regret her choice. She was betrothed on the 1st of June, and the nuptials were celebrated on the 20th of November following. It is worthy of remark, that both on the day of the betrothal and wedding an English courier arrived in Berlin, bringing the most flattering proposals for a union of the princess Wilhelmine with an English prince. As the courier arrived too late on both occasions, we may fairly suspect the sincerity of England.

The king had made a promise to his daughter, as a reward for her submission to his will, that Frederick should be liberated from all restraint immediately after the solemnization of her nuptials. On the fourth day of the wedding festivities the king gave a grand ball in the state apartments of the palace: as a minuet was commencing Frederick entered. Much changed in manner and appearance,—for he had grown taller and stouter—and attired in his simple gray suit, he remained some time unnoticed, standing amongst a crowd of royal servants near the door. No one, except the king, was aware of his admission, and a considerable time elapsed before he was recognized. At length the queen was informed of his presence by the mistress of the household: throwing down the cards she held in her hands, she rushed to meet him, and clasped him in her arms. The princess Wilhelmine was completely overcome with joy on learning his presence from Grumbkow, with whom she happened to be dancing at the moment; her eyes wandered long round the room before she could recognize him. After having cordially welcomed him, she threw herself at her father's feet, and testified her gratitude towards him in so affecting a manner, that he could not restrain his tears. The cold behavior of Frederick contrasted strongly with all this

THE RECONCILIATION. 63

warmth, so much so as to procure him a passing rebuke
from his father. Frederick's motive in pursuing this line
of conduct was, in part, a determination to avoid in future
that appearance of caballing which had formerly given
so much offence to his father; but in truth, his thoughts
were at present engrossed by more serious matters than
pleasures or gaieties. The princess remarked this estrangement with pain, but ere long the brother and sister
were as ardently attached as ever.

A few days afterwards, all the superior officers quartered in Berlin, with the Prince of Dessau at their head,
solicited the restoration of the prince to the military service. On the 30th of November he received the uniform
of an infantry regiment, and was appointed its future
commander. During the winter he was, however, obliged
to resume his civilian dress, and return to his former
duties at Cüstrin. With increased ardor, and daily more
and more to the satisfaction of his father, he discharged
the various duties committed to him. His tours of inspection became more extended, and he availed himself of the
proximity of certain glass-works to increase his stock of
knowledge. He applied himself with so much ability to
this latter subject, as to effect a considerable improvement
in the proceeds of the establishment. He drew up a plan
for the management of the various works of the kind
throughout the kingdom; and the king, to whom every
increase of revenue was a subject of high satisfaction,
directed that all glass-works situated on royal domains
should be conducted on the prince's plan. Military
affairs likewise engrossed a considerable share of his attention; from the king he solicited a copy of the military
text-book, and exerted himself, by diligent study, to become an expert tactician. In January, 1732, he had a
severe attack of fever; and in February was, on his recovery, summoned to Berlin to assume the command of
the Goltz regiment, and the town of Ruppin allotted him
as his headquarters. As Frederick was paying his fare-

well visit in Cüstrin, to the President de Münchow, the latter inquired, what they, who had acted unkindly towards him during his melancholy differences with his father, had, one day, to expect: "I will heap burning coals upon their heads," was his reply.

CHAPTER IX.

MARRIAGE.

Domestic peace was now fully re-established between the father and son; yet neither neglected the necessary precautions to preclude the possibility of future disagreements. The king, seeing that nature had formed Frederick in quite a different mould from himself, was apprehensive of the consequences of their living together, and this was the reason of his selecting Ruppin, a town ten leagues distant from Berlin, for Frederick's residence, in preference to Berlin itself. Here Frederick, provided he discharged his military duties with zeal, was in other respects master of his own actions. The consequences of this prudent arrangement were, that the reciprocal confidence which existed between the father and son daily increased and their trivial differences, wholly unavoidable from the different temper of their minds and the irascibility of the king's disposition, were readily adjusted, without being attended with any serious consequences.

The son's complete submission to his father's will had now to undergo one of the severest tests. In order to do away with the most important source of dissension, the father had resolved on Frederick's marrying. The preliminaries had been adjusted during the residence of the latter at Cüstrin. The Austrian party, who still maintained a complete ascendency over the king's mind, and were still opposing with all their might every remnant of English influence, proposed Elizabeth Christine, a princess of Brunswick-Bevern, niece of the empress, for the king's approval. Frederick William was the more inclined to this proposal from the circumstance of his entertaining a particular regard for the father of the princess. The prince royal gave his consent, but in a spirit of desperation; the princess having been described to him as ugly and without intellect: and he, in the first bloom of youth, devoted to all the pleasures of existence, feeling reluctant to submit to the restraints of a tie which was doubly opposed to his inclinations, looked round for some expedient to break off the negotiations.

The princess Catharine of Mecklenburg, niece and adopted child of Anna, Empress of Russia, seemed more suited to his wishes. However, on his communicating his ideas on the subject, as this choice did not altogether suit the views of the Austrian party, their exertions in favor of the Princess of Brunswick were now redoubled, and the will of the King of Prussia unalterably resolved.

As early as the month of March, 1732, during a visit of Duke Francis Stephen of Lorraine, the emperor's future son-in-law, to the court of Berlin, the members of the Brunswick royal family were amongst others invited to meet him, and the betrothal of Frederick with the Princess Elizabeth Christine took place. Frederick then found, to his great satisfaction, that he had been deceived in the accounts he had heard of his bride. So far from being ugly, her person was most prepossessing, and the extreme diffidence of manner, which gave her an air of simplicity, Frederick conceived would in time wear off. He was, notwithstanding, too prudent to avow this change in his sentiments, in order that his father might estimate the more highly the sacrifice he made. Austria exerted herself to the utmost to render the princess a worthy object of Frederick's affections. Care was even taken to engage an eminent dancing-master for her, in consequence of a remark on her dancing made by Frederick, who himself excelled, and was passionately devoted to this amusement. The solemnization of the marriage was fixed for the following year; the Austrian court strove to expedite matters as much as possible, from a fear of losing the advantages already gained, in case of the king's death, an event which, from his delicate health, seemed not improbable.

On the conclusion of the festivities the prince returned to Ruppin. The tranquillity which he here enjoyed was balm to his soul. Unremitting were his exertions for the efficient discipline of his regiment, and the procuring of the tallest and finest recruits, to render it as imposing in the eyes of the king as possible; and although he by no means neglected the civil duties which his father had likewise entrusted to him, yet his hours of recreation were not few, and these he devoted to the acquisition of knowledge, to reading and music. He could now apply himself more seriously than hitherto to the sound scientific culture of his mind. All the great heroes of by-gone ages, whose deeds were reflected in the mirror of history, arose before him, challenging him, as it were, to an imitation of their glorious exploits. Even the soil in the immediate vicinity of Ruppin was classic ground. At Fehrbellin the prince royal's ancestor, the great elector, had, half a century before, routed the hosts of Sweden, and restored freedom to his country. Frederick visited the field of battle, inquiring all the particulars of this glorious deed; foreseeing, perhaps, that the future might render such a study desirable. An old citizen of Ruppin, who had been present at the engagement in his youth, acted as his guide. Having completed the tour of inspection, Frederick asked the guide whether he could not inform him as to what had been the cause of the war. The old man frankly stated that the great elector and the Swedish monarch had in their youth studied together in Utrecht, that they could not agree, and had settled their differences on the plains of Fehrbellin. Little did the old man know that a similar ill-feeling between the prince royal's father and the English monarch had almost led to a similar catastrophe, and had exerted considerable influence on the destinies of Frederick.

But the age in which he lived was likewise destined to afford him a glorious example, and one the more calculated to make a deep impression, as it was his own father who challenged his admiration. It was in 1732 that Frederick William offered his royal protection to the inhabitants of Salzburg, who had been the victims of religious persecution, and promised them a home and protection within his states.

Taking advantage of this offer, upwards of twenty thousand of these emigrants settled on the friendly soil, where, in the provinces of Prussia and Lithuania, large and fertile tracts of land, which had been depopulated by the plague, were assigned them. Many had left their goods and chattels behind them, and this excited the charitable inhabitants of the districts through which they passed to be more zealous in their endeavors to relieve their distresses. The example which the king had set was not lost upon the meanest of his subjects. Frederick's feelings are sufficiently depicted in the letters written by him about this period. "My heart impels me" (he thus addresses Grumbkow from Ruppin) "to become acquainted with the sad lot of these unhappy exiles. The resolution with which they endure all their privations rather than relinquish the only creed which instructs us in the doctrines of our Saviour, cannot be, in my opinion, sufficiently rewarded. I would part with my very shirt to divide it with these unhappy beings." And again, "I assure you," (he says in another letter,) "when I think of the miseries of these emigrants my heart is ready to burst. Procure me, I beseech you, the means of assisting them: I will give as much as I can possibly spare from my small means with all my heart." We have no proofs of how much the prince in reality did for these unhappy creatures; but we have so many instances of his generosity upon record, that there can be little doubt that these expressions of commiseration were accompanied by solid acts of kindness.

In one of the above passages from his letters Frederick

solicits Grumbkow, who had insinuated himself into his confidence, to procure him pecuniary aid, of which he stood but too much in need. The income allowed him by the king was exceedingly limited; and in spite of all the exertions of his father, he had not as yet learned economy in his household arrangements; from the numerous expenses which, from different causes, he was obliged to incur, the amount of his debts again became very considerable. The gigantic recruits, now absolutely necessary for his regiment, could only be procured at a great expense. His sister, married to the hereditary Prince of Baireuth, was likewise in a very uncomfortable position; she could not obtain a sufficient provision either from her father-in-law in Baireuth or her father in Berlin. His old tutor, Duhan, was likewise in distress in his place of exile: both sister and tutor were tenderly loved by Frederick, who, regarding himself as the cause of the displeasure with which they had been visited by the king, gladly shared all he had with them. This state of things exactly suited the wishes of the Austrian court, as affording an opportunity of attaching him, who was one day to sway the destinies of Prussia, more firmly to their interests than they had been hitherto successful in effecting. They made him considerable advances, which soon assumed the shape of a regular annuity; the Princess of Baireuth was provided for in the same way, as her influence over Frederick was well known; Duhan was also provided with a trifling situation in Wolfenbüttel, and had a small pension likewise secured to him. These arrangements were effected with the greatest privacy, in order to evade the observation of the king. Frederick could see through the conduct of the Austrian court clearly enough; but accepted, notwithstanding, that which his necessities imperiously demanded. That the conduct of Austria was anything but disinterested or deserving of gratitude, became but too soon apparent.

The principal aim which the whole policy of Charles the Sixth, Emperor of Germany, had in view, was the ratification of the Pragmatic Sanction, securing the succession to his daughter. The alliance with Prussia had been entered into because Frederick William had promised his adhesion to the Sanction; the feeling towards England was hostile, because opposition was apprehended from her. These relations became altered when England acceded to the Sanction. Every effort was now made to win the English court, and Prussia was to be made the tool. The King of England still wished to have one of his daughters future Queen of Prussia; this wish was hardly expressed, when the whole tactics of the Austrian party became reversed, and the same zeal and energy which had been formerly displayed in bringing about Frederick's marriage with the Princess of Baireuth was now directed to forward the views of England. Other objects were not lost sight of; the Princess Elizabeth Christine, a niece of the emperor, was to be united with an English prince. This diplomatic zeal was pushed to such a length, that on the very eve of Frederick's marriage the most urgent representations were made to the king. For once, however, the arts of Austrian diplomacy were foiled by the German honesty of Frederick William, their only result being to make the king suspect the aims of England, and awaken even some doubts as to the real sincerity of Austria. Even Frederick testified little approbation of the new scheme, attributing, as he did, the union of his favorite sister with the Prince of Baireuth mainly to the misconduct of England.

The marriage of the prince royal with the Princess Elizabeth Christine was solemnized without opposition on the 12th of June, 1733. The Prussian court went for this purpose to Salzdahlum, one of the palaces of the Duke of Brunswick Wolfenbüttel, who, as the grandfather of the princess, provided the wedding entertainments. The marriage service was read by the celebrated Mosheim. The festivities were arranged on an unusual scale of splendor, but gaiety of heart was wanting. The Queen of Prussia was now in desperation, seeing all her plans had been baffled: the bride submitted to the dictates of her relatives, her natural reserve being still further augmented by the formal pageantry. Frederick, though no longer entertaining the same aversion to her, found it advisable to continue to play his game before the eyes of the world; and the king appeared moody, in consequence of the conduct of his son; whilst the Anglo-Austrian propositions were exactly calculated to complete the general gloom. Some days afterwards the various members of the royal families of Prussia and Brunswick returned to Berlin, where they attended various grand military displays, and then made a solemn entry into the city in procession. The festivities were then resumed, and closed with the celebration of the marriage of the Princess Philippine Charlotte, a younger sister of Frederick, with the hereditary Prince of Brunswick.

The present royal palace (then the Government House) was given up to Frederick during his residence in Berlin; and in order to render his sojourn in Ruppin with his regiment as agreeable as possible, the king purchased for him the Rheinsberg palace, situated about two miles from thence: expending a considerable sum of money in repairing and putting it in order, and thereby gratifying one of Frederick's favorite wishes.

CHAPTER X.

FIRST SIGHT OF ACTUAL WARFARE.

FREDERICK's knowledge of warfare had been hitherto purely theoretical; he was destined, however, soon to see the stern realities of actual strife.

The war, in which Prussia now took part, was occasioned by a contest for the possession of Poland. King Augustus II. had died on the 1st of February, 1733. He had, in contravention of the constitution of Poland, which recognized not an hereditary but an elective monarchy, sought to render the crown an heirloom in his family. His efforts had been, certainly, unsuccessful; but his son, afterwards known as Augustus III. who had succeeded him as Prince Elector of Saxony, came forward as a claimant for the throne of his father, and his pretensions received the most energetic support from the courts of Russia and Austria. His claims were contested by Stanislaus Lesczynsky, father-in-law to Louis XV., King of France. Stanislaus had, some years previously, been decked with the Polish crown, on the occasion of Augustus II. being obliged to yield to the power of Charles XII. of Sweden, and his pretensions were supported by his son-in-law. Poland itself was split into factions; once a mighty realm, it had long ceased to be capable of enjoying freedom and independence, and had been long swayed by foreign powers. Augustus III. triumphed through the military power of his allies, whilst Stanislaus could obtain from France nothing beyond empty promises. But the occasion seemed to France to be favorable for declaring war against Austria for this infraction of the Polish freedom of election, in order to have an opportunity of once more extending its dominions at the expense of some portion of the Germanic empire—this had been the policy of France for more than a century. The formal declaration of war took place in October, 1733.

Frederick William had some time previously joined Austria and Russia in their plans respecting Poland, in consideration of Berg being, with other advantages, secured to him. On perceiving, however, that no decisive arrangement was to be expected, he had abstained from interfering further in the affairs of Poland; but on the declaration of war by France, he offered the emperor the aid of forty thousand troops, on condition of his demands being complied with. He again received nothing but evasive replies, and consequently sent but ten thousand men, that being the contingent, which, according to a former treaty, he was bound to supply as a subsidy to the emperor. This corps joined the imperial army in the spring of 1734. The combined forces were under the command of Prince Eugene, of Savoy, who had grown gray in the service of Austria, and had reaped so many laurels in former contests. The King of Prussia was glad at thus having an opportunity of initiating Frederick in the arts of war, under the guidance of so renowned a tactician; the prince royal was accordingly attached to the Prussian regiment as a volunteer. The king also set out shortly afterwards for the camp.

The French army, which had advanced with rapidity upon Germany, were besieging the Imperial fortress of Philippsburg on the Rhine. Eugene's army advanced to the relief of the fortress: the headquarters of the latter were at Wiesenthal, a village almost within gun-range of the French lines. Frederick arrived here on the 7th of July. Immediately after his arrival he sought out Prince Eugene, in order to obtain a view of this aged warrior, then the most brilliant star in the horizon of German fame, and still living in the national poetry of the German people. Frederick asked to be allowed " to see how a hero gathers laurels." Eugene repaid this courtesy in kind: he lamented that it had not been his good fortune to have made the acquaintance of the prince at an earlier period, as he might, in that case, have been able to have given him an insight into things possibly of advantage to a commander: " For," said he, with the look of a connoisseur, " everything about you tells me that you will one day become a valiant leader."

Eugene invited the prince to dinner. Whilst at table the French commenced a furious cannonade; but this was unheeded, and the conversation continued in unbroken gaiety. Frederick was delighted, on proposing a toast, to hear it responded to by the roar of the enemy's guns.

Eugene took a lively interest in the youthful prince; the spirit, sagacity, and manly bearing of the latter won upon him. Two days after Frederick's arrival he paid him a visit, in company with the Duke of Wurtemburg. Frederick, who had known the latter previously, embraced and kissed him. Eugene turning quickly towards him, said: " Will not your Royal Highness kiss my old cheeks too?" Heartily did Frederick comply with this request.

Prince Eugene testified his attachment to Frederick by presenting him with four picked recruits. Frederick was summoned to every council of war; and strove to prove himself worthy of this consideration, by a zealous discharge of his military duties, and an active participation in military toils. He shared the fatigues of the camp, and attentively studied the mode of treatment of the men. He also rode daily along the lines, during the whole period of the siege, and was always present when anything of importance was going forward.

Of his undaunted courage he now gave a striking proof. He had, on one occasion, ridden out, attended by a pretty numerous staff, to inspect the lines of Philippsburg. On his emerging from a thinly planted grove, he became so exposed to the enemy's fire, that several trees on either side of him were shattered to pieces; he still maintained his quiet pace and even the hand in which he held the bridle betrayed not the slightest nervousness. It was likewise observed, that he continued in unbroken conversation with the general who rode beside him; and his whole bearing, in the midst of dangers to which he was wholly unaccustomed, excited universal admiration and astonishment.

The most flattering testimony to Frederick's good conduct was afterwards borne by Prince Eugene, on the arrival of the father in the camp, coupled with the assurance, that the prince would become one of the most distinguished warriors of his day. This praise, from the lips of so renowned a hero, afforded the king the highest delight: he declared his satisfaction to be the greater, as he had always doubted Frederick's entertaining any inclination for military renown. He began from thenceforward to regard him with more favorable eyes.

The deep impression which the appearance of the venerable hero of Savoy had made upon Frederick, is attested by a poem which he composed during his stay in the camp, and which is one of the earliest of his metrical productions that have been preserved. And although he here gives utterance to his emotions in that rhetorical style which characterized all the French poetry of the period, yet, as evidence of his feelings, it is a singular document. It is an ode addressed to Fame, as the parent of everything great, achieved by the sword or the pen. He adduces historical examples, and after recounting the glorious exploits of Prince Eugene, concludes with an allusion to his own future career. The important concluding strophe might be rendered, (the original poem, like all Frederick's writings, is in French,) perhaps thus:

> " O Fame, for whom I now resign
> Pleasure's guilty glittering crown;
> O Fame, I'm now entirely thine!
> Then lend my life its fair renown!
> And though Death's terrors me await,
> Thou canst at least perpetuate

The spirit that now lives in me;
Ope with thy hand thy portals wide,
Me on thy path direct and guide—
For thee I live—I'll die for thee."

A second poem, written about the same period, is of less importance: in it Frederick seeks to depict the horrors of war, and avers his having maintained his sensibility unimpaired in the midst of them.

This campaign was, notwithstanding, but little calculated to shed the glory which Frederick coveted, upon those engaged in it. The Austrian troops were badly disciplined, and afforded a striking contrast to the admirable condition of the Prussians, inferior as the latter were in numbers. Frederick was himself, on his return home, completely disgusted at the vauntings and unmartial bearing of the Austrians—a circumstance which influenced, beyond a doubt, his subsequent line of policy towards Austria. Eugene had lost the fire of youth, and did not care to hazard his well-won laurels. To this is attributable the fact, that instead of taking advantage, by some decisive movement, of the disadvantageous position of the French, the allies looked calmly on, whilst the French captured the fortress, on the eighteenth of July. With this event all hopes of valiant deeds vanished.

During his sojourn in the camp, Frederick and some congenial spirits engaged themselves in making a singular experiment. It struck them, that sleep was a great curtailment of existence, the dispensing with which would give life double duration. The attempt was made, and their good intentions seconded by doses of strong coffee. Four days had been thus passed without sleep, when nature demanded its rights. Sleep came upon the innovators during their avocations; and Frederick was on the point of falling ill, when the resolution of resting content with the ordinary period of existence was arrived at.

Frederick William had left the army as early as the month of August, in disgust at the ill success attending its operations; but did not reach Berlin until September,

FIRST SIGHT OF ACTUAL WARFARE.

having been attacked by a dangerous disease on the way thither. The prince was commissioned to conduct the Prussian troops to their winter-quarters: this he did with the more dispatch, in consequence of the illness of his father; and October found him also at home. The king testified the confidence he reposed in him by authorizing him to attach his own signature to all papers, instead of the royal sign-manual. From his illness, dangerous as was its character, the king recovered in the spring, although the root of the evil was never completely eradicated. In June, 1735, the king marked his approbation of Frederick's conduct by promoting him to the rank of Major-general.

Austria, in the meantime, testified but little gratitude to the king of Prussia for his services. She, on the contrary, now made demands founded on the duties of the Prussian kingdom, as component part of the Germanic empire. She likewise required the surrender of the person of Stanislaus Lesczynski, who, on being defeated in his designs on Poland, had entered the Prussian territories, and there met with a hospitable reception from Frederick William, by whom he was personally esteemed;—a demand which, as it could not in honor be complied with, was refused by the king; but Frederick William was equally deaf to the tempting overtures of France, made to win him over to the cause of Stanislaus, in reliance on the strong regard which the monarch personally entertained for the latter. The Austrian court, conceiving they could now dispense with the Prussian monarch's aid, declined all further conference. Propositions were made to France, assigning the dukedom of Lorraine to Stanislaus for life, and on his demise, to fall to France; the Duke of Lorraine being, on the other hand, indemnified by receiving Toscana. This ignominious termination of the war was hailed by the Germanic empire with joy. The emperor had obtained, through this arrangement, France's recognition of the Pragmatic Sanction. In this compact Prussia had been completely overlooked; no notice had been given of the progress of the negotiations, much less any indemnity for the losses incurred or the sacrifices made. Nay, the very laws of decorum were so far outraged, that the Prussian monarch received no notification of the marriage of the emperor's eldest daughter, Maria Theresa, with the Duke of Lorraine, which took place in the year 1736. There was now no longer any reason for Frederick William's withholding his long-repressed indignation against Austria. He commented, in a tone of bitter irony, upon the conduct of the Austrian court; and on one occasion, in prophetic anticipation of the future greatness of his son, and his own increasing infirmities, pointing to Frederick, used the following words: "There stands one who will avenge me."

In the beginning of 1739 Austria actually concluded a compact with France, by which Jülick and Berg, the succession to which was claimed by Prussia and guaranteed by former treaties, were made over to the then Prince of Sulzbach. Austria had assumed the initiative in this treaty, and its protection against Prussia was expressly stipulated for by France.

CHAPTER XI.

RESIDENCE IN RHEINSBERG.

In the midst of the severe illness by which the king was attacked at the close of the Rhine campaign of 1734, Frederick, with tears in his eyes, exclaimed, " Willingly would I give one of my arms that the king might live for twenty years to come, only provided he would allow *me* to live as *I* wish myself." This sacrifice proved unnecessary for the attainment of a happy change in his circumstances and mode of life. The king granted him thenceforth perfect freedom; and there followed a succession of far happier days than he ever afterwards enjoyed, as his subsequent life was much more devoted to advancing the happiness of his subjects than his own.

Rheinsberg, that delightful retreat near Ruppin, with which Frederick had been presented on his marriage, formed the centre of his joys. His domestic arrangements were here on a princely scale, but without any excess of splendor; and he drew around him here the men whom he most highly prized. His feelings towards his princess were of the tenderest kind: her exterior had become delicately beautiful; her timidity had expanded into the purest feminine mildness; whilst her entire devotion to her husband excited the warmest reciprocal attachment; but unhappily their union was not blessed with issue. Of Frederick's friends we may particularize the following: Baron Keyserling, a lively, agreeable man of the world, who had been assigned him as a companion in early days, by the king, and between whom and Frederick there existed the closest intimacy; Knobelsdorff, to whom Frederick had reason to be grateful for services rendered during his sojourn in Cüstrin, who had been at that time a captain in the army, but had since left the service, and devoted himself to the cultivation of his taste for architecture, for which he displayed great talents; Jordan, formerly a clergyman, but now devoted to belles-lettres, and remarkable for his conversational powers. Then followed a number of distinguished officers, young and old; artists, among whom Pesne, the court-painter, was of some importance; musicians, as, for instance, the well-known Graun, and many others who paid but passing visits to Rheinsberg; while intercourse with distant friends was kept up by a lively correspondence.

We find in the letters of a contemporary, Baron Bielfeld, who had been likewise received into the number of Frederick's friends, a very animated sketch of Rheinsberg, the beauty of the scenery, and the gaiety of the life there led. We cannot give his description better than in his own words:

"The situation of the palace (Bielfeld writes thus in October, 1739,) is delightful. A large lake reaches almost to its very walls, beyond which a grove of oaks and beech rises in the form of an amphitheatre. The former palace consisted of the principal building and one wing, at the end of which stood a tower. This building and its situation were well calculated to give scope for a display of the prince royal's taste, and the talents of Knobelsdorff, who is inspector of the building department. (The first plan of the alterations did not, however, emanate from him.) The main building was enlarged and improved with arched windows, statues, and all kinds of architectural embellishments. A second wing was erected at the other extremity of the building, and both were connected by means of a colonnade, with vases and groups of figures. This gave the whole the appearance of a quadrangle. It is entered by a bridge crowded with statues, which serve as supporters for lamps. The handsome portal leading into the courtyard bears the inscription, conceived by Knobelsdorff: *Friderico tranquillitatem colenti.* The interior of the palace is splendid and tasteful. Sculpture richly, but not injudiciously, overlaid with gold, everywhere meets the eye. As the prince has a dislike to gaudy colors, the furniture and tapestry are of a bright violet, sky-blue, bright-green, or fawn-color, edged with silver. The saloon which will form the chief ornament of the palace, is not yet completed; it is to be wainscotted with marble, and furnished with mirrors and bronze. The celebrated Pesne is engaged in preparing a centre-piece for the ceiling, representing the rising sun. On one side you see Night wrapped in a dense veil, and attended by the night-birds and the Hours. Night appears retiring to make way for the Dawn, at whose side the morning-star appears in the form of Venus. You see the white steeds of the chariot of the Sun, and Apollo shooting forth the first rays. I consider this picture as allegorical and typical of an event which may not now be far distant. The gardens in Rheinsberg have not yet attained maturity, as they have been laid out but two years since. The plan is grand, the execution will depend on circumstances. The principal walk terminates in an obelisk, in the Egyptian style, with hieroglyphics. Groups of trees, arbors and shady seats everywhere abound. Two pleasure-boats, built by order of the prince, float upon the lake, and bear the wanderer, who is fond of sailing, to the edge of the wood."

The writer next proceeds to notice and describe the characters of the different persons composing the society of Rheinsberg, who, from the variety of their peculiar habits of mind, contributed to diversify and enliven social intercourse. He then proceeds:

"All who reside within the palace enjoy the most unconstrained liberty. You see the prince royal and his consort only at meals, balls, concerts, or other recreations in which they take part. Every one thinks, reads, draws, writes, plays, amuses or engages himself in his room until dinner. He then dresses himself neatly, without any os-

tentatious display, and adjourns to the dining-hall. All
the engagements and amusements of the prince mark the
man of taste. His conversation at table is delightful: he
speaks much and well. It seems as if no subject were new
to him, or above his comprehension: he is always ready
with a store of original and judicious remarks. His wit
resembles the perpetual flame of Vesta. He bears contradiction with calmness, and is even 'the cause of wit in
others,' by his tact in calling forth judicious remarks.
He jests and jokes at times, but without bitterness, and
does not take offence at a witty repartee.

"The library of the prince is admirably arranged; it is
situated in a tower of which I have spoken, and commands
a view of the lake and garden. It contains a numerous and
well-selected collection of the best French works, in glass
cases, ornamented with carving and gilding. In it is suspended a full-length portrait of Voltaire. He is the prince
royal's favorite author; but, indeed, all the good French
writers, in verse or prose, are held in high estimation by
him.

"After dinner the gentlemen adjourn to the saloon of
the lady whose turn it is to do the honors at the coffee-table. The mistress of the household is the first in order,
and the others follow in their turn, there being no exception made, not even in favor of visitors. The whole household assembles round the coffee-table. We chat, joke, and
amuse ourselves, and this hour is generally the pleasantest of the whole day. The prince and princess take their
coffee in their own room. The evenings are devoted to
music, a concert being given by the prince in his saloon,
for which an invitation is necessary. Such an invitation
is always regarded as a special mark of favor. The prince
generally performs upon the flute, of which instrument
he is a perfect master, displaying much feeling, with a
rapidity of fingering and execution singularly effective.
He has himself composed several sonatas. I have often
had the honor of standing behind him whilst playing, and
have been particularly enchanted by his adagio. In fine,

Frederick excels in all he undertakes. He dances elegantly, with ease and grace, and is partial to every honorable amusement, with the exception of the chase, which he regards as destructive of time and mind, 'and,' as he says, 'not more profitable than cleaning a chimney.'"

The writer then proceeds to speak with rapture of the beauty, amiability, grace, and feminine character of the princess.—" We have lately had " (he mentions amongst other things) "a most delightful ball. The prince, who usually appears in uniform, wore a rich green silk dress, trimmed with broad silver edgings and tassels. The waistcoat was of silver tissue, and richly embroidered. All the cavaliers of his suite were similarly, but less expensively, attired. Everything was rich and festive, but the princess glittered as the most brilliant star amidst the throng. My life here is complete enchantment. A royal table, wine fit for gods, delicious walks in gardens and groves, excursions by water, the delights of arts and science, agreeable conversation—everything combines, in this fairy palace, to give zest to life."

The writer has forgotten to mention one kind of entertainment, which added much to the pleasure of Rheinsberg and exhibited Frederick in a new character—the performance of plays, the different characters in which were sustained by the various visitors. Thus Frederick himself appeared in Racine's Mithridates, and as Philoctetes in Voltaire's Œdipus. Masquerades were likewise held.

The poetic inspiration which formed the soul of the enjoyments of Rheinsberg was cultivated in various ways. Thus the tradition connected with the place itself became a source of pleasure. The antiquarian assertion, which had been ventured centuries before, that Rheinsberg was originally termed Remusberg, from Remus, the co-founder of the Roman empire, who, after being expelled by his brother Romulus, had here founded a new empire, and that he lay interred in Remus Island, which was situated in the adjoining lake, had now become a subject of popular tradition. The discovery of some old blocks of marble, which had been dug up in the island, is said to have given rise to this assertion; while lately, some Italian monks are said to have searched on the Remusinsel for the ashes of the Roman hero, in consequence of hints contained in a recently-discovered manuscript. Many relics of antiquity found upon the island seemed to give a color of truth to the affair, and no one ventured to criticize the rights of the classic island too closely. The letters written from this place are generally dated Remusberg; and the visitors, partly in jest, partly in earnest, were designated by names more harmonious than those which they bore in common life: thus Keyserling was generally called Cæsarion; Jordan, Hæphestion or Tindal, and others in the same way.

These poetic tendencies assumed a more important shape in the foundation of a new order of knighthood, which included many princes, relatives and friends of Frederick, and several of the prince royal's more immediate military friends. The patron of the order was Bayard, the hero of French history. The badge consisted of a sword resting on a laurel wreath, encircled by Bayard's well-known motto: "Without fear and without reproach." Fouqué, who afterwards became so distinguished under Frederick, was the grand-master. The number of the knights was limited to twelve; and the object of the order was to invite to military ardor, but more especially with a view to the improvement of military tactics. The knights wore a ring fashioned to represent a bent sword, with the motto: "The man that never surrenders." The members had each a distinctive appellation: Fouqué was the Chaste; Frederick, the Resolute; while the Duke of Bevern was called the Knight of the Golden Quiver. To the absent members of the order, letters, conceived in the old French style of chivalry, were sent; and there is evidence that up to the period of the seven years' war, nay, even later, the fellowship of the order was regarded with the same pleasure, and its forms observed with almost the same exactitude, as in its infancy.

It is possible that a similar poetic charm may have induced Frederick to enrol himself amongst the Masonic brotherhood. The mysterious gloom in which this society was then wrapped, and the increased necessity for secrecy which was then felt, owing to the religious intolerance of the church, must have possessed an irresistible charm for the prince's peculiar tone of mind. His reception into the body took place in 1738, on his visiting the Rhenish provinces, in his father's suite. The king had here spoken in a very disparaging tone of freemasonry; but Count Lippe, who happened to belong to that brotherhood, defended the institution with such courage and eloquence, that the prince privately requested of him to procure his enrolment in a society which numbered such eloquent and fearless advocates amongst its members. In order to meet the wishes of the prince royal, it was arranged that his initiation into the mysteries of the craft should take place upon his arrival in Brunswick, on his way back; and members of the brotherhood from Hamburg and Hanover, with the necessary apparatus, were summoned thither. His reception took place at night, as great circumspection was necessary to elude the vigilance of the king. Frederick insisted on being treated as an ordinary person and without any regard to his rank; he was accordingly enrolled in the usual form. The courage, calmness, elegance, and address which he displayed during the performance of the ceremonies, excited as much admiration as his talents and conversation, when taking part in the masonic labors. Some members of the brotherhood (and amongst others the above-mentioned Bielfeld) were invited to Rheinsberg where the mysteries of the craft were afterwards continued, but in the greatest secrecy.

Consecrated as was the life of Frederick, during his sojourn in Rheinsberg, to the pleasures of the imagination, and though he even made several attempts at poetical composition, yet subjects of a more serious character were far from escaping his attention. The hours which were not passed in society—and these were by far the more numerous—he devoted to the most varied occupations; for, as the scientific culture of his mind had been previously neglected, he was now resolved to apply every minute to the repairing of this neglect,—not knowing the instant when a more busy sphere of action might withdraw him from the peaceful tranquillity of Rheinsberg. Frederick possessed the peculiar talent of extracting their learning from the learned, either through the medium of conversation or epistolary correspondence, and making the information thus acquired completely his own. He thus, from a correspondence with Grumbkow obtained an insight into all the secrets of Prussian diplomacy; he was instructed in the same way by the Prince of Anhalt-Dessau and other distinguished warriors, in the most approved arts of warfare, and maintained a similar intercourse, from the same motives, with physicians, theologians, and divines. His course of reading was very discursive; much of his attention was engaged by the works of the ancient authors, more particularly the historians of antiquity, with whom he made himself acquainted through the medium of French translations.

Frederick applied himself also, with considerable perseverance, to the consideration of those subjects which affect the weightiest interests of mankind; he sought to obtain some satisfactory views as to the relation of the finite to the infinite, of the present to the eternal, of man to God. That complete religious prostration, with which he had been overwhelmed at Cüstrin, had gradually passed away, as he regained his strength and faculties; but the impression which it had left upon his mind was sufficiently vivid to incite him to a study of the great problem. Precepts enjoined in a mysterious form of creed were not sufficient to satisfy him; his quick and acute mind required conviction. He began with the works of the most distinguished French divines; he next sought, by means of written and verbal communication with the ablest French preachers in Berlin, from whom he demanded answers to particular questions, to have his doubts satisfied and removed.

Amongst the preachers here alluded to, was one, the venerable Beausobre, who inspired him with strong feelings of regard. A sermon, which he had heard him preach in March, 1736, so completely enchanted him, that he sought his acquaintance. Beausobre was well calculated, by his imposing exterior and his polished address, to make an impression. After their first greeting was over, Frederick, despising all preliminary forms, abruptly inquired, in what study the preacher was at present engaged. "Ah, monseigneur," replied Beausobre, in his habitually impressive tone of voice, "I was this moment reading a delightful and really divine passage the influence of which I still feel." "And what might that have been!" "The opening of the Gospel of St. John." The answer came unexpectedly upon Frederick, and he feared that the biblical divine might not comprehend his wants. But Beausobre succeeded, in the course of conversation, in so entirely captivating Frederick, that the latter, at the conclusion of the interview, volunteered the adoption of the divine's eldest son. Unhappily this venerable pastor died not long afterwards,—too soon for his youthful pupil. Frederick, however, kept his word to the deceased's son.

The prince also called in philosophy to aid him in the solution of his theological difficulties. Wolff, the celebrated scholar whom Frederick William had expelled from Halle, occupied the foremost rank amongst the philosophers of his day, and his writings were received by the learned with delight. Frederick's attention had been called to them by his friends. Wolff's Logic, Ethics, and Philosophy were translated into French (he had already accustomed himself to frame his thoughts in that tongue only,) for his use, and he was actively engaged in appropriating to himself the results of the other's investigations, and even, wherever he thought he could himself detect errors or imperfections, in correcting or supplying the deficiencies. He returned to that doctrine of predestination of which he had formerly entertained so crude a conception; but he sought to strip it of its merciless rigor, and reconcile it with human energy. From such a religious conviction alone could that entire defiance of death, which accompanied all the mighty actions of his after life, arise.

But, on the whole, he did not acquire any considerable relish for philosophical speculations, and he soon abandoned such attempts altogether. Nature had not formed him for meditative tranquillity, but for energy and action. Thus those elements only of philosophy, ethics, for instance, which exert a more immediate influence on life, brought him in connection with that science. All his works, which do not refer to historical subjects, are devoted to disquisitions on ethics. It would accordingly appear as the irony of chance, that just as a fair copy of the French translation of Wolff's metaphysics was ready, one of the monkeys, which Frederick then kept, seized it, and calmly thrust it into the fire.

The man who excited the strongest and most powerful interest in the breast of Frederick, was the same who raised himself to the pinnacle of literary glory in France —and consequently throughout Europe—Voltaire. It was not, unquestionably, any depth of knowledge, nor the fire of enthusiasm, which had raised Voltaire to his brilliant position;—it was that unceasing war which he waged, with all the weapons of raillery and knowledge, against the antiquated pretensions, whether of the church or the schools;—it was that brilliant torch of sound common sense, which he hurled into the darkness of superstition;—it was that universality of genius which rendered every department of knowledge, history, physics and philosophy, and even every poetical form, subservient to the dissemination of the new doctrines, rendering them comprehensible to the many;—it was, in fine, that command of language, that equally witty and captivating dress in which he veiled the creations of his playful fancy, that enchained the attention of his readers. Everything he wrote had a specially practical character; therefore it was that Frederick found in Voltaire the man who gave expression to the undefined ideas which he felt within his own breast. Frederick had long derived instruction from Voltaire's writings: in the year 1736, then in his twenty-fourth year, he addressed a letter to this literary lion, then in his forty-second year, testifying his admiration, and offering his friendship; a correspondence was thus opened between these two great men, which, with some interruptions lasted to the close of Voltaire's life, a period of forty-two years. Frederick submitted his philosophical studies and practical essays to his friend, with a view to derive instruction and advice. His admiration knew no bounds: Voltaire's productions were prized by him beyond everything; his portrait, suspended over Frederick's writing-desk, constituted the chief ornament of his library: he was in the habit of comparing it with the statue of Memnon, in its life-diffusing properties. Of Voltaire's Henriade he intended to publish a splendid edition, with copper-plate engravings, for which Knobelsdorff was to furnish the drawings—an undertaking which remained, however, unaccomplished. He was in the habit of asserting that a single thought in the Henriade was worth the whole of Homer's Iliad. He made Voltaire many valuable presents: nay, he actually sent, in Keyserling's person, an ambassador to him, to present him with his portrait, painted by Knobelsdorff, and in return to procure Voltaire's last works, particularly such as were withheld from publication. This acquisition Frederick was wont to call his Golden Fleece.

Thus Frederick passed his time in Rheinsberg, actively preparing himself for that high post which he was soon to occupy. But some extraordinary fruits of these studies appeared even during this period; writings, in which he expressed his views and sentiments for his own guidance and that of others. His poetical effusions of this period are of less moment. They, at least the earlier ones of which we are now speaking, display the same defect that is observable in his philosophical essays—an attention to the mere practical part, being mostly ethical disquisitions. Such only of his poems as were written during the seven years' war, when the hand of tribulation was heavy upon him, and braced every dormant energy of his mind to action and resistance, display anything like deep or heartfelt emotion. Far more important and curious than these, his early poetical inspirations, are two treatises which he composed during the period of his residence in Rheinsberg.

One of these, written in the year 1736, is entitled, "Considerations on the present State of the political Relations of Europe." Frederick here discusses the critical position of Europe, arising out of the coalition of France and Austria; and with a degree of intellectual acumen, surprising in a youth of twenty-four years of age, he draws his deductions, based on the constant policy of these kingdoms—the unceasing aggrandizement of France, and Austria's struggle for absolute supremacy over Germany,—and points out the probable results of such coalition, provided no new power be developed amongst the other states. This treatise was conceived with a foreboding of that new power which was to be evolved in his own person. He concludes with emphatically reminding princes, "that their weakness hitherto has been the result of their absurd reliance upon themselves, and that nations have not been made for princes, but princes for nations."

Such were the novel doctrines which Frederick was resolved to reduce to practice and make the foundation of his government, and to which he remained faithful during the whole course of his life. Indeed, Frederick intended to have this treatise published in England, but abstained from doing so from certain motives; it was not discovered until after his death, when it was found amongst his posthumous works.

The second treatise, which is of a more comprehensive nature, was written by Frederick in the year 1739. This is the well-known work, which, under the title of "Anti-

Machiavelli," was intended as an answer to the celebrated one, written by the eminent Florentine historian Nicolo Machiavelli, in the beginning of the sixteenth century. Machiavelli's work—which must certainly be regarded as a masterpiece, considering the relations which it was intended to affect, and the object which the author had in view—lays down precepts for the attainment and maintenance of unlimited sovereignty, with particular reference to the Florentine state of that period. Frederick regarded the author as the apostle of despotism in general, and viewed the doctrines inculcated, not alone as base but even slanderous of the exalted duties of rulers. Replying to each argument of the Italian he triumphantly demonstrated, that instead of despotic or criminal acts, virtue, justice, and benignity should form the basis of government, as these latter can alone secure permanent happiness to the monarch. His whole line of reasoning is based upon the maxim with which he concluded the former treatise, namely, that the monarch is not to be regarded as the unlimited lord of the people he sways, but as the first servant of that people. The reader is not to expect in the above work a dispassionate historico-scientific review of the arguments which the prince sought to combat; but as containing an explicit statement of the views of an heir to a mighty monarchy, and that, too, at a time when his succession to the crown could not, in the course of nature, be far distant, this book cannot fail to awaken considerable interest. Nor did it at the time of its appearance in Holland, where Frederick had it printed under the inspection of Voltaire, but without Frederick's name being appended to it, attract any mean share of attention. The author's name did not remain a secret long, and the world waited, with impatience, an opportunity of judging in how far Frederick's practice would coincide with his precepts. He was already in possession of the crown.

CHAPTER XII.

DEATH OF THE FATHER.

DELIGHTFUL as were the days passed in Rheinsberg, yet they were not wholly unclouded. Onerous duties in Ruppin, visits to the court of his father in Berlin, excursions to the distant provinces of the kingdom, caused but too frequent interruptions; they however served, on his return, to heighten the enjoyment derivable from society, science, and art.

The principal aim of Frederick's life was now, by the zealous discharge of his various duties, to win the monarch's applause. Unremitting in his exertions that his regiment should appear on field-days and reviews as one of the handsomest and best disciplined, he had the gratification of seeing himself complimented by his father in presence of his staff. This military zeal was of all things that best calculated to neutralize the expressions of disapproval which Frederick's social and scientific engagements would at times elicit from his parent. Frederick exerted himself, likewise, to procure from all quarters of the globe the tallest and handsomest recruits for the regiment, which the king in person commanded. He also sought, by means of small presents for the king's table, the produce of the gardens or shambles of Rheinsberg, to give so many tokens of attention and respect. All this was dictated by prudence; but it emanated still more from a feeling of veneration for his father, whose unquestionable services to the state had exalted him to a high rank in Frederick's estimation.

DEATH OF THE FATHER.

A considerable change had likewise taken place in Frederick William's character during the latter years of his life. Frederick himself, writing to a friend, in December, 1738, mentions the fact of the king speaking in praise of the sciences. "I am quite charmed and delighted," he writes, "at what I have seen and heard. I feel all the sentiments of filial love redoubled within me, when listening to such rational and correct views from the lips of the author of my being." A year afterwards he was enabled to announce to another friend a still more important change in the character of the king; in effecting which the superior abilities of the son were, perhaps, partially instrumental. "The news of the day is," such are his words, "that the king spends three hours daily in reading Wolff's Philosophy, for which God be praised!" It was a compendium of Wolff's Natural Theology which the king was then reading. Frederick William was likewise most anxious, towards the close of his days, to make amends for the errors of his former life, and procure the return to his kingdom of the banished philosopher. This remained, however, for his successor to effect.

But Frederick's feelings of admiration for his father's virtues became perfectly enthusiastic, on accompanying him, during the summer of 1739, on a tour through Prussia, and perceiving the blessings which the monarch had diffused over a completely desolated province—the same which had been assigned to the Salzburg exiles. Frederick's feelings are best expressed in his own words. "Here we are," he thus writes from Lithuania to Voltaire, "arrived in a land which I regard as the *ne plus ultra* of the civilized world. This province is but little known, and may be said to have been called by the king, my father, into being. Lithuania was ravaged by the plague; twelve or fifteen depopulated cities and four or five hundred uninhabited villages, formed the melancholy spectacle which here met the eye. The king spared no expense in the execution of his humane design. He rebuilt, remodelled, and induced several thousand families from all parts of Europe to settle here. The soil was tilled, the land peopled, trade flourished, and this province, which is one of the most fertile in Germany, is now as thriving as ever. And all this has been solely the work of the king, who spared neither money, labor, trouble, promises, nor rewards for effectuating an object, not alone devised but carried into execution by himself, whereby he has secured peace and prosperity to a million of sentient beings, who are indebted to him for their weal and good government. To me there seems to be something heroic in the completion of so noble an undertaking—in thus colonizing a desert and rendering it fertile and prosperous; and I feel confident that you will coincide with me in this opinion." During this tour the prince royal received a particular and perfectly unexpected mark of the king's favor, in the shape of a present of an extensive establishment for breeding horses, which produced an annual sum of ten or twelve thousand thalers. This act of generosity was the less expected, inasmuch as the king had, but a short time previously, given utterance to a feeling of dislike towards Frederick —and that in no very measured language; this token of undiminished affection came, therefore, so completely unaware, that he could not find words to express his gratitude. This accession to his income was the more welcome, as his expenditure far exceeded his receipts, and he had been forced to raise considerable sums of money, by way of loan, in foreign countries. This source of uneasiness and embarrassment was thus removed for the remainder of the monarch's life.

But the days of the king were now drawing to a close. Every vestige of disunion between the father and son had, however, disappeared, and had been superseded by feelings of mutual esteem. Frederick William could commit the fortunes of his subjects, without a fear, to the hands of his son. He suffered an attack, during his tour through Prussia, of his old disorder, but with redoubled virulence, and attended by the worst symptoms of dropsy.

DEATH OF THE FATHER.

During the entire winter his sufferings were extreme. Frederick passed the greater part of his time in attendance on him. The letters written by the son to the father during this period give evidence of the kindest attention.

As spring drew on the situation of the king seemed to exhibit signs of improvement, and Frederick returned to Rheinsberg. An express, announcing the approaching dissolution of the monarch, summoned him from thence. Frederick hastened to Potsdam, where the king had chiefly resided during his illness. On Frederick's arrival his father had partially revived, and was seated in front of the palace, in a chair on wheels, in which he was moved about, as he had long lost the use of his limbs. The king was inspecting the laying of the foundation-stone of a neighboring house. On recognizing the prince some distance off, he extended his arms to clasp him, and his son was soon wrapped in his embraces. They remained a considerable time in this position, without either speaking. "He had certainly been always harsh," he admitted to his son, "but still he had ever loved him with a parent's love; it was a great consolation to have been able to see him once more." Frederick replied in terms suited to the strong excitement he labored under. The monarch was conveyed to his chamber, and conversed there for more than an hour, in private, with the prince, informing him, with unusual vigor, of the internal and external relations of his kingdom. He continued these discourses during the few remaining days of his life. On the second day, as the prince and several of the higher officers of state happened to be present, he exclaimed, addressing the latter: "Has not God been very kind to me in giving me so good and noble a son!" On this Frederick arose and kissed his father's hand; but the king drew him towards him, and, embracing him affectionately, exclaimed: "My God! I die in peace, as I possess so worthy a son and successor!"

A few days afterwards the king commanded the presence of his whole household, the ministers of state, and the superior officers of his own regiment, in his antechamber. On being wheeled into this room in his chair, he appeared exceedingly feeble, and scarcely able to articulate. His kingdom and the command of his regiment he solemnly resigned to Frederick, by proclamation of one of the officers present, and exhorted his subjects to testify towards his son the same fidelity and allegiance which they had ever exhibited towards himself. He was so exhausted by this exertion, that he had to be conveyed to his bed. The prince and queen attended him thither. He resigned himself calmly to the last agonies, and expired, whilst offering up a pious prayer, on the 31st of May, 1740.

The king had left directions in his will that his interment should be unattended with pomp. The prince royal obeyed these instructions; but being apprehensive that the public might put a false construction upon his acts, and, in ignorance of the wishes expressed in the monarch's will, attribute his conduct to the former differences which had existed between them, he subsequently arranged a solemn funeral procession in memory of his father. Frederick has himself, when writing his father's life, spoken of these differences in a spirit of filial duty, alluding to them in these words: "We have passed over the domestic crosses of this great prince in silence. Some lenity is due to the faults of the children in consideration of the virtues of their parent."

CHAPTER XIII.

FREDERICK'S ACCESSION.

FREDERICK was seized with the bitterest anguish as he gazed on the closing eyelids of his dying parent. Every fond feeling of his childhood, which late years had awakened, crowded upon him; the virtues which had distinguished the government of his father seemed to fling an additional hold round his memory. But he did not surrender himself, whilst surveying the past, to vain regrets. He paid the best tribute of sincere veneration to the shade of his father, by following boldly in the path which the latter had marked out for him, and by laboring to improve the mechanism of the state, which the master-hand of his father had called into being; making only such additions as, in accordance with the freedom of his own spirit, would liberalize its institutions. Mastering his grief, he devoted himself with the most restless energy to his high vocation; and even the few first days of his government indicated in how far his future policy was likely to be conservative or innovatory—how, in short, he was resolved to reign.

The line of conduct which the king pursued, was to many productive of the bitterest disappointment, whilst to others it was a source of unexpected delight. Every one had expected that considerable changes would now take place in the state; that the men who had enjoyed the especial confidence of the preceding monarch would now play a more subordinate part. But Frederick felt little inclination to act harshly towards real merit, in order to gratify any personal dislike, arising from their former conduct towards himself as an individual. An instance of his conduct in this respect is related, with reference to the old warrior, Prince Leopold of Dessau, who had formerly belonged to the Austrian court party, and who, on his paying a visit of condolence to Frederick, entered the presence-chamber in tears, and besought the king to permit himself and his sons to retain their posts in the army, and their former influence and consequence. To this Frederick replied, that he would not deprive him of his former rank, as he expected that the prince would continue to serve him as faithfully as he had served his father; but at the same time added: "that as to influence and consequence, no one under his government should possess either but himself." It created still more surprise, that Frederick should not only continue in office the former minister of finance, de Boden, who had been accused of unworthy practices, and seemed to be by no means a favorite, but that he should even present him with a splendid, newly-built, and fully-furnished palace.

Others, on the contrary, found themselves sorely disappointed in the hopes which they had conceived themselves warranted in building on Frederick's accession to the throne. In this way the meritorious Lieutenant-general De Schulemburg found himself exposed to a sharp rebuke from the youthful king, in consequence of his having from a friendly feeling, and in order to offer his personal congratulations to the new monarch, left his regiment without having first obtained leave of absence. In this way a number of adventurers, allured by the more lively turn of Frederick's mind, crowded in upon him, whilst nothing was further from Frederick's thoughts than to lend himself to their absurd schemes. The bundles of congratulatory poems which were transmitted to the royal poet repaid the labor of versification but poorly. Several of his former favorites had likewise to discover that they had formed but a very false estimate of his character. One of these could find nothing more important to do, than to write immediately to a friend in Paris, inviting him to come to Berlin, with the assurance that there was now every prospect of his making his fortune there, and of leading the merriest life in the world in Frederick's society. Unfortunately, Frederick had entered the chamber of the Berlin correspondent unobserved, and had read the letter. He took it out of the writer's hand, tore it, and said very calmly, "The farce is now at an end."

But those amongst Frederick's friends whose real fidelity, merits and capabilities had been tested, saw an honorable path to fame now opened before them. Frederick took care to provide each with a situation suiting his peculiar capacity, and in which his services might be rendered most available to the state. Those who had innocently suffered on his account were now nobly recompensed. The father of the unfortunate Katte was created count and field-marshal: the other relations of Katte received likewise particular marks of the king's favor. The trusty Duhan was recalled from his place of banishment, and Frederick took care to make a competent provision for his tutor's declining days. Keith also returned to Berlin, and was raised to the rank of captain and lieutenant-colonel. The president De Münchow, had, from the time of the termination of Frederick's captivity in Cüstrin, been exposed to many crosses, as an indemnification for which both he and his sons were honored with special marks of Frederick's approbation.

Frederick entertained the same solicitude for the welfare of his brothers and sisters; in particular for the suitable education of his younger brothers. To his mother he testified the tenderest regard up to the hour of her death. On her addressing him at the funeral of his father by the title of "Your Majesty," he interrupted her, and said, "Call me your son; I am prouder of this title than that of king." He conducted himself with the same deferential regard towards his wife, although the report was soon spread that, as his marriage had not been blessed with issue he intended to be divorced from her, and proceed to a second alliance. But Frederick thought not of divorce. On the contrary, it is stated that after his accession to the throne he presented her to his assembled court with the words : "This is your queen!" and embracing her tenderly in presence of all assembled, kissed her affectionately. But that cordiality which had existed between Frederick and his consort during the happy days of their sojourn in Rheinsburg, had fled forever : they soon lived separate from one another, and only met on occasions of public ceremony. The gentle, feminine piety which formed the very soul of this rare princess suited, perchance, but ill that severity of reasoning which Frederick was accustomed to apply to the revelations of religion : Frederick took care, notwithstanding, that she should enjoy all the honors which were her due as reigning queen ; and was most scrupulous in seeing that she was treated by the foreign embassies with all the courtesy due to her rank. She repaid these attentions with the most touching tenderness and devotion.

As to the mode in which Frederick wished the administration of affairs in exchequer matters to be carried on, his language was sufficiently explicit. Immediately after his accession, on the occasion of the ministers of state appearing before him, on the 2d of June, to do homage, his high-minded declaration, of which he never lost sight during his whole reign, was as follows: "Sincerely grateful though we be (he thus addressed the ministers) for the faithful services you have rendered our dearly beloved father, yet it is not our pleasure that you should enrich us at the expense of our poorer subjects ; you shall, on the contrary, consider yourselves bound by virtue of the present command, to provide with the same care for the happiness of the country at large as for our own ; the more particularly as we do not wish to recognize any distinction between our own individual interest and that of the land in general, the latter of which you

FREDERICK'S ACCESSION. 101

are as little to lose sight of as the former; nay the advantage of the country at large is to have precedence of our own in the event of their clashing."

These sentiments, which were at that period but rarely to be met with in princes, were soon practically exemplified by Frederick in a manner that gained him universal love. The preceding winter had been one of unusual severity and duration; scarcity and famine were, in many places, the consequences. But the voice of misery was not long in reaching the ear of the youthful sovereign. On the very second day after his accession he ordered the well-filled granaries to be opened, and the corn retailed to the people at moderate prices. Wherever the supplies were insufficient, large quantities were procured from the neighboring kingdoms. The game killed in the royal preserves were likewise sold at low prices. Several taxes, which pressed heavily upon the necessaries of life, were for a time wholly remitted. In fine, several sums of money, which had been spared by retrenchment in the expenses of the household, were, distributed amongst the most needy. The shouts of joy with which the presence of the young king was everywhere greeted in consequence of these acts came really from the hearts of the people. But Frederick did not overlook, even during the few first days of his reign, the importance of those causes of national prosperity which operate silently; several ordinances were issued, having for their object the increase and improvement of manufactures; skilful artizans, who would consent to immigrate to Prussia, were secured in many privileges.

Frederick was not the less alive to the advantages which a powerful standing army could fail of ensuring to the scattered dominions of the Prussian monarchy. Little as the severity of military service seemed originally consonant to his nature, yet his energies were now, nevertheless, carefully directed to its discipline and development. Only in such superfluous expenditure as tended to no practical purpose was retrenchment made. This military reform opened with the disbandonment of the Giant-guard, which the late king had maintained in Potsdam for his own pleasure. It is even said that Frederick William, shortly before his death, communicated to his son an account of the vast sums which the maintenance of this corps had cost, and had even recommended its disbandonment. This body appeared for the last time in the funeral procession, as guard of honor to the late king's remains: it was immediately afterwards dissolved, and the men distributed amongst the other regiments. Frederick obtained thereby the means of adding more than ten thousand men to his army. In other respects provision was made for the splendor of the military career. All the flags and standards of Prussia were now decorated with the Prussian black eagle, grasping the sword and sceptre in his claws, with the inscription: "*Pro Gloria et Patria!*"

The most important changes which Frederick introduced were in those elements of life which had met with the least attention from his father. Frederick struck off the shackles from the mind, and thereby conferred a degree of moral power far more potent than swords or any engines of war. Freedom of speech had been prohibited by his father; newspapers, at first wholly forbidden, had been subsequently tolerated under oppressive restrictions, and dragged on a wretched existence. Shortly after Frederick's accession two journals were published at his instance, which soon became of importance, and to which he himself contributed some articles. An Academy of Sciences was founded, and literary men of eminence invited from different countries to Berlin. Frederick was particularly anxious to regain the services of Professor Wolff: he said in a letter to Provost Rheinbeck: "The man who seeks and loves truth must be esteemed by every community;" and that it was his opinion that Wolff's being induced to return would be a great moral victory. Wolff yielded to the solicitation of his noble disciple, and returned to Halle, where he was received with every honor. Contemporaneously with the above appeared a royal edict, restricting government situations to such only as had spent two years at a Prussian university. The society of Freemasons was now publicly acknowledged: Frederick himself held a solemn lodge shortly after his accession, in which he took the chair as master. The more enlightened character of his mind was favorable to a freer development of other relations of life. Religious toleration was one of the most important maxims which Frederick enforced from the commencement of his reign, and with which he opposed all the abuses of narrow-minded bigotry. A second point at which he aimed was the attainment of a purer and more rational administration of the law. But to effectuate this object, a complicated structure, the result of mature deliberation and judicial wisdom, was absolutely essential. The first rays of that light which Frederick was destined to shed, appeared in the form of some new ordinances. One of these, which was promulgated on the third day of his reign, was the abolition of torture, except in some extraordinary cases; and even in these it was abolished some few years subsequently. The neighboring states did not imitate his example until much later.

Every change thus introduced by Frederick in the very commencement of his reign, was altogether his own work; his ministers but carried his orders into execution. By means of the most extraordinary activity, and an exact subdivision of his time, he succeeded—a thing hitherto unheard of—in observing, examining, and conducting everything himself. And yet he found time to devote some hours of recreation to the arts, poetry, and, in particular, to music; and these enjoyments served but to give, in turns, a greater elasticity to his mind. The strongest evidence of his unusual activity in the discharge of business is to be found in the dispatches of the foreign ambassadors then resident at the Berlin court. They complain that the king is his own minister, and that there is no one of whom they can make a confidant, and through whom they can attain influence; adding, that it would be most advisable to act with frankness towards this young king, unusual as such a course might be.

About the middle of July Frederick proceeded to Königsberg, in order to receive the homage of the Prussian chambers. His grandfather had there assumed the Prussian kingly crown. But Frederick William had been averse to ceremony, and had neglected the form of a coronation. Frederick, likewise, saw no necessity for reviving all the forms. "I am now travelling (he thus expresses himself in a letter to Voltaire) to Prussia, there to receive homage, but without the holy oil-bottle, and the idle and empty ceremonials which ignorance devised and custom has hallowed." The coronation took place on the 20th July. Frederick had himself instructed in all the necessary formalities by a friend well acquainted with such matters. He afterwards asked this person whether he had acquitted himself tolerably. "Oh, yes, sire," replied the person interrogated, "but there was one who acquitted himself still better." "And who might that be?" "Louis the Fifteenth." "But I," added Frederick, with a smile, "knew a person who did the thing still better." "And who was that?" "Baron!" (a well-known French actor.)

On the whole, Frederick was very well satisfied with his few days' residence in Königsberg. The coronation sermon, preached by the court preacher, Quandt, met with his decided approbation: he had heard Quandt previously with pleasure, and in a work on German literature, which he wrote in the evening of his life, he makes mention of Quandt as one of the best public speakers which Germany ever possessed. He derived particular pleasure from a torch-light procession, which the Königsberg students arranged in his honor; in return for which he provided them with a plenteous entertainment. The manœuvres of the Königsberg troops were likewise completely to his satisfaction. He marked his approval by conferring several favors as well upon the town as upon the whole province, mindful of the motto, which the medals distributed at the coronation bore—" The Prosperity of the People."

On Frederick's return to Berlin on the 2d of August, he received the homage of the Curmark chambers; and on his appearing in the balcony after the coronation, the people gave three joyous shouts for "King Frederick!" Contrary to custom and etiquette, he remained half an hour gazing fixedly and intently upon the myriads collected in front of the palace, and apparently absorbed in meditation. The medals distributed in Berlin bore the inscription:—" For Truth and Justice."

A short time afterwards Frederick left Berlin a second time, to receive the homage of the Westphalian provinces. He first paid a visit to the Margravine of Baireuth, his eldest sister, in her capital. From thence he made a rapid detour to Strasbourg, in order to touch French soil and see French soldiers. For the purpose of escaping observation, he had assumed the name of Count De Four, and was accompanied by but few attendants. The whole cortége consisted of two carriages. On their arrival at Kehl (on the German side of the Rhine, opposite Strasbourg) the landlord directed the attention of Frederick's valet to the fact of its being necessary to produce the passports immediately on their arrival at the other side. The latter made out a passport accordingly, and presented it to Frederick for signature, who appended the royal seal. The hotel-keeper, to whom this process appeared unusually summary, quickly suspected from whom alone it could emanate; and it was a matter of much difficulty to purchase his silence.

On his arrival in Strasbourg, in order that his appearance might be more completely French, he ordered some clothes to be made in the newest French fashion. He became acquainted in a coffee-house with some French officers, and invited them to supper; they were charmed with the information, grace, and elegance of their host, but sought in vain to penetrate his secret. Frederick visited the parade on the following day. He was here recognized by a soldier, who had been formerly in the Prussian service; the fact was immediately communicated to the governor, Marshal De Broglio, and Frederick had much difficulty in evading the honors intended for him by the marshal. The news soon spread throughout the city, and the people were overjoyed at having the young king, of whose fame they had already heard so much, in the midst of them. The tailor who had made the clothes would not consent to accept of payment: being satisfied with the honor of having worked for the Prussian monarch. Bonfires blazed during the evening throughout the streets, and from all sides rang the shout, " *Vive le Roi de Prusse!* "

From Strasbourg Frederick proceeded down to Wesel. This tour was not quite of so melancholy a character as that which he had made as a prisoner ten years previously, but he derived little enjoyment even now, owing to his suffering from an attack of fever. This fever was the cause of Frederick's abandoning his original intention of visiting Voltaire at Brabant, where the poet was then residing. Frederick had, however, but to express the wish, and Voltaire came to meet his royal admirer at the palace of Mayland, in Cleves. Frederick was so enfeebled by disease, that he apologized for not being able to receive so great a genius as he deserved. He was now as much charmed with the man as he had been hitherto with his books. "Voltaire," says Frederick in a letter to Jordan, written shortly after this visit, "is as eloquent as Cicero, as agreeable as Pliny, as wise as Agrippa: he unites in his own person all the virtues and talents of the men of antiquity. His mind is perpetually at work, and every drop of ink that flows from his pen is pregnant with wit. He has read us his noble tragedy of Mahomet: we were enchanted. I could only admire and be silent. You will find me," adds Frederick, "on my return very talkative; but remember, I have seen two things which I always admired—Voltaire and French troops."

On his way back Frederick was present at the betrothal, in Salzdalum, of his brother, Prince August William, with the sister of Frederick's wife, the Princess Louisa Amelia of Brunswick.

Frederick's visit to Westphalia had given rise to a political demonstration, which served to illustrate very forcibly the future political conduct of this monarch. A similar incident had even previously occurred during the three first weeks of his reign. The Kurfürst of Mayence had made an unjust claim to a part of the territory of the Landgrave of Hesse Cassel, an ancient ally of the house of Brandenburg. Frederick sent a serious remonstrance to the Kurfürst, cautioning him against disturbing the peace of the empire: the consequence of which was that the latter withdrew his troops.

The second incident was more important. Prussia had become possessed, by inheritance, of Hirstal, a place situated in the see of the Bishop of Liège. The inhabitants of Hirstal had rebelled during the lifetime of Frederick William, and had been protected by the bishop, who coveted its possession. Frederick William had in vain endeavored to arrange the matter amicably. Hirstal now refused to swear fealty to Frederick, and was sustained in this line of conduct by the bishop. Frederick thereupon sent one of his higher officers of state, to obtain a distinct declaration from the bishop on the subject, and at the same time to point out the consequences to which he might expose himself by his conduct. This declaration could not be obtained, and 1600 Prussian troops invested the bishop's territories. The latter applied for aid to all the neighboring princes, and in particular to the emperor. His imperial majesty wrote emphatically to Frederick, to the effect that, instead of redressing his own wrongs, he should bring his complaint before the Diet. But Frederick, well aware of the futility of such a proceeding, defended his conduct in his reply, and refused to withdraw his troops. The bishop was now compelled to come to terms; and on the 20th of October a treaty was entered into, by which Frederick assigned Hirstal to the bishop for a considerable sum of money. The isolated position of Hirstal was the chief inducement for disposing of it in this manner.

Thus Frederick had, within the first five months of his reign, given sufficient evidence of the principles which were to guide his future government. But the freedom and independence which were manifest in his actions were altogether too strange and extraordinary for his contemporaries to comprehend or properly estimate. The hour had, however, already arrived, when the sword was to open a more brilliant path to fame, and bring his name into the mouths of men.

CHAPTER XIV.

OPENING OF THE SILESIAN WAR.

UNUSUALLY cheering was the prospect which the commencement of autumn ushered in. Voltaire had come, on Frederick's invitation, to Berlin, where they could now communicate more freely than at their first hasty interview. Besides Voltaire, many other distinguished men had gathered round Frederick. His two sisters, the Margravines of Baireuth and Anspach, had also come upon a visit. The pleasures of intellectual enjoyment, concerts, and festivities seemed to promise a long course of gaiety.

Just at this moment a courier arrived with intelligence that the Emperor Charles VI. had expired, on the 20th of October (1740). Frederick was at Rheinsberg, whither he generally resorted to recover from the periodic attacks of fever to which he was subject. Shaking off the fever perforce, he began to meditate on the execution of that which had long occupied his thoughts. "Now is the time," he writes to Voltaire, "in which the old political system may be made to undergo an entire change; the stone is loosed which shall fall on Nebuchadnezzar's statue of many metals, and crush them all."

The figure which Nebuchadnezzar had seen in a dream, and which the prophet Daniel had been summoned to interpret for him, was nobly wrought in metals, but its feet were of iron and clay, so that it could withstand no shock. Such was likewise the constitution of the Austrian dominions. This vast empire possessed no internal strength;

an unfortunate war with the Turks had exhausted its last resources. Prince Eugene, long the prop of the state, was dead. Charles VI. had devoted his whole life to obtaining the acquiescence of the principal sovereigns of Europe in the succession of his daughter Maria Theresa. Eugene's advice, to rely on an army of 180,000 men for carrying the Pragmatic Sanction into effect, rather than on any promises made by princes, had been unheeded. Prussia was, on the contrary, in all its pristine vigor. Frederick William had been, no doubt, frequently ridiculed for expending such large sums upon his army, and yet not venturing into the field; but the fact of the existence of an army was undeniable, and that it was in point of discipline second to none, was equally so. Prussia's provinces were flourishing, its revenues proportionably large, the state was encumbered by no national debt, and there were nearly nine millions of thalers in the royal exchequer. With such resources at command, a powerful, manly spirit might look fortune in the face, and venture in search of fame and greatness.

Austria had been for centuries playing a very double game as regarded Prussia. We have seen the emperor acknowledging its claims to Jülick and Berg, and at the same time favoring those of her rivals. Frederick might have now supported his claims by force of arms; but he saw the extent of the danger he incurred, in arousing the hostility of so many competitors, and his being necessarily obliged to leave his kingdom comparatively unprotected, from concentrating his forces at a point so distant. He therefore preferred urging other claims, manifestly just, attended with less danger, and of more solid advantage to the state. Several principalities in Silesia had at different periods become the property of his ancestors by inheritance, but had been unjustly withheld from them by Austria. Such were Jägerndorff, Liegnitz, Brieg, and Wohlau. This circumstance had led to many former quarrels. Under the government of the Great Elector, when Austria stood in need of his aid against the Turks, a species of arrange-

OPENING OF THE SILESIAN WAR. 111

ment had been entered into, to the effect that, instead of the above principalities, others, known as the Schwiebusian district, but of less extent, should be ceded to Prussia ; but Austria succeeded at the same time in extracting (by means of the most wily representations) a promise from the son of the great Elector, that these dominions should be restored to Austria on his accession. On the latter (afterwards King Frederick I.) coming to the throne, he informed his ministers of the promise he had given, and exposed the duplicity of the Austrian diplomacy. He was compelled, however, to keep his promise, but did so with the protest, that he left it in the hands of his successors to prosecute their just claims. "If God and our necessities ordain it so, we must be content; but should God dispose it otherwise, then my successors will know what it will be their duty to do."

Frederick was well aware of what it was his duty to do. That undefined feeling, which impelled the youthful monarch to glorious deeds, had now found a worthy direction : he therefore resolved to embrace the favorable opportunity that now presented itself for regaining by his might, that which he felt to be his inalienable right.

Frederick did not require much time to put his military operations on a proper footing. His plan was communicated to but few confidants. The unusual activity which his dispositions required, the marching of troops, the movements of the artillery, the erection of magazines, all announced that something important was going forward. All was wonder and curiosity; the most contradictory rumors were in circulation; the diplomatists despatched and received couriers without being able to obtain any distinct information as to the king's designs. The latter had so arranged the marches of the troops, as to appear desirous of attacking Jülick and Berg, rather than Silesia. He was much amused with the false impressions which were rife amongst the public. "Write to me all the comical things that are said, thought, and done, (he says in a letter written by him from Ruppin to Jordan.) Berlin shall look like Madame Bellona in labor, and I trust that a pretty babe will see the light; and that I, by some bold and successful stroke, shall win the confidence of the public. I shall then be in one of the happiest periods of my life, and perhaps lay the foundation for future fame."

It could not, however, long remain a secret that the Prussian troops were being concentrated on the Silesian frontier. The Austrian court was informed of its danger through its ambassador in Berlin; but the cabinet council of Maria Theresa replied, that it neither could nor would credit such things. A second ambassador, Baron Botta, was sent, notwithstanding, from Vienna to Berlin, to observe the motions of Prussia more closely. He saw through Frederick's plan clearly enough. On his being presented to Frederick, he took occasion to remark impressively on the bad state of the Silesian roads, through which he had just passed, and which were then rendered almost impassable by the floods. Frederick saw his object; but not desiring to give any further explanation, drily replied, that the worst thing that could happen to a person on such roads, was to be dirtied by the mud.

In December everything was ready for opening the campaign. The design of occupying Silesia had ceased to be a secret. Frederick afterwards sent an ambassador, Count Gotter, to Vienna, to advocate his claims to Silesia and propose conditions. Before setting out for his army he informed Botta of his intentions. "Sire," said the latter "you will hurry Austria and yourself into perdition." Frederick replied that it would be for Maria Theresa to accept of his proposals. After a momentary pause, Botta remarked to Frederick, in an ironical tone: "Sire, your troops are, unquestionably, very fine-looking men—much finer looking than ours; but ours have stood fire before now. Weigh well, therefore, I beseech you, the step you are about to take." The king, becoming impatient, replied sharply: "You seem to approve of the appearance of my troops: you will soon have an opportunity of judging of their conduct!" All further representations on the part

OPENING OF THE SILESIAN WAR.

of the ambassador were met by Frederick with the remark that it was now too late, as he had already passed the Rubicon.

Before Frederick's departure for the seat of war, he summoned the general officers of his army once more into his presence, and bade them farewell in the following terms: "Prussians, I have ventured on the present war with no other allies to sustain me than your gallantry and devotion. My cause is just—and I rely on fate to aid me in my enterprise. Be ever mindful of that high renown which your ancestors have achieved on the battle-fields of Warsaw and Fehrbellin under the Great Elector. You are the arbiters of your own destiny: honors and rewards await the execution of glorious deeds. But there is little need of my exhorting you to the pursuit of that which is ever present to your thoughts, the one object worthy of your toils—Glory. We shall have for adversaries troops that have already attained the highest renown under Prince Eugene. This prince is, certainly, now no more; but our glory, in the event of victory, will not be the less, as we have ventured to cope with soldiers so famed. Fare you well. Start for your different posts. I shall follow without loss of time to the theatre of that fame which awaits us."

On the 13th of December there was a grand masquerade in the royal palace. Whilst the violins and the trumpets were challenging to the dance, and the motley maskers moving to and fro through the saloons, preparations were silently making for the departure of the king. He stole unobserved from the capital, and hastened towards the Silesian frontiers. On the 14th he arrived in Crossen which is situated on the borders of Silesia. On the same day the belfry of the principal church in Crossen gave way, a circumstance which was regarded by the king's troops as a bad omen and portending future disasters; but Frederick had sufficient tact to turn the circumstance to a good account. He told his men to be of good cheer; for the lofty should be humbled, as they saw in the case of the bell. Austria was, of course, as compared with Prussia, the lofty, and by a simile so apt he revived the courage of such as had begun to despond.

On the 16th of December Frederick set foot for the first time on Silesian soil. He was here met by two deputies, who had been sent by the Protestant inhabitants of the fortified city of Glogau to entreat him to graciously abstain from attacking the city on the side on which the Protestant church stood. This church lay outside the line of fortifications; and the commandant of the town, Count Wallis, had resolved on burning it down, (he had already committed all the other buildings to the flames,) with a view to prevent it from forming a basis for Frederick's operations. Frederick had ordered his coachman to halt, on the approach of the two deputies. "You are the first Silesians," said he, addressing them, "who have ever asked a favor at my hands, and it shall therefore be granted you." A messenger was immediately dispatched to Count Wallis, with the assurance that Frederick would abstain from attacking the town from the side alluded to, and the church was accordingly spared.

The Prussian arms had as yet encountered no opposition; the troops, on whom the defence of the land devolved, were hardly numerous enough to garrison the principal fortified towns. No considerable reinforcements could arrive within so short a time from Austria. The couriers and messengers, perpetually dispatched by the government of Breslau to Vennia, imploring aid with increased urgency as the danger became more imminent, could effect nothing. The final resolutions issued by the cabinet in Vienna to the government officers in Breslau, consisted in a recommendation to spare themselves the expenses of the couriers, and not to give way to such inordinate apprehensions.

Thus no more considerable impediments opposed the invasion and conquest of Silesia, than the badness of the weather and the wretched state of the roads, of which the Marquis of Botta had drawn, in truth, no very exaggerated picture. But the troops retained their ardor, and Frederick did not neglect to keep this spirit alive by the distribution of manifold rewards. Manifestos, addressed to the inhabitants of Silesia, were published, confirming the inhabitants in their property, rights, and privileges, promising the strictest discipline on the part of the invading army, but declaring it to be the intention of the king to maintain his rights by force against the claims of any third party. These declarations, and the admirable conduct of the troops, and perhaps, more than all, the hopes of the Protestant inhabitants of Silesia, who considered Frederick in many respects as their deliverer, gained amongst the people many friends to the Prussian cause. The answering protestations of the Austrian government were, on the other hand, but little heeded, if not totally disregarded.

It was certainly at first rather difficult for the Silesians to know how to act between the fealty they had so long maintained towards the Austrian government, and that which was now demanded from them by their new masters. One mode of escape from this dilemma is worth mentioning. In Gruneberg (the first considerable town in Silesia assailed by the Prussian arms) the gates were found closed. An officer was immediately dispatched to the burgomaster to demand in the king's name the surrender of the town; the messenger was conducted to the town-hall, where the burgomaster and the council were assembled in their civic robes. The officer demanded the keys of the city gates. The burgomaster begged to be particularly excused: he could not and dare not give the keys. The officer threatened to burst open the gates; and explained that in the event of the town not accepting the gracious offer of the king, ulterior measures would be resorted to, of which it might afterwards have reason to repent. The burgomaster shrugged his shoulders. "There are the keys upon the table," said he; "but I will not give them to you on any account. If you are inclined to take them, I certainly cannot prevent you." The officer smiled, took the keys, and opened the gates. On the arrival of the troops within the walls, the Prussian general notified to the burgomaster, that he was now, according to the custom of war, at liberty to take back the keys. The burgomaster refused to comply. " I have not given away the keys," said he, " and I will consequently not send for them, nor take them. But if the general be kind enough to replace them, or have them replaced on the spot from whence they were taken, I shall certainly not object." The general mentioned the circumstance to the king, much to the amusement of the latter, who ordered that the keys should be carried back to the town-hall by a detachment of soldiers, with bands playing and banners streaming.

The first fortified town, the garrison of which checked the progress of the Prussians, was Glogau. The fortifications were not in particularly good condition, but the commander had made every disposition, which was possible within the time, for its defence. Frederick, in order to be enabled to continue his march, and in particular, as the unfavorable season of the year rendered a regular siege impracticable, left a detachment of his army behind, for the investment of the town, and then pushed on for Breslau.

Breslau enjoyed, at this period, free, almost republican institutions: it had been even relieved from the presence of a garrison. As an Austrian corps was about to enter, the citizens became turbulent; and the disorder being still further heightened by the proposition to burn down the suburbs, the inhabitants resolved on defending the ramparts themselves; but the Prussians had got possession of the suburbs, and assaulted the town much sooner than had been expected. The citizens were insufficiently provided with ammunition and provisions; while the trenches being frozen over, exposed the town to be stormed; and in that event it was feared that if taken it would be handed over to the mercy of the soldiers. The besieged were therefore not indisposed to negotiate; and the propositions for an arrangement were hurried to a precipitate conclusion by the violence of the Protestant section of the inhabitants, who, at the instigation of a fanatical shoemaker, pressed the senate to come to a speedy decision. Frederick granted the town neutrality; it was obliged to open its gates, but was not required to maintain a garrison. No provision had, however, been made in this capitulation with respect to the Austrian directory: Frederick, on entering the town, immediately dismissed all its members.

On the 7th of January, 1741, Frederick made a solemn entry into Breslau. The procession was opened by the royal carriages and mules, the latter decorated with cymbals and blue saddle-cloths, ornamented with gold-fringe and eagles in embroidery. Next came a body of gens-d'armes, and after these the royal state-coach, lined with yellow velvet, and containing a magnificent blue velvet mantle, trimmed with ermine, as the symbol of royalty. After the coach came the princes, margraves, and counts of Frederick's army; and, finally, the king himself, surrounded by a small staff, and ushered in by the town-mayor. The crowd was unusually great, and the king most graciously acknowledged the salutations with which he was on all sides received. The deputies of the council and the nobility were invited to the royal table. After dinner, Frederick rode through the town. On arriving at a splendid palace erected by the Jesuits, he observed, that he was not much surprised at the Emperor being in want of money, as he permitted the clergy to spend such vast sums in this manner.

Two days afterwards a large ball was given, which Frederick opened with a lady belonging to one of the highest families in Silesia. But he soon disappeared from the groups of dancers, and hastened, without loss of time, to his troops, who had already advanced considerably further. Ohlau and Namslau were speedily captured; Brieg, a fortress, was, like Glogau, invested; Ottmachau, in Upper Silesia, was taken. Neisse, the most considerable fortress in Silesia, was now the only important point which was not in the hands of the Prussians: the main strength of the royal army was accordingly concentrated here for its reduction.

These rapid successes, the conquest of a fertile land, almost without a blow, raised Frederick's spirits to the highest pitch, and appeared to promise a glorious future. His letters to Jordan, of this period, are instinct with singular gaiety and humor; and, indeed, his whole correspondence with Jordan, which extends over the period of the first Silesian war, is remarkable for more easy grace than that of any other period. He everywhere breathes forth the tenderest sensibility; not, however, without occasionally a touch of satire, at the pacific virtues of his friend. From Ottmachau he dispatched the following humorous epistle.

"My dear Mr. Jordan, my sweet Mr. Jordan, my mild Mr. Jordan, my good, amiable, peace-loving, most philanthropic Mr. Jordan! I have to announce for your satisfaction, that Silesia may be regarded as conquered, and that Neisse is already bombarded! I wish to prepare you for mighty projects, and to announce the greatest success to which fortune's womb has ever given birth. Let this satisfy you for the present. Be my Cicero in defending my acts: I will be your Cæsar in their execution. Fare thee well; thou art thyself best aware of the hearty love which I, thy true friend, bear thee."

A few days afterwards he again addressed him, as follows: "I have the honor to announce to your philanthropy, that we are making the most Christian-like arrangements to bombard Neisse; and that, in the event of the town not surrendering of its own accord, we shall find ourselves under the necessity of battering it to the ground. On the whole, we have been as successful as possible, and you will soon hear nothing further from us; for in ten days everything will be over, and in about fourteen I shall have the pleasure of seeing you again." The conclusion of this letter is as follows: "Farewell, Mr. Councillor; amuse yourself with Horace, study Pausanias, and raise your spirits with Anacreon: as regards me, I have nothing further to amuse me than loopholes, hurdles, and casemates. Indeed, I pray God to grant me soon some more pleasing and peaceful occupation; and you health, happiness, and everything your heart desires."

The conquest of Neisse did not, however, prove so easy of execution; the fortress withstood the bombardment, and all attempts at storming were baffled by the judicious arrangements of the commandant; the outworks were put in good condition; the environs, with all their fine buildings, burnt down; the frozen trenches were every morning freed from the ice; and the ramparts, being drenched with water, speedily presented the appearance of an inaccessible wall of glass. As the season of the year precluded a regular siege, and the Prussian troops were exhausted by the severity of their winter-marches, Frederick was compelled to abandon the undertaking: but the remaining portions of his army had simultaneously pushed on through the whole of Upper Silesia, as far as Jablunke, on the frontiers of Hungary. The Austrian troops, arriving too late to defend the land, had retired upon Moravia, being too weak to offer any effectual resistance. The Prussians had therefore time in their winter-quarters to recover, in some degree, from their exhaustion. On the 26th of January Frederick had already returned to Berlin.

CHAPTER XV.

CAMPAIGN OF THE YEAR 1741.

WITH the rapidity of lightning the tidings spread through Europe of the wholly unexpected occupation of Silesia. Nothing could equal the amazement which the daring of the young sovereign, who had ventured with his insignificant resources, to enter the lists against the might of Austria, everywhere excited: by some his conduct was regarded as imprudent, by others, pronounced to be actual insanity. In the opinion of the English ambassador at Vienna, Frederick deserved to be declared under the ban. The most obtuse could indeed perceive that the peace of Europe, which had been but lately established, must be, by his acts, long interrupted; for other powers would likewise step forward with pretensions to the inheritance of Charles VI., and pay but little respect to the provisions of the Pragmatic Sanction. As a proof of this, the Elector, Charles Albert, of Bavaria, who had never recognized the Sanction, already laid claim to the vacant imperial throne: he was, however, too weak to enforce his pretensions with anything like a prospect of success. Greater dangers were to be apprehended from France, as it was easy to foresee that this power would not neglect an opportunity so favorable for renewing its inveterate hostility to Austria.

Meanwhile, the demands and propositions of Frederick were conveyed by Count Gotter to the cabinet of Vienna. He made an offer of Frederick's friendship, army, and aid for the protection of the Emperor's daughter, and also his vote for the election of her husband, Duke Francis of

Lorraine, as Emperor; but he demanded, in return, the whole of Silesia for his master. Such a proposition met with no very favorable reception: to part with one of Austria's best provinces for such questionable advantages seemed but too irrational. The chamberlains at Vienna tauntingly remarked, that it was not seemly that a prince, whose office it was, as grand-marshal of the empire, to present the Emperor with the wash-hand-basin, should attempt to dictate terms to the Emperor's daughter. The negotiations were not, however, wholly broken off; it seems probable that it never was Frederick's intention to insist on the cession of the whole of Silesia, for the further he advanced the more he yielded in his demands; he soon, in fact, claimed less than his just right; but all his overtures were disregarded. England used its best endeavors to procure the compliance of Austria; but Maria Theresa and her ministers would agree to no concession as long as Frederick occupied any portion of Silesia. If he would consent to evacuate the land, forgiveness and immunity for the past were offered him; the negotiations terminated without producing any satisfactory result. Frederick had nominated thirty chaplains to provide for the spiritual wants of the Protestant inhabitants of Silesia: this step awakened the jealousy of the Pope, who appealed to the Catholic powers of Europe for protection against the heretic "Margrave of Brandenburg." Frederick published a declaration in reply, in which he promised to protect every one within his states, and in particular in Silesia, be his creed what it might. This tended to pacify men's minds, and the Pope's appeal was disregarded. Frederick succeeded also in winning over the Russian court to his views; and even France expressed itself in friendly terms towards him. England (Hanover) alone, and Saxony allied themselves with Austria; but both these states were unprepared for war, and a corps of observation, which was stationed on their frontiers, under the command of the old Prince of Dessau, deterred them from taking any active measures.

Towards the end of February the Austrian army was concentrated in Moravia, under the command of Field-marshal Count Neipperg, and advanced on Silesia, a detachment being sent to cover the province of Glatz. Preparations were now commenced for a decisive struggle.

Frederick had already arrived in Silesia, and his first object was to inspect the quarters where his troops were lodged, and procure further information as to the nature of the land itself. On the 27th of February he visited the piquets, which were posted on the ridge of hills that separate Silesia from the province of Glatz. He was attended by an inconsiderable escort, and his want of caution had nigh cost him dear. Small bodies of Austrian hussars had very frequently passed the Prussian posts, and carried on a system of predatory attacks. They had learned, through spies, the presence of the king in the neighborhood, and could they only succeed, by a bold stroke, in getting possession of his person, the war must have terminated at its very outset. But the party sent on this service missed the object of their search, and came in contact with a body of Prussian dragoons. The latter suffered a considerable loss; but the Austrians were obliged to return without having effected the object of their mission. Frederick had heard the firing, and quickly hastened to the relief of his dragoons, with such troops as he could muster at the instant, but arrived too late to render any service.

On the 9th of March the fortress of Glogau fell beneath a rapid and well-organized assault, led on by Prince Leopold of Dessau. The garrison were made prisoners of war. The fortifications were immediately put in the best possible state of defence.

The two remaining fortresses, which were still in the hands of the Austrians, became now the subject of Frederick's next operations. He proceeded to the camp in Upper Silesia, where General Schwerin—the most experienced general in the Prussian army, and one who had served under Eugene and Marlborough in the Netherlands

—was in command. At Jägerndorf, ten leagues distant from Neisse, he learned, for the first time, from some deserters, that the main body of the Austrian army was close at hand, under the command of Neipperg, and intended to attempt the relief of Neisse. Orders were immediately given to concentrate the scattered detachments, and the Upper Silesian regiments were retired to Jagerndorf. A junction with the Lower Silesian detachment was to be effected at the river Neisse. Simultaneously, and at no very considerable distance, the Austrian army put itself in motion; it reached Neisse before the Prussians, and actually prevented Frederick from being able to join the Lower Silesian corps at the above point. Frederick was, therefore, compelled to advance further northwards, in order to command the nearest point for crossing the stream; but the Austrians were again in motion in a similar direction on his left, and deserters informed him that Ohlau was the point aimed at, as the Prussian cannon, which were laid up there, promised a considerable booty. Frederick's situation had now become very critical; he was cut off from all connection with the main body of his army; his communication with his own states was intercepted, and important points in Silesia were either in possession of the enemy or in danger. To increase his embarrassment, a heavy fall of snow rendered it impossible to observe the enemy's motions, or make the necessary dispositions. But the Austrians were equally unaware of the proximity of the Prussians.

Frederick had now no other alternative than to come, as soon as possible, to an engagement—one in which the discipline of the Prussian army and the strategic studies of its leaders were to be, for the first time, brought into serious operation, and the results of which must prove of the utmost importance as regarded the whole future character of the war. Fortune favored the opening; the sun rose brightly on the 10th of April; the ground, although covered with snow, presented, at least, no further impediments. The Prussian troops advanced in readiness for battle in the same direction as the Austrians, who were moving on before them. Information was obtained from some prisoners, that the centre of the Austrian army lay encamped in the village of Mollwitz, not far from Brieg. Mollwitz was reached by noon without the Austrians being aware of the Prussians' approach. The Prussian army here formed in order of battle, awaiting the enemy's advance from the village. It had been possible to have taken the enemy by surprise; but the old system was adhered to, its absurdity not having been, as yet, sufficiently established. The Austrians advanced into the field under a raking fire from the Prussian guns; the left wing of the admirable Austrian cavalry was the first to arrive, under the command of General Römer. This officer, perceiving the danger of hesitation, and his regiments demanding to be led on out of the showers of shot to which they were exposed, made a sudden charge on the Prussians' right wing, but being rather impeded, and in a somewhat unfavorable position, was obliged to give way, and falling back upon the lines of infantry, carried the Austrians with it. The confusion consequent on this sudden assault was great. Frederick, who commanded the left wing in person, in endeavoring to rally the fugitives, was borne along in the retirade. He succeeded, at length, in collecting a few scattered squadrons: with these, and shouting, "Brothers! Prussia's honor, your monarch's life!" he charged the enemy's lines. But this small body of men was speedily overpowered, and a general rout ensued, it being impossible to recognize friends or foes.

The battle now seemed lost: Frederick rode up to Fieldmarshal Schwerin, who was in command of the left wing, and was by him impressively reminded of the great danger which existed in that quarter, of their being cut off from the remaining portions of the army, although, at present, the battle was by no means decided. "If," said Schwerin, "your majesty will consent to leave the battlefield, and hasten to the opposite bank of the river Oder, and bring up the considerable corps, with which every effort has been made to form a junction, it will not fail to be of the utmost importance; I, in the mean time, will use my utmost efforts for the success of the battle." Frederick was, at first, undecided; but the Austrians pressed forward anew, and he at length yielded, with a heavy heart, to the advice of his experienced general.

In order to pass the Oder, Frederick was obliged to take the road to the distant town of Oppeln, where he conceived that one of his regiments must have been stationed. He proceeded with a very trifling escort,—a body of gendarmes following him in the rear; but he rode so hard that the latter could not keep pace with him. In the middle of the night he arrived, with his small suite, at the gates of Oppeln, which were found shut. On the challenge of the sentry, the answer was given, "a Prussian courier;" but the gates still remained closed. The matter now assuming a serious aspect, Frederick commanded some of his attendants to dismount, and inquire why the gates were not opened. This demand was replied to by several musket-shots from the loopholes, as the town was held by a troop of Austrian hussars. The Prussians speedily turned their horses' heads, and retraced their steps with the utmost haste. At break of day, Frederick had arrived at Lowen, a small town situated between Mollwitz and Oppeln. Here he found the gendarmes who had followed him the preceding evening, and also an adjutant with news of the successful issue of the battle. He immediately returned to the field, having ridden seventeen leagues without dismounting. The efficiency and precision, as well as the courage and unflinching resolution of his infantry, as soon as it was possible to bring their strength into play, had wrung the victory from the Austrians. Neipperg had retired, with considerable loss, in the direction of Neisse. A want of unanimity in counsel, and the approach of night, prevented the victors from taking full advantage of their success.

Frederick has subsequently, when writing the history of his own times, severely criticised his first military operations, and particularizes the numerous faults committed in the battle of Mollwitz. But he remarks, in conclusion, that having gravely considered the various faults committed by him, he would seek to avoid them in future, as indeed he did.

As an immediate result of this victory the Prussians were enabled to conduct the siege of Brieg without fear of interruption. The garrison capitulated after a short resistance. A camp was then formed at Streheln, thus covering the whole of Lower Silesia. Frederick employed the two months, which he here passed, in reinforcing his army, and improving the discipline and efficiency of his cavalry.

The importance of the victory did not consist so much in the actual success, as in its moral influence upon the general character of Frederick's troops. It was now apparent that the soldiers who had been bred in the school of Prince Eugene were not invincible, and that the Prussian army, which had been hitherto efficient only on parade, was equally good under an enemy's fire. The belief was even entertained that the colossal empire of Austria would soon fall to pieces, and the Prussian state seemed, like a new constellation, to ascend in the political horizon. In truth, Frederick obtained considerable weight in the council of Europe, through the blow he had struck. Ambassadors hastened to his camp from England, France, Spain, Sweden, Russia, Denmark, Bavaria, Saxony, and Austria, and here formed a species of political congress. France was the most anxious to court the Prussian king's favor, as England had allied itself with Austria. A treaty had been already concluded between France and Bavaria, according to which France promised to support the Elector, Charles Albert, in his claims upon Austria and to the imperial crown: it was now proposed to Frederick, that he should take part in this alliance, on his being secured in the possession of

Lower Silesia. Frederick hesitated to assent, hoping, perhaps, that Austria, after its late defeat, would be more inclined to come to terms. But these hopes proved visionary: a powerful alliance for the protection of Austrian interests seeming to be in train. The Hanoverian troops, which had remained hitherto inactive, were now reinforced by Danish and Hessian regiments in English pay: Saxony likewise prepared to unite its forces with the former; and Russian troops were being concentrated in Liefland. Any further hesitation appeared now fraught with danger, and Frederick accordingly, on the 5th of July, joined the Nymphenburg league.

Frederick's connection with France was kept a secret until the military resources of the latter were fully developed, and its army fit for action. The intelligence of this league came upon the Austrian cabinet completely by surprise; for they could not bring themselves to believe that Frederick possessed anything like diplomatic talent. The English ambassador at Vienna, who was present at the ministerial council, reported, that the ministers, on receipt of the news of this alliance, sank back in their chairs as if they had been paralyzed. It soon became known that two French corps had already entered Germany,—the one in the south, for the support of the Elector of Bavaria, the other in the north, to hold England in check,—and to crown all, little reliance could be placed in Russian aid, as that power had become suddenly involved in a war with Sweden. This state of things decided Maria Theresa, who had hitherto refused all compliance with Frederick's demands, to have recourse to negotiation. The English ambassador was sent from Vienna to Frederick's camp, to solicit him to accept, in lieu of all his claims on Silesia, two millions of florins and the province of Geldern.

Frederick, in the history of his own times, describes the progress of these negotiations with much humor. The English ambassador, a perfect enthusiast in favor of Maria Theresa, whose personal charms and powers of fascination were unquestionably great, made his insignificant offer in a tone of considerable bombast, and gave it as his opinion, that the king should congratulate himself on making such admirable terms. But Frederick felt little sympathy with the romantic feelings of the ambassador, the singularity of whose manner induced him to reply in a similar strain. His answering speech surpassed that of his English rival in point of ridiculous hauteur. He inquired how he, as king, after consenting to such ignominious terms, could venture to stand in the presence of his army! and how should he excuse himself for delivering up his new subjects, the Protestants of Silesia, again to Catholic tyranny! "Were I," continued he, in an elevated tone, "capable of so mean, so dishonorable a compromise, the graves of my forefathers would yawn before my eyes, and as they ascended from their tombs, they might well address me, 'No, thou art none of our blood! What! thou, whose duty it is to struggle for those rights which thou hast inherited from us, wilt thou barter them for gold? Thou hast stained that honor which we have bequeathed thee as thy noblest patrimony! Unworthy of the name of prince, unworthy of the royal throne, thou art but a contemptible pedlar who prefers profit to fame.'" He concluded by stating, that he would rather see his army for ever buried beneath the ruins of Silesia, than expose himself to the stigma of an act so dishonorable. Then, without pursuing the discussion any further he took up his hat and retired into an inner chamber of his tent, leaving the ambassador completely stupefied, and obliged to return to Vienna without accomplishing the object of his mission. Frederick played his part so admirably, that in the report made by the English ambassador to the cabinet in London, the effects of Frederick's high-sounding speech are quite apparent.

The camp in Strehlen became not merely the sphere of diplomatic negotiation or military organization: the arts of peace, science, poetry, and music occupied Frederick here, as if the happy days of Rheinsberg had returned.

His letters to Jordan of this period evidence his gaiety and high spirits. At times he finds prose insufficient for his epistolary purposes, and has recourse to all the sparkling imagery of poetic inspiration. As his arms prospered, and in proportion as he felt his growing importance in the political world, his wit and humor expanded. His letters remind us, at times, of the inimitable humor of the great British poet; and it must ever remain inexplicable, that, despite the æsthetic relations of the age, Frederick did not recognize in Shakespeare a kindred spirit.

We have already remarked that Jordan's pacific disposition had been frequently the subject of ironical remarks from Frederick. An incident occurred, subsequently to the battle of Mollwitz, which gave a fair opening for satirical banter. After the battle a call to arms was, by accident, beaten, where Jordan, who had been summoned to Frederick's camp, was stopping; Jordan no sooner heard the first sounds than he fled precipitately from the camp, and took refuge in Breslau. This act exposed him perpetually to the shafts of Frederick's satire, notwithstanding all his attempts to justify his conduct. Frederick always returned to this subject at intervals, and in one of the letters, which he wrote in the year following, makes these reflections on Jordan's courage : "Prudence," says the writer, "an attribute of which your gallantry largely partakes, is by no means the least considerable of your admirable qualities :

> Prudence is valor's real source and firmest hold!
> The rest is nought but blind and senseless rage,
> By which, betrayed through animal instinct low,
> So many fools so fascinated seem,

"You are perfectly aware that real courage consists in facing such dangers as our prudence points out to us to be inevitable or proper to be hazarded. But you are singularly cautious and provident, and consequently never expose yourself at all, from which it is clear, that few heroes equal you in point of true valor. Your courage is still intact; and as everything new surpasses the old, your gallantry must be really astonishing. It is as a bud about to unfold its leaves,—one which has never experienced either the scorching rays of the sun or the keenness of the northern blasts; in a word, an object as deserving of respect as metaphysics, or the treatises on the nature of fire, written by the Marchioness,—(a friend of Voltaire's, whose scientific pursuits Frederick frequently ridiculed.) You want nothing further than a white plume to overshadow the banks of your valor, a long sabre, spurs, and a somewhat louder voice, and then my hero would be perfect. I must really congratulate you, valiant and heroic Jordan! and entreat you to cast a look, from the pinnacle of your fame, upon your friends, who are here wallowing in Bohemian mire."

Meanwhile a plan was being silently matured, which might have been productive of the worst consequences to Frederick. A considerable number of Austrian and Bohemian old ladies residing in Breslau, and entertaining an equally marked aversion for Prussian soldiers and the Protestant faith, kept up a correspondence with the Austrian army through the aid of monks. In collusion with some of the members of the Breslau common-council, they formed the plan of delivering the city into the hands of the enemy. Field-marshal Neipperg entered into their views; he resolved on seducing Frederick from his favorable position by means of some aggressive movements; and then advancing by forced marches on Breslau. But Frederick discovered the plot; he succeeded in introducing a traitress into the political meetings, which were held by these ladies every evening. Through this channel the king discovered the whole intrigue, and was enabled to take his measures accordingly.

The neutrality of Breslau was fraught with too much danger to admit of its further continuance. The resident foreign ambassadors were summoned to the camp in Strehlen, in order that they might be removed from the scene of action in the event of any disorders occurring. A Prussian corps, under the command of the Prince of Dessau, requested leave to march through the town; the municipal guards were under arms to conduct them through. Whilst this corps was in the act of entering at one gate, another Prussian troop burst in unexpectedly at a second, and barred the entrance. The town-major remonstrated with the Prince of Dessau, but was advised to sheath his sword and return home as fast as his horse could carry him. No attempt at resistance was made, and in less than an hour, without one drop of blood being shed, the town was in the hands of the Prussians, the citizens were obliged to take the oaths of fealty to the Prussian sovereign, money was flung amongst the populace, and a general shout of joy rang through the streets.

Neipperg had already begun to put his troops in motion, in order to cut Frederick off from Breslau. On hearing of the rapid occupation of the town by the Prussian troops, he resolved on retiring; but took up his position with so much adroitness, that he covered Upper Silesia; whilst Frederick, breaking up his camp, moved on Neisse, which was still in the hands of the Austrians. Each army kept the other for a time in check by their marches and countermarches; but this petty warfare led to no decisive issue.

The French and Bavarians had already advanced considerably further, and Saxony had joined the Nymphenburg league, in the prospect of being recompensed for its services by the acquisition of Moravia. The Austrian cabinet was now necessitated to make some concessions. The English ambassador was a second time sent on a mission to Frederick. He brought with him a plan of Silesia, on which the cession of a considerable part of Lower Silesia was indicated by an ink-line. He was, however, informed that what at one time might be very acceptable, might at another be by no means so. His second offer of the whole of Lower Silesia and Breslau was likewise rejected. Austria's embarrassments daily increased; Linz was already in the hands of the Bavario-

French army; the Viennese were already preparing for flight, and the court itself about to retire from the city. A simultaneous movement on Silesia was made by Frederick; and by the capture of Oppeln he forced Neipperg to retire from Neisse.

Through the mediation of England the Austrian court was induced to acquiesce in the cession of Lower Silesia and Neisse, on the condition that Frederick should forthwith withdraw his forces. Frederick accepted of this proposal, although the proposition did not meet his full approbation. But he wished to avoid enfeebling Austria to such an extent as to aggrandize France, and thereby convert an independent ally into a dependent slave. On the 9th of October a private interview took place between Frederick and Marshal Neipperg, to which a few trusty officers and the English ambassador were admitted. It was here arranged that Neisse should, in fourteen days, be nominally invested; that the garrison should be withdrawn, and the fortress handed over to Frederick; that one portion of the Prussian troops should take up their winter-quarters in Upper Silesia, and that, merely for appearance sake, a few desultory attacks should be made from time to time; that the treaty should be fully drawn up and ratified within the year, but that these preliminary stipulations should remain an inviolable secret,—a precaution which Frederick's position, as regarded his allies, rendered necessary. He expressed the liveliest sympathy for Maria Theresa, and even hinted that he might be possibly induced to take up her cause.

In consequence of this arrangement Neipperg retired with his army to Moravia. Neisse surrendered after a twelve days' siege; the Austrian garrison had actually not been withdrawn before the Prussian engineers were busy drawing up the plans for the new defences. One section of the Prussian army now encamped in Upper Silesia, another moved on Bohemia, and some regiments were detached to blockade Glatz.

On the 4th of November Frederick arrived in Breslau,

whither the several princes and estates of the dukedom
of Lower Silesia had been summoned to pay their homage.
The solemn entry of the king was the first of a series of
festivities in which the higher and lower classes of the
town joyfully took part. The populace were highly gratified by the present of a roasted ox, tricked out with gar-
lands and stuffed with poultry and game. The 7th of
November was appointed for the doing homage. An immense procession moved through the streets to the council-
house, where the ceremony was to take place in the prince's
saloon. The town had not seen any of its regents within
its walls for centuries; the arrangements for the act of
homage were, consequently, on such a scale as the short-
ness of the time permitted. An old imperial throne was
repaired and put in requisition for the ceremony. The
Austrian double-headed eagle embroidered thereon was
deprived of one of its heads, and thereby converted into
the Prussian emblem, and Frederick's initials fastened
upon its breast. Frederick, clad in a simple military uniform, ascended his throne in the midst of a brilliant assembly. The marshal had forgotten the imperial sword
of state, which should have been held at the king's side,
but Frederick repaired this omission by drawing from its
scabbard the sword with which he had conquered Silesia,
and presented it to the marshal. An address having been
read to the assembly, they took the oaths of fealty, and
kissed the hilt of Frederick's sword. "Long live the King
of Prussia, our sovereign duke!" was echoed from all
sides, and this shout concluded the ceremony. The town
was brilliantly illuminated in the evening. Frederick remitted the usual coronation present of one hundred thousand thalers, and made provision for the relief of the
indigent inhabitants. He testified his gracious feelings
by the conferment of dignities and decorations. From
Breslau he returned in November to Berlin.

CHAPTER XVI.

CAMPAIGN OF THE YEAR 1742.

DURING the autumn of 1742 the operations of the Bavario-French army were attended with the most uninterrupted success, and a Saxon corps was advancing simultaneously upon Bohemia. By a bold decisive movement Charles Albert might have made himself master of Vienna. But the Bohemian crown was the real object of his ambition; and the French, in order to prevent Bavaria from becoming too powerful, confirmed him in his resolution of setting out for Bohemia, as this would necessarily awaken the jealousy of his Saxon allies. The hostile army was thus drawn off from its march of conquest, and the dangers which so imminently impended over the head of Maria Theresa were once more averted. Charles Albert, with his irresistible host, seized the capital of Bohemia, but, intoxicated with the splendor of coronation festivities, allowed the favorable moment for pushing on his arms to pass by. From Prague he proceeded to Frankfort-on-the-Main, in order to urge his claims to the imperial crown, the dearest object of his ambition. This, the choicest wish of his heart, was likewise accomplished. On the 24th of January, 1742, he was proclaimed Emperor of Germany, under the title of Charles the Seventh,—but, whilst in pursuit of the semblance of power, he allowed the reality to fall from his hands.

The cause of Maria Theresa had, in the mean time, found enthusiastic, almost fanatical supporters in the heart of her empire. The Hungarians, often as they had been obliged to submit to the harsh rule of her ancestors, were, notwithstanding, inspired with the most ardent feelings of attachment for their young and lovely sovereign. " Our swords and lives for our KING, Maria Theresa," was the cry of the magnates of Hungary, as their youthful queen appeared before them during the diet in Presburg, clad in the time-honored robes of the Hungarian kings, and bearing in her arms her infant son Joseph: the oath was not long registered ere its fruits were apparent. Her army became suddenly invested with preternatural strength; one section of the Franco-Bavarian army, which had not yet set out for Bohemia, was forced speedily to evacuate Austria; was pursued across Bavaria; and Munich, the capital of the newly-created Emperor, seized. The Austrians entered Munich on the 12th of February, the same day on which Charles had been invested with the imperial purple at Frankfort. The wild Hungarian hosts, thirsting for vengeance, perpetrated the most savage atrocities throughout Bavaria, and marked their path with blood.

This change in the state of affairs rendered it necessary for Frederick to remodel his plans, especially as Austria, so far from taking any steps towards the fulfilment of the treaty concluded at Schnelendorf, had, in contravention of the direct terms of that treaty, communicated its various stipulations, which should have been kept secret, to the different cabinets of Europe. Frederick was consequently obliged to enter into the plans of the allies with the more energy and decision. An allied corps, stationed in Bohemia, was opposed by an Austrian army under circumstances so unfavorable for the former as to render an engagement hazardous. New forces must be therefore brought up to aid the allies; and a diversion, by forced marches upon Moravia, seemed to promise considerable advantages. Frederick, anxious to spare his troops as much as possible, strove to induce Saxony to contribute the principal means for such a movement; the more particularly as Moravia was, according to former treaties, to become its portion. To effectuate this object, he proceeded without loss of time to Dresden, having made but a short stay at Berlin, where he had been present at the nuptials of his brother, Prince Augustus William.

It was, however, no easy task to obtain the consent of Augustus the Third, (Elector of Saxony and King of Poland,) or, rather, that of his minister, Count Brühl, to this measure, as the Saxon monarch felt little thirst for military fame. Brühl entertained a natural aversion for Frederick, as petty spirits generally do for those whom they feel to be their superiors: a further impediment consisted in the obligations which the Saxon minister owed to the Austrian cabinet. But Frederick was well skilled in the arts of diplomacy. A conference was held in the chambers of King Augustus, at which Brühl and some of the Saxon generals were present, and at which Frederick displayed considerable talent in meeting the objections urged. On Augustus entering, and after the interchange of the customary civilities, Brühl, well acquainted with the character of his master, endeavored to terminate the conference; he rolled up the map of Moravia, which had been made use of, and quickly laid it aside. Frederick, without heeding the interruption, calmly unrolled the chart, and endeavored to make the monarch comprehend the nature of the service for which his troops were required, and how deeply and immediately he was interested in the success of the measure. Augustus felt constrained to assent to the various arguments of the Prussian king. Brühl, embarrassed by the approbation which Frederick's remarks perpetually elicited from his master, in whose countenance he could plainly read signs of growing impatience, observed that the opera was about to commence. This piece of intelligence was of a nature by far too important to allow of Augustus continuing the conference. Frederick took advantage of the instant, and would not allow the Saxon monarch to retire until he had obtained his full assent to his various plans.

CAMPAIGN OF THE YEAR 1742.

Frederick now put himself at the head of the Saxon troops, and pushed through Bohemia and Moravia. In Olmütz, he was joined by a section of his own army, which had penetrated into Moravia from Silesia. His first successes were not inconsiderable; the Prussians burst in upon Upper Austria, and their hussars swept the plains, again carrying terror and dismay to the very heart of the capital. But Frederick, judging from his own men, had estimated the worth of the Saxon troops by a false standard, and this error was the cause of the failure of his measures. The want of energy or ardor, which the Saxons displayed, neutralized the advantages gained by the Prussians. Brünn was besieged, and Frederick demanded the necessary cannon from Augustus, but the latter refused compliance with this demand, on the ground of want of money; he had, however, just given the sum of 400,000 thalers for the purchase of a large green diamond, to adorn his "Green Vault" in Dresden. The Austrian army now advanced in turn upon Moravia, and whilst Frederick was obliged to make the most serious preparations for its protection, the Saxon army displayed nothing but cowardice, disobedience, and perfidy. Nothing therefore remained for Frederick but to abandon Moravia, and fall back upon his own troops, who were stationed in Bohemia. The Saxon minister Bülow, who had followed Frederick into Moravia, begged leave to inquire, who now was to place the Moravian crown upon his master's head. Frederick replied drily, that crowns were generally obtained by cannons.

Whilst events were proceeding in this way a second Prussian corps, under the command of the Prince of Dessau, had reduced the fortress of Glatz, and exacted the homage of the whole province. Some short time afterwards the states of the Upper Silesian district, on the other side of the Neisse, took the oaths of fealty to the king, in the presence of a commissioner.

On the 17th of April Frederick was joined by the Prince of Dessau at Chrudin, in Bohemia, and pitched his camp here in order to recruit his soldiers. The Saxons, who had likewise left Moravia, passed through Bohemia, and encamped on the Saxon frontier: it was found impossible to induce them to form a junction with the French on the Moldau, by which means a considerable counterpoise might have been opposed to the Austrian power. Frederick devoted his four weeks' inactivity at Chrudin to the pleasures of science and art. This interval was likewise, through the mediation of England, employed in new negotiations with Austria. Frederick could clearly see the little advantage he derived from his allies, for he could count as little upon the ability of the French leaders or the Bavarian army, as on the good faith of the Saxons, and he even had in his hands convincing proofs of the little reliance which was to be placed on the sincerity of a French cabinet; but England's aim in withdrawing Frederick from his allies was to be able to crush them the more easily. Frederick now claimed the whole of Silesia and the province of Glatz; but as the Austrians conceived that they had attained considerable advantages, there was no hope of the negotiations being successful.

Frederick now resolved to leave his cause to be decided by the sword. He took up a preparatory position, and reinforced his army by supplies drawn from Upper Silesia. The Austrians under the command of Prince Charles of Lorraine and Field-marshal Königseck, evacuated Moravia and marched on Prague, intending to attack the Prussians, of whose real strength they had no idea whatsoever. At the approach of this army Frederick required the commander of the French troops, Marshal Broglio, to advance from the Moldau and effect a junction with him. The latter refused, on the ground of having no orders to that effect; but declared his readiness to send speedy intelligence of the king's wishes to Paris, and he hoped that he would as speedily receive the necessary instructions.

One body of the Austrian troops had already advanced

on Frederick's flank, and evidently intended to attack the Prussian magazines. To parry this blow, Frederick put himself at the head of his advanced guard, and taking up a favorable position, awaited the arrival of the main body of his army, under the command of the Prince of Dessau. The latter had received orders to invest the town of Czaslau, but his march had been so delayed by the transport of the heavy artillery, that he had not got further than the neighboring village of Chotusitz, whilst the Austrians had already entered Czaslau. On the 17th of May, at early dawn, Frederick returned with his advanced troops to the main body of his army, which he had scarcely reached before the Austrians made their intended assault. The thunder of the guns opened the fight; the Prussian cavalry of the right wing, under Field-marshal Buddenbrock, took advantage of its favorable position, and dashed with irresistible impetuosity upon the enemy, repulsing the assailants; but the frightful cloud of dust attendant on this attack brought confusion and disorder into the ranks of the Prussians, so that the charge became comparatively useless. Königseck now led on the infantry of the Austrian right wing against the Prussian left, whose position near Chotusitz was rather disadvantageous. The Prussian horse here distinguished itself by its intrepidity and courage, but the infantry were forced to give way. The enemy availed themselves of this retrograde movement to fire the village: but this act deprived the victors of the advantages of their success, as the fire screened the enemy completely from them. Frederick now resolved on heading an assault in person upon the Austrian left wing. He drove the left back with impetuosity on the right, and charging into the ranks of both, as they occupied an unfavorable position, obliged the whole Austrian army to fly. In this way the victory which brought Frederick nearer to the object of his ambition was obtained in a few hours of the forenoon.

The negotiations with Austria were now renewed with increased ardor and Maria Theresa assented to Frederick's demands. The Prussian cabinet-minister, Count Podewils, and the English ambassador, Lord Hyndford, each provided with the necessary powers, concluded the preliminaries of a treaty of peace, on the 11th of June, at Breslau, ceding to Frederick the whole of Silesia, the province of Glatz, and a district of Moravia, the only part excepted from the treaty being a portion of Upper Silesia of about 500 square miles in extent. He on his part stipulated to pay off a debt, which was due to England, and for payment of which Silesia had been pledged. Peace was immediately proclaimed throughout the whole of the king's dominions. In the camp at Kuttenberg, which Frederick had formed after the battle, the news was not made known until Frederick communicated it at a fête, to which the princpal officers of his army had been invited; he here seized his glass, and proposed "the health of the Queen of Hungary, and that their reconciliation might be lasting." The peace was proclaimed in Berlin on the 30th of June, by a herald, who rode through the streets, mounted on a horse splendidly caparisoned, and bearing a sceptre in his hand.

Before returning to Berlin Frederick visited the Silesian fortresses. He was told at Glatz, that whilst the Prussians were besieging the place, a lady of rank had made a vow to present the statue of the holy Virgin in the Jesuits' church with a handsome robe, in the event of the siege being raised: this vow had not, of course, been fulfilled. Frederick immediately ordered a robe of the most costly materials to be made, and sent it to the Jesuits, with the remark that the holy Virgin should not lose through him the present which had been promised her. The Jesuits were politic enough to accept of the robe, and went in procession to thank the king for his gift.

On the 12th of July Frederick arrived in Berlin, and was welcomed with the utmost enthusiasm. Peace was definitely concluded on the 28th of July, and England undertook to guarantee its continuance. Saxony was included in this treaty of peace, although King Augustus knew so little of his own affairs that, on being informed by the Prussian ambassador of the victory of Chotusitz, he inquired if his troops had behaved well during the action. The news of this treaty of peace, which frustrated a series of well-devised schemes, was received in France with the greatest horror. The whole cabinet was completely paralyzed ; some fainted away ; old Cardinal Fleury, who then guided the helm of state, burst into tears. Frederick had explained to him the motives which had induced him to conclude the peace. The cardinal, in his letter in reply, remarks in a sad tone as follows : "Your majesty will now become the arbiter of Europe's destiny; this is the most glorious part you could possibly play!"

But Maria Theresa had bowed with a broken heart to the decrees of fate; she bewailed that the brightest jewel had been torn from her diadem. As often as she saw a Silesian, she would involuntarily burst into tears.

CHAPTER XVII.

TWO YEARS' PEACE.

At the conclusion of the peace of Breslau the funds of the Prussian exchequer had dwindled to the sum of 150,000 thalers. This was one of the many reasons which induced Frederick to hasten the couclusion of the war. But the acquisition of Silesia increased his revenues to the amount of three millions and a half of thalers. He was therefore bound to apply himself with ardor to the management and development of the resources of his kingdom; for the political relations were still so involved, that sooner or later a war must be the result; his utmost care was therefore devoted to preparations for the hour of need.

The next object of Frederick's attention was the ordering of the relations of his Silesian dominions. The peculiar rights of the newly-acquired provinces were infringed upon as little as possible; but such new dispositions were made as were absolutely necessary to the performance by Silesia of the duties, and participations in the advantages enjoyed by the other states of the Prussian monarchy. The administration of this land was conducted separately from that of the other provinces; the government offices were filled for the most part by natives; the system of taxation which had hitherto prevailed being most oppressive, was now reformed according to the enlightened principles prevailing in Prussia. Security was given to traffic by the introduction of the Prussian criminal code and police. The Protestant inhabi-

TWO YEARS' PEACE. 143

tants were protected in the free exercise of their religious beliefs, without the Catholic Church being in any way compromised in its rights. As regards this spirit of religious toleration, Frederick found a worthy coadjutor in the Bishop of Breslau, Cardinal Count Sinzendorff, who was at the same time the highest dignitary of the Catholic Church in Silesia. Frederick nominated him, with the approbation of the pope, vicar-general and supreme judge in all matters spiritual affecting the Roman Catholic Church throughout the Prussian monarchy. Sinzendorff issued in 1742 a pastoral letter, exhorting the zealots of his own creed to peace and toleration, and interdicting the use of the word heretic. By this conduct Sinzendorff ingratiated himself in the king's favor, and received many high tokens of royal approbation.

For the more complete protection of Silesia against any new incursion, the fortresses were repaired, and new defences added. Neisse was rendered one of the strongest holds in the land by a considerable enlargement of its fortifications. On the far side of the river Neisse, upon the elevation from which Frederick had battered the town in 1741, a strong fort was erected, and received the name of Prussia. Frederick laid the first stone in person on the 30th March, 1743, with a silver trowel and hammer; the inscription which was placed in the foundation-stone seems to refer to Frederick's character as Grand Master of the order of Freemasons.

Glatz was likewise rendered a place of considerable strength by the erection of numerous outworks. Whilst extending the line of fortification here, amongst other things were found two statues of saints,—St. Nepomuck and St. Florian,—which had been erected during the Austrian regency. Both were preserved until the arrival of the king at Glatz, and his wish learned as to what should be done with them. " Florian, "replied Frederick, " is serviceable against fire, still I feel no great interest in him ; but the patron saint of Bohemia, St. Nepomuck, must certainly receive due honor. A tower must therefore be raised upon this spot, and St. Nepomuck placed upon it." To this circumstance the round tower in the defences of Glatz owes its origin, and upon its highest platform stands the statue of St. Nepomuck. On Frederick's arriving here a second time, and finding the saint's face turned in the direction of Silesia, he remarked, with a smile, "This is not right: St. Nepomuck should have his eyes directed to the land under his protection;" and accordingly the statue was turned round, so as to face Bohemia. The fortifications of Glogau and Brieg were strengthened; and the town of Kosel, in Upper Silesia, which had been hitherto unfortified, was also provided with strong defences; by which means the frontier was secured on the Austrian side.

His exertions for the augmentation and perfect organization of the army were characterized by equal spirit. The first war had indicated many deficiencies, and laid bare many defects, which Frederick now resolved to remedy; and his cavalry, from having been of but little use in the field, through the total neglect of his predecessor, shortly became one of the most efficient arms of the service. His attention was equally directed to the fostering of the internal prosperity of his states; he made new arrangements for the advancement of manufactures and trade, and connected the Elbe with the Oder by means of a canal. The academy of sciences burst into new life and vigor, and held its first meeting in the royal palace in Berlin, when prizes were proposed for such as distinguished themselves in the various walks of science.

Amidst this general reorganization the gaieties and enjoyments of life were not forgotten; the royal palace at Charlottenburg was considerably enlarged, by the addition of a new wing, erected under the direction of Knobelsdorff. The splendid collection of antiques which Frederick had purchased, in 1742, from the heirs of Cardinal Polignac, was employed in decorating this palace. The opera-house, likewise planned by Knobelsdorff, and first opened in December, 1742, became one of the principal architectural ornaments of Berlin. The visits of foreign princes afforded opportunities for a display of the splendors of royalty; but Frederick, despite his many engagements, still found leisure to compose the first portion of the History of his Times, descriptive of the first Silesian war, and thus qualified himself for companionship with those classical historians of antiquity whose works had engaged his early attention. On the occasion of his friend Keyserling being married, in November, 1742, Frederick composed a comedy in three acts, "The World's School," as an epithalamium. Voltaire's arrival, in 1743, on a second visit to Berlin, completed the poetic charm.

This visit of the French poet is thus described by the then English ambassador at the court of Prussia, in his correspondence with the English cabinet, and seems to have been but little relished by him: "Mons. Voltaire is again here, and perpetually in company with the king, who appears resolved to afford him materials for a poem on the pleasures of Berlin. There is nothing talked of here except Voltaire; he reads his tragedies to queens and princesses until they weep, and surpasses even the king himself in raillery and sarcastic sallies. No one is considered fashionable here unless he have this poet's works in his head or pocket, or talk in rhyme."

But Voltaire conceived himself called upon to play the part of a political negotiator in behalf of the French court; however, as he had no credentials to produce, Frederick considered the whole thing as a farce, the offspring of the poet's vanity; for he had discovered, even during the poet's first visit, that his moral character was not as faultless as his rhymes. The Frenchman's avarice had been sufficiently apparent, although it had been passed over in silence; but now his vanity involved him in many petty quarrels. By a strange poetic licence he transmitted to the amiable princess Ulrike, one of the king's younger sisters, a polished madrigal, containing nothing less than a direct declaration of love. We translate it as literally as possible:

"E'en falsehood's coarsest web would seem
With threads of truth still partly wrought;
Last night myself a king I thought,—
The sweet illusion of a dream.
Princess! I loved, and dared my love for thee to own,
And then awoke, but lost not all, I deem—
I had but to resign my throne."

The princess replied in the most polished strains, composed by her brother Frederick, and enlightening the poet in the most polite manner as to the difference in their ranks: "He had raised himself to the summit of Helicon by his own natural powers, whilst she was indebted for everything to her ancestors." A second reply from Frederick treated the subject less allegorically. It ran pretty nearly as follows:

"Our dreams, by nature's law, will ever take
Their tone from what we think of when awake:
The hero dreams that he has crossed the Rhine;
The merchant asks, 'Can all these gains be mine?'
The dog, though sleeping, still the moon will bay:
But should Voltaire, in Prussia, deem, with lying art,
Himself a king—and still the fool but play,
That were indeed t' abuse the dreamer's part."

But these petty skirmishes did not prevent Voltaire's poetical powers from being enthusiastically admired; and, on his departure from Berlin, the wish to retain him altogether at the Prussian court was warmly expressed.

In May, 1744, Frederick's possessions were augmented by the addition of a new territory, East Friesland, through the death, without issue, of its then ruler. Under a title derived from the Great Elector, he took immediate possession of the land, and received the homage of his new subjects, on the 25th of June, by commission. Frederick confirmed the rights and privileges of its estates, and prosperity and peace soon reigned throughout a land, which had hitherto suffered considerably from internal feuds and misgovernment. Its favorable position for maritime purposes rendered it an object of considerable importance.

Frederick had, meanwhile, narrowly watched the train of events in the political world, and adopted such measures as were necessary for his own security. After the conclusion of the Breslau treaty, Austria directed the whole of its military resources against the French armies, scattered through Bohemia; and freed the land of their presence then, advancing on Bavaria, again expelled the emperor, who had succeeded in regaining possession of his capital. The Bavarians and the French were now driven to the borders of the Rhine; England had likewise taken up arms, and opposed a considerable army to the French force in Germany. The English were successful on the Mayne. France and the Emperor now made the most favorable propositions to the Austrian cabinet; but in vain. Maria Theresa would listen to nothing less than the ejection of the Emperor from the imperial throne, which her husband, Duke Francis, was to occupy. On the contrary, Austria, England, Holland and Sardinia entered, at Worms, in September, 1743, into league both offensive and defensive: Sardinia was induced to join, on condition of Austria surrendering up certain portions of its territories, which the latter power had hitherto held. On Maria Theresa's complaining to the King of England, that she was perpetually forced to surrender new portions of her kingdom, George II. replied, "Madam, whatever is worth taking is worth restoring." Frederick received a copy of this letter, and understood the moral which it contained for him also.

The intentions of the allies became more apparent on Saxony joining the Worms' league, with the private articles of which Frederick had become acquainted. The contracting parties had bound themselves to the mutual defence of their different territories, in pursuance of former treaties, therein recited; but no mention was made of that of Breslau. The private negotiations of this period rendered it impossible for Frederick to remain an idle spectator of passing events.

The Emperor, who dragged on a wretched existence at

Frankfort, craved his aid with the utmost importunity; and Frederick resolved on taking some decisive step. His idea was, to band the petty sovereigns of Germany together, as a counterpoise to the preponderating influence of Austria. With this view, and under cover of paying visits to his sisters in Anspach and Baireuth, he proceeded, during the spring of 1744, on a tour through the empire, and succeeded in effecting the "Frankfort Union," which was to restore to "Germany freedom—to the Emperor his rank,—and to Europe peace." But, as France refused to advance the necessary monies, the greater number of the contracting parties subsequently abandoned the Union.

Frederick's attention was now, of course, engrossed by France, the natural enemy of both Austria and England. But French politics had undergone a considerable change. Cardinal Fleury had died, and the kingdom was governed without regard to any fixed principles. Louis XV.'s reign had now commenced, attended by all the intrigues and absurdities of a government completely in the hands of abandoned women. Frederick perceived how matters stood, and alluded to the subject in the presence of the French ambassador. One evening as he was present at the opera, the curtain accidentally rose and disclosed the legs of some dancers who were practising their steps. The king turning to the English ambassador, who sat next him, whispered, but loud enough to be overheard by the French ambassador: "Look, there you have a perfect picture of the French ministry, all legs and no head."

To negotiate with a ministry so constituted Frederick felt was by no means an easy task; he therefore resolved on sending Count Rothenburg as his ambassador to Paris, who, having served in the French army, and being related to many members of the court, was best accquainted with its local relations. In order, however, to test the abilities of his representative, he summoned him; and taking upon himself the part of a French minister, advanced every possible objection to his own propositions; but Rothenburg refuted the various arguments with so much ability, that the king remarked: "If you be as eloquent and persuasive in Paris, you must certainly succeed."—And Frederick was not mistaken. Rothenburg's exertions were attended with such success, that France concluded, on the 5th of July, 1744, a treaty with Prussia, against Austria, and, on the basis of the Frankfort Union, for the protection of the Emperor. France promised to advance with two corps upon the Lower and Upper Rhine; Frederick, on his part, was to attack Bohemia, and to retain out of his conquests Austrian Silesia, and such portions of Bohemia as immediately adjoined Silesia.

Frederick's next care was to secure himself against his northern neighbors. He was very anxious to conclude a treaty with Russia, but was baffled by British gold. He succeeded, however, in having the Princess Sophia Auguste of Anhalt-Zerbst (subsequently Catharine II. of Russia), who had been brought up in Prussia, and whose father was a field-marshal in the Prussian service, affianced to the heir of the Russian throne. By this means Frederick obtained at least some influence in the Russian councils.

Prussia and Sweden became likewise more intimately connected, in consequence of the intermarriage of the Prince-royal of Sweden with the Princess Ulrike. The nuptials were celebrated with much splendor in Berlin, on the 17th of July, 1744. This was the last pageant that adorned these few brief years of peace. Frederick on this occasion exhibited all his talents for display, but the natural graces of the lovely bride far outshone the gaudy splendors of artificial pageantry. Fête succeeded fête up to the date of her departure. To drown the pain of parting, the various members of the royal family assembled at the opera, where Frederick handed his beloved sister a poem of his own composition. After the conclusion of the performance the bride set out for the Swedish capital, and Frederick returned to the field of battle.

CHAPTER XVIII.

OPENING OF THE SECOND SILESIAN WAR. CAMPAIGN OF THE YEAR 1744.

SUCCESS had in the meantime awaited the operations of the French army, which advanced in two columns. The northern army, under the command of King Louis XV. in person, had made an incursion into the Austrian Netherlands, whilst the second corps had taken up a position on the Upper Rhine, but with more equivocal success. The latter was held in check by Count Traun, one of the ablest generals in the Austrian service; who with his troops had penetrated into Alsatia, and already threatened Lorraine; so that the northern French corps was necessitated to detach a part of its strength, in order that the southern might escape disaster; whilst Frederick was compelled to hasten his operations against Bohemia.

The Prussian army put itself in marching order, and prepared to enter Bohemia in three columns; two of these were to penetrate through Saxony, and the third through Silesia, leaving two corps behind for the protection of Mark Brandenburg and Upper Silesia. A Prussian adjutant-general conveyed a requisition to the Dresden cabinet, wherein King Augustus was required by Charles VII. to grant a free passage to the Prussian troops. Augustus was in Warsaw at the time, and the Saxon ministers protested against the step; and the land put itself in a state of defence, but the only result of these measures was that the passage of the Prussians through

SECOND SILESIAN WAR. CAMPAIGN OF 1744.

the country was rendered more tedious, and consequently more injurious.

On the 15th of August, 1744, the Prussians reached the Bohemian frontier. The inhabitants having been strictly warned against offering any opposition to them, in a manifesto published prior to the incursion, allusion being made in general terms to the articles of the Frankfort Union, the Prussians met with but little resistance. The trifling embarrassments attending the march, arising from a want of water and provisions, were speedily removed; and magazines were constructed at Leitmeritz, on the Elbe, for provisioning the army, the different corps of which were concentrated round Prague on the 2d of September.

Preparations were immediately made for the siege of the Bohemian capital, which was garrisoned by a corps of 12,000 men. On the evening of the 10th of September trenches were opened in three different places. Schwerin prepared to assault the Ziskaberg; Prince Henry, the king's brother, visited the marshal during the night, and happening to inquire, in the course of conversation, the name of the chapel near which the king had encamped, the latter declared his ignorance: the prince, waving his hat, cried out: "Sancta Victoria!" "Then we must certainly do our utmost," replied Schwerin, "to become better acquainted with that saint." The assault was opened on the following day, and the Ziskaberg taken by storm. Frederick, who was standing in one of the trenches, advanced with several officers into an exposed position, in order to reconnoitre. The Austrian garrison, observing so many uniforms of rank, pointed the guns in that direction, and a luckless ball struck the Margrave William, one of the king's cousins, as he stood beside the monarch. (The margrave's elder brother had already met a hero's death in the battle of Mollwitz.) Frederick was deeply affected at the death of this prince. With the exception of this disaster the operations were signally successful, and the garrison capitulated on the 16th of

September, surrendering themselves prisoners of war, and were conducted under escort to the Silesian fortresses.

From Prague Frederick proceeded southwards, and invested the cities of Tabor, Budweis, and Frauenberg, so that he was not far from the Austrian frontiers. He was induced to advance in this direction in consequence of an arrangement with King Louis XV. that they should act in concert. But the French were not particularly scrupulous in fulfilling their engagements. They not only left the Austrian army every opportunity of effecting its retreat from Alsatia, on the news of Frederick's incursion into Bohemia, but did not even follow them as they hurried forward to oppose Frederick, although this had been expressly stipulated. Instead of this the French, with an eye to their own individual interests, commenced an attack on the Austrian possessions in Breisgau.

Frederick's position in the south of Bohemia was thus rendered critical, and other circumstances tended still further to increase his embarrassment. He found himself in a country which offered but little means for the support of his troops or for the transport of the magazines. The peasants had been commanded by the Austrian government to leave their huts on the approach of the Prussians, to bury their corn, and fly to the woods. Thus the army saw nothing but a wilderness and empty villages before it. No one could be induced to bring provisions to the camp for sale; whilst the nobility, the clergy, and officials remained faithful to the Austrian crown—religious opinions producing an insuperable hatred of the heretic Prussians. In addition, the Prussian army was on all sides surrounded by numerous swarms of hussars, who had advanced from Hungary, and so completely intercepted all communications, that Frederick could learn nothing from Prague for the space of four weeks, nor as to the place whither the Austrian army of the Rhine, under Traun, had proceeded, nor of the warlike preparations making in Saxony in favor of Austria. The Prus-

SECOND SILESIAN WAR. CAMPAIGN OF 1744.

sian scouts were invariably cut off, and fell into the hands of the enemy; and the army, as in the times of ancient Rome, were compelled to dig trenches, and confine itself within the circuit of the camp.

The want of provisions at last compelled Frederick to retire. The various fortified places which he had captured and garrisoned, were soon besieged by Hungarian troops, and being but scantily supplied with stores, were forced to surrender at discretion. After some days' marching, Frederick encountered a numerous hostile army, considerably augmented by reinforcements from Saxony. He now conceived that he had arrived at the limit of his toils, and hoped by one decisive engagement to attain such advantages as would ensure him the sovereignty of this obstinate land. But Traun took up such an admirable position, that the Prussians, as they dared not venture on an attack, were again, from want of provisions, forced to retire still farther. The Austrian army hung upon their rear; and Traun, who received ready support from the inhabitants of the country, continually repeated this manœuvre.

Thus a considerable period was wasted in marches and countermarches between the Sassawa and the Upper Elbe, until Frederick was forced, from want of provisions, the severity of the season, the harassing nature of the march, and the numerous diseases which had broken out in his army, to retire across the Elbe. He trusted that the Austrians, exhausted by their double campaign, would take up their winter-quarters on the opposite side of the stream. He therefore strove to strengthen his position on the far side, and cover the river. But the enemy were able to observe and profit by every motion of the Prussians, as they had full information of everything passing in the Prussian camp. On the 19th of November the Austrians suddenly forced a passage across the stream, at a point where they were almost unopposed. A single battalion, under Lieutenant-colonel Wedell, disputed the passage. This battalion sustained the attacks of the

Austrians for five hours with surprising hardihood and endurance, backed as the former were by fifty cannons, and repulsed the Austrian grenadiers three several times. Wedell had sent off some hussars to the Prussian camp to apprise Frederick of his position, but they had fallen into the hands of the enemy; and no reinforcement arriving, he retired, in perfect order, with the remnant of his valiant troop, to the main body of the Prussian army. This deed procured him the appellation of the Prussian Leonidas. Prince Charles of Lorraine, the leader of the Austrian army, could not avoid expressing his admiration for the chivalry of the deed. "How happy," said he to his staff, "would our queen be, had she in her army officers resembling this hero!"

The Austrians thus passing the stream decided the fate of this year's campaign. Frederick was forced to surrender Prague, as he was cut off from Silesia, and to retire upon the latter, where alone winter-quarters for his troops were to be found. The retreat was effected in three columns, and in such good order that the enemy acquired no further advantages. The rear-guard, in which Frederick was present, was during its march violently assailed by a corps of Pandoors; but the latter, on hearing the grunting of some pigs in a village, hastened without loss of time in pursuit of this welcome booty, and allowed the Prussians to continue their march without further interruption. The garrison of Prague was the only section of the Prussian army which suffered any considerable embarrassment or loss during their retreat, arising from the want of decision and energy in its leader, General Einsiedel. Frederick consequently cashiered the general, and the Prince-royal of Dessau, who had been hitherto Einsiedel's chief patron, likewise withdrew his favor. But Schwerin, who had frequently opposed the views of the Prince-royal of Dessau, so much so that Frederick was often obliged to interpose his whole authority in order to bring about a reconciliation between these two generals, sought to justify Einsiedel's conduct. Not being successful in this, he

SECOND SILESIAN WAR. CAMPAIGN OF 1744.

threw up his commission and retired from the service. On the 14th of September the king reached Silesia, from whence he returned to Berlin to make preparations for the future.

Frederick has severely criticised this campaign, also, in the History of His Times, without attempting to conceal the errors which he had committed. "The whole advantages of this campaign," he remarks, "were on the side of Austria. Traun played the part of Sertorius; the king, that of Pompey. Traun's conduct was a perfect model, which every soldier should study in order to imitate him, if possible. The king has himself acknowledged that he must consider that campaign as his school in the art of warfare, and Traun as his master. The successes of monarchs have often been pregnant with far more disastrous consequences than their reverses. The former intoxicate them with personal vanity whilst the latter teach them prudence and modesty."

Frederick had scarcely left his army, when the Austrians strove to take advantage of what they termed the fears of the Prussians. Numerous detachments advanced, towards the close of the year, upon Upper Silesia and the province of Glatz, and the Prussians retired upon the fortified towns. The Austrians published a manifesto, in which Maria Theresa declared the Breslau treaty void, as being the effect of compulsion on her part, and relieving the Silesians from their allegiance towards Frederick, reminding them of the happy days they enjoyed beneath the Austrian rule. Frederick was not slow in taking counter-measures. As Schwerin had retired from the service, and the young Prince of Dessau was dangerously ill, the illustrious father of the latter, Leopold of Dessau, who had hitherto commanded the corps which had remained behind in Brandenburg, was summoned to Silesia, and received the command of the troops serving in that quarter. A Prussian manifesto likewise appeared, refuting the assertions of the Austrians and commenting upon the alleged blessings of the former sovereignty of Austria. In spite of all the horrors of the weather the Prussians attacked the Austrians with courage and resolution, and drove them back with considerable loss to the Silesian frontier. On the 21st of Feburary, 1745, a solemn Te Deum was sung in Berlin in commemoration of the successes in Silesia. The army then took up its winter-quarters, exposed, however, to repeated attacks from the light troops of the Austrians.

On Frederick's return to Berlin he received intelligence of an event which gave him great joy. His brother, Augustus William, had a son (afterwards William II.) born to him during the campaign in Bohemia, so that there was now an heir to the throne. Frederick, as his own marriage proved without issue, had invested his brother, before the commencement of the second Silesian war, with the title of Prince of Prussia, and declared him his successor. As a mark of the weight he attached to the event above alluded to, he with his own hands suspended the order of the Black Eagle round the infant's neck.

But the political horizon was still darkened by many a tempest cloud. Towards the commencement of the year 1745 Austria, England, Holland, and Saxony concluded at Warsaw a treaty for their mutual defence. Saxony binding itself to provide a considerable army in consideration of receiving English subsidies in money, it was arranged in general terms that she should receive different provinces of the Prussian monarchy, whilst Austria was secured in the possession of Silesia and Glatz.

Frederick's position became still more critical through the death of the Emperor, Charles VII., which occurred on the 20th of January, as Austria had succeeded in inducing the Emperor's son to relinquish the war, and abandon all claims on her, in consideration of his hereditary dominions being restored to him, and even to support the Grand Duke Francis in his pretensions to the imperial crown. The Frankfort compact was consequently at an end. Immediately on the death of the Emperor,

SECOND SILESIAN WAR. CAMPAIGN OF 1744.

Frederick entreated the King of France to fulfil his obligations, and commence, in unison with himself, a series of active operations against Austria. But for this Louis felt little inclination: the Emperor's death, seeming to promise some arrangement of his disordered affairs, was rather welcome than otherwise; and Frederick whom he was taught by his confessors and mistresses to regard as the first of heretics, was the subject of his most thorough detestation. He accordingly concentrated his whole power against Flanders, and his army obtained, on the 11th of May, a brilliant victory at Fontenay.

Thus Frederick, opposed to powerful foes, saw himself reduced to rely upon himself alone. Every effort was therefore made, by means of extraordinary conscriptions, to be prepared to repel any attack that might be made. More than six millions of thalers were taken out of the treasury, a million and a half were advanced by the Estates, the greater part of the massive silver plate into which Frederick William I. had converted a portion of his treasure, and particularly the splendid silver orchestra was taken out of the Knights' Chamber in the Berlin palace, and reconverted into money. With these additional funds he was enabled to make some provision for the future sustenance of his army; and no sooner were these serious arrangements completed than Frederick returned (on the 15th of March) to the camp.

CHAPTER XIX.

CAMPAIGN OF THE YEAR 1745.

UNWILLING to expose his army a second time to the toils of a campaign like that of the last year, Frederick resolved on awaiting the enemy's attack on Silesia, and then concentrating all his forces at the point assailed. One considerable advantage for him was the recall of Traun from the command of the Austrian army, and his post being afterwards filled by less provident commanders. From the movements of the Austrians it became apparent that the blow would come from the Bohemian side, although various dispositions were made to lead Frederick to form a different conclusion. The latter was, however, not so easily imposed upon, and the desultory warfare that occurred was merely calculated to improve the Prussian cavalry, and lay the foundation for that fame which it subsequently achieved at Winterfeld.

After having visited Neisse, Frederick concentrated the main body of his army in front of the hills which separate the province of Glatz from Silesia, taking up his headquarters in the Cistercian monastery of Camenz. Shortly previous to his so doing, Frederick narrowly escaped being captured; a danger which had already threatened him in this neighborhood before. The best authorities are agreed that the circumstance to which we allude is referable to this period. It seems that Frederick had paid a preparatory visit to the monastery, and that some Austrian marauders had learned this fact. The convent-bell suddenly pealed throughout the mon-

astery; all the monks were summoned to the choir at a
most unusual hour, it being evening; and when the abbot
appeared, he was accompanied by a stranger, clad in the
vestments of their order. Prayers and matins were held,
but the chant had hardly commenced when a violent
tumult arose in the court-yard of the convent. A band
of Croats burst into the church; but as they did not
venture to disturb the divine service it continued without
interruption. At length, as soon as the confusion had
subsided, the abbot made a signal for the music to cease,
and the monks were now for the first time informed that
the Croats had been in search of the Prussian king, but
had only found his adjutant, whom they had carried off
with them.—The strange clergyman was no other than
Frederick himself. For this act of fidelity and presence
of mind the abbot of Camenz, Tobias Stusche, always enjoyed the highest favor of the king, from whom he received various presents, and amongst others a set of
splendid vestments, upon which the abbot caused the
Prussian eagle to be embroidered, and consecrated them
on the anniversary of the king's birthday. These singular sacerdotal robes are still preserved in Camenz, and an
inscription in the church informs posterity of the danger
and escape of the great king.

The enemy's motions rendered it necessary for Frederick to make the most vigorous preparations for active
warfare. The Margrave Charles was still at the head of
a division in Upper Silesia, but the whole land was so
completely overswarmed with Hungarian marauders,
that all communication between the margrave and the
king was intercepted. Ziethen, who had already distinguished himself by his gallantry in the first war, and had
rapidly advanced from a subordinate post to that of commander of a regiment of hussars, was detached with his
regiment to the margrave, with orders for the latter to
advance without delay. This commission was by no means
easy of execution; but the new dolmans, which the regiment had just received, afforded an opportunity for a

bold stratagem. These dolmans gave this regiment somewhat the appearance of imperial troops, and enabled them to proceed quietly on their march, until, by attaching themselves to an Austrian troop, they had passed through the midst of the enemy. Ziethen was not recognized until very late, and then the hussars broke through all opposition, carrying off even some officers with them as prisoners. The margrave's march to join the main army was attended with more considerable difficulties. He was opposed by far superior numbers, but regiment after regiment dashed forward, and carved themselves a path with the sword, until they reached the king's camp, where their courage met with its full meed of praise. The whole army burned to earn similar distinction; nor was the opportunity long wanting.

The Austrian and Saxon armies had formed a junction at Trautenau, and advanced from thence upon the frontiers of Silesia. Frederick fell back with his army to Schweidnitz, and took up a favorable position between Schweidnitz and Striegau. In order to deceive the enemy, he circulated the report that he was about to retire upon Breslau, and, to give this intention a color of probability, the Breslau roads were partially repaired. Frederick now recalled his advanced guard, and circulated the same report amongst them. The enemy fell into the snare, and did not take those precautionary measures which were necessary in the presence of so considerable an enemy. On the hostile armies emerging from the hills, the Austrian and Saxon generals held a council of war on the Galgenburg, near Hohenfriedberg, where the whole plain lay beneath their feet. Frederick's troops were, however, so concealed by brambles and mud-walls as to be almost invisible. This confirmed the enemy in their mistake, and plans for the capture of Silesia with the least possible trouble were here debated. The troops then got under arms, and continued their march.

The following night Frederick mustered his troops near Striegau, in perfect silence, and in such a position as

CAMPAIGN OF THE YEAR 1745. 161

was best adapted for receiving the enemy. At break of day the troops formed in line of battle. Before this manœuvre could be executed, the Saxon army had received orders to seize Striegau, and had descended the heights. The Prussian right wing now advanced with such impetuosity upon the Saxons that they were borne down and routed before the Austrians could obtain intelligence of the event. The Prince of Lorraine, who was commander-in-chief of the Austrian army, had heard the firing, but conceived that it was the attack upon Striegau. He was now informed that the plains were strewed with Saxon dead, and was forced to prepare for battle without a moment's delay, but the repeated charges of the Austrians were met with the same heroic fortitude. Not a Prussian corps gave way; each steadily advanced, and every man vied with his fellows in acts of gallantry and daring.

The morning sun shone upon a well-fought field.

The dragoon regiment of Baireuth, under the command of General Gessler, distinguished itself particularly, by routing upwards of twenty battalions of the enemy, taking two thousand five hundred prisoners, and capturing sixty standards and four guns. Frederick himself had set his troops an example of the most determined contempt of death, by advancing with three battalions in the face of the Austrian guns, which mowed them down by his side in lines, so that but three hundred and sixty men reached the heights; where he headed a charge with fixed bayonets upon a battery. The Austrians lost in this battle, which bears the name of Hohenfriedberg, or Striegau, eleven thousand men,—seven thousand prisoners, and four thousand slain,—together with many standards and guns; whilst the loss on the Prussian side amounted to but eight hundred rank and file, inclusive of prisoners and slain. The Baireuth dragoon regiment was invested by the king with extraordinary decorations in memory of its gallant exploits on this occasion; and Frederick remarks in the History of His Times, alluding to the victory of Hohenfriedberg, "The globe does not rest more securely upon the shoulders of Atlas than Prussia upon such an army as she now possesses."

The French ambassador, the Chevalier de la Tour, who had come to announce the victory of Fontenay, and was present at this defeat of the Austrians, had some time previously asked Frederick's permission to accompany the Prussian army for a short period, when the latter inquired, "Do you wish, then, to see who shall retain Silesia?" "No, sire," replied the French chevalier, "I only wish to see your majesty chastise your enemies and defend your subjects." He now received a letter, directed to his master, King Louis XV., in which the following words occur: "I have honored at Friedeberg the draft which you drew upon me at Fontenay." The bitter tone of this remark was elicited by Louis's conduct. Frederick had not neglected to make every exertion to induce him to take more active steps against Austria, but in vain. He excused himself by pointing to the victory of Fontenay. Frederick replied by remarking that the Austrian forces opposed to the French in Flanders hardly exceeded six thousand men; that the French victories were, no doubt fraught with glory for the King of France, but about as useful to his allies as a victory on the banks of the Scamander or the capture of Pekin. Frederick received a cold and haughty answer in reply, and the friendship which had hitherto subsisted between the French and Prussian monarchs seemed at an end.

After pursuing the enemy to the heights of the hills, Frederick halted, as his troops were completely exhausted by their previous night's march and their exertions during the engagement; besides which, before proceeding further, it was necessary to bring up his provision, ammunition, and stores which had been left behind at Schweidnitz. Thus the pursuit of the foe was necessarily suspended until the following day, when the advance-guard coming up with the enemy's rear, which had not taken any part in the previous engagement, attacked it and put it to the rout, the Austrians retiring

CAMPAIGN OF THE YEAR 1745.

with considerable loss and the utmost expedition, upon Bohemia.

On Frederick's arrival in Landshut he was surrounded by two thousand peasants, who entreated permission to slay all the Catholics of the neighborhood. This was intended as an act of retribution for the harsh treatment which the Silesian provinces had to endure from the Catholic priesthood. Frederick reminded the clamorous miscreants of the words of the gospel: to bless those that calumniate them, and pray for those that persecute them. The peasants, struck by such expressions of clemency, declared the king to be in the right, and refrained from the execution of their barbarous design.

Frederick, in pursuance of the plan which he had adopted previous to the battle of Hohenfriedberg, pursued the Austrians to Bohemia, in order to destroy, as far as possible, their means of support, and thus hinder them from again taking up their winter-quarters in the neighborhood of Silesia. He did not, however, venture to penetrate deeper into Bohemia, being obliged to draw the whole of the provisions for his army from Silesia. The Prince of Lorraine had formed an intrenched camp at Königingrätz. Frederick's positions were equally strong: first at Jaromirz and afterwards at Chlumetz. Here nothing beyond a species of petty warfare between the light troops of both armies, and some desultory attacks upon the convoys of provisions occurred to relieve the dull monotony of camp-life. Sometimes an opportunity for a display of humor and originality, or, may be, gallantry would offer. Thus, on one occasion a detachment of Prussians stationed at Schmerschütz played off an admirable *ruse de guerre* upon their Pandoor enemies, in order to cure the latter of their propensity for perpetually attacking the trenches. Some Prussian grenadiers constructed a wooden figure, and dressing it up in their own costume, placed it at a point which was generally held by the outermost piquet. They then concealed themselves behind some brushwood, and put the wooden soldier's limbs in motion by pulling certain cords. The Pandoors remarking from afar the jollity of the supposed sentry, shot at him until they brought him down, and then rushed forward to strip the slain of his worldly goods. But they were received by a hot fire from the ambuscade in the brushwood, and several prisoners were taken, while those who escaped so frightened their comrades that similar attacks were not for some time repeated. Proofs of chivalrous feeling were likewise given at times. Thus some officers belonging to an Austrian detachment, having been engaged with a Prussian corps, remarked to the officers of the latter, "It is a pleasure, gentlemen, to fight with you; we can always learn something from you." The Prussians replied, with equal politeness, that the Austrians were their masters, and that if they had learned to defend themselves vigorously, it was owing to their having been always vigorously attacked.

It now became necessary for Frederick to act with more caution, and make better provision against any unforeseen attack, inasmuch as he had considerably diminished his strength by detaching several corps. No sooner had Upper Silesia been evacuated by the Prussian troops, than the Hungarians began to spread themselves over the face of the country, without meeting any opposition; until Frederick, upon receiving intelligence that the fortress of Kosel had fallen into their hands through the treachery of one of the officers of the garrison, sent some troops thither, who speedily recaptured it, and freed the province from the presence of its enemies. A second corps was then detached to reinforce the Prussian army stationed at Halle, under the command of the Prince of Dessau, in order to enable it to withstand any attacks that might come from Saxony; renewed preparations for war having been made by that power, which had called forth a most serious remonstrance from Frederick. This movement caused the greater portion of the Saxon troops, who had hitherto served with the Austrians in Bohemia, to be recalled.

CAMPAIGN OF THE YEAR 1745.

Frederick did not, however, proceed to aggressive measures against Saxony in the first instance, in the hope of being able to arrange matters amicably. The English court had, in consequence of a change in the ministry, become more peacefully disposed, and on the 22d of September a convention was signed at Hanover between Frederick and the King of England, wherein the latter guaranteed anew the possession of Silesia to Frederick, and promised to induce, if possible, both Austria and Saxony to come to terms, in consideration of Frederick promising to acknowledge the Grand-duke Francis as emperor. The latter had been elected on the 30th of September at Frankfort, no regard having been paid to the protestation of the Prussian ambassador. But the haughty soul of Maria Theresa, swelling with ancestral pride and the brilliant recollections of her imperial descent, would stoop to no compromise. She considered it incompatible with her dignity to negotiate with the prince, whom she regarded as a rebellious subject, and publicly declared that she would rather part with the garment from her back than with Silesia. Saxony felt equally little inclination for peace. King Augustus aimed at rendering the Polish crown hereditary in his family, and conceived that the increase of his power and the connection of his Saxon possessions with Poland, by means of some Prussian provinces, was admirably calculated to effect this purpose.

New reinforcements were sent to the Prince of Lorraine, together with a few generals to aid him in drawing up his plans. The Austrians did actually attempt some unusually violent measures, which were, however, parried by the gallantry of the Prussian troops. Frederick's camp was too strong to admit of being attacked with success; he therefore contented himself with surveying from his tent, which was situated upon a height, the motions of the Austrian generals, as they daily advanced to consult together, and opened their long telescopes to reconnoitre his position, and then retired, in the hope of the future inspiring them with better counsels.

Meanwhile Frederick found himself obliged to take up a new position; he advanced more to the north, in order to strip that portion of the Bohemian hills lying between Lower Silesia and the province of Glatz of its provisions, and thus form a complete line of partition, so as to protect Silesia, during the approaching winter, from any hostile incursion. For the occupation of the mountain-passes he was again obliged to weaken his army, by detaching several corps, so that the total amount of his collective forces did not now exceed eighteen thousand men, whilst the Austrians who watched his movements amounted to forty thousand.

As he was about to advance from his camp in the village of Staudenz, he was suddenly attacked at early dawn by the Austrian army, which advanced in order of battle upon him. His position was unfavorable, and he had not sufficient troops to hold the important points. But the Austrians were likewise on rather unfavorable ground, as they could not bring the whole of their forces into play. Frederick took advantage of this circumstance, and instead of retiring, as the Austrians expected he would, and thus allowing himself to be attacked possibly in a still more disadvantageous position, he rapidly expanded his whole army in one line, so as to prevent himself from being outflanked. This manœuvre was executed under a shower of hand-grenades from the enemy, but not a soldier blenched or flinched from his position. Frederick rode for a quarter of an hour beneath this shower of shot, but without being wounded: one ball must have struck him, were it not that it passed through the head of his horse, which at that instant was in the act of rearing. The Austrians permitted this disposition to be made without any further interruption. The Prussian cavalry now charged the enemy, broke their first lines, and drove them back upon the second, and these again upon the third; fifty squadrons were thus overpowered by twelve, through the impetuosity of the assault, and were prevented from rallying by the unfavorable nature of the ground. The Prussian right wing then stormed the battery with which the Austrians had opened the battle; whilst a single battalion of the left wing put a strong column of the enemy to the rout. The Prussians pressed irresistibly forward, leaving but one steep ascent in the centre of the engagement in the hands of the Austrians, and this was soon escaladed and captured likewise by the Prussian Guard. Fate ordained that two brothers should be here opposed to each other in mortal combat; Prince Lewis of Brunswick commanded the Austrians at this point, whilst his younger brother, Prince Ferdinand, headed the Prussian Guard, and here first displayed that heroism for which he became afterwards so distinguished. The routed Austrians made a last effort to rally upon the heights of the mountain-land; but the Prussians again pressed forward upon them, and forced them to take refuge in the adjoining woods. Frederick checked the pursuit at the village of Soor, from which the battle derives its name. The victory was complete, but Frederick lost a great part of his baggage, it having fallen into the hands of a Hungarian corps. This circumstance, however, rendered the victory so much the more easy, as the Hungarians were so occupied with the booty that they neglected to fall upon the Prussian rear, as they had been instructed.

The further pursuit of the enemy was rendered impossible through the intervention of a wood, as the Prussians would there be necessarily exposed to every species of danger, and without the prospect of any equivalent advantage. The immediate inconvenience arising from the loss of the baggage was soon forgotten in the general joy at the victory itself. The king had lost the whole of his camp-stores and furniture. He was even obliged to send the news of the victory to Breslau on a small slip of paper, written in penciling; and when he was about to sup, it was discovered that but a few bottles of wine remained, and not a loaf of bread was to be had. An officer was accordingly sent out to procure some bread, and after a long search a soldier was discovered who had one loaf left. For this he was offered a ducat, which he, however, refused, rejecting even still higher offers ; but on being informed that the bread was wanted for the king's use, he resolved on bringing his majesty the half of it. Frederick accepted this valuable present with gratitude. But this state of things was speedily remedied. The king also had fresh books sent him, to replace those which he had lost, in order to fill up his leisure hours.

A pretty little greyhound belonging to the king had likewise been carried off with the royal baggage. This was the only loss which affected the king sensibly. The animal was a particular favorite of his ; and, indeed, he was generally surrounded by some favorite dogs. The enemy testified their commiseration for the king's loss by sending back the greyhound. The story goes, that Frederick had just seated himself at his writing-desk when the greyhound entered the apartment unobserved, and springing upon the table, placed its fore-paws upon the king's shoulders. Frederick was so affected by this unexpected meeting that he is said to have shed tears.

The battle of Soor left the continuance of the campaign completely at Frederick's discretion. Feeling little inclination for any new enterprise in Bohemia, he, after remaining five days upon the field of battle as undisputed victor, proceeded to ravage the neighboring country, and then set out for Silesia. His march was considerably impeded by the murderous attacks to which his army was exposed in its progress through the narrow defiles of this mountain-land, but the loss sustained was comparatively insignificant. On its arrival in Silesia the main body of the army encamped, under the command of the Prince-royal of Dessau, at Schweidnitz ; and Frederick, on learning that the Austrians had separated into three bodies, and were likely to become even still more dispersed, returned to Berlin.

CHAPTER XX.

CONCLUDING CAMPAIGN OF THE SECOND SILESIAN WAR.

In Berlin Frederick was received with all the honors due to a conqueror. He now hoped that the favorable moment had at length arrived when his enemies would lend a more willing ear to his overtures of peace. But Austria and Saxony were far from sympathizing in these sentiments; and Count Brühl, who had felt his pride severely wounded by some expressions contained in Frederick's manifesto against Saxony, had, on the 8th of November, the same day on which the trophies won at Hohenfriedberg were suspended in the churches of Berlin, been raising a new storm round Frederick's head. Private intelligence had been conveyed to Frederick, to the effect that the armies of Austria and Saxony were about to form an immediate junction, for the purpose of attacking him in Mark Brandenburg. Further corroborative intelligence was soon received, announcing the erection of considerable magazines in Saxon Lusatia, for the support of Austrian troops; one section of the Austrian army being held in readiness to attack Silesia on the Bohemian side, whilst a corps of the Austrian army of the Rhine, under the command of General Grunne, was already marching upon Berlin.

But with the same rapidity with which these new dangers had been conjured up, were Frederick's dispositions made to meet the coming foe. The venerable Prince of Dessau was again invested with the command of the army stationed at Halle, with orders to make an incursion upon Saxony; whilst Frederick, at the head of the Silesian army, attacked it on the Lusatian side. It was Frederick's intention to march from both points straight on Dresden. A garrison was left in Berlin for its defence, and a considerable number of the citizens enrolled themselves in a brigade to aid in repelling any sudden assault; the capital was further put in a state of defence by digging trenches and throwing up outworks.

Frederick reached Liegnitz, the headquarters of the Silesian army, on the 15th of November. Whilst the Austrians were penetrating into Lusatia he employed the same manœuvre which he had already played off with such success at Hohenfriedberg. He circulated reports as to his being concerned for the safety of his own territories, and its being his intention to return with his army in order to cover them, and took several steps to give a color of truth to these reports. The Prince of Lorraine fell a second time into this snare. Frederick reached Lusatia quite unexpectedly, and came in contact, on the 23d of November, at Hennersdorff, with the Saxon regiments which formed the advanced guard of the Austrian army. The Saxons were attacked and beaten, and their loss produced such confusion in the body of the Austrian army that the latter retired from place to place. Görlitz, which had been stored, was obliged to surrender to Frederick, and soon afterwards Zittau, where the Austrian rear-guard had sought refuge, was likewise taken, and with it the Austrian baggage. In a very short time the whole of Lusatia was in Frederick's hands; the Austrian army having fallen back upon Bohemia. An attack of the Austrians on Silesia had been likewise repulsed with loss. The whole of Saxony became panic-struck, and General Grunne's corps, which was just on the edge of Brandenburg, was recalled with all expedition to the Saxon main army.

Frederick employed these new successes in endeavoring to induce King Augustus to conclude a treaty of peace, based on the terms of the Hanoverian convention with England. But Augustus, or, rather, Brühl, insisted, as a preliminary, on the immediate suspension of all hostilities, and the payment of all damages occasioned by the incursion of the Prussians. This condition was of course rejected by Frederick, and the negotiations were shortly afterwards suspended. Brühl had wisely transferred his master from Dresden to Prague on the first approach of danger, and thus spared him a sight of the horrors of war, in order that his voice alone might reach the monarch's ear.

The war was now carried on with increased vigor. Frederick entered Saxony, and accelerated the movements of the Prince of Anhalt, who had hitherto been rather tardy, either from caprice or age. The latter now moved forward, invested Leipzig on the 30th of November, and reached Meissen on the 6th of December. Frederick kept likewise moving in the same direction. The Prince of Lorraine had in the meantime again evacuated Bohemia, and formed a junction with the Saxons at Dresden; but the Saxon ministry had quartered the army in such an absurdly scattered manner that it required twenty-four hours' time to muster it; the prince's protestations against such an arrangement being unheeded. Count Rutosky, also, who held the command of the Saxon army which was to cover Dresden from the first attacks of the Prussians, upon being requested to give information to the Prince of Lorraine with all possible dispatch, in the event of his being attacked, replied, that he required no aid; and thus the Saxons by their infatuation became themselves the instruments of their own destruction.

On the 15th of December the Prince of Dessau marched on Dresden. Frederick at the same time invested Meissen, which formed the communication between both banks of the Elbe, so as to be prepared for all attempts of the enemy on either side of the stream. He here received a letter from the Saxon ministry, consenting to the terms he had formerly offered, and informing him of Maria Theresa's wish for peace. He had hardly read the letter when the heavens seemed lit up with flame, and the thunder of a furious cannonade burst upon his ears. The battle had begun between the Prince of Dessau and the Saxons.

Prince Leopold had taken up an admirable position near Kesselsdorf. The left wing of the Saxons, which rested on this point, seemed assailable, but was strongly sheltered by a powerful battery. The other wing of the Saxon army stood on the edge of a precipice, whose heights were so covered with ice and snow as to appear inaccessible;—but the more daring the deed the brighter the renown. The day had come on which this aged warrior was to crown his brilliant career of half a century by one glorious exploit. His dispositions were made with the most perfect coolness and indifference. He could well rely on the undaunted courage of men who were ready to follow him whom they deemed invulnerable, whithersoever he chose to lead them: and having offered up a short prayer, which was well calculated to strengthen his resolution—" Heavenly Father!" such are his words, " graciously aid me this day: but if thou shouldst not be so disposed, lend not, at least, thy aid to those scoundrels, the enemy, but passively await the issue!"—he gave the signal for the assault. The charge was twice beaten back by heavy showers of grape. The Saxons advanced in pursuit, but immediately received such an overwhelming shock from a regiment of Prussian dragoons that they were instantly borne down. The village was speedily seized, the battery taken, the hostile cavalry dispersed, and a general rout ensued. The Prussian left wing, which had stood opposite those sheets of rock, now pressed forward, escaladed the heights by a dangerous path, and again put the foe to flight. Count Rutowski arrived with the remnant of his routed army in Dresden, just as the Prince of Lorraine was engaged in mustering the Austrian forces. The latter proposed to the count that they should make a joint attack upon the Prussians the next day, but the latter was so disheartened that he would attempt nothing further. He demonstrated to the Prince the necessity which then existed for withdrawing their troops, and falling back upon the Bohemian frontiers, a measure which was accordingly put in execution.

Frederick paid a visit on the following day to the field of battle, and saw with astonishment the almost miraculous successes of his army; the Prince of Dessau, who accompanied him, receiving the most flattering eulogies. On the 18th of December Frederick entered Dresden, the town having surrendered at discretion. A body of militia, which had been left in the town after its evacuation by the army, was disarmed, and employed, together with other prisoners, in completing the Prussian army. Frederick, immediately after entering, proceeded to the palace, where King Augustus's children still remained. He endeavored to console them: and as they kissed his hand, embraced them affectionately, assuring them that they should be secured in all the honors due to their rank; at the same time placing the palace-guard at their command. He treated the ministers with the same courtesy, and in the evening visited the theatre, where the opera of Arminia was performed. This was one of the operas in which Brühl strove to pander to the passions of the king.

It contained an allusion to the league between King Augustus and Maria Theresa. But the singers prudently omitted the chorus which was intended to allude to Frederick's conduct, the moral of which was now applicable to King Augustus himself; one passage denouncing as guilty that ambition which sought to erect a throne upon the ruins of foreign power. Frederick was present, the following day at a solemn Te Deum, which was sung in the Kreuzkirche.

The negotiations now progressed with somewhat more expedition, as an ambassador had been sent by the Austrian cabinet to Dresden, and peace was concluded at the latter city on the 25th of December. The various articles of the Breslau treaty were introduced into it, but Saxony was forced to pay Prussia a subsidy of a million of thalers; Frederick recognizing the election of the Grand-Duke Francis to the imperial purple.

On the 28th of December Frederick made his solemn entry into Berlin, amidst the enthusiastic shouts of his subjects, who hailed their youthful monarch as a hero. He was met by various processions, and conducted within the walls amidst cries of "Long live the king! Long live Frederick the Great!"

The king, who was pensive and deeply moved, returned the salutations with which he was on every side heartily greeted, betraying at the same time the greatest anxiety to prevent any accident occurring to those who crowded round his chariot. The town was brilliantly illuminated from evening until break of day; and thousands of devices were displayed at the windows, almost every house bearing the inscription, "Vivat Fredericus Magnus!" Military salutes were fired during the whole night, while the crowds of people that filled the streets made the welkin ring with their joyous acclamations.

Frederick had proceeded, in the company of his brothers, through the streets during the evening, in order to be a spectator of the rejoicings of his people: but he had a dear and sad office likewise in view. In a retired street he stopped his carriage, entered a house, and ascended its narrow staircase. This was the residence of his old and faithful tutor, Duhan, whom he found confined to his bed in the last stage of sickness. Frederick approached the couch of the dying man: "Beloved Duhan," said he, what pain it gives me to find you in this state! Would to God that I could procure your convalescence or assuage your sufferings; you should then see what sacrifices my gratitude would be ready to make." "To have once again beheld your majesty," replied Duhan, "is the dearest consolation which I could have possibly desired. Now I shall die more happily." He made a motion to grasp the king's hand and imprint a kiss upon it. Frederick would not permit him, but bidding him farewell, in the deepest sorrow, hurried away. On the following day

CONCLUSION OF THE SECOND SILESIAN WAR.

Duhan expired. There were others, too, unable to congratulate Frederick on his successes. His best friends, Jordan and Keyserling, had died during the foregoing year. "They were my family," said Frederick, announcing their death to Duhan. "I consider myself now childless and fatherless, and in deeper mourning of heart than any dress could indicate. Take care of your health, and remember that you are now the last of the friends I have left me." Frederick took a father's care of the children of the deceased.

The war between Austria and France continued unabated, and only terminated on the 18th of October, 1748, in the treaty of Aix-la-Chapelle, when Frederick received a new guarantee for his possession of Silesia. His position as regarded the King of France was by no means of a friendly character, although the treaty existing between them was not to expire until the year 1756. Frederick had had recourse to the King of France for aid on the approach of the dangers impending from Austria and Saxony, but had received an answer in which unfriendly feelings were but thinly disguised in phrases of empty courtesy. The victory at Dresden was accordingly announced in a similar style, and, to use the words of an English ambassador, who was negotiating with Frederick previous to the treaty of Aix-la-Chapelle, and addressed by him to his cabinet: "The king's heart is truly German, despite the French filagree which decks its surface."

CHAPTER XXI.

FREDERICK'S ADMINISTRATION UP TO THE SEVEN YEARS' WAR.

Much of Frederick's attention was now engrossed by cares for the internal welfare of his people. His exertions, his advice were ever ready at hand; and the eleven years of peace, which now succeeded, produced such indubitable proofs of the prosperity which his government had everywhere diffused, that he had good reason to feel satisfied with the fruits of his labors.

Through the conquest of Silesia, he had added a third to the extent of his kingdom; but he was fully as zealous in making equally extensive conquests in the heart of his own empire. Waste lands were reclaimed and colonized; and, in the year 1746, those stupendous works were commenced, which converted the marshes of Oberthal into arable and pasture land. On the completion of these works, Frederick could with justice exclaim, as he stood upon the dam of Oberthal, and surveyed the flowery meads that had sprung up, as it were, by enchantment: "There is a principality which I have won, and which needs no soldiers for its defence.

With a view to advance internal navigation, several canals were cut, connecting some of the principal rivers. A harbor was constructed at Swinemünde, and Stettin thereby elevated to the rank of an important seaport. Emden was declared a free port, and an Asiatic and Bengal trading company was there chartered. Still greater exertions were made for the advancement of manufactures and trade, and the population and revenue of the Prussian state soon increased to a very considerable extent.

Frederick bestowed particular attention on a reform in the administration of justice. The state of the law called loudly for amendment. Thousands of abuses had crept in, and suits lingered on from year to year, wrapped in such a maze of technicalities, that it was wholly impossible to obtain the desired relief; whilst the expenses attending the institution of the legal proceedings had become ruinously large. This state of things naturally awakened in Frederick the most unlimited disgust, and he resolved to interfere with promptitude, and apply some strong remedy to these abuses. His views were ably seconded by his minister, Cocceji, a man fully equal to the task of amending the defects in the Prussian code. An experiment was made in the province of Pomerania, where particular disorder was known to exist in the administration of justice; and the result was, that in the short period of eight months, an enormous number of lawsuits, amounting to two thousand four hundred, some of which had been pending for years, were decided; so that not one single suit of longer duration than one year remained undetermined. A particular code was then prepared for Pomerania, and Frederick was so satisfied with the fruits of Cocceji's labors, that he nominated him his high-chancellor, and commissioned him to effect a judicious reform throughout the whole Prussian monarchy. Cocceji, despite his advanced age, devoted himself with the most unwearying perseverance to this gigantic task, and in one year succeeded in removing all such judges and advocates as were inefficient, from their different posts, and supplying their places with men of acknowledged ability. In pursuance of Frederick's plan, an ordinance was published, limiting the duration of a lawsuit to one year. At length, the most arduous part of the undertaking, namely, the reducing of the law to clear and determinate principles, was effected; and in the year

1749, the draft of a new Prussian code, entitled, "Draft of the Corpus Juris Fredericiani," appeared. Frederick, in commemoration of these beneficial reforms, which became the subject of wonder and imitation throughout the whole of Europe, had a medal struck off, on which the Goddess of Justice was represented, holding in her hands a pair of scales, one of which was considerably depressed, whilst Frederick was in the act of restoring equilibrium by laying his sceptre in the other. Cocceji received one of these medals in gold, together with many other proofs of royal approbation. Frederick told him, that his virtues and integrity were worthy of the most glorious days of the Roman republic, and his learning and wisdom such as to fit him, like a second Trebonian, for the task of legislating with advantage for his fellow-men.

The peculiar constitution of the Prussian state rendered unceasing attention to the affairs of the army absolutely essential. Frederick never relaxed in his exertions for the improvement and discipline of his troops; large camps were formed every year, and the most complicated manœuvres executed. The infantry were exercised in the various evolutions requisite for attack and defence; in pontooning and the usual routine of military tactics. Particular care was likewise bestowed upon the cavalry, and Frederick labored unceasingly to render this arm of the service worthy of its calling and its great importance in war. Not content with officers trained in the Prussian school, he summoned some of the most distinguished cavalry-officers from Hungary, to instruct his men in all such manœuvres as required a combination of superior daring and skill. Immediately after the second Silesian war in 1746, a large camp was formed at Potsdam. Frederick proposed rewards for such hussars as distinguished themselves by their courage and stratagems; and the following anecdote will throw some light upon the nature of these exercises, while it illustrates the innate goodness of Frederick's heart. He had, in order to keep the officers and men stationed at the outposts always on the *qui vive*, given instructions to the hussars to hover round the outskirts of the camp, and carry off the shakos of such men as they found off their guard; a ducat being offered for each shako so taken. An aged officer of Cuirassiers, Major Leopold, overpowered by the heat and his exertions during the day's manœuvres, had set up a camp-chair in the middle of his troop, and incautiously fell asleep. A hussar observing the circumstance crept softly forward, and carrying off the shako of the slumbering warrior, brought it to the king. The latter inquired to whom the shako belonged, evidently much displeased at the misconduct of the owner; but, on hearing the name of the officer, his brow quickly relaxed. The following morning he summoned the major to his presence: the latter entered much depressed, and the king advancing towards him, addressed him in a friendly tone. "Look ye," said Frederick, threatening him with his finger; "no one should sleep upon guard; you will act most prudently by quitting the service, as you are so advanced in years. I shall give you a pension of five hundred thalers. You have a son in the regiment, an ensign—have you not?" The major replied in the affirmative. "Your son," continued the king, "is likely to become an able officer; but in order to prevent him from imitating the bad example of his father and sleeping upon his post, I shall take him with me to Potsdam as a cornet of the guard."

The most remarkable of these manœuvres was a grand one held at Spandau in 1753, to which several foreign personages of distinction, together with all the principal general officers in the Prussian army, were invited. None but such as were specially invited were permitted to be present, as Frederick did not wish to have the results of his own experience made indiscriminately public. The piquets were posted as in actual warfare; and the patrols had orders to commit some slight depredations on the persons of such over-curious individuals as transgressed the king's injunctions. This tended to heighten the general interest and curiosity felt by the public; and

Frederick published a mock account of the manœuvres, in which he drew largely on his fancy, but which was received by many as a valuable contribution to the science of military tactics.

In matters of religion, Frederick was faithful to those principles and maxims which he had already enunciated in his writings. "Religious intolerance is a tyrant that depopulates a land; but religious liberty is a tender mother that cherishes and fosters her children." And, in truth, his adherence to these principles contributed materially to the prosperity of his states. Frederick paid, no doubt, more attention to the matter than the form of any creed; but we have sufficient evidence of the deeply religious tone of his mind and the strength of his religious sentiments, although he might at times give utterance to an expression derisive of things which are generally considered sacred. One of the best proofs of our assertion is the prayer which he ordered to be offered up during the second Silesian war, both by the army and in the churches. This prayer had been hitherto as follows:—"But, especially, we recommend unto thee, O God, his majesty, our most beloved king;" (here the king's name was particularly mentioned.) Frederick had objected to this formula, even while prince royal; this pompous display of earthly grandeur, whilst addressing the Supreme Being, appeared to him to be as improper as the particularizing by name the subject of the prayer was superfluous. He therefore directed that the following words should be substituted for the foregoing: "Especially, we recommend unto thee, O God, thy servant, our king."

As Silesia was an eminently Catholic land, Frederick had a full opportunity for the exercise of that religious toleration which he advocated; and, indeed, he proved as considerate a father to his new Catholic subjects, as he had hitherto been to his Protestant children; he naturally required that this feeling should be reciprocated, in order to embrace all denominations of his subjects in one bond of unity and love. The pope was highly pleased with Frederick's treatment of his Silesian subjects, and did not omit to give him proofs of his approbation; and with this view he admonished Cardinal Sinzendorff's successor, Count Schaffgotsch, to consult in every way the wishes of a prince so well disposed towards the Catholic Church. His holiness was particularly pleased at Frederick's granting permission to the Catholics of Berlin to erect a splendid church in that city, and his presenting them with a suitable plot of ground and a portion of the building-materials. On the 13th July, 1747, the foundation-stone was laid for this edifice, amidst all the pomp and ceremony prescribed by the Catholic ritual, in the presence of a royal commissioner.

But Frederick did not in the meanwhile forget his high vocation as the most powerful Protestant prince of Germany, and the protection which it was his duty to afford to the Protestant church. The hereditary prince of Hesse-Cassel had embraced the Catholic faith; Fredrick, in common with the King of England, guaranteed to the estates the continuance of the evangelical creed as the state religion. He likewise stipulated that the future sovereigns of Wurtemberg should profess the evangelical creed, on the intermarriage of the Catholic prince, Eugene of Wurtemburg, with a Prussian princess. The Protestants of Hungary enjoyed his special protection at their own suit. He even addressed a protest to the cabinet of Vienna, in which he distinctly declared himself the protector of Protestantism; and threatened the queen with making reprisals on the Catholics of Silesia for any severities inflicted on the Protestants of Hungary. In Vienna his representations were received with anything but approval: it was even asserted that no religious wrongs existed in Hungary. As these remonstrances proved ineffectual, and as the Hungarian Protestants were subjected to still greater persecutions after the close of the second Silesian war; on the appearance of a pamphlet from the Bishop of Vesprim, in which the queen was in terms required to annihilate the Hungarian heretics, Frederick, in the year 1751, sent a serious remonstrance to the Prince-Bishop of Breslau, requiring him to interfere. This document is full of the deepest feeling. Frederick shows clearly that his only motive was religious toleration, as he could owe but little gratitude to the Hungarians; inasmuch as they had committed the greatest depredations upon him during the late wars; and further depicts the melancholy consequences that must ensue from the imitation by Protestant sovereigns of the conduct pursued by Austria toward subjects of a different persuasion. The prince-bishop applied to the pope; and the interference of the latter caused the barbarous pamphlet of the Hungarian bishop to be withdrawn from circulation.

The severity with which the Hungarian Protestants were treated, and the reluctance displayed by the court of Vienna to accede to Frederick's demands, gave rise to a rather amusing incident, in the shape of a reprisal, and evinces the humorous, rather than harsh nature of Frederick's heart. It occurred in the year 1750. Frederick was one day walking in the gardens of Potsdam, when he met a young man, in rather an unusual garb, and on inquiring, was informed that his name was Hedhessi; that he was of the reformed faith; an Hungarian; had studied theology at Frankfort on the Oder; and had been anxious to see the capital of Prussia before returning to his native land. Frederick conversed with him, and being pleased with the ready, rational answers which he received to his questions, proposed to him to remain in Prussia, and promised to provide for him. The candidate being obliged for family reasons to reject this offer, Frederick told him, as he could not remain, that he was at liberty to demand some favor of him. The candidate could think of no request which he wished to make of the King of of Prussia. "Can you think, then, of no favor," repeated Frederick, "which I can grant you?" "One thing your majesty," replied the candidate, "could do for me, perhaps, if you would graciously condescend. I have purchased several theological and philosophical works, which I know are forbidden in Vienna, and which will certainly be taken from me, as the Jesuits superintend the revision of books, and they are strict. If your majesty would but graciously "——" Take the books," said Frederick, interrupting him, "in God's name, with you; and purchase such others as you think most strictly forbidden in Vienna, but of use to you; and, do you hear? should they take the books from you in Vienna, tell them that I have made you a present of them. The fathers will not respect them the more on that account, but that is no matter. Give up the books, but go directly to my ambassador, and tell him the whole of what I tell you. Afterwards go to the best hotel, and live in right expensive style. Never spend less than a ducat a day, and remain there until the books are sent back to you, as I will take care they shall be. Rely upon my word—but never spend less than a ducat a day." The king then ordered him to wait; went into the palace, and returned with a slip of paper, and upon it the words, " The bearer to remain at our expense in Vienna. FREDERICK." The king commanded the candidate to present this paper to the ambassador, again reminded him not to spare money, and promising to obtain for him the best living in Hungary, wished him a happy journey. It turned out just as had been foreseen: the books were taken from the candidate on his arrival in Vienna and confiscated. Hedhessi applied to the Prussian ambassador, who had already received instructions to conduct the candidate to the best hotel, and then report to the king how matters stood. The king immediately issued orders that the valuable library of the Breslau Jesuits should be closed, and sentries posted at the doors. The Jesuits were completely confounded, as no one could assign any reason for this act of royal displeasure. They therefore resolved on sending a deputation to Potsdam. On arriving there the deputation was obliged to wait several weeks before the members were admitted to the royal presence, and on their obtaining an audience, Frederick referred them to his ambassador at Vienna, and gave them a letter of introduction to the commissaries superintending the revision of books in Vienna.

They were therefore obliged to return to Breslau without having effected their object, and then to send a second deputation to Vienna. The Prussian minister in that capital expressed to them his great regret at not being able to give them any information on the subject, but informed them that there was a young Hungarian stopping at an hotel in the city, from whom the Jesuits had taken a box of books. A sudden light now broke in upon the deputies, and hardly an hour elapsed before Hedhessi was in possession of his books. But before leaving Vienna they had to pay the candidate's expenses at the hotel. They now hastened back to Potsdam, where they were received in the most gracious manner by the king, who gave them a cabinet-order for the reopening of their library. The rector at the same time received a special letter from Frederick, stating that in the event of Hedhessi, or his family, or the Hungarians in general being insulted or persecuted, or if the candidate did not receive the best parish in Hungary, the Jesuits' college at Breslau would be held responsible for the same. But everything was managed agreeably to the king's wishes.

The architectural embellishment of his palaces was an object of Frederick's particular care, regarding it as a means of bringing the coin of the realm into more general circulation amongst the lower orders. He consequently felt comparatively little annoyance when the Charlottenburg palace was burnt down in 1747; and, amidst the general confusion which prevailed, Frederick quietly paced the terrace in front of the palace, remarking: "It is a misfortune—but the artisans of Berlin will earn something by it." His only care was that no one should be injured in attempts to save the building. The edifice containing the valuable collections of the Academy of Arts and Sciences had also fallen a prey to the flames in

FREDERICK'S ADMINISTRATION. 185

the year 1742, but a spacious building, devoted to the same purpose, was soon erected in its stead; to which other handsome structures were in a short time added.

We have already mentioned the erection of the Opera-house; we must now mention that of the Invaliden-house, an extensive building, constructed soon after the conclusion of the second Silesian war. A new cathedral was likewise erected in the Lustgarten, at Berlin, which was consecrated in September, 1750. The old cathedral had served as the sepulchre of the reigning family; but on the completion of the new edifice it was devoted to this purpose, and the coffins of the departed members of the royal house of Brandenburg were conveyed to their allotted places of rest within its walls. Frederick was present at this solemn translation; and on the coffin of the Great Elector being brought in he had it opened. There lay the Elector in his robes of state, wrapped in the electoral mantle, and wearing the peruke which he had adopted toward the close of his life; round his neck was a large frill, while richly-worked gloves and yellow boots completed the costume of the deceased monarch. His features were still to be recognized, and Frederick long surveyed this beloved corse in silence; then, with the tears starting in his eyes, seizing the Elector's left hand, and turning towards his suite, he exclaimed with deep emotion: " Gentlemen, this man wrought much."

Not in Berlin only, but in other cities, particularly in Potsdam, various buildings were erected at Frederick's expense. Both these cities were likewise embellished by the construction of a considerable number of private residences for the citizens. Of the Palace of Sans-souci, at Potsdam, we shall have occasion to speak more particularly hereafter. Frederick frequently drew the plans for the buildings himself, and the works of Palladio, Piranesi, and other masters supplied him with the ideas. The architects had sometimes no very enviable task in carrying out the designs of this royal dilettante.

His patronage was likewise extended to the stage; the

opera and ballet were much cultivated, and became the leading recreations of Berlin. The best singers and dancers were engaged, and amongst others the fascinating danseuse Signora Barbarina, whose personal attractions and refined parts were so enthusiastically admired, and to whom royalty itself did not refuse its homage. Frederick was in the habit of taking tea with her after the conclusion of the opera; and sometimes even invited her to supper amidst a select circle of his friends. This was a singular tribute of respect, as about this period he held hardly any intercourse except with male friends. At the present day there are several portraits of the lovely danseuse, painted by Pesne, to be found in the royal palaces at Berlin and Potsdam, in which she is drawn in various positions, generally in a dancing attitude, with a tiger's skin suspended over her shoulders, and the tympan, which she flourishes in her hand, marking the character of a bacchanal. Even in the great historical paintings which were executed under Frederick's orders her features are discernible. This lady, who first came to Berlin in 1744, where, in 1749, she married the son of the high-chancellor, from whom, however, she was subsequently divorced, was raised to the rank of countess, but not until after Frederick's death.

Frederick devoted his particular and personal attention to the interests of the stage. He was present at many of the rehearsals, and even took part in the management. He himself wrote many librettos, and composed several musical pieces. But it must be recollected that in Frederick's time the stage was essentially an appurtenance of the court, and its principal province was to heighten the splendor of court pageantry. Many descriptions have reached us of those pageants, which carry us back to the merry enjoyments of that happy period. A festival which Frederick arranged in honor of his sister, the Princess Auguste of Baireuth, on the 25th of August, 1745, is one of the most memorable. An equestrian tournament was held in the Lustgarten, at Berlin, by night; the whole space being encircled by platforms for spectators, and lit up by myriads of lamps. Four bands of knights, in costumes sparkling with gold, silver, and precious stones, and clad as Romans, Carthaginians, Greeks, and Persians, each headed by one of the royal princes, advanced by torchlight, and entered the lists. The Princess Amelia, one of Frederick's younger sisters, distributed the prizes, and Voltaire who was then present in Berlin, composed some elegant verses in honor of the champions and the fair umpire. Frederick was so satisfied that he subsequently arranged a repetition of the festival by daylight.

The same year another but somewhat different spectacle was presented in Berlin in honor of a Tartar aga who arrived as the representative of the Crim Tartar, the Sultan of Budziak, to pay homage to the King of Prussia, whose fame had already reached those distant parts.

Frederick was the soul of every measure for the improvement of the administration, the discipline of the army, social intelligence, and, in short, everything appertaining to the general weal. We have already alluded to this subject, and shall here particularize his exertions more closely. The spirit of his government was purely monarchical, as it had been under his father, but his energy and talents gave it strength and permanence. In place of the chambers, which had hitherto aided the monarch as a deliberative council, officers were now appointed, whose duty was confined to the mere execution of the monarch's orders. All affairs of state passed immediately under the eye of the king. Seated alone in his chamber, he took personal cognizance of everything passing; the cabinet-ministers merely submitting the various matters to his notice in order to learn his pleasure, while the other ministers attended to the executive, according to the different departments over which they presided. Frederick was guided in this by a consciousness of his own powers, and a sincere desire to be the most active in providing for the welfare of his people. The most insignificant of his subjects were permitted to have recourse to him, and none but those whose propositions bore absurdity on the face of them had need to be apprehensive of neglect. He considered the state as an artificially constructed machine, each member of which was bound, according to the position which he held, to provide for the welfare of the whole. In his own hand he held the various threads which kept the entire machine in its proper motion. He examined everything, was aware of everything, and his extraordinary memory alone preserved him, as far as it is possible for erring nature to be preserved, from the danger of making dispositions at variance, at least in subordinate points, with the settled organization of the state.

History has preserved many characteristic traits illustrative of the mode in which he directed the whole machinery of state, by a minute control of its most subordinate parts, and which likewise fully evidence how entirely his heart was set upon the welfare of his people. We shall here record but one of the many instances of his thorough knowledge of the most trifling details connected with the administration of affairs, and at the same time of the sterling qualities of his heart. A document was once laid before him for signature, confirmatory of a justice of the peace in his office. On reading the name, the king paused and desired the minister to be summoned. To him he expressed considerable annoyance at the selection of such an individual, whilst the minister endeavored to defend the appointment, by recounting the high qualfications of the person selected. The king desired that a particular document should be brought him from one of the law offices; and after perusing it addressed the minister: —" Look ye, this man has carried on a lawsuit with his own mother about a few acres of land; and she has been obliged on her very death-bed to take an oath respecting such a paltry matter. How could I expect from a man with such a heart, that he should care for the welfare of my people! Away with this thing; let another be chosen!"

Such extraordinary mental activity, amidst no unfrequent interruptions, arising from the attention he bestowed both on art and science, would nevertheless have been unavailing, if not seconded by the careful husbandry of every moment of his time. A register lay upon his table, in which his various duties were noted. His subdivision of time admitted of no deviation from its fixed routine. His constitution requiring but little sleep, he commenced his labors at break of day: the forenoon was entirely devoted to affairs of state, whilst the greater part of the afternoon was consecrated to social enjoyment and study. It is rather singular, that he filled up the pauses, intervening between his different occupations, by playing on the flute; generally, during those intervals pacing his chamber, and extemporizing on that instrument. He told a friend, that whilst so engaged, he has been often weighing different matters in his mind, without attending to the tones he was evoking; and that frequently some of his happiest thoughts occurred to him whilst thus employed. Thus we see that it was art, which, perhaps without being aware of it himself, expanded the energies of his mind, and sustained his spirit in its native strength.

As each day had its peculiar destination, so each year was devoted to some particular object. The principal epochs consisted of his travels, and the reviews of his troops, in the distant provinces. These tours were fraught with much good for all parts of his kingdom; for he not only looked after his troops, but everything connected with the administration of the provinces. Rapidly as he travelled he always halted sufficiently long at different points to allow of conversation with the various officials, who were expressly commanded to meet him, and were sometimes required to accompany him a part of the way. He was also glad to meet merchants and men of business on such occasions, and entered with much interest into their affairs. On the Silesian highlands, he addressed the deputies of the mercantile classes as follows: "Only apply to me; I am your prime minister." Even the time which he passed in his carriage was not lost. If there were nothing on the road to interest his attention, he employed himself in reading; and if prevented by the jolting of the carriage from being thus occupied, he was in the habit of reciting passages from his favorite poets, with whose works his memory was richly stored.

CHAPTER XXII.

THE PHILOSOPHER OF SANS-SOUCI.

BEFORE setting out for the second Silesian war, Frederick had been so captivated by the beauty of the scenery round Potsdam, that he resolved on erecting a palace there; and had himself drawn the plans. The side of a hill was cut into six terraces, and the foundation-stone of the palace, which was to crown this eminence, laid in April, 1745. This palace, which was completed in two years, received the name of Sans-souci. It was immediately adopted by Frederick as his place of residence, and formed his retreat from the cares of life, and the scene of his social enjoyments, up to the hour of his death. Frederick's name is inseparably connected with that of Sans-souci. All his private letters written here are dated from Sans-souci, whilst those on business are dated from Potsdam. In his literary works, which he published during his life, he calls himself "The Philosopher of Sans-souci." His residence at this palace resembled that at Rheinsberg, with the exception of the buoyancy of youth being now gone. Rheinsberg, which was too distant for royal residence, had been presented by him to his younger brother, who now occupied it.

The scenery round Potsdam presenting, as it does, bold sheets of water, deeply embosomed within shady groves, with rippling streams, that seem to sport round the basis of each verdant height, forms a delightful oasis amidst the sandy flats of Mark Brandenburgh. From the period of Frederick's residing there, the princes of his line have never ceased to heighten the charms of nature by the cherishing and ordering hand of art. Grassy lawns encircle the town, palaces and villas now glitter on hill and dale; exhilarating and refreshing odors are wafted far and wide on the zephyrs; but the residence of the great king remains untouched; and to this day recollections of him, who has long since passed away, seem borne on every breeze that sweeps those winding terraces.

Frederick associated with the name of 'Sans-souci,' a hidden, deeper meaning. Beside the palace, he had constructed a vault, which was one day to receive his mortal remains. It was lined with marble, and its purpose playfully veiled by a statue of Flora reclining on a polished slab. This vault, the existence of which no one dreamed, was properly speaking, that to which the name 'Sans-souci' alluded. He once mentioned this in conversation to a friend and said, alluding to the vault, "Quand je serai là, je serai sans souci." From the windows of his bed-chamber he could daily gaze upon the guardian of his grave, the goddess Flora.

Several anecdotes connected with Sans-souci are told, which throw light upon the peculiar character of this rare king. The history of the windmill, which stands beside the palace, and the land around it, which Frederick wished to have included in his garden-grounds, is well known. Frederick, we are told, had the miller summoned to his presence, and inquired how much he required for his mill. The latter replied, that he had inherited it from his father, and he wished it to descend as an heirloom to his children. The king promised him to build him a better mill in another place, with water-power, and everything free of expense, and to pay him down such further sums as he might demand. But the miller remained unalterable in his resolution. Frederick became angry. "Know you not," said he, in a threatening tone, "that I can take your mill from you, without giving you a farthing?" "Yes," replied the miller, "provided there was no such thing as a council-chamber in Berlin." On receiving this reply, Frederick no longer persisted in his demand, and altered the plan of the garden. To this day the arms of this mill sweep over the royal palace, a memorial of the submission of a king to his own laws. The other anecdotes are pretty similar.

In Sans-souci Frederick drew around him men of congenial sentiments and minds. To such of his old friends as still survived, and who had once brightened the happy days of his Rheinsberg retreat, others equally valued were soon added. Amongst the latter we must especially notice the Marquis D'Argent, a native of Provence, who found an asylum here from the persecutions to which he was exposed in his own country; his agreeable manners, cultivated taste, and above all, his faithful and entire devotion to the king, procured him in return such esteem, that he soon occupied the same place in Frederick's heart which Jordan had once filled. Frederick's literary secretary, Darschet, was equally remarkable for his fidelity and attachment. As an old and valued friend, we must likewise mention Baron Pöllnitz, who had served under King Frederick I., and whose varied talents and inexhaustible conversational powers strongly recommended him; but owing to the volatility of his character, he never gained Frederick's entire confidence. He had, in 1744, completely forfeited the king's patronage through his inconsiderate acts; and was only again received into favor after formally signing certain strict conditions. These latter consisted in a promise never to hold any intercourse with any ambassador; never again to disturb the pleasures of the royal table; and in Berlin it was publicly forbidden to lend him even the most trifling sum of money, under a penalty of a hundred ducats. Pöllnitz was a species of court buffoon; and the French surgeon, De la Metrie, figured in a somewhat similar capacity in Sans-souci.

The king's military friends formed likewise a part of this social circle, but were never permitted to forget the duties they owed the service. Professional faults were severely censured; but this censure did not affect the friendship that subsisted between them and their monarch. Winterfeld enjoyed the king's special favor; but being adjutant-general, his time was altogether occupied in business. Count-Rothenburg, who had received several wounds at the battle of Craslan, became a second Keyserling to Frederick. He likewise died early, and his death revived all the pangs which the king had experienced at the loss of his beloved Keyserling. Frederick exhibited the most marked sympathy for Rothenburg during his last illness. It was in the month of December that he received intelligence that the count was on his death-bed. Half-dressed as he was, he rushed across the street to his friend's lodging, where finding the physician in despair, Frederick wept, and on its being proposed that, as a last resource, the patient should be bled, he held the basin during the operation. As this was not attended with the desired effect, Frederick left the dying man, and giving way to his feelings of grief, did not appear in society for several days.

Colonel De Forçade, who had been wounded in the battle of Soor, received many marks of Frederick's favor in consideration of his high merits. As the colonel was one day present at a levee in the Berlin palace, paying his respects to the king, he happened to lean against the window to support himself, being lamed by a wound in the foot, which Frederick perceiving brought him a chair, and addressing him, said: "My dear Colonel De Forçade a man of your worth and valor deserves that even a king should bring him a chair."

Frederick attached much importance to the acquisition which he made in gaining two men, one of whom he respected as much as he esteemed the other. We allude to the two brothers Keith, natives of Scotland, who had left their native country in consequence of their attachment to the Stuarts. The younger of the two, James, had been immediately invested with the rank of field-marshal he having been the first to enter Frederick's service; the elder brother, George Keith, who had been Earl-marshal of Scotland, came some time afterwards, and was one of the few whom fate spared to gladden Frederick's declining years.

The venerable field-marshal Schwerin, who had left the army on the close of the second Silesian war, was likewise induced to rejoin the service. Frederick made the first advances towards a reconciliation by inviting Schwerin to pay him a visit. The latter obeyed the summons, and on arriving at the palace, and learning that the king was in good humor, he announced his presence through the officer-in-waiting. The officer received no reply to his announcement: on the contrary, Frederick took up his flute, and paced his chamber for a quarter of an hour extemporizing; then, laying it down, he girt on his sword, and desired the marshal to be ushered into his presence. This done, the king received him courteously, and gave the attendant a hint to leave the chamber. The latter, on reaching the ante-chamber, heard the conversation between the king and Schwerin grow gradually louder, and at length so violent that he began to feel uneasy as to the issue. The storm, however, soon subsided, and the conversation gradually resumed its former subdued tone. The door then opened; Schwerin took his leave, with evident gaiety and satisfaction depicted in his looks, and the king addressed him in a friendly tone: "Your excellency dines with me to-day." From thenceforward the good understanding between the king and his general continued uninterrupted. What passed in that hour no third person has ever heard.

With the most unbounded enthusiasm was that man greeted by Frederick—whose genius unceasingly, and far beyond that of any other, commanded his admiration, and whom he made such repeated attempts to attach permanently to his person—Voltaire. The French poet received, in the year 1749, the following letter from Frederick: "You are like the white elephant, for whose sake the Shah and the Great Mogul war with one another, and which forms one of the titles of him who may be fortunate enough to win it. If *you* come here you shall stand at the head of my titles : ' Frederick, by the grace of God, King of Prussia, Prince Elector of Brandenburg, and possessor of Voltaire.' "

This letter dissolved the ties which bound the poet to his home, and he accepted Frederick's oft-repeated invitation. On the 10th of July he arrived at Sans-souci to reside permanently with the king. He was appointed lord-chamberlain, knight of the order of Merit, and received the splendid salary of five thousand thalers. Frederick paid him the most decided homage; princes, field-marshals, and ministers of state vied in courting his favor. Voltaire's presence lent a charm to the residence of Sans-souci which was everywhere felt. The extraordinary powers of the poet produced a spirit of emulation in all. Poetry and science were universally cultivated, and princes and princesses sought to realize the ideas of the master in the impersonation of his tragedies. All etiquette and ceremony was banished from this social circle. Voltaire had sufficient leisure to complete those labors which he had been obliged to suspend in France in consequence of the restrictions there imposed on the liberty of the press. He was free to live as he pleased, and was only required to give hilarity by his presence to the social evening meetings. These banquets were indeed remarkable for "the feast of reason and the flow of soul," and Voltaire and Frederick stood side by side as in the realms of fancy.

That Voltaire was neither a man to whom Frederick could attach himself warmly, nor one for whose moral character he could entertain any real respect, was a fact sufficiently apparent; but Frederick had not sought for him in the capacity of an intimate friend; he desired his society as a man of congenial powers, and one whose critical judgment and refined taste he hoped to render available in the execution of his literary labors. Voltaire gladly rendered him these services, and Frederick profited considerably from his intercourse with him. He now completed many of those important works which he had carelessly composed in intervals of peace, and others, the fruits of the literary leisure which he now enjoyed. The second portion of his History of His Times, describing the second Silesian war, had been written in the year 1746. The year following he commenced his Memoirs of the House of Brandenburg, portions of which were read to the members of the Academy, and printed in their Transactions: a handsome edition of this work appeared in the year 1751. Several of his minor compositions, in poetry and prose, odes, letters in verse, a poem on the art of war, and a comic epic, entitled "The Palladium," were published, in the year 1750, under the general title of "The Works of the Philosopher of Sanssouci." In these labors he was considerably assisted by Voltaire. Of the former works, especially the poems, but few copies, for private circulation amongst his friends, were printed. A private printing-office had been fitted up in the tower of the Berlin palace, from which circumstance such works as were here printed bear on the title-page the words: "Au Donjon du Château." The title-pages of the poems are further marked—"With the privilege of Apollo."

His hours of recreation were enlivened, as in former times, by music as well as literature. The hour before supper was generally appropriated to concerts, at which Frederick performed on his favorite instrument, the flute. At the appointed hour he entered the concert-room with the music-books under his arm, and distributed them himself on the different stands. He played none but concert-pieces, sometimes of his own composition, and arranged by Quantz, who had entered his service immediately on his succession to the throne. His performance, especially in adagio parts, was peculiarly expressive, and his compositions evince considerable proficiency in the science of music; but his attachment to the strict rules of the art was not such as to make him lose sight of the beauties resulting from an absence of technical restraints. He ventured to introduce a peculiarity in his recitativo, which was attended with the best effect. While once performing one of those recitativos he succeeded in expressing the act of weeping so perfectly as to excite universal admiration. "I pictured to myself," said he, "the mother of Coriolanus, as she on her knees implored of her son to spare and protect Rome."

His old master, Quantz, enjoyed special privileges at these concerts; he was the only person who ventured to applaud the king's performance, and though he did not presume to dispraise, yet by withholding his approbation he contrived at times to give vent to his feelings of disapproval. Frederick was once performing one of his own compositions, in which several faulty passages occurred. Quantz hemmed pretty loudly. Frederick saw his meaning, but took no notice of the circumstance: a few days afterwards he consulted another musician as to the faulty passages, and on being set right by the latter he corrected the faults, remarking, "We must not give poor Quantz a catarrh."

Thus all the elements of social enjoyment were concentrated at Sans-souci; but this happy state was destined to be speedily interrupted, and that, too, by one whose talents had hitherto lent it its chief charms. Voltaire, dazzled by the splendor of the position in which Frederick had placed him, forgot the respect which he owed alike to his royal patron and himself. Instead of his ambition being satisfied by the honors paid him, he became daily more greedy of power, and sought to employ the position which he occupied for the annihilation of every rival in the world of letters for pecuniary profit and the attainment of political importance. He himself had recommended a young Frenchman, D'Arnaud, to assist the king in his literary labors. But now feeling his pride somewhat wounded by the flattering terms in which Frederick addressed the youthful poet, he speedily procured his dismissal from his post. His jealousy was

THE PHILOSOPHER OF SANS-SOUCI. 199

still more aroused by the talents of Maupertius, the naturalist, who had been likewise on his recommendation appointed president of the newly instituted academy. Between these two men a bitter feud sprang up, which every day threatened to explode. A disgusting lawsuit, in which Voltaire had been engaged with a Jew merchant, tended likewise to place his integrity in rather an equivocal light. The Jew accused Voltaire of having imposed upon him with false jewels; and although the sentence of the court was in favor of the latter, it did not altogether clear up the matter. His character was still more compromised by his purchasing at low rates, in Leipzig, Saxon securities, (in direct contravention of the king's edict,) and then, by virtue of his right as a Prussian subject, demanding payment in full for the same, according to the terms of the Dresden treaty. At length he forgot himself so completely as to hold intercourse with foreign ambassadors, in such a way as Frederick could not possibly tolerate in a person holding such intercourse with him. All this was observed by Frederick with growing disgust, and he sent the poet some serious remonstrances which seemed likely to put an end to their intercourse forever. Voltaire sought to justify his acts, but perceived too clearly that Frederick valued him for nothing else than his talents. "I shall want him at the utmost," said he, "for another year: we squeeze the orange and then throw away the peel."

Such are the expressions which Frederick is said to have used when speaking of Voltaire. The latter attributed the loss of Frederick's favor to a calumny said to have been circulated by Maupertius, who was asserted to have given currency to a report, that a general on Frederick's staff happened to call on Voltaire to request him to look through a manuscript which he had just completed; that at the same instant a servant arrived with one of Frederick's poems, and that Voltaire dismissed the general with the words, "My dear friend, some other time: the king has just sent me some of *his* soiled linen; I will wash yours afterwards."

Despite these various causes for disagreement, these two great spirits could not keep long apart. Reproaches the most violent were followed by expressions of esteem the most flattering. Frederick admired the powers of the poet too highly, not to view the former follies of the man with much charity. As a proof of this, we must mention a passage from an ode, which he addressed about this period to Voltaire, seeking to console him for the approach of age, by pointing to his growing reputation. The ode closes with the following words:—

> "How bright the future that awaiteth thee,
> Whose master mind unveiled each mystery.
> Ages to come at thy shrine shall bow!
>   The heralds of fame
>   Already proclaim
>   Immortal art thou!"

But new events occurred to widen the breach and bar all hopes of reconciliation. Maupertius had promulgated, in a learned dissertation, what he considered to be a new natural law. Another author insisted that this law had been long since enunciated by Leibnitz. A hot contest ensued, and the Berlin Academy took a decided part in favor of its president. This seemed to Voltaire to be a favorable opportunity for striking a deadly blow at the reputation of a rival, and accordingly he wrote an anonymous letter, which was eminently calculated to throw ridicule on Maupertius. Frederick, who felt little inclination to see the president of his academy the subject of ridicule, wrote a reply, in which the author of the anonymous letter was harshly dealt with. A second work of Maupertius' called forth from Voltaire a satire, entitled, "History of Doctor Akakia:" Frederick had read this production in manuscript; its pointed wit had amused him much, but he required that the work should not be printed. Voltaire made him a promise to that effect; but the work soon appeared in Dresden, to the great delight of the president's enemies. Frederick was naturally incensed at this conduct of the poet; although the latter denied that it had been done with his sanction. However, to regain Frederick's favor, he was obliged to sign a written declaration, in which he promised to act more prudently in future. But the matter did not end here. On the 24th of December, 1752, he was forced to look on, from his window, whilst the public hangman burnt his Akakia in the open street.

Voltaire was not prepared for such unheard-of ignominy. He packed up his pension-warrant, order, and gold chamberlain's key in a parcel, which he sent back instantly to Frederick. On the wrapper of the parcel he wrote the following lines:—

> "I now restore each token,
> For which I once had fondly strove;
> As one, whose heart is broken,
> Returns the likeness of his love."

A letter soon followed the parcel, describing, without disguise, the poignant anguish which the poet felt. This letter had its desired effect:—on the same day the marks of royal favor were returned, and the attempt was once more made to renew their former friendship.

But Voltaire soon saw the impossibility of being again restored to Frederick's confidence, and therefore begged to be permitted to visit France on a bathing excursion. This favor was granted him, and he set out from Potsdam on the 20th March, 1753. He had, however, hardly arrived in Leipzig, when he committed new insulting matter to the press; for this he was obliged to atone in Frankfort on the Main. Frederick had directed him, before setting out, not to take with him either the warrant, order, or key, nor the copy of Frederick's poems which the latter had presented him with. This injunction had not been heeded, and accordingly, at the instance of the Prussian ambassador, he was detained in custody at Frankfort for the space of sixteen days, until his luggage arrived from Leipzig. This incident naturally gave rise to many a biting satire in verse and prose; but still, before any very long period elapsed, these two men, Voltaire and Frederick, had renewed their intercourse. Frederick could not, however, be again induced either to recall Voltaire or re-invest him with the chamberlain's golden key.

Much more clearly than Voltaire did another French scholar, D'Alembert, to whom Frederick paid likewise much homage, perceive the danger with which propinquity to a throne is fraught for a man of independent mind. Whilst Frederick had been making a tour through the western provinces of his kingdom, he chanced to meet D'Alembert, to whom he made the most flattering proposals to induce him to take up his residence in Berlin; but these offers were respectfully declined; D'Alembert consenting, however, to accept of a small pension, in consequence of the many privations to which he was exposed in France. The correspondence which now opened between Frederick and D'Alembert is of considerable importance.

After this interview with D'Alembert, Frederick made a most agreeable excursion into Holland, mainly with a view to examine the treasures of art which were collected there, intending to adorn Sans-souci with a large picture-gallery. In order to be relieved from all restraint, he laid aside, this time also, every emblem of royalty, and succeeded in preserving his incognito somewhat better than on the former occasion at Strasburg. He assumed the character of a wandering musician; his suite consisting of but two persons, Colonel Balbi, a connoisseur, and a page: he wore a simple black wig and a light brown dress with gold buttons.

Several laughable scenes are said to have been occasioned by this incognito. Thus, whilst stopping at an inn in Amsterdam, he happened to order a very expensive kind of pasty, which was there regarded as a great dainty. Mine hostess, who usually drew her conclusions, as to the finances of her guests, from externals, begged leave to inquire whether he was prepared to pay for so expensive a delicacy. She was informed that the individual in question was a virtuoso, who could earn by his performances the price of more than ten such pasties. Her curiosity being awakened by this statement, she hastened to Frederick, and would give him no peace until he consented to play something for her on his flute. At length, enraptured by the beauty of his performance, the Dutch woman exclaimed, " That'll do, sir! that'll do ! You can indeed pipe beautifully, and I dare say earn a few halfpence: I'll get the pasty ready."

From Amsterdam Frederick proceeded in a common passage-boat to Utrecht, and here became acquainted with a Swiss, Le Catt, who acted as tutor to a young Dutchman: he invited the Swiss to dine with him, and was so pleased with his intelligence and information, that he requested his address, telling him at the same time, that he might hereafter have occasion not regret their meeting. Three months subsequently, Le Catt received an invitation from Frederick to come to Berlin and act as his secretary. This offer he could not, however, accept, as he was then ill ; but three years later, he received a second invitation, which he accepted ; and for twenty years remained faithfully attached to Frederick's person.

CHAPTER XXIII.

POLITICAL RELATIONS PREVIOUS TO THE SEVEN YEARS' WAR.

During the years succeeding the conclusion of the treaties of Dresden and Aix-la-Chapelle, Europe enjoyed repose, but it was the calm of a sultry summer's day. Angry clouds were gathering on the horizon, and the dull sounds of distant thunder might be at intervals heard. These harbingers of the coming storm did not prove deceptive:—the sweeping tempest again burst forth and with redoubled violence.

The jealousy which the other states of Europe felt at Prussia's growing power was the immediate cause of this political convulsion. They could not reconcile themselves to the idea of Prussia, whose rank as a monarchy they had hitherto considered as a mere bubble,—the gratification of an innocuous pride,—now becoming so powerful, as to have an important voice in the council of nations. That the "Margrave of Brandenburg," as Frederick was still derisively styled, should have attained such power as rendered it by no means improbable that he would become a most dangerous neighbor, caused no little chagrin. That his thoughts were set on further aggrandizement was assumed as a self-evident proposition. And further, there was many a personal pique to be gratified; so that between public jealousy and private malice open war was the natural result.

Maria Theresa could not teach herself to forget Silesia. The rising prosperity of the land beneath Prussia's rule, and the considerably increased revenue which Frederick derived from it, rendered her grief at the loss but so much the more poignant. Considering her surrender of Silesia as an act to which she had been forced by the imperious nature of her necessities, her whole thoughts were employed in devising schemes for regaining her lost possessions. Nor did she give way to mere vain regrets, but with masculine energy concentrated the strength of her empire, and sought, by intimate alliances with foreign powers, to attain still further security. Her administration was so judicious, that, notwithstanding the many territorial losses which she had sustained, her revenues were more flourishing and larger in amount than they had been under her father, Charles VI.; and so unremitting were her personal exertions for the improvement and discipline of her army, that she soon inspired it with fresh feelings of confidence and resolution. As one of her ministers who was peculiarly efficient in council, we must mention Count Kaunitz. He had been appointed chancellor of state, and sympathizing with his imperial mistress in her hatred of Frederick, his high talents were wholly devoted to the effecting of judicious combinations with foreign powers. Maria's husband, the Emperor himself, was the only one who was wholly inefficient. He took no part in the administration of public affairs. His attention was chiefly engrossed by money transactions, for which he betrayed considerable aptitude; indeed, to such a degree did he carry his taste for speculation, that on the war breaking out between Prussia and Austria, he actually supplied Frederick at first with different necessaries on being paid in money for the same.

Saxony, particularly Count Brühl, continued, even after the treaty of Dresden, to entertain the same hostility to Frederick; but much caution was here necessary, from Saxony's lying so exposed to Prussia. In Russia, the personal feelings of the Empress Catherine as well as those of her all-powerful minister, Bestuscheff, were not less inimical to Frederick. Austrian diplomacy was not slow in taking advantage of this state of things, and a treaty of mutual defence was concluded in the year 1746 between Austria and Russia, in which it was stipulated by a private article that, in the event of Frederick attacking either of those powers, his right to Silesia became forfeited, and that steps should be instantly taken to restore it to Austria. Saxony was invited to join the league, and testified the utmost readiness to accede to the proposition; but at the same time urged the difficulties of its position, as a reason for the other cabinets not insisting on a formal declaration of adhesion: of the sentiments of the Saxon cabinet and court there could be little question. Austria and Saxony now directed their joint energies to inflame Russia against Frederick, and in this they were eminently successful. Frederick had allowed some expression to escape him, reflecting on the dishonorable policy of the Empress and her minister: this had been speedily conveyed to the ears of the individuals alluded to, together with a number of fictions, and calumnies, and the result was that the Russian cabinet formally decided, in 1755, that war was to be declared against Prussia the moment any of Russia's allies assailed that power.

English gold had likewise contributed to sway the Russian cabinet to this decision. The friendship which had hitherto subsisted between Austria and England had grown somewhat cold, in consequence of the former power regarding the latter as, in some measure, the cause of the surrenders which it had been obliged to make. England having been previously allied with Russia, now held it advisable to join this league against Frederick, viewing him still as the ally of France, with which country a war threatened to break out, on account of some differences in North America. In that event, Hanover would be, as England conceived, best protected against any attempts on the part of Prussia.

These machinations of his enemies were not long a secret to Frederick. The Russian crown-prince was one of his most ardent admirers, and had often given him important information, without being able, however, to take any active steps in his behalf, as he was studiously excluded from all part of the administration by the Empress. Frederick had other channels also through which he derived information, as to everything that was going forward. One of the most important of these was an official in the Saxon government, through whose treachery he obtained complete copies of all the secret correspondence carried on between the cabinets of Saxony, Vienna, and Russia. He was thus enabled, at the first approach of danger, to take the most judicious measures for meeting it. He took a calm, general view of his complicated relations and the embarrassments of his position. In 1753, just about the time his fantastic account of the Spandau manœuvres appeared, he wrote his "Anonymous Letters to the Public," in which he admirably parodied the diplomatic intrigues of the day. The Berlin court, it was therein stated, had refused to permit the minuets of a musician from Aix-la-Chapelle to be performed at its fêtes, preferring to dance to its own airs; that several barbarous courts had taken up the musician's cause; and that divers and sundry treaties, alliances, and so forth, had been concluded, and that consequently a most frightful war might reasonably be expected. Voltaire remarked, on the appearance of these "Letters," that the king had written them solely with a view to prove that he was not dependent on him; and, in truth, they evince so much satirical power in their author, that they would go far to show that the writer hardly needed the aid even of a Voltaire Frederick had, however, in all probability, something else in mind besides the French poet.

But England saw that it would be clearly her interest, in the event of a war with France, that the continent should be at peace; and further, that Austria was the most active in enkindling this continental war, whilst Frederick was equally anxious with herself for the maintenance of peace, from an apprehension of endangering the acquisitions which he had made in the former wars: he had given a sufficiently strong proof of his pacific intentions, when summoned by France, in 1754, to join in an enterprise against Hanover. "You have a prospect of plunder there; such were the words used towards the Prussian ambassador in Paris: "the King of England's exchequer is well filled, the King of Prussia has only to carry it off." To this Frederick replied, that such considerations might be inducements in the eyes of some persons, but he begged that there might be a distinction drawn between him and others. This induced England to make advances to Prussia, and their interests so coalesced, that a treaty for their reciprocal defence was actually concluded in 1756 between these powers. This alliance had been certainly entered into on a calculation, which the cabals in the Russian cabinet rendered by no means improbable, that Russia would side with England, and, by consequence, with Prussia.

Just about the period of the conclusion of this treaty, an ambassador arrived from France, offering Frederick a renewal of the treaty which was about to expire with that country, and holding out to him, as an inducement, an offer of sovereignty over the island of Tobago, in the West Indies. This last proposition, savoring so strongly of romance, was viewed in the light of a joke by Frederick, who at the same time distinctly declared, that he desired nothing but the maintenance of peace, and that this had been his actuating motive in concluding the treaty with England. This declaration gave much offence to the French cabinet, and loud complaints were made of the "treachery" of the Prussian king.

An alliance between France and Austria was now speedily brought about. Kaunitz, who had long since observed that England's sympathy was waxing cold, had taken the very means to bring about this result. Indeed, no sooner had the treaty of Aix-la-Chapelle been concluded, than he made proposals of this nature, which, though at first rejected by the French ministry, had at least the effect of suggesting the possibility at some future day of such a change in the policy of France. But these propositions met with a different reception from the moment that Kaunitz succeeded in gaining the support of Madame Pompadour, the King of France's mistress. She entertained a thorough hatred of Frederick, as his kingly pride would not stop to court the royal harlot. His ambassador was the only foreign minister who did not pay her his respects. Voltaire, on returning to Sans-souci in 1750, had brought Frederick many tender greetings from the marchioness, which Frederick replied to, by remarking drily, that he did not know her. Indeed, he evinced the most marked contempt for the entire mistress-government of France, and used to divide its different epochs according to the ruling petticoat, into "Cotillon 1, 2, 3." That the French monarch's personal feelings towards Frederick were of no very friendly nature, has been already mentioned. The Austrian party left, on the contrary, no means untried for gaining the favor of the all-powerful Pompadour. Even Maria Theresa so far sacrificed her pride to her hatred of Frederick, as to condescend to address the harlot in private letters, under the titles of "Princess," "Cousin," and "Dearest Sister." But Pompadour was also deeply interested in a war, as being the only means of providing for her creatures; besides feeling assured, that if once the European powers found their policy concentrated in her person, they would take care to banish every rival from the king's presence. Regular conferences were held at her summer palace during the autumn of 1755, which led to the conclusion of a treaty of mutual defence between Austria and France, on the 9th of May, 1756, to serve as a counterpoise to that existing between England and Prussia.

The calculations of England and Prussia, as regarded Russia, had been founded on a false assumption. The influence of English gold was outweighed by the hatred entertained by the empress and her minister towards Frederick, and the bribery resorted to by Austria. Russia refused to enter on any alliance with Prussia, and abandoning England likewise, joined the opposite party. To increase still further the number of Frederick's enemies, a revolution had broken out in Sweden, throwing the whole government into the hands of the imperial council, which was completely in the pay of France. Frederick's sister, the then Queen of Sweden, as well as her husband, were thus robbed of all power and influence.

A naval war had in the mean time broken out between England and France. Considerable preparations for war were likewise going forward in the immediate neighborhood of Prussia. Extraordinary levies of troops were being made in Bohemia. Magazines were erected, and such dispositions made as could have no other purpose than war. In Liefland a considerable Russian army was being drawn together. Frederick had obtained information of all those movements, and, likewise, that there was no danger of an immediate invasion, owing to the dispositions not being as yet in a sufficient state of forwardness. He likewise learned that it was the intention of the allies to raise a large army in Saxony, where no preparations for war had been as yet made; and that there was nothing further desired than that Frederick should be induced to take some hostile step, in order to give a color of justice to the acts of his enemies. His system of defence consisted in being always prepared for war, and the anticipating the motions of his enemies; but wishing to leave no means untried for the maintenance of peace, he, on the 12th of July, 1756, demanded a public declaration from the Empress of Austria, as to the object of the present equipments. The answer which the Empress returned, under the dictation of Count Kaunitz, was to the effect, that at the present momentous crisis, her own safety and that of her allies imperiously demanded that she should take every precautionary measure possible for preserving intact the honors and dignity of her crown. This reply was designedly conveyed in words, the exact purport of which is rather vague, and at first sight not very intelligible. On the 2d of August, Frederick demanded a less equivocal explanation, as also a distinct declaration that he should not be attacked either during the current or following year. But the answer to this demand was expressed in equally vague terms; and the latter part of it entirely disregarded. On Frederick's again applying for a further explanation, his request was replied to in a tone of insulting hauteur. Frederick regarded this threefold refusal as a formal declaration of war, and resolved on devoting the remainder of the year to the most active preparations, to prevent his enemies attacking him at a disadvantage.

On the outbreak of the war, Voltaire sent Frederick an epistle in verse, forewarning him that he would now lose the laurels which he had hitherto reaped, as a punishment for thus fanning the slumbering embers of discord into a flame: this was of course the interpretation put by his enemies on his conduct. Frederick replied likewise in verse, asserting his love of peace in preference to war; but at the same time remarking, that he knew full well the duties which Providence had imposed upon him. "Voltaire," he proceeds, "may well, in the safety of seclusion, enjoy the repose of the philosopher;" and concludes with the words:—

"'Tis mine, destruction to defy,
To boldly meet the coming storm;
As king to think, to live, to die."

CHAPTER XXIV.

FIRST CAMPAIGN OF THE SEVEN YEARS' WAR.

FREDERICK had embraced the resolution of anticipating the motions of his enemies, and, by assuming the aggressive, averting the war from his own territories. As to Russia, he had positive information of there being no danger of an attack from that quarter during the present year; nothing was therefore necessary as regarded it further than to augment the garrisons lying in the eastern provinces of the Prussian monarchy. The main strength of the Prussian forces was to be directed against Saxony and Bohemia. In Saxony Frederick was resolved to intrench himself strongly, in order to cover Brandenburg, and at the same time to have a firm basis for his operations against Bohemia. His dispositions were conducted with as much secrecy as they were executed with dispatch; none but the most trustworthy of his generals received information of his designs; nor were the generals of brigades informed of their destination until the very eve of their departure for the field.

On the 29th of August 60,000 Prussian troops advanced on Saxony. No one was prepared for so sudden an outbreak of the war. Saxon troops to the number of 17,000 were drawn from their cantonments, and formed a fortified camp at Pirna. King Augustus and his minister, Brühl, becoming completely stupefied in the midst of the general confusion, abandoned Dresden, and sought refuge in the camp at Pirna. It was first resolved that the Saxon army should fall back on Bohemia, there to form a junction with the Austrians, but on the advice of the French ambassador it was determined to take advantage of the strength of the position and cover Austria, in order to give the latter time to collect its scattered forces, complete its equipments, and march to the relief of Saxony. The extensive plateau lying between Pirna and Königstein, twenty miles in circuit, was accordingly occupied by the Saxons, the precipitous nature of the ground securing them from all danger, whilst the approaches were all blocked up by barricades formed of trees.

Frederick on his arrival found the whole land in a pitifully defenceless state. Wittenberg, Torgau, Leipzig were occupied without resistance. On the 9th of September he entered Dresden, in the immediate vicinity of which the different corps of the Prussian army took up such a position as cut off the Saxon camp from all connection with the interior.

He now declared that he was compelled to regard Saxony as a pledge for his own security, and accordingly had the contents of the well-supplied arsenals of Dresden, Weissenfels, and Zeitz transferred to Magdeburg. Torgau was fortified and garrisoned by Prussian troops The Saxon officials were suspended from their duties, the offices closed, the privy chambers shut, and a Prussian executive established in Dresden. All monies belonging to the king were seized, but the property of the subject was in every way respected. The conduct of the Prussian troops was exemplary. Frederick was particularly gracious in his conduct towards every one in Dresden: to Augustus's wife and the royal family he showed the most marked civility and attention.

But this sudden occupation of Saxony had excited the amazement of the world; and Frederick's enemies strove hard to represent the act as a breach of the general peace. The Emperor of Germany addressed a remonstrance to him, requiring him in the most paternal terms to "desist from his unexampled, highly criminal, and most culpable rebellion; to pay adequate compensation to the King of

Poland, and quietly return home." At the same time the
generals and colonels of the Prussian army were required
to abandon their impious lord, to avoid participation in
his guilt, provided they did not wish to expose themselves
to the vengeance of the supreme ruler of the empire. As
a reply to those charges, which he had anticipated, Frederick resolved on publishing the whole series of documents
obtained from the Dresden archives; and to preclude the
possibility of any question as to their authenticity, he
determined on seizing the original documents. The
Saxons had, however, taken precautions to prevent this.
The archives, which were to have been sent to Poland for
security, had been transferred into the queen's chamber,
and the key of the presses handed over to her majesty,
who was as inveterate an enemy to Frederick as even
Brühl himself. She was, however, obliged to surrender
the key: her tears and supplications availed her nought;
the presses were opened, and the records sent off to Berlin.
A few days afterwards a detailed statement, taken from
the original documents, appeared in print. A number of
statements were published in reply, not impugning, however, the accuracy of the records, but excepting to the
conclusions which Frederick had sought to deduce from
them.

From the time of entering Saxony Frederick kept up
an uninterrupted correspondence with Augustus, from
whom he demanded either the clearest and most unequivocal guarantees for his remaining neutral in future, or that
he should join him against Austria. It was a singular
circumstance that the position of the Saxons was such
that they dared not venture to attack the Prussians nor
the Prussians them. The storming of the camp itself
appeared, if not altogether impracticable, at least attended
with too much bloodshed to admit of the experiment being made; but the Saxons were so completely hemmed in
on all sides that there was no possibility of their obtaining supplies, the want of which they had already begun
to feel very sensibly, as nothing was permitted to pass,

except such things as were intended for the royal table. Frederick had consequently every hope that famine would soon force them to surrender. But Augustus would not consent to acquiesce any further in Frederick's demands than by giving him a general assurance of his intention to remain neutral; a promise which Frederick was little inclined to place such implicit reliance upon as to expose himself, by advancing on Bohemia, to the annoyance of having a hostile army in his rear. He consequently continued a strict blockade of the Saxon camp; but as these operations required the presence of the greater part of his troops, he was prevented from acting with due energy against the Austrian army in Bohemia.

The latter had, although not completely equipped, advanced in two columns towards the frontiers of Saxony and Silesia. One of these corps was opposed by a separate Prussian army under Schwerin, which advanced from Silesia; but the Austrians took up their position with so much tact, that it was impossible to force them to an engagement, and nothing beyond mere skirmishes took place between the two armies. Augustus had in the meantime found an opportunity of conveying intelligence to the Austrian court of the imminent peril in which he stood, and solicited instantaneous relief. Upon which the second Austrian corps, under Field-marshal Browne, received orders to take decisive steps for the relief of Saxony. Browne immediately concentrated his forces at Budin, and prepared to cross the Eger.

Frederick sent a body of his troops to watch the movements of this Austrian corps. These troops possessed themselves of the narrow passes connecting Saxony with Bohemia, and informed Frederick of all the enemy's motions. Frederick's chief aim was to prevent a junction of the Saxons and Austrians. He therefore resolved to attack the latter with the troops which he had hitherto employed merely as a corps of observation, inconsiderable as they were in numbers. He hastened in person to assume the command, and led them from the mountainous heights into the open plains. The hostile armies encountered each other at the village of Lowositz, on the Elbe, which is situated at the foot of a ridge of hills. Neither army had any idea of the proximity of the other, but Frederick had the advantage of being able to take up a strong position between the hills which flanked both his wings.

On the morning of the first of October Frederick formed his troops in line of battle; the plain was, however, so completely enveloped in a dense fog, as to render it impossible to distinguish the different objects. Lowositz was half veiled from view, and at its side nothing beyond a few troops of hostile cavalry was discernible. The Prussian left wing, as it advanced and ascended the heights to the left, was received with a heavy fire, which was sustained from some vineyards that descended to the brink of the Elbe. This attack came from a few thousand Pandoors, who had concealed themselves behind the walls of the vineyards. Frederick conceiving from this that he was not engaging the whole of the hostile army, but merely its advanced guard, directed that his guns should be pointed so as to play on the Austrian horse, and this proving ineffectual, he sent twenty squadrons of dragoons to put them to the rout, and thus terminate the contest. The Prussians charged boldly forward on the foe, overthrowing every obstacle in their way; but whilst engaged in the pursuit they were suddenly assailed on the flank by a well-sustained fire, which obliged them to retire. Frederick, who now saw that he had to deal with the entire of the enemy's forces, which were double the number of his own, immediately dispatched an adjutant to the dragoons, to direct them to take up a different position; but they, in connection with the cuirassiers, had made a joint charge on the enemy's cavalry, and, in the face of the fire to which they were exposed and the unfavorable nature of the ground, had again routed it. The fire which now opened upon them became, however, so murderous that they were again obliged to retire, but

FIRST CAMPAIGN OF THE SEVEN YEARS' WAR. 217

in perfect order; thus matters came to no decisive issue on either side. The fog began, however, to clear away, and the combatants were enabled to make the necessary dispositions. Frederick sought out the most favorable position that the overwhelming numbers of his foes would permit, and strained every nerve to secure the victory. The chief attention of the enemy was now directed to the Prussian left wing, which they sought to dislodge from the elevated position which it had taken up. But the Prussians pushing forward with undaunted courage, and gaining wall after wall within the vineyards, descended into the plain in pursuit of the enemy, one portion of which fled towards the Elbe, whilst the other intrenched itself in Lowositz. The Austrian reserves were now brought up against the Prussians, who had expended almost the whole of their ammunition during six hours of continual firing: the Duke of Bevern, who commanded this division of the Prussian army, observing this movement, called out gaily to his troops: "Boys, take no heed of it! for what other reason have you been taught to attack the enemy with the bayonet?" These words enkindled the enthusiasm of his men, who, notwithstanding the enemy were perpetually reinforced, overthrew everything in their charge, and penetrated into Lowositz: here, advancing amongst the houses, which had caught fire, they drove the whole of the Austrian army from their position, and put it to flight.

This victory was achieved before two o'clock in the afternoon, but not without considerable sacrifices. Frederick's losses exceeded those of the Austrians; and such was the skill with which Field-marshal Browne covered the defeat of his right wing with his left, that he was able to retire without any further loss. The Prussian right wing, commanded by Frederick in person, had, with the exception of such brigades as had been detached to reinforce the left, not been able to take any part in the engagement. The story goes, that Frederick, after the conclusion of the battle, worn out from fatigue and want of rest, not having slept during three successive days and nights, got into his carriage to take some slight repose. On a sudden a heavy gun loaded with ball was fired by the Austrians, through mistake, as a signal for the retreat; the ball struck the bottom of the carriage in which Frederick lay, and passing through it, would have carried off both his legs, were it not that he had providentially placed them upon the opposite seat.

It was considered unadvisable to pursue the Austrians, as Frederick was anxious to terminate the affair with Saxony, and especially as he was not strong enough to follow the enemy with effect. The battle of Lowositz had likewise shown him that he had no longer to deal with the old Austrians, but with a much better disciplined army. He could at the same time remark with pride, as to his own men, "Never have my troops done such wonders, since I have had the honor of commanding them." The victory had at least the effect of preventing a junction of the Austrians and Saxons. Leaving one division of his victorious army in a fortified position, he set out on the 14th of December for Saxony.

Things had, however, assumed another complexion in Saxony. Notwithstanding the severe privations to which the Saxon soldiers were exposed, they remained faithful to the last. As the thunder of the guns from the surrounding heights proclaimed the victory the Prussians had achieved, all hope of relief vanished, and their only remaining prospect of salvation lay in the possibility of eluding the vigilance of the Prussians, and then, sword in hand, fighting their way through their foes. Private messengers were dispatched to Browne, who immediately put a corps, consisting of six thousand men, in motion, to take the Prussians in the rear, and by an active co-operation relieve the Saxons. He arrived on the spot at the hour appointed on the 11th of October, but the first attempt of the Saxons to cross the Elbe failed. Preparations were made to ford the stream on the following night; and on a given signal from the heights, the Austrians were to attack the Prussians, in order to cover the passage. Unfortunately, the fury of the elements on that night prevented the signal from being recognized, and Browne remained in position. No sooner had the Saxons left the heights, than the Prussians ascended, and the Saxon rear-guard and baggage fell into their hands. The Prussian posts on the other side of the Elbe were now strengthened, and the Saxons again hemmed in on all sides. Browne remained in his position, which became every moment more critical, until the 14th of October, and then retired upon Bohemia. Seventy-two hours were passed by the exhausted Saxons under the naked canopy of heaven, without either food or sleep. Brühl and the king, who were in the enjoyment of every luxury in the fortress of Königstein, directed that a desperate sally should be made; but the generals saw the utter impossiblity of its success. The Saxons next sought to regain their freedom by an honorable capitulation. Count Rutowski, as commander-in-chief, sent an officer to propose conditions to Winterfeldt; but the latter declared that he had no authority from the king, and to dispel the last shadow of hope, led the officer along the Prussian posts, telling him to give Rutowski an accurate description of what he had seen. Nothing now remained but to surrender themselves at discretion as prisoners of war. Every regiment was obliged to lay down its arms. Frederick rode along the lines, treated the hostile generals, who advanced to meet him, with courtesy, and invited them to dinner. Bread was plentifully distributed amongst the half-famished soldiery. The Saxon officers, on giving their parole that they would not again serve against Prussia, were permitted to return home. The privates were obliged to swear fealty to the Prussian flag, as there was no other mode of providing for them. They were clad in the Prussian uniform, and partly distributed amongst the different regiments. Frederick thereby considerably augmented the number of his troops, but had formed a false estimate of the strength of Saxon national feeling, for the services which the Saxons rendered him were trifling, and on several-occasions whole regiments fully equipped deserted to the enemy.

Such was the issue of the first campaign. King Augustus, who had been a spectator, from the heights of Königstein, of the captivity of his army, demanded passports from Frederick; and setting out with his youngest son and Brühl for Warsaw, sought there to drown the memory of defeat in the distractions of court revelry. His royal consort remained in Dresden, and continued to entertain the most bitter animosity towards Frederick, up to the time of her death in the year following. The Prussian troops were withdrawn from Bohemia, and a frontier line formed for the protection of their winter-quarters.

The first campaign was, however, but the prelude to the awful struggle which was yet to come. The promptness and decision with which Frederick had neutralized the plans of his enemies, converted their jealousy into the most furious animosity. The Emperor, regarding the conquest as one involving the existence of the Catholic church and the German empire, declared Frederick under the ban, and actually raised the "speedy executionary army of the empire," which was placed under the command of Prince William of Hildberghausen. An unfortunate misprint in the proclamation for raising this army, converted the term *eilende*, meaning speedy, into *elende*, wretched; and, indeed, its subsequent operations were much more correctly characterized by the latter than the former of these epithets. The German empire had long since become but a mere shadow.

The danger which Prussia had to apprehend from foreign powers was more considerable than that to be feared from the "speedy imperial army." France declared Frederick's invasion of Saxony to be a breach of the treaty of Westphalia, the maintenance of which it had guaranteed. New combinations against Frederick sprang up. The Queen of Poland was the mother-in-law of the

French Dauphin; and Madame Pompadour found in her an active ally against Frederick; further, the French ministry were now anxious to convert the naval war with England into a continental one against Hanover. An immense army was accordingly raised, to be conducted against Hanover and Prussia. Sweden was forced to adopt the policy of France; and it was arranged that North Pomerania, which had been ceded by Sweden to Federick's father, should be now regained by force of arms. Russia concluded a new league with Austria, against Prussia in January, 1757.

Frederick had but few allies. Some few petty princes in English pay sided with him. His treaty with England was renewed on the 11th of January, 1757, and the English people testified the most enthusiastic admiration of his genius; but the leaders of the English ministry were divided in their views, and lost sight of the important struggle which was now approaching. The English cabinet thought of nothing beyond securing the Hanoverian frontiers from the dangers of invasion; nor could Frederick induce the Hanoverian minister to send an army across the Rhine to oppose the march of the French, and as he could not consent to weaken his own forces, he was obliged to surrender Wesel, his strongest hold in the Westphalian provinces.

To strengthen his power, he had recourse to Saxony, which he obliged to supply him with considerable subsidies, recruits, and provisions: the salaries of the public officers were either curtailed or altogether withheld; the vast supplies of porcelain lying in the Meissen manufactory were sold, and the money so obtained appropriated to the exigencies of the Prussian state. The royal palace at Dresden, with its immense treasures of art, which King Augustus had collected at an enormous expense, was, however, spared. During the winter, the greater part of which Frederick spent in Dresden, he repeatedly visited the picture-gallery, with a view to the collection which he intended to form at Sans-souci. The attendants in the gallery, who saw, in imagination, the pictures stript from the walls and packed up for Berlin, were, on the contrary, handsomely remunerated on such occasions; and on Frederick's desiring to have Batoni's Magdalene copied, he first applied to the Saxon royal family for permission. The opera and concerts afforded him particular pleasure, as music was highly cultivated in Dresden. The Queen of Poland and her son were always treated with the most marked courtesy; although Frederick would not permit her to have any part in the administration of affairs; and on his discovering that she carried on a secret correspondence with Austria, he ordered a guard to be placed at the entrance of her palace: a severe scrutiny shortly after led to the detection of a packet of letters, enclosed within a sausage, which she had sent as a present to a friend. The consequence of this discovery was, that more circumspection was used in future in the transmission of these female dispatches.

CHAPTER XXV.

OPENING OF THE CAMPAIGN OF 1757. **PRAGUE AND KOLLIN.**

SUCH was the way in which the winter passed preparatory to that serious contest which was to decide the fate of the Prussian monarchy, and which was soon to commence. Frederick had, according to the most liberal calculation, 200,000 men at his command, whilst the combined forces opposed to him amounted to 500,000. But neither France, nor Russia, nor Sweden were as yet prepared; Austria was the only power which had already assumed a threatening aspect. Frederick resolved on having recourse to his old manœuvre of anticipating the movements of his enemies, and attacking them in detail, before their measures were fully concerted or matured.

The supreme command over the Austrian army had been delegated to Field-marshal Browne. It was his intention to attack Frederick in Saxony, and thus attain the same advantages which Frederick had hitherto won by the rapidity of his movements. He accordingly made a judicious disposition of his troops, and constructed magazines in the neighborhood of the Saxon frontiers. Frederick acted as if it were not his intention to interfere with Browne's operations; he fortified Dresden, and circulated reports that he was about to await the attack of the Austrians. Browne was now superseded in the command of the army by Prince Charles of Lorraine, the emperor's brother, who had felt a longing for this post. Prince Charles made some considerable changes in the system of operations, which were rather variations than improvements. This was exactly what Frederick desired; he proceeded with his masked measures, and lulled the enemy into a feeling of entire security. Just when such an event was least expected, his army burst from different quarters, like so many mountain torrents, down upon Bohemia, sweeping the isolated Austrian corps before it, and carrying off the magazines. Only one corps offered any considerable resistance, and this was routed near Reichenbach by the Duke of Bevern, who was advancing from Lusatia upon Bohemia.

The discomfited Austrians rallied round Prague, and thither Frederick pushed his troops likewise, in order to come, if possible, to a decisive engagement. On the 6th of May the main strength of the Prussian army, in three divisions, under Frederick, Schwerin, and the Duke of Bevern, took up a position on the left bank of the Elbe, below Prague, whilst a fourth corps, under Prince Moritz of Dessau, received orders to proceed along the left bank, cross the stream, and turn the enemy's flank. Frederick explained to Schwerin his intention of immediately attacking the Austrians, who had derived their first information as to the propinquity of the Prussians from some musket-shots discharged by the latter at a band of Croats. Schwerin remonstrated, urging that the troops were fatigued by the march of the foregoing night, that it was not possible to reach the enemy, except by a circuitous path, and that they had no accurate knowledge of the nature of the ground. On Frederick persisting in his resolve, the old field-marshal, pulling down his hat over his eyes, as was his habit, cried out: "If we shall and must have an engagement to-day, I'll attack the Austrians in the first place I meet them." This was not, however, so easy of execution, for the Austrians had taken up a very strong position upon a rising ground, protected by a marsh. General Winterfeldt was dispatched, notwithstanding, to reconnoitre, and soon brought back word that it would be no very difficult matter to turn the enemy's flank, as there was a very accessible approach, formed by a plateau and some corn-fields which ran between the dykes. The Prussian army accordingly deployed, whilst the Austrians made a movement in a similar direction.

But what Winterfeldt had taken for corn-fields proved to be in reality a morass, which considerably impeded the motions of the Prussians, especially the left wing, under Schwerin, whose duty it was to open the attack on the enemy's flank. Some few of the soldiers found narrow ridges of dry ground, along which they crossed in small bodies; while the greater number were obliged to wade across, sinking at every step, and unable to bring up the requisite number of cannon to bear upon the enemy. Notwithstanding the delay and disorder occasioned by this mode of transit, each battalion, as it reached the opposite side, gallantly charged the enemy, but was received with such murderous discharges of grape that they were forced to halt. The Austrians, led on by Browne, who had patriotically accepted of a subordinate command, now advanced, and repulsed the first lines of the Prussians. Schwerin did all in his power to rally his men; snatching a banner from an ensign, he again led on his troops, in the face of the enemy's fire, but had scarce advanced a few paces, when he was dashed to the ground from his horse, no less than five grape-shot having entered his body. Browne was at the same moment so severely wounded that he had to be carried off the field. A cavalry charge on the left wing had been attended, although not without the most obstinate resistance, with more success. The enemy's horse were completely routed. The Prince of Lorraine, struggling in vain to rally the scattered squadrons, was borne down in the mêlée, and being seized with a cramp in the breast, was likewise borne in a state of insensibility off the field of battle. The Prussian left was now reinforced, and charged with redoubled impetuosity, to avenge the death of its fallen leader. The Austrians were soon forced to give way. The Prussian army had by this time crossed over at all points, and bore down upon the enemy. The most heroic courage was displayed on both sides, in the many minor struggles which the conjunctures of the day gave rise to. The Austrians, notwithstanding the resolution they displayed, were everywhere forced to yield. The want of a leader precluded anything like unity in their operations. Frederick now brought the battle to an issue: he observed that a chasm had occurred in the centre of the Austrian army—thither he rushed, notwithstanding a furious cannonade which opened on him from all quarters, cutting down many from his side, and at the head of three battalions completely routed the enemy. The retreat of the Austrians was a general flight, the main object being to seek safety behind the gates of Prague. One body of the Austrians not succeeding in reaching the city, dispersed. The rout of the enemy would have been complete had Prince Moritz of Dessau been able, in pursuance of his instructions, to cross the river with sufficient speed and take the fugitives in the rear.

The victory was gained, but with much and serious loss. Prussia had lost 12,000 men. Of Schwerin's loss Frederick afterwards remarked: "His death has blasted the laurels of victory." Besides Schwerin a considerable number of other distinguished officers had either fallen or been wounded. The losses on the side of the Austrians were still more considerable. In Browne they lost one of their ablest leaders. Frederick had testified to the latter, who expired some weeks afterwards from the wounds he had received, his extreme commiseration, and notified to him Schwerin's death. The main body of the Austrian army having secured itself in Prague, Frederick embraced the bold idea of executing here on a grand scale what he had already effected at the Saxon encampment near Pirna. This extensive city was to be invested, and the army forced to surrender. On the very evening after the battle he summoned the town; but the summons being disregarded, he drew a cordon around it, and raised a series of works for carrying on a blockade, hoping between fire and hunger in a short time to complete its reduction. The red-hot balls which he fired into the city kept up a perpetual conflagration. The congregated masses began to feel the effects of famine; diseases and death committed frightful ravages. The courage of the Austrian army appeared completely gone, and some feeble sallies which had been attempted were repulsed without trouble. Frederick sent spies into the town, and the intelligence they brought back confirmed him in the hope of a speedy fulfilment of his wishes. The court in Vienna trembled for the issue of the contest, which seemed inseparably bound up with the fall of Prague. The Germanic empire tottered to its base, for a daring body of freebooters had penetrated from Bohemia into Bavaria, and spread on all sides the terror of the Prussian name; thoughts were even entertained as to how the hitherto invincible Prussian king was to be propitiated by new concessions.

But the army shut up within the walls of Prague sustained, in the hope of speedy succor, the horrors of the blockade with wondrous fortitude. One of the Austrian corps which had stood under arms in Bohemia, having advanced some days later than the others towards Prague, had been several miles distant during the battle. This corps was under the command of Field-marshal Daun, who now retired further on the road towards Kollin, where he was joined by the numerous bodies of Austrians who had been routed in the engagement and cut off from Prague. Frederick first sent General Ziethen with his hussars against him, but as the enemy was in greater force than had been expected, a special corps of observation, under the Duke of Bevern, was united to that under Ziethen. The latter corps advanced against Daun; but he, although the stronger, retired, permitting the Prussians to capture Kollin with its well-stored magazines, and even to invest Kuttenberg. But by this retiring he approached nearer the central provinces of the Austrian monarchy, and by perpetually incorporating the reinforcements which were sent to him, the number of his troops soon became very considerable.

More than five weeks had now elapsed since the battle of Prague had been fought, but without Frederick's having been able to bring matters to a decisive issue. Just as his operations of the previous year had been retarded by the tedious reduction of the camp in Pirna, so he was now detained by the siege of Prague from following out his measures. Delay was in the present instance fraught with proportionably greater danger, inasmuch as the safety of considerable masses of troops was now at stake, and the perils which from every side impended were becoming momentarily more imminent. The French had crossed the Rhine with a powerful army, and were already in Westphalia; the Russians, Swedes, and the army of the Germanic empire were likewise preparing to march. An overwhelming spirit of dejection took possession of the soul of the great king. The victory of Prague would, to all appearance, have obviated all these embarrassments, had the Prince of Dessau appeared on the field of battle at the proper moment. That the prince's absence was not attributable to any fault of his own was a circumstance overlooked by Frederick. Indeed, the Duke of Bevern might even then, as Frederick maintained, by a rapid movement disperse Marshal Daun's corps; but that this corps was superior to the Prussians in number, and that the Austrians were not likely to yield so readily were two facts which Frederick would not consent to believe. He resolved on attempting that in person which Bevern would not take upon himself to hazard, and taking with him all the troops not absolutely engaged in the siege of Prague, left the camp on the 13th of June to join Bevern.

Daun had, in the interim, feeling himself in sufficient force, again advanced, and given express orders that every exertion should be made for the relief of Prague. This was a third fact which Frederick, who had now joined Bevern, could not bring himself to credit. All dispatches confirmatory of this intelligence were received with so much displeasure that after a time no one dared to interfere, and it was with the most painful forebodings that those more immediately around his person observed his faculties, hitherto so clear and unobscured, seemed now wrapt in the most impenetrable gloom. Zieten, whose hussars had obtained accurate information of the real state of things, openly declared that the situation of the king and army was becoming every moment more critical, and that the consequences would be in the last degree disastrous. At length, on the afternoon of the 17th of June, Frederick, on visiting his outposts, saw before him the whole Austrian army, far superior to his own in point of numbers, and strongly intrenched between Kollin and Panian. He promptly adopted the resolution of attacking the enemy next day, being determined to bring matters to a speedy issue, and apprehensive lest, by seeming to shun an engagement, he should be forced to relinquish all the advantages hitherto obtained.

The morning of the 18th of June dawned, and the Austrian army a second time disappeared from before the Prussians. It being impossible to ascertain whether Daun had merely shifted his position or had really retired under cover of night, Frederick determined on marching to Kollin, where he was certain in every case to come up with the enemy. But on ascending the heights near Panian he again came in view of the hostile army, which had taken up a strong position, and formed in order of battle. Frederick still pushed forward on the road towards Kollin, in order to discover the most assailable point for attacking his foes. At nine o'clock he reached an inn on the road-side, the upper windows of which afforded a commanding view of the Austrian position, and here he drew up the plan of the battle. The enemy's left wing being protected by a precipitous steep was wholly unassailable, and the centre lines appeared to promise but little hopes of success if assaulted. The right wing alone seemed to present no local impediments. In this state of things Frederick resolved on making an effort to outflank the enemy, and then charge them with all his disposable force in the rear. His troops, although completely overpowered by the heat of the weather and the toils of the march, were permitted to rest but till noon, when orders to march were again given. The Austrian leader recognizing Frederick's intention, took the necessary steps to strengthen his right wing.

The Prussian van opened the battle. Zieten's hussars and the grenadiers who formed this advanced body attacked the enemy in the rear, and in spite of a most obstinate resistance obtained considerable advantages. But Frederick, suddenly altering his plans, ordered the remaining portion of the army to halt, and commanded the infantry of his left wing to advance and attack the enemy's centre. Prince Maurice of Dessau, who commanded the main body, represented the dangers to which they would be necessarily exposed by so perilous a movement, but without being able to induce the king to alter his resolves. The prince, after repeated remonstrances, insisted that, without a breach of duty, and taking the most serious responsibility upon himself, he could not venture to execute the order. Opposition of this nature was more than the temper of Frederick could bear, and riding up to the prince with his drawn sword in hand, he inquired in a threatening tone, whether the prince meant to obey his orders or not. The latter yielded, and his regiments charged the enemy. Was it some new storm of impetuosity—was it defiance of fate, that thus warped Frederick from the execution of his first plans, so wisely and maturely laid?

At first it did seem as if he had not placed too much reliance on the heroism and valor of his warriors. Despite the raking fire that swept their ranks, they dashed gallantly amongst the Austrian lines, and joining the regiments that had formed the onset, rushed upon a frightful battery. The enemy's right wing began to waver, and victory appeared to incline to the side of the Prussians. Daun had actually given the order for a retreat, but a subordinate officer, perceiving at this critical moment that the battle appeared to take a more favorable turn, withheld the order from circulation. The Prussian centre had, contrary to the express commands of the king, through the imprudent zeal of its general, joined in the battle, and advancing on a village which was held by Croats, drove them out, and strove to escalade the heights of the Austrian position; but owing to the precipitous nature of the ground, which was covered with slippery, parched grass, every step was insecure, whilst they were at the same time exposed to a frightful shower of grape from the heights. The valiant Prussians were mowed down in lines, and through this disastrous attempt the left wing and van were deprived of the necessary support. Frederick dispatched the cuirassiers and dragoons to their aid, to assist them in retaining the advantages they had already gained. But these valiant horsemen, after advancing twice in the teeth of a furious cannonade, were each time forced to retire. The third charge was led on by Frederick in person but proved equally ineffectual.

The heroic Prussian troops, who had now stood for two hours the brunt of the battle, had by this time exhausted their ammunition, and it was impossible to send them any succor. The Saxon cavalry, which had issued from Poland and joined the Austrians, now advancing upon them, followed by Austrian troopers, a general butchery ensued. The Saxons, goaded on by the memory of the defeat they had sustained twelve years before, shouted in triumph at every sabre-stroke, "In return for Striegau!" The Prussians made a desperate resistance, but with so much loss that those who remained were compelled to betake themselves to flight. Once more did Frederick endeavor to defy fate; he followed the fugitives, striving to rally them, and then, attended by a body of but forty, advanced, in the hope of being joined by others, against the hostile battery. In vain! These few devoted soldiers were again forced to fly beneath a shower of bullets. Frederick, not observing that he stood alone, attended by but a few aides-de-camp, was standing in front of the battery, when one of the officers at length inquired : " Sire, do you mean to capture the battery single handed ? " Hereupon Frederick reined in his steed, and drawing out his glass, calmly surveyed the works, from whence the bullets fell thick as hail ; then, turning his horse's head, rode slowly and silently toward the left wing of his army, which the Duke of Bevern commanded, and here gave the signal for retreat.

The right wing had as yet taken no part in the action, and was consequently now employed in covering the retreat of the rest of the army. But before this retreat actually commenced, the right wing became engaged with the Austrian left, and a new struggle ensued, which was contested with as much ardor as any of the previous ones of this sanguinary day. The Prussians had again to yield to the murderous fire of the Austrians—whole regiments were swept away. At length, towards eight o'clock in the evening, the right wing of the Prussian army succeeded likewise in retiring. Daun, contenting himself with holding the field of battle, and resting satisfied with this his first victory over the Prussian arms, permitted Frederick's army to retire over Planian to Nimburg, and in a truly chivalrous spirit sent the vanquished such of their wounded as they had been obliged to leave behind them in Planian.

Frederick, as soon as he saw that the battle was irrevocably lost, retired, attended by a small escort, towards Nimburg. This evening's ride was accompanied with much peril, as the neighboring villages and woods swarmed with troops of Austrian hussars and Croats. Indeed, in the middle of this journey the report was suddenly spread that some hussars were advancing, and the king was obliged to proceed for half-an-hour in full gallop. It became necessary to make a short halt in a village in order to water and breathe the panting steeds. Here an old trooper advanced to the king, and offering him a cool draught which he had taken from a horse-bucket, addressed him: "Drink, your majesty! and let battles be battles: it's well that you are safe. Let us trust in God that it will soon be our turn to conquer!" These words must have been consoling to the ear of the king, but there were few in the army who re-echoed them. On the arrival of the officers belonging to Frederick's staff, they found him seated on a water-pipe, his eyes intently fixed upon the ground, describing figures in the sand with his cane. No one ventured to interrupt his train of gloomy reflection Springing up soon after, with an air of composure and forced gaiety, he gave the necessary orders for the night. At sight of the small remnant of his much-cherished Guards, the tears started in his eyes. "Children," said he, "this has been a sad day for you!" They replied, that they had been badly led on. "Have but patience," said Frederick, "and I'll set all to rights." This was the first battle which Frederick had lost. His losses amounted to nearly 14,000 men, while those of the Austrians hardly exceeded 8,000. But Frederick's chief loss was the loss of confidence and self-reliance now observable throughout an army which had hitherto deemed itself invincible, and whose confidence could only be restored by future victories. On news of the defeat being communicated to the officers of the army in front of Prague, a sullen silence of several moments' duration ensued, and Prince William of Prussia, although of a particularly mild disposition, broke out into loud complaints at the conduct of his royal brother.

All idea of carrying on an offensive war in Bohemia had to be now relinquished, and the siege of Prague raised. On the second day after this defeat the besieging army abandoned its intrenchments, under sound of trumpet and drum; and the Prince of Lorraine, who commanded the Austrians in the town, and had received intelligence of the victory from a sutler who had come from Kollin, interposed no obstacles in the way of its departure. It was not until the last divisions of the Prussian army, which had been too dilatory in their movements, were filing off, that the besieged ventured on a sortie, which was certainly productive of considerable loss. Daun felt still less disposed to pursue the Prussians; being snugly intrenched in his camp, he contented himself, whilst the two Prussian corps were forming a junction, with singing pæans of victory, and then advanced with his army towards Prague to join the Prince of Lorraine.

With a view to embarrass the future operations of his enemies by consuming all the provisions in the northern part of the country, Frederick remained as long as possible in Bohemia; for this purpose he divided his army into two corps, which took up fortified positions on both sides of the Elbe; that on the east side, which was afterwards to retire towards Lusatia, being under the command of his brother, the Prince of Prussia. The Austrian army remained for several weeks inactive, and then directed its main strength against the corps under the command of the Prince of Prussia. The latter, on the danger becoming imminent, sent Frederick frequent details of the enemy's motions; but Frederick was now as little disposed as he had been previous to the battle of Kollin, to listen to statements regarding the strength or courage of the Austrians; the consequence was, that Prince William found himself under the necessity of retiring hastily on Zittau, where considerable magazines had been collected. He, however, unfortunately selected a route which, from passing through a chain of mountains, offered many obstacles to his progress, and so impeded the retreat of his army as to cause it considerable loss, whilst the enemy, who had taken a shorter path, reached Zittau contemporaneously with the Prussians. Prince William avoided an action, but the Prince of Lorraine so bombarded the town of Zittau, where the Prussian stores were but feebly defended, that nothing soon remained of it beyond a heap of ruins. Intelligence of his brother's retreat did not reach Frederick until he had set out with his army for Saxony. After securing the frontiers here he marched with the main body of his army to the succor of his brother, and came up with him in Bautzen, where a very unfriendly meeting took place. The prince, and the several generals of his army, with the exception of Winterfeldt, whom Federick had appointed in a measure the prince's adviser, had to listen to the severest reproaches for the losses occasioned by their retreat, and Frederick distinctly informed the generals that every one of them deserved to lose his head. Prince William, in consequence of this, retired from the army, proceeded to Berlin fell sick, and died the following summer.

CHAPTER XXVI.

CONTINUATION OF THE CAMPAIGN OF 1757.

In the meantime, the horizon had become gradually more and more overcast; new dangers began to crowd in on all sides, and Frederick could desire nothing more ardently than to be able to come to an engagement with the Austrians now stationed in Upper Lusatia; but the Prince of Lorraine had taken up so admirable a position, that any attempt to dislodge him was evident madness, and Frederick's feigned marches, intended to draw him from this strong position, proved fruitless, as the Austrians did not move. Another species of stratagem which Frederick put in requisition proved equally unsuccessful. Whilst supping one evening in the open air, in company with several of his general officers, nothing was talked of but the attack which was to take place on the following day, and the conversation was sufficiently loud to be overheard by such as crowded round the royal table, amongst whom it was natural to suppose that some spies were present. Preparations were even made during the night for the threatened attack. Numerous deserters passed over to the Prince of Lorraine, but he did not allow himself to be deceived by this *ruse de guerre*.

There was now no further time to be lost for the defence of Saxony, unless Frederick would consent to surrender it to the French and imperial armies who were in full march upon it. Accordingly, leaving the greater portion of his army behind him, under the command of the Duke of Bevern, to protect Lusatia and Silesia against the Austrians, he proceeded in person, at the head of twelve thousand men, in the direction of Dresden, intending to draw from thence such troops as might be stationed there, and then march towards the river Saale. Winterfeldt, whose courage and experience rendered him an object of Frederick's special favor, was associated with the Duke of Bevern in the command of the army thus left behind. The Austrians, who had hitherto remained inactive, now, on the arrival of the chancellor, Count Kaunitz, in the camp of the Prince of Lorraine, made, in order to afford the favorite of the Empress a proof of the activity of the army, a sudden attack on an isolated Prussian corps, to which it was of course far superior in numbers. Winterfeldt, who commanded this corps, was, during the engagement, shot in the breast, and died within a few hours. The Austrians obtained a victory in an unequal contest, but its fruits were comparatively insignificant. The Duke of Bevern, however, becoming apprehensive lest the Austrians might cut him off from Silesia, proceeded in that direction, and the Prince of Lorraine, after having first permitted his adversary to cross the different streams which divide Lusatia from Silesia, prepared to follow him. On Winterfeldt's death being communicated to Frederick, he exclaimed in anguish, "The numbers of my foes have never appalled me, but where shall I find a second Winterfeldt!"

The successes of his numerous enemies were now such, that any other person except Frederick must have given himself up to despair. On the Lower Rhine a powerful French army, under Marshal D'Estray, had entered Westphalia; its progress was opposed by an army composed of Hanoverians, Hessians, Brunswickers, and other Germans under the command of the Duke of Cumberland. Some Prussian troops, which had been until then incorporated with the allies, were now, as the army under the Duke of Cumberland advanced towards the Weser, drawn off and employed to strengthen Magdeburg. In Hastenbeck, at no great distance from Hameln, an engagement

ensued between the French and allied armies. The losses
and advantages on both sides were pretty equal, and
both leaders supposing themselves vanquished, beat a
retreat at the same moment; but the French, the more
cunning of the two, soon discovering their error, took
rapid possession of the field of battle, and thus appeared
as victors. The Duke of Cumberland retired in all haste,
pursued by the French army, and considered himself so
completely destitute of aid, as to conclude an ignominious
treaty on the 8th of September, in pursuance of which
the whole allied army engaged to disperse. The Hanoverians were permitted to take up their cantonments near
Stade. Brunswick was occupied by the French, who
poured into the Prussian provinces of the Elbe, and committed every species of barbarity. The Duke of Richelieu, who had been sent from Paris to supersede Marshal
D'Estray, was not slow in taking advantage of this state
of things for recruiting his shattered finances.

Somewhat subsequent to the incursion of the French
army, a considerable Russian corps had entered Prussia.
The wild hosts of Asiatic barbarians who accompanied
this army laid the land waste, and inflicted indescribable
hardships on the inhabitants. Memel was captured. The
Russians advanced as far as the river Pregel, where they
encountered a Prussian army not much more than a
quarter of their number, under Field-marshal Lewald.
On the 30th of August a battle ensued near Gross-
Jaegerndorf. The steady discipline of the Prussians appeared likely to prove victorious over the brute force
of innumerable barbarian hordes, until the advantages
which had been already won were again lost through the
incapacity of the Prussian leader. The Prussians were
obliged to abandon the field of battle, but without being
pursued by the Russians, whose losses amounted to at
least double those of the former.

A Swedish army which had landed at Stralsund, after
ravaging Pomerania and Uppermark, having been concentrated with the imperial executionary army under Prince

Hildburghausen, and a special French corps, under Prince Soubise, furnished towards the close of August, in pursuance of a treaty with Austria, now took possession of Erfurt.

Thus every point of Frederick's kingdom was now assailed, and hostile armies had already taken up fortified positions in the very heart of his dominions. To this frightful combination of hostile forces, he had nothing to oppose beyond a small army, already in part melted away, and which, through the defeat at Kollin and the retreat from Bohemia, had become entirely dispirited and disheartened. According to all human calculation, escape from destruction was now impossible; and to complete the measure of his misfortunes, whilst his enemies were making the most rapid advances upon him, and whilst the best and the bravest of his friends were falling around him, another calamity occurred which affected him the most severely of all—the death of his mother, which took place shortly after the battle of Kollin. Her energetic and decided character had attached him to her more closely and sincerely than any one could have believed. A morbid melancholy now seized his mind and although by immense efforts he succeeded in disguising the torpor of his feelings, and appeared even cheerful and gay, yet those who were more intimately attached to his person shuddered, when they recollected that he always carried a deadly poison about his person, and knew him to be resolved not to outlive the downfall of his kingdom. In the poems composed by him about this period death forms his only theme; in it he hopes to find shelter from the storms of fate; and dwells with gloomy satisfaction on the pleasurable feelings evoked by a voluntary exit from this world of care and strife.

But the king still retained the power of clothing his grief in words, of wrapping his thoughts, as it were, in an artificial dress, and this it was which saved him. Poetry was the anodyne which preserved him from taking the last frightful step, and we soon find in his poems another tone than that of complete prostration. Desperate as was his situation, the poetic temperament of his mind enabled him to look out from the dark canopy of the present at the coming brightness of the future, and in a spirit of prophecy to announce the glorious results of that frightful contest in which his kingdom and himself were then engaged. Thus, in an ode dedicated to his younger brother, Prince Henry, he holds up the conduct of the Roman people, who had likewise to wade to sovereignty and power through a thousand adversities and dangers, as an example to the Prussians, and endeavors to impress upon the minds of his people the fact, that no nation ever yet attained supremacy or fame without having first passed through the fiery ordeal of privation and suffering. He likewise expresses his entire confidence in the brilliant future reserved by destiny to gild the name and fame of Prussia. And though he concedes the possibility of *his* being neither the architect nor contemporary of his country's greatness, yet by an oracular prescience, inspired by the yearning of his heart, he gives utterance to a prophecy, the verification of which was the work of his own hand. From this moment may be dated the most heroic achievements of the great king.

CHAPTER XXVII.

CONTINUATION OF THE CAMPAIGN OF 1757. ROSSBACH.

NUMEROUS petty skirmishes delayed Frederick's progress towards Erfurt. He at length arrived, but the combined army of imperial troops and French had retired on the appearance of the Prussian van, and evacuated the town. The combined troops were further forced to abandon Gotha and retire with loss on Eisenach. But Frederick was again obliged to weaken his petty army by dispatching two corps, one to oppose the French under Richelieu, and the other, the Austrian army, which had penetrated into Lusatia and threatened Mark Brandenburg. With a view to conceal the paucity of his numbers from observation, divisions of the Prussian troops were scattered through the villages and obliged to change their quarters repeatedly, every regiment entering its cantonment under a new name. The spies faithfully reported the number and names of the regiments, and informed the Prince of Soubise of the strength of the Prussians, who was thus deterred, in spite of his great numerical superiority, from hazarding any decisive step.

As soon, however, as Soubise learned that Frederick had occupied Gotha with but a few cavalry regiments under General Seidlitz, and had retired with his main forces towards Erfurt, he resolved on again advancing on Gotha. Seidlitz, who by his brilliant achievements at Kollin had already obtained the highest military reputation, immediately withdrew from the town, but it was not in his nature to leave his enemies an undisputed mastery;

he drew up his little army at some short distance, in order
of battle, and in such a manner that at first view it would
appear to be pretty numerous. A dragoon was dispatched
to the town to play the character of a deserter, and state
that the king was approaching. In consequence, as soon
as the French and imperial troops, after occupying Gotha,
advanced to give battle, and saw before them long lines
with, as they conceived, infantry mixed amongst the
cavalry, (Seidlitz having made a couple of squadrons of
hussars dismount in order to deceive the enemy,) they
did not doubt for a moment that they were now about to
encounter the whole Prussian army. Seidlitz gave the
signal for attack, and the enemy speedily retired. A
body of Prussian hussars and dragoons dashed in full
gallop towards the town, when Soubise and his generals,
who were being entertained at the ducal table, mounted
their steeds in all haste, and narrowly escaped being made
prisoners. Besides an immense number of prisoners, the
whole baggage of the French fell into the hands of the
Prussians. The hussars were much amused with the
pomatum, the powdering-cloaks, the queues, the dressing-
gowns, shawls, and parrots, which were found in numbers
amongst the baggage of the French officers. The attendants, servants, cooks, hairdressers, mistresses, and players
were sent back without ransom. Seidlitz pursued the
hostile army as far as Eisenach. Frederick paid the
highest tribute of praise to this daring exploit: it was of
little positive advantage to him, but he thereby became
acquainted with the character of his enemy, and his little
army derived confidence from the conduct of the French;
but Frederick was again obliged to fall back on Thuringia,
in consequence of intelligence that the Austrian army,
stationed in Lusatia, was marching on Mark Brandenburg, that a corps of Hungarian hussars under Haddig was
already in advance on Berlin, and it seemed likewise not
improbable that the Swedes would make a simultaneous
attack on the province of Mark. On receiving this intelligence, Frederick proceeded to Torgau, whilst Prince

CAMPAIGN OF 1757. ROSSBACH. 243

Maurice of Dessau, at the head of a special corps, endeavored to check General Haddig's march on Berlin. The latter had, however, arrived a day earlier than his adversary; the court had fled in all speed to Spandau, and the town had paid a contribution of two hundred thousand thalers, besides giving twenty-four pairs of ladies' gloves as a present to the Empress. The latter were carefully packed up, but on the chest being opened, they were found to be all for the left hand. Haddig retired rapidly on the approach of Prince Maurice, the main Austrian army remaining quietly encamped in Bautzen.

A danger so considerable had now blown over without any proportionable loss, and more favorable tidings soon arrived from other quarters. The Russians had taken no advantage of their victory, but after leaving a garrison in Memel, had again crossed the Russian frontier. The reason of this movement was, the sudden indisposition of the Empress Elizabeth. Bestuscheff, hostile as he was disposed towards Frederick, conceived it good policy to ingratiate himself by this movement with Elizabeth's successor. For this step, however, the all-powerful minister, on the Empress, contrary to all expectation, recovering, was sent to Siberia. The Swedes had met with an unexpected resistance from the Pomeranian militia, which had of its own accord assembled in considerable numbers in that province. By its exertions Stettin, although very feebly garrisoned, was protected against the Swedish army, and the latter detained from its march on Berlin. Throughout the whole course of the Seven Years' War, these militias, at a time when standing armies only were known, formed a peculiar and remarkable feature, and played an important part in the defence of the land and its fortresses. For this reason, as well as from other proofs of Pomeranian fidelity, Frederick declares his wish in his political testament, "that his successors should chiefly rely on the Pomeranians as the principal pillars of the Prussian state." In imitation of this Pomeranian militia, similar corps were instituted in the provinces of Mark and Magdeburg. On the Russian army retiring from Prussia Proper, Frederick ordered up the corps stationed there to support the Pomeranians against the Swedes, who were speedily compelled to fall back on Stralsund.

Frederick had in the meanwhile opened negotiations with the Duke of Richelieu. The latter did not belong to the Pompadour faction, but to that smaller section of the French court, who desired the continuance of the old league which had subsisted between France and Prussia The flatteries contained in Frederick's letters, and an acceptable present of a hundred thousand thalers, rendered the French minister disposed to enter into his views. The articles of the agreement were not exactly such as could be communicated to the French court, but Richelieu readily entered into a compact not to take any further measures at present. To the King of England Frederick had likewise written, on receiving intelligence of the disgraceful treaty of Seeven, requiring the monarch not to abandon him, now that the Duke of Cumberland had submitted to such a treaty. In this letter Frederick touched the weak point in the character of George, for the latter had heard of the convention with the greatest indignation, and publicly addressed the Duke of Cumberland with the words, " Here is the son who has destroyed me and disgraced himself! " The consequence was, that England entered into Frederick's views with energy and alacrity, and all manner of excuses were invented for the non-ratification of this disgraceful treaty.

An enemy, which in former centuries had been the most dangerous of any, was now got rid of in a very simple, almost comical manner. We mean the imperial ban, which the *Reichshofrath*, then assembled in Ratisbon, were busy in pronouncing against the King of Prussia, as he appeared to be now completely prostrated. On the 14th October, the grand advocate, clad in the robes of an imperial notary, and accompanied by two witnesses, presented himself at the residence of the Prussian ambassador in Ratisbon, "to insinuate to the latter the fiscal citation of the ban." This consisted of a "summons of the Prince Elector and Margrave of Brandenburg, to see and to hear how he was about to be declared under the ban of the empire, and deprived of all fiefs, rights, graces, freedoms, and expectancies whatsoever." Baron Plotho, the Prussian ambassador, received the notary in his dressing-gown. The result of this citation is detailed in an official document, conceived by the delegate in the following words: "And thereupon his excellency, Baron Plotho, did fall into violent rage and fury, so that he, the same, could not hold nor govern himself, but with trembling hands and burning looks stretching both his arms towards me, and holding the fiscal citation in his right hand, did burst out into the following formalia: 'What, you scoundrel! insinuate?' Whereupon I replied, 'This was my duty as notary, which I must fulfil.' But in spite of this, he, the aforesaid Baron von Plotho, did fall upon me in all rage, seize me by the front parts of my mantle, with the inquiry whether I would retract. Whereupon, and on my refusing so to do, he, the said baron, did drive and push the said citation between the folds of my gown with all violence, and holding me by the mantle, did drive me out of the room, and called to two attendants, with the command to pitch me down the stairs." The matter rested here for the present; for Frederick soon obtained new victories, which induced the imperial council to act with more caution.

Frederick now intended to set out for Silesia, where the Duke of Bevern was hard pressed. But he suddenly received intelligence that the allied army, composed of imperial and French troops, and strengthened by a division of Richelieu's army, had abandoned their former state of inactivity, were advancing on Saxony, and had actually arrived in the neighborhood of Leipzig: he accordingly resolved on first turning his arms against this foe and driving it back on Thuringia, in order that it might not take up its winter-quarters too close to the Saxon electorate: he therefore concentrated the different corps of his army with all expedition, and covered Leipzig. The enemy retired to the Saale, and in order to prevent the Prussians from crossing this river, took possession of Halle, Merseburg, and Weissenfels. Frederick followed his enemies with all speed, and even penetrated, at the head of his advanced guard, into Weissenfels, whilst the enemy fled across the stream, and hastily setting fire to the handsome bridge, in order to cut off the king's approach, threw a considerable number of their own troops into the hands of the Prussians. Frederick wished to save the bridge, but as it had been filled with conbustible matters, it was in an instant completely wrapt in flames, and sharp volleys of musketry prevented the Prussians from being able to extinguish the fire. As Frederick was here riding along the bank of the river reconnoitring, he escaped, through the chivalry of the French leader, the Duke of Crillon, the most imminent peril. The latter had directed two officers to take up a post on a small island in the Saale, and watch the motions of the Prussians; one of these hurried forward with intelligence of the king's being in the neighborhood, and requested permission to fire on him from the brushwood, but was reprimanded by the Duke, who informed him, that he had not been posted there for that purpose, and that the sacred person of majesty should always be respected.

Two corps, led on by Frederick from Weissenfels in the direction of Merseburg, found the bridges broken down, and the enemy in retreat, encamped a few miles on the opposite side of the Saale, at Mücheln. The Prussian troops not having been interrupted in their operations of pontooning and crossing the Saale, likewise encamped on the other side. The position of the allied troops had been selected with so little tact, that the Prussian hussars found opportunities of penetrating into the hostile camp, and carrying off horses and even soldiers out of their tents. Frederick had resolved on coming to an engagement; but on advancing, the day following, the 4th of November, he discovered that the enemy, warned by the daring of the Prussian hussars, had taken up a very strong position during the night. He accordingly gave up all idea of attacking an enemy so far outnumbering him, and retiring, formed a camp in the neighborhood of Rossbach. This fancied flight of the Prussian king was a subject of great joy in the enemy's camp. Trumpet and drum resounded from every height, as if in celebration of some great victory. The French officers became witty, and asserted that much honor was done the Marquis of Brandenburg by their entering into a war of this kind with him. Messengers were dispatched to Paris to announce Frederick's capture. They did not recollect that, superior as they were in numbers, they were deficient in that spirit which Frederick had breathed into the Prussian army: that the jealousies existing between the leaders of the German and French troops must necessarily prevent them from acting in concert or with decision; and that on the troops of the empire, which formed a motley mass, devoid of all military organization and discipline, no reliance whatsoever could be placed; that the discipline of the French troops was anything but exemplary; and, further, that pride is generally the precursor of a fall. The morning of the 5th of November dawned, and Frederick received intelligence that the enemy had abandoned their position, and were advancing in an extended curve round his army, whilst a single corps remained directly opposite to him. It was evidently their intention to cut off this retreat, and by encircling him on all sides to completely annihilate him. Frederick remained the whole of the forenoon perfectly tranquil, as if wholly unaware of the danger which impended, ordered dinner, and sat down to table with his generals. The enemy were delighted at this improvidence of the Prussian army, whilst the leaders of the latter, who surmised the king's object, had made every preparation for departure. At length, about half-past three in the afternoon,

Frederick gave orders to break up the camp, and the French officers could not refrain from expressing their astonishment at the rapidity with which this manœuvre was executed : they compared it to the shifting of an opera scene. Becoming now apprehensive that the Prussian army might escape them, the enemy put their columns in full motion. But Frederick advanced in the same direction; the cavalry, headed by Seidlitz, formed the van, and got out of view of the enemy beneath a ridge of hills, whilst the infantry became partly covered by some marshy ground. The Prussian cannon were now posted on the most considerable of the surrounding heights, and their thunder opened the fight, their position rendering them very effective, whereas the enemy's gun's were totally inefficient from their low range. By some extraordinary chance a great number of hares happened to be shut in between both armies, and being startled by the roar of the guns, made repeated efforts to escape in different directions. As soon as the first French bullets had killed a hare in front of the Prussian lines a joyous shout arose from the latter, declaring the French were butchering one another. The French columns, with the cavalry at their head, were pushed on in order to outflank the Prussians; but Seidlitz had, without being perceived, already outflanked them, and suddenly halting with his valiant squadrons on a height, took advantage of a favorable moment, and made a general charge without waiting for the infantry. His squadrons were no sooner drawn up in serried array, than he advanced in front of the lines, and in presence of the whole division tossed his tobacco-pipe into the air, as a signal for the onset :—in an instant his men fell upon the hostile cavalry, who in vain strove to unfold their lines. They were completely overthrown; some regiments attempted to rally, but in vain. A general flight ensued, and the narrowness of the path impeding their progress, a vast number of prisoners fell into the hands of the victors; such as escaped continued their flight unceasingly as far as the river Unstrut. But Seidlitz was now in the rear of the enemy's infantry. Against it Frederick had now likewise directed his left wing with the guns, and like the cavalry it had no room to deploy its lines. The Prussian grape carried death and destruction into the middle of the ranks. The Prussian infantry charged on the flank, and the cavalry in the rear. At length all took to flight, and whole masses of fugitives were captured. The battle had not lasted two hours, when darkness coming on precluded all further pursuit. The Prussian army, which was not quite 22,000 strong, had lost 165 dead, and 376 wounded, whilst the enemy, whose numbers amounted to 64,000 had lost between 600 and 700 dead, more than 2,000 wounded, and upwards of 5,000 prisoners, together with a great number of guns, standards, flags, and the greater part of their baggage. Moreover, the whole of the Prussian army had not been by any means engaged in the action—but seven battalions had taken part in the fight, while ten battalions had not fired a single shot. The rejoicings of the Prussians were of course great. Frederick formally thanked his army, and Seidlitz, whose arm had been shattered by a musket-ball, received the most rare mark of favor—the order of the Black Eagle—and was promoted to the rank of lieutenant-general.

On the following day the Prussian army went in pursuit of the enemy, and a multitude of stragglers were captured. But the greater number of the enemy had fled so fast that it was impossible to overtake them. Many of the French did not halt until they had reached the Rhine, and perpetually fancied that the Prussian hussars were at their heels. In order to indemnify themselves in some measure for their disaster, they marked their path with acts of rapine and violence of every kind. But they thereby roused the peasantry to some acts of severe retaliation.

Frederick treated the French prisoners with the greatest kindness; he consoled such as were wounded, and, touched by his condescension, they declared him the most perfect of conquerors; one who not only enchained

the limbs but the hearts of his foes. On their asking his
permission to send unsealed letters to France, he replied,
"I cannot bring myself to regard you as my foes, and
feel no jealousy towards you; consequently you are at
liberty to seal your letters, and you shall have your answers back with seals unbroken." General Custine, who
had retired to Leipzig, having been severely wounded,
was honored with a personal visit from Frederick, and
the latter depicted the lively interest he felt in the
French nation with such ardor, that Custine, raising
himself slowly from his couch, uttered the words, "Sire,
you pour oil upon my wounds."

But in Germany—even among Frederick's opponents
—the victory of Rossbach was received with the greatest
joy, as a humiliation of the French, who were not very
popular. The fire of enthusiasm, which had been long
since kindled by the acts of the German hero, now burst
into flame. On all sides were heard songs proclaiming
the victory of the Prussians, and deriding their opponents. The German once more felt the pride of being a
German.

These chants of victory were, of course, poison to those
who could not forego their hatred towards Frederick. The
Queen of Poland, whose intrigues in Dresden against him
were without end, could not endure her feelings of exasperation any longer. One evening, having dismissed
her household in anger, she retired to rest, and was found
dead in her bed the following morning.

The enthusiasm of the Germans was loudly re-echoed
in foreign climes, even by the French nation, who re-
regarded it as a defeat of the court party, and who vented
their resentment in the most violent invectives against
Prince Soubise. In the coffee-houses of Paris Prussia became for a long time the popular theme. The court endeavored to console Prince Soubise by raising him to the rank
of marshal. The sympathy which the people of England
testified for Frederick knew no bounds. He was wor-
shipped by the people; his portrait suspended in all the

London shops, and his victories commemorated by general illuminations. Contemporaneously with the news of the victory of Rossbach a favorable change in the English ministry took place; refusals to ratify the treaty of Seeven on the ground of the French having first broken it by renewing the war followed; and as the English were in want of a good general, Frederick recommended them the Duke of Brunswick as the best of his leaders. The duke was, in truth, immediately summoned, and taking the command of the Hanoverian army and its allies, obtained during the winter several advantages over the great French army, which was thus averted from the Prussian frontier, and Frederick thereby fully secured in this quarter.

CHAPTER XXVIII.

CONCLUSION OF THE CAMPAIGN OF 1757. LEUTHEN.

UNCONQUERED and unconquerable, Frederick had freed himself from all grounds of apprehension as to one of his enemies; it now remained to repel the second, but far more dangerous foe. The Duke of Bevern had retired from the borders of Lusatia on Breslau, and had taken up a fortified position in front of that city. The Austrian army, under the Prince of Lorraine, so very superior to his in number, had followed in his rear. A special corps had invested Schweidnitz, which had been but lately fortified, and was considered by Frederick as the key of Silesia. After a brief interval of repose, Frederick broke up his camp and hastened to the aid of the Duke of Bevern. The Austrian corps which was stationed in Lusatia was to be first driven from its position, in order that the march of the Prussian army might not be retarded; and Field-marshal Keith received orders to execute this manœuvre, and make an incursion with a small corps on Bohemia. Keith conducted this expedition with such courage and skill, that the Austrians were not alone forced to evacuate Lusatia, in order to cover Bohemia, but an immense number of their magazines and a considerable quantity of plunder fell into Keith's hands.

But whilst Frederick was yet in Lusatia, he received intelligence that Schweidnitz had capitulated on the 14th of November; whereby a whole corps, a magazine, a quantity of munitions of war, and a military chest had fallen into the hands of the enemy, who thereby obtained the command of the Bohemian highlands. On the 25th of November news arrived that the Duke of Bevern had been attacked and beaten by the Austrians, and that the duke himself had fallen into their hands. Two days afterwards Frederick learned that Breslau had likewise surrendered to the enemy, and that the whole garrison, amounting to 5000 men, had gone over to the Austrians. The remnant of Bevern's army had been conducted by General Zieten to Glogau. Silesia seemed now irrecoverably lost, and it appeared altogether vain to expect that Frederick could prevent the Austrians from taking up their winter-quarters in the heart of the country. Such of the inhabitants as were favorably disposed towards Austria exhibited the greatest glee; and many of the officials paid their homage to the Empress: even the Prince-Bishop of Breslau, Count Schafgotsch, who was indebted solely to the King of Prussia for his dignity, and had been the object of numerous acts of kindness, so far forgot himself as to treat his benefactor with the most contemptuous scorn, and trod under foot the order of the black eagle with which he had been decorated.

Despite all this Frederick did not blench. In defiance of the wretched state of the roads, he hurried by forced marches on to Breslau, and on the 28th of November arrived in Barchwitz, and there took up his camp on the opposite side of the Katzbach, in order to give his troops some short period of repose. The Austrians were encamped in an admirable situation in front of Breslau, but Frederick was resolved to attack them wherever he should meet them; were it even, as he himself expressed it, on the top of the Zobtenburg. Near Barchwitz he was joined by Zieten with the remnant of Bevern's army. "This army was altogether dispirited," says Frederick himself, "and entirely broken down from the effects of its late defeat." The officers were reminded of their duty, of their former exploits; and to dispel those gloomy visions which were of but so late an origin, even wine was used. The king conversed with the soldiers, and ordered provisions to be distributed freely amongst them. In a word, every possible means were employed to awaken that spirit of confidence in themselves, without which all hopes of victory were illusory. The countenances of the men began to brighten up by degrees, and those who had beaten the French at Rossbach, persuaded their comrades to be of good cheer. A little rest invigorated their exhausted strength, and the army was soon in a position to wipe out the stain on its honor inflicted on the 26th of November.

But the king did not rest satisfied even with this. His situation was, notwithstanding all his exertions, one of extreme danger. His whole army amounting to but 32,000 men, was opposed to from 80,000 to 90,000 Austrians far better disciplined than the enemy encountered at Rossbach, and feeling within themselves, from their former successes, the elements of victory. Summoning his generals and the officers of his staff to his presence, Frederick addressed them in the following words, which have peen preserved in the annals of history:

"Gentlemen, you are aware that Prince Charles of Lorraine has succeeded in becoming master of Schweidnitz, beating the Duke of Bevern and possessing himself of Breslau, whilst I was necessarily absent, having been obliged to check the advances of the French and their allies. A part of Silesia, its capital, and all the munitions of war there stored up have been lost; and my disasters would be regarded by me as fully crowned and insurmountable, were it not that I place the most unbounded confidence in your gallantry and courage,—in that resolution,—in that love of country, which you have on so many occasions, and so nobly evinced. With the most heartfelt gratitude do I acknowledge these services rendered to your father-land and myself. There is not one amongst you who is not distinguished by some great, some chivalrous exploit. I can consequently flatter myself in the hope that, when occasion offers, you will not fail to satisfy the demands which your country now makes upon your courage and devotion. The decisive moment is approaching, and I should consider that I had accomplished nothing, if I left the Austrians in possession of Silesia. Rely then on this, that contrary to every rule of art, I shall attack the army under the command of Prince Charles, though it be three times my own strength, wherever and whensoever I may meet it. The number of the foe,—the strength of their position, are here matters of but secondary importance; all these must, I feel confident, yield before the unflinching bravery of my troops, and the judicious execution of my orders. I must venture on this step, or all is lost. We must beat the foe, or be buried beneath their batteries. These are my feelings, and my acts shall be in accordance. Inform the different officers of the army of my purpose and resolves; —prepare the private soldier for the events which are about to follow. Impress upon his mind that I am justified in demanding the most implicit obedience from him. In conclusion, recollect but that you are Prussians, and your acts will certainly be in accordance with that high distinction. If there be, however, any one amongst you who fears to share those dangers with me, he can this day demand his dismissal without being exposed to the slightest reproach from me."

This address from the monarch penetrated, as we are informed by an eye-witness, to the hearts of his hearers, and fanned anew the fire of enthusiasm into flame. All became inspired with the determination to sacrifice their lives for their great sovereign, who saw with inward satisfaction the ardor he had enkindled. A pause ensued— and the resolution which he read in the countenances of his hearers, bore ample witness of the entire devotion of his army towards him. With a friendly smile he continued : " I feel already perfectly assured that not one of you will leave me. I calculate on your aiding me valiantly,—and on victory. Should I fall, and thus be disabled from acknowledging your services, you must look to the gratitude of your country for your reward.

Return to the camp, and communicate to the regiments what you have now heard from me." Frederick had spoken in a tone of confidence to awaken the enthusiasm of his hearers; but now that he had convinced himself of the irresistible force of his words, he again addressed them in his character as king, alluding to the punishments which would necessarily follow any breach of duty. "That cavalry regiment," said he, "which does not immediately, on being ordered, burst impetuously on the foe, I shall immediately after the battle dismount, and convert it into a garrison regiment. The battalion of infantry which, be the obstacles what they may, for a moment halts, shall lose its standards and swords, and I shall cut the facings from its uniform. Fare you well, gentlemen, for the present. We shall soon have beaten the enemy, and meet again."

The ardor and devotion with which Frederick inspired the assembled officers, soon spread throughout every man belonging to the army; joyous shouts rang through the Prussian camp; the hoary warriors who had won so many fights under Frederick grasped each others hands, swore steadily to stand by their comrades, and conjured their youthful brothers in arms not to flinch from the foe, but boldly, in spite of every obstacle, dash into the thickest of the throng. An internal feeling of resolution and self-confidence, the ordinary precursors of coming success, was plainly to be read in the countenances of all.

On the 4th of December the Prussian army broke up its camp. Whilst marching towards Neumarkt, Frederick, who led the van, learned that this place was already occupied by Austrian hussars and Croats. Deeming it advisable to gain possession of the heights on the opposite side, he stormed, without waiting for his infantry, the gates of the town, and took the greater number of the enemy prisoners. Having then occupied the heights, he awaited the arrival of the main body of his army. Towards the evening of the same day, intelligence was brought him that the Austrians had abandoned their entrenchments, and advanced across the Schweidnitz: the Prince of Lorraine considering it beneath his dignity to meet the attack of the Berlin parade, as the Austrians termed the little Prussian army, in fortified entrenchments, had abandoned them; but Frederick regarded this unexpected and imprudent step of his opponent as an omen of victory. On entering the chamber where he wished to distribute the pass-words, he said with a smile to those present, "The fox has left his den, and I will punish his arrogance!" He then rapidly distributed the orders for attack, which was to take place on the following day.

The morning of the awful 5th of December came, and the army quickly got under arms to meet the enemy. Frederick could obtain no distinct information as to the Prince of Lorraine's position, but felt confident that he should soon be able to discover the enemy's most vulnerable point, and that the attainment of this knowledge would be the means of his obtaining the victory. He was prepared for every event. Placing himself at the head of his army, he selected an officer and fifty hussars to serve as his escort, and addressed them as follows: "I shall expose myself more than usual this day during the battle: you, sir, with your fifty men, are to form my body-guard. You are not to leave me for an instant, and to take care that I do not fall into the hands of the canaille. Should I fall, cover my body quickly with your mantle, and place it in a wagon, without mentioning the fact to any one. The battle is to be continued and the enemy beaten." The leading columns of the army had commenced singing some pious hymns during the march, and the commander inquired of Frederick whether the soldiers should not remain silent. "No," replied he, "let them alone. God will certainly grant me victory this day with such an army under my command."

The Prussian advanced-guard now arrived in the neighborhood of a village, in front of which some of the enemy's cavalry was drawn up in line. At first it was generally thought that this was the wing of the Austrian army; but it was soon afterwards discovered that the wing stood further back. In order, however, to be quite certain, Frederick directed an attack to be made on this line, which was speedily driven in, and a number of prisoners secured. Frederick ordered the prisoners to be conducted in front of the ranks, and led away to Neumarkt, in order to inspire his troops with fresh feelings of courage; but this was almost unnecessary, for he could scarcely control the ardor of the hussars, who had made this charge, and were now panting to engage the main body of the enemy.

Taking up a position on a hill which commanded a view of the whole field of battle, Frederick gazed upon the innumerable lines, covering more than five English miles, which opposed his march. In their centre lay the village of Leuthen. From the charge made on the cavalry, which was in advance of the Austrian right wing, the enemy supposed that Frederick would attack them in that quarter, and accordingly made rapid evolutions to strengthen it. But Frederick had discovered that by attacking the enemy's left far greater advantages were to be obtained, and accordingly deployed his army, which was sheltered by a range of hills, in a lateral direction. The Austrians noticing this movement without being able to guess Frederick's intention, conceived that he wished to avoid a battle, and Marshal Daun said to the Prince of Lorraine, " Those people are moving off; let them alone!"

Towards noon the Prussian army had arrived in the flank of the enemy's left wing, and at one o'clock the engagement commenced. Prince Charles had been so imprudent as to post Wurtemberg and Bavarian troops, on whom but little reliance could be placed, in this quarter. These were speedily routed, and flying towards Leuthen were received with frequent discharges of musketry from their own allies. This flight caused complete confusion in the left wing of the Austrian army. The Prussians immediately charged the Austrian centre, which was covered by the village of Leuthen; the latter, from its breadth, and its affording no entrance, rendered the attack exceedingly difficult, and a sharp fusilade opened on the Prussian ranks from the different courts and farm-yards. A desperate struggle ensued round Leuthen. A battalion of the Prussian guard stormed the village. The commander paused on seeing the difficulties of his situation, and was for a moment undecided as to how he should act. The senior captain, Von Möllendorf, who afterwards became a distinguished field-marshal, called out to him not to hesitate, but the former could not make up his mind; upon which Möllendorf sprang forward with the words, "Away with him! Men, follow me!" A barricaded doorway was assailed, the planks knocked in and torn down. Ten muskets lay levelled—the leader, at the head of his courageous band, dashed on. The battalion pierced through the open gateway, and breaking up into bodies, became master, but not until after an obstinate resistance, of the whole village. The Austrians tried to form in position on the heights behind the village, whilst the Prussians were now in a measure protected by Leuthen. The Prussian guns spread devastation far and wide throughout the enemy's lines, which were concentrated in dense masses, and the struggle lasted for hours without either party advancing or yielding. It was now four o'clock, when the Austrian cavalry of the right wing made a charge on the flank of the Prussians; but for this the Prussian cavalry composing the left wing had been long waiting, and, taking the former in the flank and rear, soon drove them from the field of battle. This was the signal for a general flight. The Austrian army rushed in wild confusion across the Schweidnitz, leaving behind a numerous body of prisoners; when night came on and put an end to the carnage.

Sagacity, tact, and courage had, during four short hours, obtained one of the most glorious victories recorded in history, over an immeasurably superior force. Frederick's measures were laid in the most masterly style. Like the musician, who by a slight pressure of the finger brings forth a flood of melody from the pipes of the organ, so had he brought all the movements of his army into one splendid and harmonious combination. It was *his* spirit which inspired the motions of his troops—which dwelt in their hearts and steeled their strength.

On the field of battle Frederick conferred on the Prince of Dessau, who had led on the grand attack, a high mark of distinction, by raising him to the dignity of a field-marshal, which he did in the following words: "Field-marshal, I congratulate you on the success of the battle." The prince, being busied in several duties relating to the service, did not catch the exact expressions of the greeting. Frederick accordingly repeated his salutation in a louder tone. "You don't hear me! I congratulate you, field-marshal!" The latter returned his thanks, and the king replied, "You have rendered me more assistance in this battle, and have executed my orders better than any one has ever yet done!"

A dense fog had spread itself over the field of battle, but the Prussians formed with as much regularity as was possible under the circumstances. The darkness of the night rendered any pursuit of the enemy impossible, and thus saved it from complete annihilation. But Frederick was not disposed to rest—he was determined by strong and decisive measures to secure the fruits of this glorious day. It was a main object with him to secure the bridge which crossed the Schweidnitz, near Lissa, in order to be able to continue the pursuit on the following day. To effect this object he selected Zieten and a troop of hussars, and set out with a few guns on the road to Lissa. A light was observed in an hostelry on the roadside, and after rapping at the door, a person was sent in to demand a lantern. The landlord, not liking to lose his lantern, came in person, and Frederick ordered him to hold his stirrup and serve as guide. In this way they proceeded in the neighborhood of Lissa, and Frederick directed the innkeeper to inform him of the noble guests who had passed the night in his house, and of the haughty language

they had used towards the Prussians. Every one was listening with attention to the singular and humorous details, when on a sudden between fifty and sixty shots were discharged at the lantern, and some of the horses were wounded. Frederick dispatched one of his aides-de-camp to the army to fetch some of the first grenadier battalions, and until this reinforcement arrived he made his troops halt, and examined the path, but no further danger could be discovered. The troops entered Lissa in perfect silence. The streets were empty; but frequently lights were seen, and much life was observable in all the houses. Some Austrian soldiers, who were in the act of carrying bundles of straw out of the houses, were seized, and admitted that they were carrying the straw to the bridge in order to set it on fire. This visit of the Prussians had not, however, altogether escaped attention; a body of Austrian soldiers had quietly assembled, and suddenly opened a sharp fire on the Prussians, which caused several of the grenadiers to fall by Frederick's side. The Prussians had in the interim got their cannons into play, and returned this greeting without loss of time. At the same moment a well-sustained fusilade opened from the different houses, which was answered by the grenadiers firing at the windows from whence the discharge came. All was now one scene of general confusion. Frederick quietly remarked to his staff: "Gentlemen, follow me; I am well acquainted with this ground," and immediately rode to the left, over a drawbridge leading to the mansion of the lord of the manor of Lissa, followed by his adjutants. He had scarcely arrived at the entrance of the mansion, when he was met by a number of Austrian officers of different ranks, who had just taken their supper, and having been aroused by the firing, were looking after their horses, and rushing with lights in their hands from the rooms and staircases. They remained completely petrified with astonishment on seeing Frederick and his adjutants dismount, and welcome them with the word—
"*Bon soir, messieurs!* you would not, certainly, have

expected to find me here. Can we not also find a lodging here?" They were superior in point of numbers, and might by a bold stroke have gained possession of the person of the king, but the confusion was so great that no one thought of this. The Austrian generals and staff-officers seized the lights, and conducted the king up the staircase into one of the best rooms. They here presented one another to him, and an agreeable conversation on general subjects ensued. In the meantime Prussian adjutants and other officers continued to arrive in such numbers that Frederick at last asked in surprise where they all came from, and then heard, to his astonishment, that his army was on its way to Lissa.

In the enthusiasm of victory the whole army had set out on its march, as soon as the order arrived for the battalions of the grenadiers to follow him to Lissa. The troops had silently and seriously broken up the camp, and each man marched forward, buried in deep reflection on the importance of this bloody day. The cold night-breeze swept along the fields, carrying with it the groans and the wailing of the wounded and the dying. A grenadier set up the old German chant, "*Nun danket alle Gott*," (Now thank ye all the Lord,) which was soon taken up by the whole army, consisting of more than 25,000 men. The darkness and tranquillity of the night—the horrors of the battle-field, where at every step the foot trod upon a corpse—lent a degree of awful solemnity to the song; and even the wounded forgot for a time their sufferings whilst taking part in this general act of thanksgiving. A new spirit of strength sustained the weary warriors, when on a sudden a loud and long-continued shout burst from every tongue on hearing the cannonade in Lissa, and each vied with the other as to who should be the first to come to the aid of his sovereign. Such of the enemy as were in Lissa were instantly taken prisoners.

The Austrians had on this day alone lost 27,000 men, 116 guns, 51 flags, and 4,000 wagons; whilst the loss on the part of the Prussians amounted to little more than

6,000 men. But at dawn of the following morning the Prussian army pushed irresistibly forward to secure the advantages acquired through this victory. The foe was pursued in all directions, and large bodies of prisoners and an immense quantity of booty fell into the hands of the Prussians. An Austrian corps of 18,000 men had thrown itself into Breslau. Frederick laid siege to the town with 14,000 men, bombarded it, notwithstanding the extreme cold, and on the 21st of December the Austrians were forced to surrender. Great quantities of ammunition, and a well-stored military chest fell into Frederick's hands. A few days afterwards Liegnitz, which had been but slightly fortified by the Austrians, likewise surrendered; a large quantity of stores fell here into the hands of the Prussians, but the garrison was allowed to retire. Schweidnitz was now the only place of which the enemy still retained possession, and it was deemed unadvisable to assail it, as the frozen state of the ground prevented the necessary breaching operations. The place was, however, closely invested, and towards the end of the year, with the exception of Schweidnitz, the whole of Silesia had been evacuated by the Austrians. The Prussians now entered their winter-quarters, and of the gigantic Austrian army only 37,000 men reached the frontiers of Bohemia.

CHAPTER XXIV.

OPENING OF THE CAMPAIGN OF 1758. THE EXPEDITION TO MORAVIA.

WELL might Frederick now hope, that after a year of such bloody toil—after the fatal blow which he had just inflicted on Austria, and which, as it were, annihilated all its plans of vengeance,—well might he hope, we say, that Maria Theresa would not be wholly indisposed to listen to overtures of peace; and in fact, some such disposition did at first appear recognizable in the conduct of the imperial cabinet. The tone of the language used in the documents which still continued to issue from the imperial cabinet and court-chamber of the empire became somewhat more subdued, and assumed a less indecorous and insulting character; and further, Count Kaunitz displayed considerable activity and zeal in warning Frederick of a conspiracy which had been formed against his life. The latter treated the affair of the conspiracy as a mere fiction, but wrote, notwithstanding, a letter of thanks for the communication which had been made; not forgetting, however, to add, that there were two modes of assassination,—the one stabbed its victim with a dagger, the other with calumnious lampoons. As to the first mode he felt little anxiety, but as to the second he was somewhat more sensitive. He, however, neglected no means, as far as in him lay, of courting peace. He sent the captive Prince Lobkowitz to Vienna to open negotiations, and wrote personally to the empress on the subject. "Were it not for the battle of the 18th of June," he said, in this letter, "in which fortune frowned upon me, I should probably have had an opportunity of paying you my homage in person. It is likewise probable, though against my nature, that your beauty and high accomplishments might have conquered the conqueror; it is possible that we might have found some means of becoming reconciled. You had achieved some slight advantages in Silesia, but this was not of long continuance; and the last battle was attended with so much bloodshed, that I cannot think of it without feelings of horror. I have taken advantage of my success, and shall be in a condition to advance again on Bohemia and Moravia. Consider well, my dear cousin, this state of things, and weigh maturely the characters of those in whom you are about to repose your confidence. It can hardly escape your own observation, that you are plunging your kingdom into misery, that you are the cause of the shedding of so much blood, and that you cannot conquer him, who, if you would but consent to accept of him as a friend, as he is your near relative, could, if joined with you, make the whole world tremble. I write this in the fullest conviction of my heart, and trust that it may produce the effect which I desire. But should you be resolved on pushing matters to their worst, I am equally resolved on exerting all my powers and energies to meet the struggle. I cannot, however, refrain from assuring you, that I should with pain see the downfall of a princess so well worthy the admiration of the whole world. If your allies remain as firmly devoted to your interest as is their duty, my overthrow is, I admit, certain; but in this there will be no disgrace; and history will record it to my praise, that I have striven to shield a fellow prince-elector (Hanover) from oppression, that I have not aided in aggrandizing the power of the house of Bourbon, and that I have resisted the combined exertions of two empresses and three kings." It were indeed difficult to use more convincing language.

Of course the most wily measures had been taken in Vienna to prevent Maria Theresa from being made properly aware of the horrors and miseries which the war had entailed upon her subjects, and of the disgrace which had been, on the 5th of December, inflicted on the Austrian arms. This was carried, in fact, to such a pitch, that the events of the battle of Leuthen were treated in their details with the utmost poetic licence, in order to excuse the catastrophe; and as French policy at this critical moment contributed its quota for the perplexing and baffling of all peaceful counsels, the old thirst for vengeance and inveterate international hatred which Maria Theresa had so long cherished in her bosom burst forth anew. The negotiations with the Prince Lobkowitz were declined with a degree of hauteur, which would almost have led one to think that the King of Prussia, and not the powerful Austrian army, had been beaten at Leuthen.

The alliance between Austria, France, and Russia became, on the other hand, more close. France promised new levies and further subsidies to Russia. The Russian Empress sought to make amends for the evacuation of Prussia by her army, which had taken place during her illness and against her will, by ordering a second incursion on Prussia to be immediately undertaken. Frederick, who had but just taken up his winter-quarters, could not prevent the execution of this measure. The Russian army had already set out from Memel, under the command of Field-marshal Fermor, on the 16th of January, and meeting no opposition, entered Königsberg with great solemnity six days afterwards. The town was obliged to do homage to the Russian Empress on Frederick's birthday. All public monies were seized; the administration was placed under the guidance of Russian officials, and the whole of East Prussia regarded as a Russian province. Fermor was raised to the rank of governor-general, and was invested with the dignity of an earl.

Frederick's alliance with England was necessarily strengthened by this state of things. William Pitt, who was then at the head of the government, clearly recognized Frederick's greatness; and taking advantage of the

CAMPAIGN OF 1758. EXPEDITION TO MORAVIA.

popularity of the Prussian cause with both people and parliament, succeeded in concluding, on the 11th of April, 1758, a new treaty of alliance and subsidy, by which England engaged to reinforce the Hanoverian army with English troops, and to pay an annual subsidy of six hundred and seventy thousand pounds. Frederick engaging on his part to augment the same army by the addition of some Prussian regiments. The acceptance of subsidies from foreign nations did not quite accord with his chivalrous feelings, and he would have preferred that an English fleet had been dispatched to operate in the Baltic. This latter was, however, declined by England, and as the dukedom of Prussia and the Westphalian provinces were in the hands of the enemy, Frederick found himself imperatively constrained to accept of the pecuniary assistance. Nay, he actually found it unavoidably necessary, in order to meet his most pressing emergencies, to still further increase this sum, by having it re-coined and re-issued, so as to form ten millions of thalers of depreciated value. For, notwithstanding that Saxony paid very heavy contributions, and Mecklenburg, whose sovereign duke betrayed the most determined hostility to Frederick, and was of all German sovereigns the most urgent in requiring that he should be declared under the ban, was obliged to submit to still harsher fiscal measures; yet all this was insufficient to complete those equipments which the overpowering numbers of his foes rendered indispensable.

The greater part of the time which Frederick passed in Breslau was devoted to the reorganization of the army and its restoration to its former footing. The severe engagements of the previous year, the oppressive marches, the pestilent diseases engendered in the hospitals, had reduced his forces to but two-thirds of their original number. It was now a principal aim to fill up the ranks with all possible expedition, and to make the host of raw recruits as well acquainted with the minutiæ of the Prussian drill as was practicable in so limited a period; but the ordering of the administration in Silesia was not forgotten. A severe scrutiny and investigation into the conduct of all such as had proved traitors on the entrance of the Austrians was threatened, and the property of the fugitives confiscated. The revenues of the Prince-Bishop Count Schaffgotsch, who had passed over the frontier, and whose more than equivocal conduct had rendered even the cabinet of Vienna deaf to his overtures, were seized.

Whilst the Prussian soldiers were as yet refreshing themselves after the toils of the last year's campaign, and the recruits were being disciplined, Ferdinand, Duke of Brunswick, at the head of the Hanoverian and allied troops, had already opened the campaign with the French. As early as the month of February he had broken up his winter-cantonments, freed Hanover, and driven the whole French army before him. The fugitives fled without pause or intermission across the snow-covered plains of Westphalia back to the Rhine, and did not even halt until they had arrived in Wesel; 10,000 of the enemy fell into Ferdinand's hands. The conqueror granted his troops here a short interval of repose, and awaited the reinforcements from England. Through the brilliant success of this action Frederick was relieved from all dangers impending from France; and subsequent events kept the French at a distance from his territories. On the 1st of June Frederick crossed the Rhine, and beat the French army, which had been strongly reinforced, on the 23d near Crefeld. After several other successes he was finally compelled to retire, on the entrance of Soubise and his army, into Hessen; but the manner in which he effected the passage of the Rhine was so brilliant, that it tended but to heighten his glory. Soubise's army, although twice victorious over isolated corps of the allies, did not succeed in obtaining any solid advantage for France. Ferdinand's marches and positions were so judicious, as to prevent the two French armies from forming a junction, and compelled them, towards the close of the year, to take up their winter-

CAMPAIGN OF 1758. EXPEDITION TO MORAVIA.

quarters on the Rhine. Soubise took up his position on the German side, whilst the French army encamped between the Rhine and the Meuse.

That this year's campaign should be conducted on the same system that had proved so repeatedly successful hitherto, was one of Frederick's earliest resolves. Instead of awaiting an attack, or allowing time for a junction of the hostile armies, he cherished the idea of being able to throw himself unexpectedly on some one of his many foes, and through its discomfiture to be in a position to rout the second. That it was impossible for him to prevent the Russians from occupying Prussia Proper was perfectly clear, but separated as this was by means of Poland from his other provinces, he considered himself warranted in assuming that the Russian army, which was as yet wholly unprovided with the necessary stores or magazines, would be so impeded in its movements as not to be prepared to assume the offensive till the following summer. He accordingly determined on directing his strength in the first instance against Austria. Prospects of success seemed here more probable, inasmuch as the Austrian army, enfeebled by the losses and disasters of the former year and the epidemic diseases which had broken out amongst the men, would certainly require much time and pains ere it could be possibly put in an effective state.

It now became a paramount consideration to compel the Austrians to evacuate Schweidnitz—the only point in the whole of Silesia which was still in their power. As soon as the season permitted, which was about the beginning of April, a regular siege was laid to the town, trenches were opened, and on the 18th of the same month the garrison, consisting of a corps of about 5,000 men, surrendered, in consequence of the capture by storm of one of the forts.

The Austrian army stationed in Bohemia was now in momentary expectation of Frederick's attempting an incursion on that country. Field-marshal Daun had been

invested with the sole command of the Austrians, a post
which Maria Theresa wished to see filled by the Prince of
Lorraine; but the latter, from feelings of disappointment at the numerous reverses which the Austrian arms
had under him sustained, became disgusted with the
service, and retired from this post. Daun's levies were
at this moment very far from being complete; and owing
to this circumstance, as well as the superabundant foresight which characterized all his acts, he deemed it necessary to throw up enormous entrenchments along the
Bohemian frontiers. Whole woods were hewn down for
the purpose of forming glacis and abattis Frederick did
all in his power to confirm his adversary in the unnecessary apprehensions in which the latter indulged, and
in the meantime made all necessary preparations, in perfect secrecy, for the execution of a far different project
from that which had caused his opponent such a gratuitous
expenditure of time and labor. Hardly had the month of
May opened, when, before any one had the least idea of
it, his army was drawn up in Moravia, and dispositions
were being made for the immediate siege of Ollmutz.

In exact proportion to the rapidity with which the
main body of the Prussian army had entered Moravia,
was the tediousness attending the motions of the heavy
train of artillery and battering-ordnance intended for the
siege. Daun, in consequence of this delay, gained sufficient
time to follow the king into Moravia and assume a
threatening attitude. He remained satisfied, however,
with harassing the Prussian army with his light troops,
looking forward to more favorable circumstances for more
decisive success. The preparations for the siege had
been in the interim pushed forward with much vigor, but
errors of a very serious nature had been committed by
the officers entrusted with its conduct. The first line of
batteries had been raised at such a distance from the
enemy's works that but few of the guns took effect, and
on new batteries being raised, more within range, it was
found necessary to wait for fresh arrivals of ordnance, so

that but very little progress was made, and thus the besieged gained sufficient time to repair such breaches as were from time to time made; and, further, the Prussian army being too weak for an effective investment of the town, a connection between the latter and Daun's army was maintained, and means were even found to effect a considerable reinforcement of the garrison.

All hopes of success now rested on the timely arrival of a large convoy from Silesia, which was to bring all the necessary munitions for the Prussian army. Zieten had been dispatched with his corps to strengthen the escort of the same. But in this case Daun had adopted the most admirable measures for the destruction of his adversary. A corps far superior in numbers to that under Daun assailed the convoy in the narrow mountain-gorges through which it had to pass. Pieces of heavy ordnance were brought to bear on the barricades which the Prussians, by overturning some of the baggage-wagons, had hastily erected. The powder-tumbrils were blown up, the horses shot, and the escort became mobbed and thrown into frightful confusion. A considerable number of recruits from Pomerania and Mark formed part of the escort; but few of them were taken prisoners, the greater proportion maintained the struggle to the last, and their lifeless bodies, which strewed the ground, bore ample witness to the dreadful nature of the struggle, and fully justified their proverbially high character for fidelity and unswerving fortitude. Zieten was compelled to retire towards the Silesian frontier, and was, during this regressive movement, exposed to repeated skirmishes with the enemy's light horse.

Nothing now remained for Frederick but to raise the siege, abandon the entire enterprise, and withdraw his army from Moravia. But the most frightful difficulties were to be encountered in the execution of this movement. Summoning all the higher officers to his presence at headquarters, he informed them of his determination, and addressed them as follows: "Gentlemen, the enemy has found means to destroy the convoy which was on its way from Silesia. In consequence of this disastrous circumstance I am compelled to raise the siege of Ollmutz. Officers are not, however, to suppose that therefore all is lost. No; you may be assured that all shall be repaired, and the enemy have occasion to remember this circumstance. Officers are to breathe courage into the hearts of their men, and not permit murmurings of any kind. I entertain no apprehension whatever that any of my officers will display anything like pusillanimity; but should I, contrary to all expectation, find this to be the case in any individual instance, I shall visit it with the utmost severity. I shall now march, and wherever we meet the enemy I will attack him, be he posted where he may, in front of one or several batteries. Yet"—here the king paused, and rubbing his brow with the handle of his Spanish cane, continued—"I shall do nothing without consideration and forethought; but I cherish the conviction that every officer, and, indeed, every private, will, when opportunity offers, do his duty as he has hitherto done it."

And, certainly, matters had now assumed a character which made the most mature and deliberate calculation, coupled with the most heroic valor, absolutely essential for escape from dangers of such magnitude. But on a dispassionate survey of the acts of this mighty monarch, we find that he then invariably commands our highest admiration when dangers begin to thicken, and his fall seems, according to the calculations of ordinary prudence, inevitable. In such cases the powers of his mind seemed to expand to a degree baffling all human calculations, and his genius was almost always found equal to the emergency. He was now with his little army, whose march was in the last degree impeded by the number of the guns and a convoy of 4,000 wagons, to retire from the centre of a land, in which every point of egress was held by hosts of enemies, and whose inhabitants were actuated by feelings of no ordinary animosity towards him. The whole world

CAMPAIGN OF 1758. EXPEDITION TO MORAVIA. 273

watched with anxiety the solution of this grand difficulty. But Frederick's arrangements bore the stamp of a mastermind. Daun naturally supposed that his enemy would take the shortest path in his return to Silesia, and Frederick strove to confirm him a second time in his false assumption. To this end he dispatched a trooper to the commandant of Neisse, with written orders to have bread and provender in readiness against the arrival of the army. The trooper played his part so skilfully that he fell into the hands of the enemy, who, not suspecting any stratagem, speedily made themselves masters of his person and his apparently important dispatch. Daun now turned all his attention to the occupation of every road and pass leading to Silesia, and Frederick thereby gained several days' time for effecting his retreat upon Bohemia, a direction almost diametrically opposed to that which Daun felt satisfied he would take. On perceiving himself outmanœuvred, Daun hastened with all expedition to repair his error, and pursue the enemy. The Austrian light troops now attempted to oppose the progress of the Prussian columns through the defiles of the Moravian hills. But all such assaults, despite the varied difficulties of the ground, were invariably repulsed. Frederick gained Bohemia, and pitched his camp near Königingrätz on the 12th of July, without having suffered any considerable loss, and without Daun being in a condition to come to a general engagement. From thence Frederick dispatched his cumbrous battering-train to Glatz. He would now, as soon as his army had recovered in some measure from its fatigue, and been slightly reinforced, have gladly concluded the whole expedition with a decisive battle, but Daun was too prudent to abandon the strongly-entrenched position which he had taken up in face of the Prussian lines. Frederick therefore fell back on Silesia, about the beginning of August, to the astonishment and admiration of the world, after having effected a retreat only comparaable to the memorable one of the 10,000 Greeks under Xenophon. The imperial court caused a medal to be struck in honor of its field-marshal, who had remained a modest spectator of the successful retreat of the Prussians, on which he is honored with the title of the German Fabius Maximus, with the inscription underneath, "Thou hast conquered by thy procrastination; continue to conquer!"

Perhaps it was during this retreat that the incident occurred, in which Frederick, by his extraordinary presence of mind, escaped most imminent personal peril. He had ridden forward, attended by a small escort, for the purpose of reconnoitring the line of march, when some Pandoors, who lay concealed in a thicket, discharged several shots at the small party. Frederick had taken no notice of this interruption, till one of his escort suddenly called out to him that a Pandoor was concealed behind a tree close by, and was aiming at him. Frederick looked round, caught a glimpse of the Pandoor as he stood with his piece levelled, and raising his cane, which he always carried, even when on horseback, called out in a threatening tone, "You, sir!" The Pandoor lowered his musket in a fright, and uncovering his head, remained in an attitude of homage until the king passed by.

CHAPTER XXX.

CONTINUATION OF THE CAMPAIGN OF 1758. ZORNDORF.

ESSENTIALLY characteristic of the Seven Years' War, and the peculiar relations which gave Frederick so many opportunities for a display of his talents as a tactician, was the circumstance, that he was ever hurried from enterprise to enterprise; that no other means was left him of combating the foes, which from every side assailed him, than the ceaseless execution of the most rapid and distant marches, and the compensation in activity for the small number of his troops. The year that had just closed had seen him in Bohemia, Lusatia, Thuringia, Saxony, and Silesia; and now, though but just returned from Moravia and Bohemia, he was obliged to direct his steps without loss of time in an opposite direction. The Russians, under the command of Field-marshal Fermor, having put their ponderous army in motion, were advancing through the northern provinces of the then Poland, (West Prussia and Posen,) and had, on the 2d of August, crossed the frontier of New Mark, threatening the heart of Frederick's kingdom, with all the horrors which uncivilized warfare brings in its train; for moderate as their conduct was on the occupation of Prussia Proper, which had been from thenceforward considered as a Russian province, the savage barbarities perpetrated by them on such places as they regarded as hostile territories knew no bounds. Fire, bloodshed, and havoc marked their path; the blooming meads through which they passed became instantly transformed into desolate wastes; the simoom, or sirocco, was not more desolating in its effects.

As the Russians approached the borders of Mark, a Prussian corps, which had previously fought in Prussia, and now, under the command of Count Dohna, held the Swedes locked in at Stralsund, advanced to meet them. Too weak to attempt any decisive step in the face of an enemy so superior, Dohna took up a position on the Oder, and contented himself with covering the left bank of the stream, and strengthening the garrison in the fortress of Cüstrin, before Fermor advanced with his main strength upon it. The nature of the ground, which was marshy, prevented a regular siege; but Fermor confidently hoped that the garrison would be induced to surrender on a bombardment, and that he should thus obtain a strong depôt for arms on the Oder. An immense number of bombshells and grape were accordingly thrown into the town on the 15th of August, which soon set the houses on fire. The inhabitants and a number of the peasantry who had sought refuge behind the walls of Cüstrin from the barbarian hordes, saw all their goods become a prey to the flames, and could save nothing beyond their lives, and even these but by flying across the Oder. Fermor continued to bombard the town while a shot remained in his tumbrils; but his intentions were nevertheless frustrated. The fortifications remained uninjured, and on the commandant being summoned on the sixth day, with the threat that in the event of his not surrendering the town should be stormed, the latter declared his determination to hold out to the last man.

A special corps of the Russian army had been in the meantime sent against Pomerania, and the Swedish army was summoned to join the Russians. The danger had now reached its height; but the Swedes were too tedious in their movements; they delayed setting out for some time, acting on the advice of the French ambassador, who wished them to join the French army on the Elbe; but the deliverer was already at hand. On the 21st of August Frederick arrived in the camp of Count Dohna before Cüstrin, bringing with him 14,000 picked men of the

Silesian army, with whom he had hurried forward, on receiving intelligence of the dangers that impended, in flying marches from the Bohemian frontiers. Immediately on his arrival he mustered Count Dohna's corps. The stately parade in which the former passed in review surprised him, and turning to Dohna, he remarked in a loud tone, alluding perhaps to their defeat of the former year, "Your men have been polishing themselves tremendously; I have some with me who look like adders, but they bite!"

Deep was the sorrow and fiery the thirst for vengeance which must have seized the heart of the king, as he gazed on the smouldering ruins of the town, and the desolation which barbarian hordes spread through his land, and listened to the miserable tales of the inhabitants as they demanded him to have their cruel distresses relieved. He kindly consoled the unhappy sufferers. "Children," said he, as he listened attentively to the minute details of their misfortunes, "children, I could not come sooner, otherwise this misfortune had never occurred. Have but patience, and I will build up everything anew!" And he kept his word. He immediately ordered a sum of 200,000 thalers to be distributed amongst them to meet their most pressing necessities, and calmly resolved on bringing the enemy to a speedy and severe account. Whilst the guns were playing on the Russian entrenchments in the neighborhood of Cüstrin, and every one expected that he would here make a serious attack, he had given orders to his army to hold itself in readiness, so as to be able, on the approach of night, to cross the Oder unobserved, a short distance below Cüstrin. As the army was preparing to set out, he rode once more along the lines, and greeting his valiant veterans, called out to them in a friendly tone, "Children, will you join me?" A universal shout of "We will!" was the response. One of the men said to him, "If we had but those Russian pack-horses, we should get on faster!" The king replied jokingly, "We shall soon get them!"

On the 23d of August the passage across the stream was effected, and the enemy outflanked by deploying in a wide circuit. The whole army was bursting with feelings of the most indignant rage at the horrors which they had seen perpetrated. As far as the eye could reach nothing was to be seen but burning or smouldering villages. The wretched inhabitants lay crouching within the recesses of the woods, robbed by the enemy of their last means of subsistence. The humanity of the soldier gladly shared his bread with them, and in return received from the peasant water to quench his burning thirst; while in many places large casks and vessels of water were, out of a kind feeling of precaution, placed on the roadside, devoted to the same purpose.

On the morning of the 25th of August Frederick had so completely turned the position of the Russian army, as to be able to assail it in the most vulnerable point. An extensive plain gave him ample room for an unimpeded assault, whilst the marshy moors in the enemy's rear and flank, and a small arm of the Oder, kept them hemmed in. The bridges over the latter had been broken down by Frederick's order, to cut off all retreat. He hoped to annihilate the whole hostile army, and with one blow seal its fate in blood. There was no time for hesitation, as he must expect that the Austrians would soon take advantage of his absence, and attempt some dangerous enterprise; for this reason he had not attacked the enemy's baggage, which was stored up within a barricade of wagons at some distance from the army, and of which he might readily have made himself master, and thus compelled the foe, without further bloodshed, to leave a land in which it could no longer support itself; but the execution of this design would have required several weeks for its accomplishment.

The Prussian army consisted of 32,760 men, that of the Russians about 52,000. The latter had, on Frederick's approach, formed an immense quadrangular figure, with the cavalry and followers in the centre. This disposition had been found very efficient during the wars with the Turks, in checking the disorderly assaults of irregular troops, but was not very valuable when opposed to a well-disciplined European army. Frederick resolved on advancing with his left wing against the encumbered mass of the enemy's lines, hoping by an impetuous shock to break in at its angle, and from thence to spread confusion and devastation throughout its thickly crowded members. Between the two armies lay the village of Zorndorf; hosts of Cossacks swarmed all round and had set the village on fire, the smoke of which was impelled into the face of the Russians, and prevented them from perceiving the enemy's dispositions.

At nine o'clock the attack commenced; the advanced-guard and left wing of the Prussian army moved on the Russian right flank, which was separated by a marsh from the main army. A frightful cannonade then opened, carrying unheard-of devastation through the deep Russian lines. One ball alone is said to have swept down not less than forty-two men. The camp-followers in the centre now fell into confusion. The horses with their wagons burst out on all sides, breaking the lines; and it was with much difficulty that they were afterwards drawn up in the rear of the army. The Prussian infantry, taking advantage of this confusion, quickly advanced, and keeping up a well-sustained fusillade, overthrew the Russian foremost ranks; but this onslaught was attended with many inconveniences. The men were at one time separated, at another led on in bodies too feeble to prove effective. The enemy's generals took advantage of this; the Russian infantry and cavalry burst with the wild shout of "Arra, arra!" (victory!) upon the Prussians, whose infantry retired in confusion. The Prussian cavalry under Seidlitz had, up to that moment, been calmly advancing, but as the Russians were commencing a disorderly pursuit of their enemies, Seidlitz, taking advantage of the propitious moment, gave the signal to charge, and in an instant his warriors rushed in regular array on the hostile mass. A frightful struggle now ensued, being almost without parallel in the history of European warfare. For though the first ranks of the Russians were hewn down, line after line held its ground without flinching. As successive battalions were cut off, new masses congregated together, and with their bodies opposed such a bulwark against the advance of the enemy, as could only be carried by a complete massacre. Although the whole of their ammunition was already spent, still they did not yield one pace until they sank sabred by their adversaries. This massacre lasted for hours; whole detachments of Russians fell upon their own baggage, plundered the provision-wagons, and staved the casks of spirits, thirsting for their intoxicating contents. The officers emptied the casks; when not a few threw themselves on the earth, and putting their mouths to the ground, drank up the liquor from out the dust; whilst others, in a wild spirit of disappointment, turned their arms against their commanders, and murdered those who spilt the inebriating liquor. At length, about noon, the battle ceased on both sides. Such of the Russians as were not slain were driven into the marshes; and Seidlitz withdrew his valiant hosts from before the hostile cannonade, which was now opened upon him from the opposite side.

The other sections of both armies had not as yet taken any part in the combat; but Frederick, who was present in the right wing, now made his disposition for a general assault, and advanced. In his front stood a Prussian battery, which, as a considerable space intervened between it and the lines, was covered by a special battalion. Upon this a vast body of the enemy's cavalry now rushed, took both the battery and the battalion captive, and then advanced against the main body of the army, but was here received with so hot a fire as to be speedily obliged to retire. On this the captive battalion broke away, and shouting, "Victory! Long live the king!" rode back to the Prussians. Frederick advancing to meet them, cried out, "Children, do not shout victory awhile; I will tell you when it is time for that!" At the same instant new hosts of Russian cavalry rushed on the Prussian left wing, which was composed of the regiments under Count Dohna, some of whom had already fled on the first assault on the left wing. A panic seized them a second time, and they once more fled most shamefully from the field of battle. It was here again reserved for Seidlitz, the hero of the day, to ward off the imminent danger which now threatened. Dashing with his valiant troops down upon the enemy, he drove the Russian cavalry back in wild disorder, and in the face of a well-sustained fire of musketry and grape, charged such of the Russian lines as still stood. Frederick, too, soon came on with the veteran battalions of his infantry; and now a second butchery ensued, similar to that which had already crushed the left wing of the Russians. The fight was now carried on man to man, it being impossible for either division to retain its ranks. Russians and Prussians, cavalry and infantry, all were compressed into one dense mass. Frederick was himself engaged in the middle of the affray, and his pages taken captive, wounded, and killed by his side. The frightful dust of this burning day, together with the smoke perpetually issuing from the cannons' mouths, made it impossible to recognize the face of friend or foe. His troops could recognize their king solely by his voice. Neither party surpassed the other in point of valor, but the discipline of the Prussians eventually prevailed. Their leader succeeded in again drawing them from out the wild mingled mass, and as evening sank, such of the Russians as had not been slaughtered were driven from the field of battle.

Whilst Frederick was mustering his army for the night, the Russians, in single bodies, were seeking safety in flight. But as the bridges were everywhere broken down, the entire dispersion of the army, which their leaders sought in every way to rally, was prevented. A body of some thousand Russians had again taken up a place on the field of battle, and Frederick marched his troops once more against them. But this last attack, which was every way unimportant, proved unsuccessful, partly from want of ammunition, and partly owing to the fact of the assailants belonging to those battalions of the left wing which had previously disgraced themselves, now for the third time flying before the enemy's fire. This petty, and, as regarded the fate of the day, perfectly immaterial success, served the Russian leaders as a basis for the braggart announcements of victory which they transmitted to Petersburg and the allied courts, where they met with full credence, and excited bright but deceptive hopes.

During the night the Russians had rallied, and on the following morning again appeared in battle array. It seemed as if a second engagement were about to ensue, in fact, a cannonade was opened, which lasted four hours. But the exhaustion on both sides was so great, and the want of ammunition so complete, that no serious engagement took place. Fermor now applied for a truce of a few days, ostensibly to bury the dead; which Frederick refused, replying that this was the duty of the conqueror. Fermor took advantage of the following night to creep round the left wing of the Prussian army, and regain his baggage, where he entrenched himself for the present.

The number of prisoners taken on the day of the battle of Zorndorf on either side was very insignificant, as quarter was neither given nor taken. We are even told that this was by the express directions of Frederick. It was not until the following day that a very considerable number of the discomfited Russians fell into the hands of their adversaries. The losses on the whole were very considerable. Frederick had lost upwards of 11,000 men, and the Russians double that number, together with 103 guns, and 27 ensigns and standards. "Heaven has this day granted another splendid victory to your majesty," said the English ambassador, who had accompanied Frederick, to the field, addressing the latter after the battle.

"Were it not for this man," replied Frederick, pointing to Seidlitz, " matters would now have worn a very gloomy aspect!" But Seidlitz modestly declined the compliment paid him, attributing the whole merit to the valor of the cavalry. Frederick felt bound to inform Marshal Daun of the real result of the battle of Zorndorf. A letter of the latter, addressed to Fermor, had fallen into his hands, and in it the Russian general was advised to avoid an engagement with so subtle an enemy, and one with whom he was not acquainted; he should rather wait until Daun's expedition against Saxony was concluded. Frederick now wrote to Daun, in allusion to the subject of this letter, " You were quite right in advising General Fermor to be on his guard against a subtle and crafty foe, whom you know better than he, for he has hazarded a battle and has been beaten."

Amongst the prisoners there happened to be five Russian generals: on their being presented to the king on the field of battle, he gave them to understand the sincere pain it caused him not to have a Siberia whither he could send them as a punishment for their barbarous mode of carrying on war, and gave orders that they should be treated with the same severity as Prussian officers experienced in Russia. They were thereupon lodged in the arched cellars under the fortifications of Cüstrin. On being led thither they protested strongly against so unseemly an abode, but the commandant of the town referred them to the declaration made by the king—" Gentlemen, you have not done me, but this poor town, the honor of battering it down; you have not left a single house standing. You must, consequently, content yourselves with the present lodgings for want of better." Frederick granted, however, some few days afterwards, permission to the Russian generals to leave the cellars, and hire lodgings in the suburbs of Cüstrin, which were not burnt down. Nay, on receiving intelligence that the Prussians were treated with more humanity in Petersburg, he even permitted them to go to Berlin, and there take part in all the court festivities. At that time prisoners of almost every European nation paid their homage to the queen on court-days in Berlin.

The Prussian and Russian armies having remained a few days in inactivity, Fermor retired to Landsberg, and Frederick moved after him in the same direction, but was obliged on the following day to desist from his original intention, and set out with a division of his army for Saxony, where his presence had become very necessary, a corps consisting of 16,000 men remaining behind to watch the movements of the Russians. Fermor now advanced into Pomerania, and joined to his other forces that division of his troops which was to have acted in concert with the Swedes. He then sent another corps to the coast of the Baltic to besiege Kolberg. The garrison of this fortress was very weak, but the militia and even the entire of the citizens took part in the defence. Repeated bombardments proved ineffectual, and even a storm was successfully repelled, although the Russians had already penetrated into the covered way. At length towards the close of October, the siege was raised, and the whole of the Russian army entered their winter-quarters on the other side of the Vistula. A special Prussian corps was dispatched, after the battle of Zorndorf, to check the motions of the Swedes.

CHAPTER XXXI.

CONCLUSION OF THE CAMPAIGN OF 1758—HOCHKIRCH.

As soon as Frederick had left the Bohemian frontiers, and advanced against the Russians, his enemies conceived it proper that so favorable an opportunity should not be neglected for incursive operations on his territories. The Prussian troops stationed in Saxony and Silesia not being very considerable in point of numbers, it would be easy to oppose such masses to them as must quite overwhelm them, and the absence of Frederick, who was in himself a host, was too advantageous a circumstance to be thrown away. The army of the empire, which had taken up its winter-quarters in Franconia, and had augmented its strength very considerably, now advanced on Bohemia, and proceeded in the direction of the Saxon frontier. Daun moved with the main body of the Austrian army towards Lusatia, and there erected his magazines. He could here, according to circumstances, either act in concert with the army of the empire in any operations against Saxony, or he could invade Silesia, or co-operate with the advancing Russians. With a view to this latter object he detached a corps of light troops, under General Loudon, which was to spread itself over Lower Lusatia, as far as the banks of the Oder. Loudon met with no considerable difficulties in this expedition, and was soon in a condition to take up a strong position in Peitz, a small old fortress, situated on an arm of the Spree, and thus to cover his future military operations. But this entry of the town did not take place without shedding new lustre on the Prussian name. Peitz was held by but fifty old Prussian pensioners. On the Austrians attempting to enter without any ceremony, they were repulsed, with the loss of several men. The Austrian leader now made preparations for a more regular assault, and summoned the commandant in due form to surrender. The latter, acting in accordance with the customs of honorable warfare, before coming to any decision made it a primary condition that he should be allowed to send two trusty officers from the fortress, with permission from the enemy to reconnoitre and examine whether the hostile corps were justified by its strength in demanding the evacuation of the place. The enemy granted the commandant's condition. The officers dispatched returned, and confessed their full belief in the superiority of the enemy's strength. The commandant accordingly capitulated, having made terms that he and his fifty veterans should be permitted to proceed to Berlin, and leaving to the conquerors nothing beyond a few accoutrements of little value.

Prince Henry, the king's brother, was commander-in-chief of the Saxon army. By means of small movable columns, he had succeeded in delaying the advance of the army of the empire. But so superior was the latter to him in point of numbers, that he could not venture to undertake any decisive measure against it, as it now entered Saxony, and was obliged to content himself with taking up a strong position in an intrenched camp near Dresden, whilst the hostile army selected Pirna for its position. Meanwhile, the Silesian army, commanded by the Margrave Charles, had likewise got under arms, and taken up a position well calculated to protect Silesia from any attempts Daun might choose to make from Lusatia. General Zieten was also dispatched in the same direction, in order to oppose the further march of the corps under Loudon. Under these circumstances, and as the Russians did not display any great willingness for co-operation in a conjoint attack, Daun suddenly embraced the resolution of directing his arms against Saxony. He soon advanced in front of Dresden, determined on attacking Prince Henry in the rear, whilst the army of the empire was to make a simultaneous attack in front, so that the small Prussian army must be completely overwhelmed by its two foes, so vastly superior in numbers. Prince Henry was, however, so prudent as to take up such a position as rendered it impossible to assail him, and tidings soon arrived that Frederick, after the victory of Zorndorf, was approaching in all haste to the Saxon territories. On the 10th of September, after uniting himself with the army of the Margrave Charles and Zieten's corps, and forcing Loudon to a retrograde movement towards the main strength of the Austrian army, Frederick arrived in the neighborhood of Dresden. Here, within the space of ten miles, four hostile armies stood opposed to one another, and each day appeared to promise a bloody termination to these peculiar relations. Frederick desired nothing more heartily than a decisive engagement; but Daun did not share in this feeling, and being a master in the art of conducting defensive warfare, he soon took up such a strong position as to be completely inaccessible, unless attacked at a great disadvantage. The army of the empire was likewise perfectly secure in the camp of Pirna. A considerable time elapsed in this way without matters coming to any issue. All the various manœuvres of Frederick to draw his enemies from their entrenchments proved fruitless, and each day increased his anxiety, for another Austrian corps had advanced on Upper Silesia, and had already invested the fortresses Oppen and Neisse; news had actually arrived of all the necessary preparations being made for a formal siege of Neisse.

Frederick now took a speedy resolve. Finding his attempts to bring the enemy to an engagement ineffectual, he determined on making a rapid movement towards Silesia, and thus prevent the Austrians from obtaining a firm footing in that province; besides which, this movement he saw would endanger the Austrian magazines erected in Lusatia, from which Daun drew his supplies.

He succeeded, by sending a small corps in advance, in securing Bautzen, and followed in person, a few days afterwards, with his army. But Daun was equally alive to the dangers attendant on the capture of his magazines, and with a view to prevent both this and Frederick's march on Silesia, he put his forces in motion in a similar direction, before Frederick's whole army had been able to break up. On the 10th of October, as Frederick was advancing from Bautzen, and had gained the village of Hochkirch, he saw his movements impeded afresh by the whole Austrian army, which was encamped directly in his front.

The position which Daun had selected was, as usual, singularly felicitous. With a range of extensive and thickly-wooded hills, which surrounded the village of Hochkirch, for his camp, it was impossible for Frederick to advance, and delay in Hochkirch seemed pregnant with danger. Frederick, who did not conceive it honorable to turn round at the mere glance of an enemy, or believe the Austrian general likely to take any bold step on the offensive, gave orders for an encampment in Hochkirch. The several Prussian generals present saw the rashness of such an act, and Prince Morrisco of Dessau took the liberty of making representations to the king on the subject: but Frederick paid no attention to such remonstrances. The quarter-master-general of the army received orders to mark out the lines; but the latter refused to execute the order, and thus become instrumental in the destruction of the army. For this he was punished with arrest. A lieutenant of the engineers was obliged, under Frederick's special direction to mark out the lines, although those engaged in erecting the tents were already greeted by showers of shot from the Austrian guns. Batteries were erected on two sides, for the protection of the camp; one of these was raised in front of Hochkirch, on the side of the hill which was crowned by the village. Frederick's effective strength amounted to 30,000 fighting men, that of the Austrians to 65,000.

The ground occupied by the Prussians was the more dangerous, as, from the low position of the camp, it was impossible to learn anything of the movements of the enemy on the heights; whilst they could readily observe everything that took place in the Prussian camp; besides which, all the woods at the base of the hill so completely swarmed with Austrian troops, that the Prussian videttes and patrols dare not venture any distance from their posts, whereas the Austrians enjoyed every facility for making unexpected assaults. Amidst this host of adverse circumstances, Frederick remained unalterable in his idea, that Daun would not risk an attack, and even neglected to take the necessary precautionary measures, permitting the troops to sleep in their tents unaccoutred. Field-marshal Keith, who happened to be present in the camp, told him distinctly, that "if the Austrians allowed them to remain there in quiet, they deserved to be hung." Frederick replied with a smile, "We must hope that the Austrians are more afraid of us than the gallows!" He was still further confirmed in his fatal resolution by the false statements of a spy. He had, as he stated, in his pay an Austrian officer, through whom he learned everything that passed in the enemy's camp. The medium of this correspondence was a basket of eggs, one of which invariably contained a letter. It so happened, however, that Daun one day met the bearer of the eggs, and ordered him to bring them to his own kitchen, when the secret was discovered. Daun had the traitorous correspondent immediately summoned to his presence. The latter had of course forfeited his life; but this was spared him, on condition that he continued to write similar letters, but under Daun's dictation. Frederick received, consequently, daily intelligence of the approaching departure of the Austrians, and their intended retreat on Bohemia; and every feeling of apprehension, which he might have previously entertained, was altogether removed, and his reliance on Daun's timidity fully confirmed.

This departure, however, not taking place as soon as he had expected, Frederick determined to deploy round the Austrian army, in order to escape from this state of inactivity; but to the execution of this manœuvre certain previous preparations for the sustenance of his army were necessary; and owing to a combination of circumstances, his march was necessarily deferred until the 14th of October. But Daun had already taken his measures; indeed, it would have been altogether unpardonable had he hesitated any longer to take advantage of so propitious a moment, when the whole Austrian army regarded the conduct of the King of Prussia as a formal insult; and it was universally declared that the generals, one and all, deserved to be cashiered if they refused to accept of so reckless a challenge. In order, however, to go the more securely to work, a nocturnal assault was agreed upon, to take place on the night of the 13th of October; the chief blow was to be aimed at the heights on which Hochkirch was situated, which were occupied by the tents of the left wing, and formed the most important point in the Prussian position. Broad ways were opened through the thickly wooded declivities which the Austrians held, in order that the troops might meet no obstacles in forming at the given points, from whence the left wing of the Prussians was to be on all sides assailed. Care was likewise taken to preserve the appearance of erecting fortifications on the heights, in order to conceal the intended assault, and lull the Prussians into false security.

Night came on, and the section of the Austrian army selected for the assault got under arms in perfect order and silence. Care had even been taken that neither the sound of footsteps, nor the rattling of cannon should reach the ear of the Prussian outposts. A number of workmen were continually employed in the woods, and keeping up a perpetual noise by felling timber, and by loud cries and songs, they succeeded in completely drowning every other sound. This tumult was heard in the

Prussian camp, and was considered as corroborative evidence of the zeal with which the fortifications were being erected. Free from every apprehension the men laid themselves down to rest,—the convivialities of the officers began gradually to abate,—dark night and deep slumber soon brooded over the entire camp; the church clock of Hochkirch had just struck five, when sudden and repeated volleys of musketry were directed against such of the Prussian posts as stood outside the alignments. The shots were at first unheeded, for hardly a night passed without repeated skirmishes between the Pandoors and the Prussian outposts. As the firing, however, became more violent, such of the battalions as lay in the neighborhood grasped their arms, and hurrying, for the most part without boots or knapsacks, to the scene of action, succeeded in repulsing the assault. Croats and other Austrian troops had, however, crept into the camp, and kept firing on the Prussians, who were every instant more and more assailed from without. A frightful struggle ensued. Man to man—the darkness precluding all possibility of mutual recognition—every one sought to defend himself by striking round him, indifferent whether his blow reached friend or foe. The men sought to discover their comrades by their helmets; the metal helmets of the Prussians and the grenadier caps of the Austrians being the only distinguishing marks. It was not without great loss that the Austrians broke their way to Hochkirch. Fresh battalions came on to oppose them, but were continually repulsed, and being attacked on all sides were obliged to retire. The Austrians captured a battery which stood in front of Hochkirch, and which was intended to cover the left wing of the Prussian camp; turning the guns round, they opened a hot fire on the village. The cannon-balls committed frightful devastation in the Prussian battalions, as the latter pressed forward to the struggle through the narrow village lanes. The red volleys of the artillery had lit up

the night, but when morning dawned a dense cloud long
wrapped the whole scene in darkness.

The thunder of the guns at length roused the various
sections of the Prussian army from their repose. Frederick's head-quarters lay to the left of the centre, in the
village of Rodewitz. He, too, was now awake, and hurried
on his dress; but had scarcely left his quarters when he
received intelligence of the losses sustained by his right
wing, and as he mounted his horse he was greeted with
the balls fired from his own guns. Still Hochkirch was
not as yet in the hands of the enemy. One battalion
maintained its ground in the gardens of the village, and
a second had secured itself in the churchyard. Frederick
could not believe in its being a general assault, and ordered
up single brigades to the support of the right wing and
to drive the Austrians from their position. Field-marshal
Keith put himself at the head of a few battalions, and
pushing in a lateral direction on to Hochkirch, recaptured
the Prussian battery, and drove the foe back a considerable distance. But he became now locked in between
overwhelming masses, and was obliged to force his way
at the bayonet-point, until he at length sank dead on the
ground beneath a shower of bullets. The Austrians
penetrated into Hochkirch, and seized the village, which
burst forth into flames, but the churchyard was still
valiantly held by the Prussians. Prince Francis of Brunswick advanced with fresh troops to meet the Austrians,
and was at first successful, but soon compelled to retire,
and, like Keith, fell on the battle-field. Prince Maurice of
Dessau was equally unsuccessful, and was borne out of the
fight mortally wounded. New masses of troops were continually poured by the Austrians into the village until they
at length became master of the churchyard. In it, as in a
small fortress, the single battalion, under the command
of Major de Lange, had with the most resolute determination repelled the attacks of seven Austrian regiments.
Shut in on all sides, they sought to carve a passage with
sword and bayonet, but were all, not even excepting the

major, left dead or wounded on the ground which they had so valiantly defended. Frederick strove once more to rob the Austrians of the advantages they had gained; in person he led on six battalions to the charge, beneath a murderous storm of bullets. His horse was wounded —coolly mounting a second, he did not retreat from the spot, despite all the supplications of those around him, until he saw that his exertions were absolutely futile. The dense fog at length cleared away, and day brought to light the sad memorials of that night's havoc. Frederick now recalled such of his troops as had hitherto taken part in the fight, and drew them up in good order in line opposite Hochkirch. The left wing, which had as yet taken no part in the affray, was now, in pursuance of Daun's original plan, likewise assailed by various divisions of the Austrian army. After a valiant defence the Prussians were here, too, compelled to retire, and the battery fell into the hands of the enemy. But the troops formed again in line, and a special corps of Prussians, which had hitherto held a distant point, and had successfully repelled many attacks on the Austrians, arrived on the field of battle; by which the position of the Prussian army was in a measure secured, and new attacks calmly defied. Daun considered it safer to retain what he had won than a second time venture on a struggle with so dangerous a foe: the attack during the night had cost him the best of his troops, and it was with difficulty that he succeeded in withdrawing his men from the confusion which prevailed, and formed them into lines. He contented himself, therefore, with taking up such a position as secured his own army against all assaults, instead of becoming himself the assailant, and remained a calm spectator of the Prussian retreat. This retirade, which the beaten army entered upon within range of the enemy's guns, was effected with as much regularity and systematic order as if it were a mere manœuvre on a peaceful parade; so much so that the Austrians themselves could not withhold their admiration at the manner in which it was executed.

The loss of life occasioned by this frightful struggle was very considerable. That of the Prussians amounted to about 9,000 men, and that of the Austrians fell little short of the same number. The former had, however, to deplore the death of their best leaders, besides the capture of 101 guns, 28 colors, and 2 standards, together with the greater part of their tents. In spite of this, Frederick proceeded but about two miles' distance from the field of battle, and here, on the heights near Bautzen, encamped, as well as this was possible without tents or baggage. He spared no pains in animating the courage of his valiant men, and had the pleasure of seeing that despondency formed no part of the Prussian soldier's character. As the regiments filed by him on their way to their cantonments, on a troop of cannoniers and grenadiers passing, he called out to them, " Cannoniers, where have you left your cannon?" "The devil carried them off last night!" was the reply. "Well, then, we'll carry them off by day," replied Frederick; "won't we, grenadiers?" "Ay," said they, as they passed, "and with interest too!" Frederick smiled, and said, "I hope to be present on that occasion." Turning to an officer, he remarked, "Daun has played me a slippery trick to-day." "It's only a flesh-wound," replied the latter, "and won't take long to heal." "Do you really think so?" said the king. "Not only I," replied the officer, "but the whole army have the fullest confidence in your majesty." "You are right," said the king, and taking the officer by the button of his uniform, as he was in the habit of doing when in confidential conversation—"You shall see," said he, "whether I don't catch Daun. I only regret that so many valiant men have lost their lives this day." Many similar remarks, in which the sad fate of the army was alluded to in terms of undaunted spirit, have been handed down to us.

But internally Frederick could fully estimate how critical his situation had become, and how great a share of the disaster, and responsibility for the loss of so many gallant officers was ascribable to his own fault. Keith was not alone his best general, but one of his most intimate friends. After the battle of Kollin, as if to increase the bitterness of his sorrow, he had received the tidings of his mother's death, and at this melancholy juncture intelligence was brought him of the decease of his fondly-loved sister, the Margravine of Baireuth. The latter had died on the day of the storm of Hochkirch. This intelligence affected him more deeply than any of his other sorrows, for the Margravine had been the sympathizing friend of his youth, the most affectionate partner of all his intellectual pleasures, and his support when his spirit drooped beneath the threatening combinations of the political world. Of that heartfelt love which he bore her we have many evidences, and amongst others a poem, which he had written but a few days previously, and in which he endeavors to console her in a sickness that threatened to prove fatal. The concluding words of the poem, in which he offers the sacrifice of his own life for the recovery of his sister's, are pretty nearly as follows:

> "If, then, stern fate, unbending and supreme,
> Demand some victim's blood, then, oh, ye gods!
> Enlighten its judicial, high decree,
> And, oh, on me let that stern choice but fall!
> Then would I wait, unmurmuring and content,
> Until grim Death, inexorable, wend
> His footsteps from my sister's weary couch,
> And blunt his sickle's ruthless edge on me.
> But if this one sole favor which I claim
> May not to mortal prayer accorded be,
> Oh, then, ye gods, in mercy do but grant
> That she and I the selfsame day descend
> To those fair meads where softest myrtle blooms,
> And gloomy cypress high its shadow flings,
> And that one grave enwrap our common clay."

The poem had not been sent off when the sad intelligence of his sister's decease arrived. It was now sent, together with some accompanying lines depicting the poignancy of his grief, to the husband of the deceased.

Some months afterwards he addressed a poem to Marshal Keith to console him for the fall of his brother, at Hochkirch, and in it the deepest feelings of sorrow at the loss of his friends is breathed forth in every line. One passage occurs, which is too characteristic of the sensibility of his heart for us to pass it over. It is, as nearly as we can render it—

> " Oft did I weep to lose both crown and life,
> But never yet has treacherous fortune deign'd—
> She who so many kings against me bands—
> To wake for me the tear in pity's eye;
> Yet will she snap the fondest, holiest ties,
> And thus, dear lord, inflict some heavy stroke.—
> Achilles' self was not invulnerable!"

Nor are other evidences wanting corroborative of the sad feelings of the monarch about this period. On the evening of the day on which intelligence of the death of the Margravine of Baireuth arrived, his secretary, Le Catt, found him reading some sermons of the celebrated Bourdaloue, and thinking to raise his spirits, addressed him jokingly: "It seems as if your majesty intended to turn saint." Frederick made no reply; but on the secretary coming to him at the usual hour on the following day, Frederick handed him a roll of black-edged paper, with directions to read it through at home. It was a sermon on some particular biblical text, which Frederick, actuated by his passing feelings, had composed. Le Catt, considering it to be his duty to offer consolation to the monarch, made every endeavor to whisper comfort in his ear, but the latter, thanking him for his sympathy, declined his attentions, assuring him, that he would make every exertion to rouse himself from his gloomy apathy; and concluded with the ominous words: " In every event I have *that* at hand with which I can terminate this tragedy." But not this strange mysterious something, (unquestionably poison, which he always carried about his person,) but the peculiar greatness of his intellect was that which soon gave a wonderful turn to the late unhappy catastrophe. As he had evinced sufficient power of mind to conquer his griefs and lend expression—strange that such expression should have been borrowed from the pulpit—to his feelings, so he had also calmly calculated all the relations of his danger, and made them subservient to his purposes. And thus, as Daun allowed the favorable moment for following up his victory to pass unheeded by, Frederick could truly and confidently assert, however vaunting these words might have appeared in the mouth of another: "Daun has let us out of the check. The game is not lost. We will remain here some days; then set out for Silesia and free Neisse."

And in truth, to the astonishment of a wondering world, Frederick soon accomplished that which, in any other person's case, must have been the fruit of a complete victory. The victorious Daun had limited his exertions to the singing of hymns and the erecting of trophies, to the ordaining of feasts and the dispatch of couriers to Vienna and the different capitals of the allied powers, and finally, to the entrenching himself with care in a strong position. So fully did he conceive himself to have hereby gathered in the fruits of his victory, that he wrote to the general who conducted the siege of Neisse, and whose operations had indeed become threatening, as follows: "Carry on your siege without fear. I hold the king fast; he is cut off from Silesia, and if he attack me, I will answer for our success."

But Frederick had given orders to Prince Henry, who still remained in Dresden, to join him with a part of the army stationed there, together with the guns, ammunition, and provisions. Both the armies met at Bautzen; the wounded were despatched to Glogau, and Frederick made some movements calculated to lead the Austrian general to believe that he was about to retire with his whole army thither, and leave Saxony free for the other's operations; but on the evening of the 24th of September, Frederick suddenly departed, and stealing round the well-intrenched camp of the Austrians, marched to Görlitz. It was not until the following day that Daun was informed of the departure of the Prussians, by which all his fine plans were baffled; he even became apprehensive for the safety of his magazines in Lusatia, which might readily fall into the hands of the enemy; and therefore, without loss of time, set out in pursuit, occupying the whole neighboring chain of hills running in a lateral direction. The King of Prussia would have willingly come to an engagement, but Daun did not descend from the heights; Frederick was therefore obliged to push forward by forced marches for Silesia, whilst Daun, as soon as he had secured his magazines, returned in the direction of Dresden, and merely employed his light troops in impeding the march of the Prussians. On the 7th of November Frederick received the glad tidings that the Austrians had raised the siege of Neisse on the first news of his approach, and had retired in the direction of Moravia. Not long after this the whole of Silesia was completely evacuated by the several Austrian corps. Frederick now visited Neisse, in order to gratify himself with a sight of those admirable defences which he himself had raised, and which had withstood the effects of the enemy's bombardment; he then made preparation for a rapid march back to Saxony.

In order to secure, in a measure, the success of this last enterprise, Frederick had left but a small segment of his army in Dresden, to strengthen which the Prussian corps, that had hitherto resisted the Swedes and Russians, was now recalled. Before the arrival of the latter, Daun had already reached Dresden, and the army of the empire, which had, up to this period, proved very lethargic, now began to give signs of life, and advanced likewise. As the Prussian army was extremely feeble, and the garrison of Dresden, under General Schmettau, well equipped and capable of sustaining a siege for a considerable time, it seemed prudent to avoid a battle and retire from Dresden, thus inviting the Austrian leader to enter on a siege, which he would afterwards, in all probability, be compelled to raise. Daun was mightily pleased with the determination to which his enemy had come, hoping by the conquest of Dresden to give a brilliant termination to the entire campaign; but on his beginning to make the first preparations for a siege, General Schmettau sent him word, that in the event of his approaching any nearer, the latter should feel it his duty to burn down the suburbs. This warning passed unheeded, and on the 10th of November the threat was put into execution; one hundred and eight houses became a prey to the flames. This conduct, which was, however, justifiable as a measure of self-defence, so infuriated the Austrian field-marshal, that he sent a message to Schmettau to the effect, " that after such unheard-of conduct in a capital, he should hold the commandant personally responsible for his acts." It is possible that Daun might not at that moment have called to mind the fact, that the Austrian army had the year before, without any necessity whatsoever, laid the flourishing town of Zittau, which belonged, besides, to their ally, Saxony, in ashes. Schmettau simply replied, that his orders were to defend the town: if the enemy approached any nearer the remainder of the suburbs should be burnt down; and that, if the Austrians persisted in approaching still closer, every street in the capital should meet the same fate, whilst he would retire from the ramparts to the palace, there to await the final result.

Intelligence now arrived that Frederick was hastening back to Saxony; and as some few enterprises, undertaken by the army of the empire against Torgau and Leipzig, had met with the most unequivocal success, partly through the resolute conduct of a corps which had advanced from Pomerania, Daun considered the answer he had received from Schmettau sufficient to justify him, under the circumstances, in abstaining from pushing matters to extremities, and thereby possibly endangering the laurels he had already won at Hochkirch. He therefore sent a message to Schmettau to state that, out of respect for the royal family of Poland, and regard for his fellow-creatures, he should abandon all further attempts on Dresden. He then retreated towards Bohemia, and as the army of the empire had previously taken the route to Franconia, Frederick, on his arrival in Dresden, found no enemy to contend with. He therefore sent the corps which he had drawn from Pomerania, back to oppose the Swedes, who had in the interim made some advances, but were soon driven back once more to Stralsund.

Thus was another campaign ended, without Frederick's losing any portions of his territories except those which were occupied in the far east and west of his dominions, and without surrendering one foot of Saxony. He could now permit his troops to take up their winter-quarters in security, there to recruit their strength after so many toils.

But for Daun a special mark of honor was in store. It was not sufficient that the empress expressed in the most flattering terms the immense debt of gratitude she owed him for the victory of Hochkirch; even the pope, Clement XIII., who had been but that year invested with the papal dignity, and who appears not to have sufficiently weighed how impartially Frederick acted towards his Catholic subjects, considered his victory as a most important event as regarded the interests of the Church. On the Austrian field-marshal he conferred a consecrated sword with a golden hilt and red velvet scabbard, a consecrated hat of scarlet velvet, lined with ermine and bound in gold, and surmounted by a dove embroidered in pearls, the symbol of that spirit which was to preside over the hallowed arms of the warrior. So unusual a mark of distinction indicated very fully the singularly strong feelings of displeasure with which the pontiff regarded the acts of the monarch of Prussia. It had never been conferred before on any, save those who, in defence of the holy doctrines of Christianity, had turned their arms against the heathen. But this act of seeming partisanship was impolitic, for, from thenceforward it became apparent that it was Prussia's future mission to enter the list for, and become the champion of dissent and the free exercise of private judgment. It had but the effect of conciliating for the great king the hearts of all opposed to Rome, without producing any of the results which its author intended that it should. For although the Prince Elector of Cologne may have been thereby induced to forbid his Protestant subjects, under severe penalties, to testify any satisfaction at the Prussian victories, yet history does not warrant us in believing that this prohibition tended materially to arrest the progress of Frederick's successes. And the latter, who fought as valiantly with the pen as with the sword, did not allow the occasion to pass over, without profiting by it, and sending forth a series of satirical pamphlets, in which he treated the act with derision, and contended, that it was more calculated for the meridian of mediæval pontifficism, than the enlightened Christianity of modern days.

CHAPTER XXXII.

CAMPAIGN OF THE YEAR 1759. CUNNERSDORF.

DURING three long years had this sanguinary contest now been waged,—many murderous battles had been fought—the blood of thousands flowed in streams—blooming meads had been laid desolate—towns and villages had sunk into sightless masses of dust and ashes—countless families, once wealthy, now wandered about in beggary. Still the jealousies of those in power had not as yet one whit abated, nor could the hope of hurling the petty Prussian monarch from a height which he had, in the opinion of his enemies, usurped, be for an instant abandoned. Frederick would have readily laid down his arms; he was no insatiable conqueror, and knew no hatred, except of the mean and unworthy. He was weary of those ceaseless, unending toils to which the vast preponderance of his enemies perpetually forced him. "At a distance," he thus writes, towards the beginning of the year 1759, to his friend the Marquis D'Argens—"my position may appear bright and brilliant; but if you were to examine it more closely you would find nothing but a heavy, impenetrable mist. I hardly know whether there be a Sanssouci in the world. Be this place where it may, for me this epithet does not exist. In short, my dear Marquis, I am old, sad, and miserable. From time to time a gleam of my former lightness of heart bursts upon me; but these are but sparks which are speedily extinguished, as there is no real fire to give them permanence. They are the flashes of lightning bursting forth from dark thunderclouds. To you I speak in all sincerity, and I assure you, that were you to see me you could not now recognize a trace of what I once was. You would find an old man, whose hairs have become gray, who has lost half of his teeth, joyless, without fire or life; in short, as unlike his former self as the remains of Tusculum, of which the architects, from the absence of ruins which might mark the real residence of Cicero, have drawn so many visionary plans. These are, my friend, the results not so much of time as of care: the sad harbingers of that feebleness which accompanies the autumn of our years. These considerations, as they render me very indifferent to life, place me exactly in that position in which a man should stand whose destiny is to fight for life and death. With this indifference to life one fights with more courage, and leaves the world with less regret."

He had employed the winter in making new preparations for war, as far as his resources admitted. But he was resolved on altering his system for the future, and abstaining from opening each campaign, as hitherto, by assuming the offensive, and made up his mind to stand from henceforth upon the defensive, husbanding his resources for the warding off of aggressions, and watching with wary circumspection each movement of the enemy.

The campaign of this year, like that of the last, was opened by the appearance on the field of the army of the allies, under Duke Ferdinand of Brunswick, and the armies of the French. During the winter the French had, under Soubise, paid a visit to Frankfort on the Main. This town, as it furnished its contingent to the army of the empire, did not think it had anything to apprehend from an ally of the empire. By the possession of Frankfort the French were able to maintain a communication with the Austrians and army of the empire, and all the necessary supplies were thereby readily obtained. For these reasons Duke Ferdinand resolved on again driving them from this important point. He pushed forward, and on the 13th of April a battle took place at Bergen, in the neighborhood of Frankfort. The French, under the command of Broglio, who had superseded Soubise as commander-in-chief, maintained their ground, and the two French corps immediately penetrated into Germany. Cassel, Münster, Minden, besides considerable numbers of the allied troops fell into their hands. But Ferdinand still commanded the Weser. In the neighborhood of Minden he encountered the northern columns of the French army, and on the first of August obtained a brilliant victory over it, whilst a special French corps was contemporaneously annihilated by his nephew, the Prince Royal of Brunswick. A series of successful engagements ensued, and the French in a short time saw themselves compelled to relinquish all their brilliant conquests of the year. The surprise of Fulda concluded the glorious campaign: it had been held by the Duke of Wurtemberg, who was in the pay of France, and had reinforced the army of the enemy with 12,000 men. But he, too, was obliged to retire with considerable loss back upon the Main.

On the Prussian side serious hostilities did not commence until summer. Frederick wished, as we have already observed, to watch the motions of the enemy, and await the most propitious moment for attack. But he remained no idle spectator. All the movements of an army being in those days dependent for support on magazines, the enemy had laid up at the different points on the frontiers of the Prussian states, where they had wintered, considerable stores for the maintenance of their future operations. Frederick, knowing that if he could but succeed in destroying these a heavy blow would be thereby inflicted on his enemies, determined on making the attempt, and as early as the month of February dispatched a corps to Poland, where the Russians had erected very considerable magazines along the banks of the Wartha. It being a main object now to counteract the operations of a Polish nobleman, Prince Sulkowski, who, notwithstanding the neutrality which the Polish republic maintained, and although his residence, Reisen, lay close

to the borders of Silesia, had organized large contributions
for the Russians, and even levied troops for their service,
both himself and his body-guard was seized and transported to Glogau. The Prussians also succeeded in destroying throughout Poland a quantity of provisions,
which would have been sufficient for the support of 50,000
men for three months. A second expedition of the same
nature was planned against Moravia, to issue from Upper
Silesia, and although not followed up, yet it was so far successful as to induce Daun, who apprehended this incursion on Moravia, to concentrate his principal strength in
that quarter, and thus expose the Bohemian territories on
the Saxon side to the inroad of the Prussians. Prince
Henry, who commanded the Prussian army in Saxony,
having already driven the advanced posts of the army of
the empire out of Thuringia, now dispatched several corps
into Bohemia, and in the short space of five days destroyed
all the magazines to be found there, inflicting on the
enemy double the amount of injury caused in Poland.
Daun sent reinforcements without loss of time towards
the Saxon border, but the Prussians had already returned
in safety. Prince Henry was not, however, content with
the execution of a single daring enterprise: with more
preparation, and still more success, he undertook a similar
one against the army of the empire stationed in Franconia,
between Bamberg and Hof. He advanced in several
columns against it, and one division of the army of the
empire fled after the other precipitately before him, and
did not rally until they reached Nuremberg. A large
number of prisoners and all the principal magazines fell
into the hands of the Prussians, who, after levying very
considerable contributions from the Franconian towns,
and having made repeated attempts to induce the enemy
to come to an engagement, returned back to Saxony,
where their presence had become now desirable. This
expedition had been organized and executed within a
month.

On the occasion of this movement on Franconia that

class of persons who felt more disposed to indulge in calumnies and slanderous attacks on the character of the Prussian monarch than in any feats of heroism received a sound warning. A Prussian officer arriving with his troops at a rapid pace at Erlanger, paid a visit to a notorious pamphleteer, and ordered a round number of lashes to be administered to the astonished publicist. Having executed this act of retributive justice, he returned to the army, with a regular receipt, which the recipient had been obliged to furnish him with, in acknowledgment of payment.

Frederick as yet remained at Landshut, watching the movements of the Austrian army, which, under the command of Daun, lay at Schurz, in Bohemia, but on its advancing northwards, in the direction of Marklissa, he followed in its footsteps, and true to his defensive system, took up an entrenched position near Schmottseifen.

This movement of the Austrian army had taken place in order to support some recent plans of the Russians, with whose operations the former had been induced to co-operate. The Russians had, as early as the end of November, crossed the Vistula, and reconstructed their magazines. Frederick now sent the greater part of the corps which had been stationed under Graf Dohna in Pomerania, with orders to attack the single columns of the Russian army whilst still on their march. Dohna did not, however, succeed in effecting this, and the whole result of his mission consisted in his carrying off a number of their magazines, whilst their different corps coalesced and advanced towards the Oder. As Dohna would not venture on a battle, Frederick conceived it advisable to appoint some more enterprising general in his stead. He selected Wedell, who had by his gallantry during the second Silesian war obtained the appellation of the Prussian Leonidas, and had already distinguished himself most brilliantly at Leuthen. But Wedell was one of the youngest generals in the army, and in order to avoid giving offence to his elder colleagues, and also with

CAMPAIGN OF 1759. CUNNERSDORF. 307

a view, perhaps, to enkindle his enthusiasm to the highest by the unusual nature of the honor conferred, Frederick formally nominated him dictator, after the fashion of ancient Rome. "Henceforward you represent my person in the army," said the king; "what you order shall be done in my name, as if I myself were present. I have learnt to prize your good qualities at Leuthen, and place the most unbounded confidence in them. You are, therefore, like many of the Romans, nominated dictator, to improve my situation on the Oder. I give you orders to attack the Russians wheresoever you come up with them; beat them soundly, and prevent their junction with the Austrians!"

Wedell came up with the Russians in the neighborhood of Züllichau, where they were very firmly entrenched near the village of Kay. Wholly disregarding the natural strength of their position, and solely mindful of the king's command, he attacked them on the 23d of July with but one third of their number. But the personal courage of the dictator and his men proved of no avail against overwhelming numbers and the disadvantages of the ground. In vain were the charges renewed till nightfall; the Prussians were eventually obliged to leave the field with a loss of upwards of 8000 men. The Russians pushed on to Frankfort, and were there joined by an Austrian corps under the command of Loudon.

The most momentous dangers now came crowding fast round Frederick. He saw no other alternative than marching in proper person to check the Russians. Summoning Prince Henry, with the greater part of his army from Saxony, he entrusted him with the command of the camp in Schmottseifen, and set out in person, at the head of a considerable body of troops, being likewise joined by the remnant of Wedell's corps on the way to Frankfort.

The Russian army, under the command of General Soltikoff, had taken up an entrenched position on the opposite bank of the Oder. Soltikoff had pitched his camp, on a ridge of hills running towards the east of Frankfort, in front of which the village of Cunnersdorf lies, and had secured the declivities with strong batteries. Frederick found it necessary to push on beyond Frankfort, and cross the stream between that town and Cüstrin; by so doing, he came in front of one face of the Russian army. On the 11th of August he took up his position here. The numerical strength of the Russian army, inclusive of the Austrian auxiliaries, amounted to 70,000 fighting men, whilst Frederick had but 43,000 wherewith to oppose them.

On the 12th of August, about two o'clock in the morning, the Prussians got under arms. They deployed in a curve laterally, as the ground was intersected with rivulets and streams, and marched through a fir-grove to face the enemy's left wing. It was eleven o'clock in the forenoon before they reached the skirt of the wood and prepared for action. The heat was oppressive, and the army had enjoyed no rest for the two preceding nights. The cannon were brought up in position, and a violent cannonade immediately opened, which was quickly responded to from the hostile batteries. The Prussian infantry now assailed the heights on which the enemy was posted. In the face of a shower of shot which fell amongst them, they valiantly climbed over the barricade erected by the Russians to protect their position, gained the heights and captured the battery. One Russian regiment after the other was overthrown, and the Prussians were soon in entire possession of the heights, which had formed the position of the Russian left wing. An immense number of prisoners and cannon were in their hands. It was not until the Russians had reached the opposite side of a ravine, with steep precipitous sides, that they rallied and opposed fresh troops to the Prussian advance; but the impetuosity of Frederick's men was not to be thus checked. Springing into the ravine they clambered up its precipitous sides: the efforts of the Russians to hurl them down proved unavailing; they forced the enemy from the ground, and made good their position here also.

It was now five o'clock in the afternoon; two-thirds of the enemy had been beaten and driven from their ground; ninety guns were in the hands of the Prussians; the victory might now be regarded as certain, and couriers were already dispatched with the glad intelligence to Berlin. It was but natural to suppose that the enemy, after receiving so severe a blow, would have retreated; but Frederick was not disposed to allow the discomfited foe to escape so easily, and as the fortune of the day had hitherto proved so propitious towards him, he trusted in his now succeeding in entirely annihilating the power of his adversaries. It was in vain that representations were made to him of how much his own infantry had suffered, of how completely exhausted they were from the heat of the day, and of the danger of driving the enemy to desperation, and the admirable position which its right wing still occupied. In truth, the heights on which the enemy's right wing still stood (the Judenberg, near Frankfort,) completely commanded the ridge of hills which had been taken. Towering in the shape of an amphitheatre above these latter, they were still held by the enemy, who was well supplied with cannon. But Frederick remained unalterable in his resolves, and gave orders to renew the fight. Both armies stood beneath a heavy fire of musketry, but the Prussians were deficient in heavy ordnance, as they could not, from the sandy nature of the ground, be dragged up the heights, whilst the enemy's cannon posted on the Judenberg began to spread frightful havoc and devastation through their ranks. Completely exhausted from heat and fatigue, they could now no longer fire with the same regularity and precision as hitherto. Without succeeding in obtaining any advantage over the enemy they still remained firm in their position. The cavalry which had, from the unfavorable nature of the ground, been hitherto unable to take any part in the conflict, now received orders to charge. But very many of the Prussian horse fell into the pits which had been constructed by the Russians;

the others were received with frightful discharges of handgrenades, and on the advance of some of the enemy's cavalry, were completely repulsed.

Thus an hour of the struggle passed. As yet but a single regiment of the Austrian auxiliaries had taken part in the contest; Loudon now perceived that the decisive moment had arrived. Bursting at once with his clouds of cavalry across a deep valley, which from that day forth bears the name of "Loudon's ground," unperceived by the Prussians, he suddenly fell upon the latter in flank and rear as they stood in broken lines, and being no longer able to maintain their ground, they were forced to retreat. Frederick did all in his power to retain the advantages of the day; he exhorted his men to steady perseverance, and led some battalions anew to the charge, but in vain. One horse had been already shot under him; several officers and adjutants had already fallen at his side, and several shots had penetrated his own uniform; still he would not yield. A ball now struck the breast of the second horse that he had mounted; and an adjutant and non-commissioned officer, the only persons near him, rushed forward and caught him in their arms, as the horse was about to plunge on its side. No fresh horse being now to be had, he mounted that of the adjutant. Another ball now struck him in the hip, but was turned aside in its course by a golden case which he carried in his pocket. Several officers now arrived with intelligence of the amount of his disasters; and entreated him most earnestly to retire from so exposed and dangerous a position. To their entreaties he replied, "We must make every attempt to regain this battle; I must do my duty as well as you." All this obstinate resistance availed not. The foe charged on impetuously anew, and the Prussians fled in wild confusion from the field of battle to screen themselves in the neighboring wood from the wrath of their enemy. In the midst of the confusion the king's voice was heard shouting in desperation: "Can then no cursed ball reach me?"

Some Prussian hussars were the last upon the field of battle. As they too were plunging their spurs into their horses' sides, to escape from the clouds of Cossack cavalry that now pressed forward, a hussar suddenly called out to the officer in command, "Captain, there stands the king!" The officer, turning round, saw the king, standing on a mound of sand, attended only by a single page who held his horse. He had driven his sword into the ground, and was gazing with folded arms on his own approaching ruin. The hussars flew precipitately towards him; but it was with the utmost difficulty that the captain succeeded in persuading him to mount his horse and provide for his personal safety. At length, giving ear to the remonstrances of the officer, he addressed him,—"Well, sir, if this be your opinion, on!" But the Cossacks were already down upon them. The captain, turning round in his saddle, shot the officer in command of the hostile troop, and checked for a moment its assaults; enabling Frederick and his hussars to get so much in advance as to be safe from their pursuers.

The night was passed in a small village on the Oder, in a ruined peasant's hut. The hussars had been sent out to rally, if possible, his shattered forces, now dispersed on all sides. A page and a single servant alone remained with Frederick, and kept guard in turn before the door. Some of the wounded who lay in the village, hearing of the king's presence, came to act as sentries, and a considerable number of troops was thus gradually concentrated round the monarch. Many believed that the king had actually fallen.

Frederick felt perfectly convinced that, if the Russians followed up their victory with the slightest vigor, all hope of escape was at an end. He had, however, fully resolved never to outlive captivity, and the disgraceful and ruinous terms which would be naturally insisted on as the price of his freedom. He accordingly took advantage of this night to make his last dispositions. Prince Henry was to succeed as generalissimo of his army, and to swear allegiance to his nephew Frederick William, the heir presumptive to the crown, then in his fifteenth year. The court and the archives were to be removed with all possible expedition from Berlin, whither he supposed his enemy to be already advancing from all sides. To Count Finkenstein, the minister of state, he wrote as follows: "I am now wholly bereft of all aid; and, to speak the truth, I believe that all is lost. I will not outlive the downfall of my native land. Farewell for ever!"

Hopeless as Frederick's condition evidently was, and fearful as the apprehensions which he must have had for his own personal safety unquestionably were, still his heart felt the liveliest sympathy for the disastrous fate which so many of his faithful subjects had that day met, and his exertions even yet to aid, where aid could still avail, were unceasing. Two young officers of his army had been frightfully wounded; a cannon-ball had torn away the greater part of the arm of one, ond a shell loaded with iron-filings had horribly shattered the arm and hand of the other: they had been conveyed into the village in which Frederick had taken up his quarters for the night, and had here somewhat recovered, but none of the surgeons would take the trouble to bind their ghastly wounds. The result of the battle was as yet unknown to them, when Frederick unexpectedly entered the chamber in which they lay saturated in their blood. "Ah, children," were his first words, "you seem severely wounded!" "Yes, your majesty," replied they; "but our sufferings would be lightly esteemed could we learn that you had conquered: we had already passed two redoubts, and had reached the third when we were struck." The king replied, "You have proved that you are invincible; everything else is chance. Keep up your courage; all will yet go well, and you will recover. Have your wounds been dressed? have you been bled?" "No, your majesty," replied they, "there is no one to bind our wounds." A surgeon was immediately summoned;

Frederick expressed his high displeasure at the neglect which had been shown, and at the same time gave strict injunctions that every attention should be paid to the wants of those gallant soldiers. The surgeon examined the wounds, shrugged his shoulders, and averred that no bandaging would be of avail, and that no surgical assistance could now be of any use, even though he were to amputate the wounded limbs. The king seized the young warriors by the hand, and turning to the surgeon, addressed him: "Look ye, no fever has as yet set in; nature works miracles when the blood is young and the heart as fresh as in them." Both officers did, in fact, recover, and continued in the service of Prussia up to the peace, when they were amply rewarded for their gallantry. Frederick, who had selected the chamber in which they lay to pass the night, gave it up to their use, and contented himself with one far inferior. Horrible visions of the future now danced in his brain, as he lay stretched upon his straw pallet: he could not sleep. An officer bringing him intelligence on the following morning that they had succeeded in saving some of the guns, he wildly exclaimed, "Sir, you lie. I have no more cannon!" No one ventured to approach him. An old colonel, Moller, was the only person to whom he imparted his grief. On inquiring of the latter how it came that his army did not now prove as successful as formerly, Moller, recollecting perhaps Leuthen, and the then pious feelings of the army, replied, that no prayers had been now for a long time said by the soldiers. Frederick the following day gave orders that divine service should be henceforth performed with strict regularity.

The Russians had neglected to cull the fruits of their victory. The staff, composed of the general officers, assembled on the evening of the battle in a peasant's hut, and held a council of war as to the expediency of pursuing the conquered Prussians. Exhausted by the extreme heat of the day, some refreshing drink had been called for, and all thoughts of further exertions were soon drowned in its intoxicating influence. Frederick suffered no further annoyance during that night, and on the following morning his scattered troops had rallied round him, and formed a body of 18,000 men. With these he crossed the Oder without interruption, and having broken down the bridges, formed an encampment between Frankfort and Cüstrin. He now saw that the enemy had still left him some hopes. Shortly previous to the battle he had received, through an adjutant of Duke Ferdinand of Brunswick, intelligence of the glorious victory which the latter had obtained at Minden, and had begged of the messenger to wait until the battle was over, in order to be able to convey to the duke similar despatches from him. He now dismissed the messenger with the words: "It grieves me sorely that the reply to such good intelligence must be so disastrous. But should you succeed in getting back, and if Daun be not already in Berlin, and Contades in Magdeburg, you can assure Duke Ferdinand from me that there has not been much lost." It required some time to be able to estimate the extent of his disasters. Upwards of 18,000 men, 127 guns, 26 colors, and 2 standards, besides the whole of the captured artillery, had been lost. Many of the best officers of the army had been severely wounded. The fate of a poet, De Kleist, whose brilliant talents had already secured him a high degree of popularity, and whose valor was conspicuous in the ranks of the Prussians, was peculiarly melancholy. A grape-shot had shattered his leg,—the Cossacks had stripped his body, and flung him into a marsh, where, after some Russian hussars had paid him some slight attention, he was again stripped and plundered by the Cossacks. Towards noon on the following day he was discovered by a Russian officer, who had him carried to Frankfort, where he died on the 24th of August, notwithstanding the most unremitting attentions had been paid to him. He was attended to the grave by a solemn procession, in which both the Russians and the members of the Frankfort University joined. A Russian officer of the staff placed his own sword upon the coffin, "that so distinguished an officer might not be buried without due honors."

But the losses sustained by the hostile army were likewise by no means inconsiderable, and somewhat exceeded 16,000 men. Soltikoff wrote to the empress as follows: "The King of Prussia generally sells his defeats dear, and should I have to communicate intelligence of a second victory of this kind, I shall be obliged to take a staff in my hand and bring the tidings myself."

Nothing, however, could banish the conviction from Frederick's mind that the enemy would, at least, in so far take advantage of their victory as to enter Mark Brandenburg and advance on his wholly defenceless capital. The passage of the Russians across the Oder, and the approach of the Austrian main army, under Daun, afforded ample grounds to justify such a conviction. Concentrating, therefore, every relic of his military strength which still remained, he ordered new guns to be forwarded from the arsenals, and took up a position in Fürstenwalde on the Spree, so as to cover as much as possible the road to Berlin. But that which every rational being must have naturally expected did not occur, for the enemy remained a considerable time in their position without attempting anything. Daun wished to throw the burden of the march on Berlin upon the Russians, and Soltikoff, who was somewhat sensitive on account of the former inactivity of the Austrian main army, contended that he had won two battles, and before exposing his troops to any further sacrifices he was entitled to await the news of two victories achieved by the Austrians. Thus jealousy and dissension sprang up between the hostile generals, and tended materially to relieve Frederick from his perilous position. This interruption of the enemy's movements was now doubly desirable, as the most imminent danger threatened the safety of Saxony likewise. The army of the empire had already advanced into that country, which was almost wholly unsupplied with troops, and had within a short time taken Leipzig, Wittenberg, Torgau, and were now preparing to

invest Dresden. Schmettau, who was in command of the
Prussian garrison in Dresden, was making his dispositions
for as obstinate a defence as that of the year before, when
he received a letter, which Frederick had written immediately after the defeat at Cunnersdorf, when in the midst
of his disasters, in which he was directed not to allow
matters to come to extremities, but to direct his principal
attention to the saving, if possible, of the royal treasure.
This order deprived him at once of all thoughts of further
resistance, little thinking that Frederick had dispatched
two corps to his relief, and that they were already close
at hand. He capitulated, and Dresden passed into the
hands of the enemy.

Prince Henry had hitherto quietly maintained his
position near Schmottseifen, on the Silesian frontier, and
had been treated with ridicule by the Austrians for his
inactivity. He now suddenly broke up his camp, and
following in the rear of the Austrian army attacked and
beat many of its isolated detachments, destroyed the
magazines from which Daun drew his supplies, and compelled the latter to turn his arms against him. Daun
strove, now that matters had assumed such an unfavorable turn, merely to prevent the prince from entering
Saxony, but the latter had anticipated his movements.
The two corps which Frederick had dispatched had
advanced with such rapidity and success that Henry
effected a union with them, and Daun, not wishing to
relinquish Saxony, against which the Austrian operations
were mainly directed, immediately abandoned his position
in the neighborhood of the Russian army, and turning
his arms against Prince Henry, a series of military
manœuvres ensued. The final result of these several
actions, which proved highly glorious for the Prussian
arms, was, that the Austrians and the allied army of the
empire lost the greater portion of their Saxon conquests,
no place of any consequence except Dresden remaining
in their hands.

The Russians had in the meantime broken up their encampment in the neighborhood of Frankfort, and were moving in a southerly direction, towards the Silesian frontier, closely followed by Frederick. On Soltikoff's learning that Daun, instead of sending reinforcements to the Russian army, as had been agreed upon, (Loudon's corps still remained incorporated with the Russian army,) had turned his whole strength against Saxony, especially as the provisions began to fall short, resolved on retiring to Poland. Daun, instead of provisions, sent him subsidies in money, which elicited from Soltikoff the reply that the Russians could not eat coin. But Daun's chief aim was to prevent Frederick's army from reaching Saxony, and with this view he endeavored once more to induce Soltikoff to prosecute his march on Silesia. He himself made preparations to besiege Glogau, but on approaching this fortress he found that he had been already circumvented by Frederick, who had taken up such a strong position as completely to block up the road thither. Soltikoff eventually fell back, towards the close of October, on Poland. Just about this period Frederick was attacked with a most severe fit of gout; he could neither ride nor drive, and was obliged to be carried about on a litter. He did not allow himself, however, to be prevented from the discharge of his kingly duties by this unexpected enemy, but resolutely defying all bodily pain, as when in perfect health, he superintended and directed every operation in person. When in Köben, a Silesian town on the Oder, he summoned the generals of his army to his presence, previous to the retreat of the Russians. They found him lying in a wretched room, his head bound in a cloth, and himself wrapped in a sable robe. In spite of the violent pains which racked his limbs, he addressed them gaily : " Gentlemen, I have summoned you to inform you of the dispositions I have made, and at the same time to convince you that nothing short of the violence of my disease prevents me from appearing personally before the army. Assure my brave troops that this is not a feigned sickness ; tell them that though I have had much ill success during the present campaign, yet I shall never rest until all be again made good—that I place the most unlimited confidence in their gallantry, and that nothing but death can ever separate me from my army." He issued his orders with the most surprising composure, and made such arrangements as his altered circumstances demanded. One division of his army was destined to cover Silesia; another was dispatched to Saxony to support Prince Henry.

The inactivity to which Frederick, partly in consequence of the movements of the Russians, and partly from his own indisposition, was doomed, had been devoted to literary recreations and pursuits congenial to the refined tastes of the monarch. Every moment that he could possibly spare from his administrative duties had been husbanded with care and employed in study; and being always provided with a small camp-library, he was able to strengthen and relieve his mind by reading and composition. Being then engaged in the perusal of a history of the life and achievements of Charles XII., the talented and adventurous Swedish king, he was induced to draw up a small and very interesting tract: "Considerations on the Character and Talents of Charles XII." Writing on this subject to the Marquis D'Argens, he says, "Being unceasingly engaged with military ideas, my mind, when I seek relief from distracting cares, naturally turns to cognate subjects of this class, so much so, indeed, that I can think of nothing else." He had this work printed during the following winter, but being intended strictly for private circulation amongst his friends, only twelve copies were printed, and these were distributed amongst the favored few.

He had hardly become convalescent when he hurried forward to Saxony, where matters had in the interim taken a most favorable turn. The hostile army had been driven back upon Dresden, and on the 14th of November Frederick reached the Prussian camp, where he highly complimented his brother, whose successful operations in

Lusatia and Saxony were mainly instrumental in giving this fortunate turn to the whole campaign, on his military talents and success. "Henry," said he, "is the only general who has committed no mistakes during this campaign." But these successes were to be now consummated by one decisive act, and the enemy driven out from the whole of Saxony. Frederick put himself at the head of his army, pursued the retreating foe, and came to a decisive engagement near the village of Krögis. Several corps were now dispatched to hang on the enemy's rear and harass its steps, and on their taking up a strong position in the Plauen Grund, one of these corps broke into Bohemia, and took ample revenge for the numerous acts of violence committed by both Austrians and Russians in their march. A second corps was dispatched, under General Fink, towards Maxen, in order to cut off Daun's retreat, or at least embarrass it. But this was a highly dangerous experiment. Fink remonstrated with Frederick on the difficulties of the enterprise, but the latter merely replied, " You know that I cannot endure the idea of *difficulties*. See that you set out." Fink surrendered himself to his fate; he saw himself surrounded by overpowering numbers, and after having in vain striven, on the 21st of November, by a bold movement to escape from his perilous position, was forced to surrender, and the whole corps, 12,000 strong, were made prisoners of war. This sudden disaster was speedily succeeded by a second. A Prussian corps, under General Dierecke, stationed on the opposite bank of the Elbe, was similarly captured by the Austrians. Dierecke made an effort, under cover of night, to fall back across the stream ; the attempt was one of extraordinary peril, and in a great measure impracticable, as the ice which covered the river's surface was in motion, and, as might be expected, but a very small remnant of the Prussians succeeded in effecting this crossing. The rest, to the amount of 1500, fell into the hands of the enemy.

Towards the close of the year matters had likewise assumed a very gloomy complexion in Saxony. Daun no longer felt any inclination to retire on Bohemia, and Frederick's army had been, through these repeated disasters, reduced to little more than 24,000 fighting men. Nothing could be now more natural than to suppose that he would be soon compelled to disgorge the fruits of his former successes. But Frederick did not retire one pace. He remained face to face with the foe in his small encampment near Wilsdruff, despite the desperate cold season that had just then set in. Four battalions of his army were alternately lodged in this encampment, the tents of which were frozen as stiff as boards. The soldiers lay within their tents stretched on each other to keep themselves warm, as the cold was most intense. The rest of the army was lodged in the surrounding villages. Here the officers sought refuge from the inclemency of the season in the different rooms and chambers, and the men lit large fires, in front of which they lay day and night. This extreme severity of the weather carried off a great number of victims, but at the same time prevented the enemy from attempting any onward movement. Daun thus saw himself necessitated to expose his troops to the same inconveniences and sufferings as his adversaries, without being able to gain anything whatever thereby. At length a reinforcement for Frederick's army arrived, under the conduct of the Prince of Brunswick. Now for the first time, it being January, were the troops allowed to take up regular winter-quarters. Freiberg was selected by Frederick for his head-quarters, and he here passed the remaining winter months.

Thus at length terminated a campaign which was productive of more disasters to the Prussian arms than any preceding one; and yet Frederick had not virtually lost any part of the territory which he had previously held, with the exception of Dresden, and a small section of the surrounding country, together with some inconsiderable

CAMPAIGN OF 1759. CUNNERSDORF.

possessions in Pomerania, which had been invested by the Swedes on the departure of the Prussian troops from that neighborhood. The combined exertions of his overwhelming enemies had not been productive of more important results.

CHAPTER XXXIII.

OPENING OF THE CAMPAIGN OF 1760. DRESDEN AND LIEGNITZ.

By dint of the most extraordinary exertions, Frederick had for the last four years been able to oppose the overpowering combinations of his enemies with the insignificant resources at his command. But he felt that the continuance of such a war, even though unattended by the unusually disastrous catastrophes of the late year, must eventually exhaust his utmost resources, and that the angry waves must sooner or later break over and engulf the fragile bark of which he was the pilot. Frederick but too clearly saw this to be the real state of things, and consequently neglected no means of allaying the wild storm, or at least giving it another direction. The King of Spain had died during the past year—Austria had claims upon the Spanish succession in Italy—these were contested by Sardinia. Frederick sent an ambassador to Turin and a second to Madrid to incite both courts to war. His suggestions met however, with no very favorable reception, and Maria Theresa allowed her Italian claims to remain in abeyance for the present, apprehensive lest their prosecution might interfere with the regaining of Silesia, on the recovery of which she had so completely set her heart as to consider all other objects but secondary to it. His efforts to bring about a peace with France proved equally fruitless. The war and the extravagance of the French court had wrought the most indescribable confusion in the French exchequer, which was almost entirely exhausted, and the court of Versailles seemed not altogether disinclined to listen to the pacific overtures of England; but on the latter power's declaring the integrity of Prussia to be an essential condition of any treaty of peace, all further negotiations were immediately suspended. The mistress of the French king, in retaliation for the contempt which she always experienced from Frederick, trifled with the fortunes and fate of the French people, and replied to every warning in wild self-confidence, challenging, as it were, that awful destiny which subsequently broke over France with these words: "After us—the flood!" Instead of the peace, so ardently desired by Frederick, a hostile alliance between France, Austria, and Russia, or, to speak more properly, for the interests of the nations were little consulted, an alliance between Pompadour, Maria Theresa, and Elizabeth was concluded.

Frederick had now no hope left him other than such as he derived from English aid, from the superiority of his own mind, the dauntless courage which animated his army, and the one circumstance, that the enterprises of his opponents had not been hitherto marked by any great spirit of cordiality or unity. He had now recourse to every possible expedient to render his ebbing resources available to the utmost, and the proceeds were employed in equipping and reinforcing his army anew. Naturally disinclined to burthen his own subjects with additional taxes, as they had already suffered very sensibly from the effects of the war, he compelled Saxony, Mecklenburg, and the principalities of Anhalt to contribute extraordinary supplies, and consequently those unhappy lands were forced to furnish very large contingents. Numerous as were the recruits which were thus obtained, as well as those drawn from his own dominions, yet they fell far short of filling up the chasms created in the ranks by the havoc of the last year's sanguinary campaign. A formal system of recruiting for the Prussian army was extended over the whole of Germany, and the Austrian prisoners of war were obliged to swear to the Prussian colors. Notwithstanding all this, on the opening of the campaign Frederick had hardly 90,000 effective men; whereas his enemies opposed him with forces exceeding 200,000. It must be likewise remarked that his present troops bore no similarity to those with whom he had commenced the war. Mere youths, who had never seen the face of an enemy, and had been drawn from the interior of the country, with others who had been enlisted abroad, did not warrant much reliance being placed upon them. He succeeded, however, in awakening a spirit of national enthusiasm, and the strict military discipline of the Prussian service, added to the peculiar eclat still attached to the Prussian arms, as well as the glorious renown of the great king its leader, were not without their influence on the efficiency of these raw levies.

In the midst of these weighty cares, science and art, which had ever proved his solace in the hour of trouble, were not neglected. In them, and their soothing influences, he sought to forget the mental torture to which the anxieties of his critical position gave birth. In poetical composition he found a vent for the emotions of his surcharged heart, and the feelings breathed forth in his poems of this period cannot fail, even to this day, to awaken in the reader sympathies of the warmest and most lively character. An "Ode to the Germans," written by him in March, 1760, is peculiarly curious. He here sharply rebukes the folly of the various German tribes, "children of one common parent," in persisting in the reciprocal slaughter of one another; in courting the aid of strangers for the purposes of bloodshed, and thus opening to them a passage into the heart of their native country. He points to the path where honorable fame may be acquired; and in conclusion, exhorts the Prussian people especially to perseverance and resolution. About this period a new and complete edition of his former poems was published by his authority, in consequence of a pirated edition having appeared in France, in which the various satirical sallies, which had been intended by him to meet the eyes of but a few trusty friends, had been invidiously applied to different political personages of the day, for the purpose of awakening the worst passions. There appears to be sufficient evidence to show that this pirated edition had been set on foot by Voltaire, who thereby hoped to inflame still further the animosities of Frederick's enemies, and thus gratify his own still unsatiated, paltry thirst for vengeance.

Feelings similar to those evinced in his poems of this period are likewise to be found in his correspondence with his friends; in these letters he describes his situation, and gives expression to his thoughts without the slightest dissimulation or reserve. In March, 1760, he wrote to Algerotti, whom he numbered amongst his most intimate friends, pretty nearly as follows:—" The Wandering Jew, if he have ever existed, never led so wandering a life as I do. I shall soon become like those village players, who have neither home nor fatherland. We run through the world to perform our bloody tragedies as often as our enemies permit us; we erect our theatre . . . . . . The last campaign has reduced Saxony to the verge of destruction: as long as fate permitted I spared that lovely land; but desolation is now abroad everywhere; and not to speak of the moral evils caused by this war, the physical ones are by no means less; and we may consider ourselves peculiarly fortunate, if pestilence does not follow in its wake. We, poor fools, who have but a moment to live, render that brief space as mutually distressing as we can, and find pleasure in the destruction of every masterpiece which time and labor have produced, leaving behind us nothing but so many hateful memorials of the havoc, desolation, and misery which we have wittingly occasioned!"

The time for active operations was now fast approaching. Frederick found himself again constrained to maintain the defensive, his forces being by no means adequate to the exigencies of an offensive war. A considerable period, however, elapsed before the enemy attempted any decisive movement. They could not agree on the plan according to which the campaign was to be opened. The Russian cabinet, acting upon the advice of Soltikoff, proposed that it should commence with the capture of Kolberg, and then, under the protection of the fleet, which it had agreed to furnish, to extend the war along the Pomeranian coast. This plan was altogether in accordance with the interests of Russia, and Soltikoff thought thereby to get rid of the disagreeable presence of the Austrians. These propositions were also in a great measure supported by France. The King of Poland, however, becoming clamorous in his entreaties that his principality might be restored to him, Maria Theresa proposed that Soltikoff should, in conjunction with Loudon, endeavor to effect the conquest of Silesia, whilst Daun kept Frederick's army employed in Saxony. This latter plan was eventually adopted; and Soltikoff, who considered himself slighted by the rejection of his counsels, felt no little annoyance at being still compelled to endure the presence of the Austrian troops.

The Prussian dispositions were as follows. Daun's army was opposed in Saxony by Frederick in person; Prince Henry commanded a corps on the Oder, which was to check the advance of the Russians; General Fouqué covered the frontiers of Silesia on the Bohemian side; and a small corps was stationed in Pomerania to oppose the Swedes.

The prelude and opening of the contest was reserved for Silesia. As early as the month of March, Loudon made an incursion upon Upper Silesia, which was protected by but few troops. General Golz, who commanded a Pomeranian regiment of infantry on the frontier, was forced to fall back upon Neisse; but the regiment had hardly got itself in motion, and joined a convoy, consisting of a hundred wagons, when Loudon's cavalry dashed in amongst its ranks, and despite the most gallant resistance, the whole was thrown into the most irretrievable disorder. Loudon dispatched a trumpeter forthwith to General Golz, requiring an unconditional surrender, as the regiment was completely hemmed in on all sides, and accompanied his message with the threat that, in the event of refusal, the whole should be massacred. The general conducted the trumpeter along his lines, at the same time informing his troops of the demand. A rather uncourteous Pomeranian reply re-echoed on all sides from the men, and the Austrian charges were recommenced with renewed impetuosity, and with equal resolution repulsed. The regiment eventually succeeded in reaching a secure position, having lost but a hundred and forty men, whilst the losses of the Austrians amounted to three hundred. Loudon himself could not refuse the tribute of his admiration to the gallantry of the brave Pomeranians.

More serious designs were in preparation. Loudon advanced, some months later, towards Bohemia, and penetrated, at the head of about 80,000 men, as far as the province of Glatz, and from thence into Silesia, where Fouqué was stationed on the border, with about 14,000 men. As the forces at the disposal of the latter were unequal to the task of maintaining his position, and in hope of being able to contend in the open country with more success against the superior numbers of his adversary, Fouque withdrew his army from the hills, and sought shelter beneath the cannons of Schweidnitz. Loudon had anticipated this movement, and took advantage of it to open the siege of the fortress of Glatz, with a view to obtain a firm footing in Silesia. Frederick was highly incensed at all this: he wrote an angry letter to his old friend, the grand master of the order of Bayard, instituted during the happy days of Rheinsberg, and still in existence, using the harsh expressions, "the devil thank you for leaving my hills. Regain me my hills, let it cost what it may." Upon receipt of this, Fouqué returned to his former position resolved to maintain it to the last man, and to sell the hills with his blood. It was, however, far from

Frederick's intention thus to sacrifice his faithful general, and he only wished that Fouqué should retard the motions of the enemy until he himself could arrive with an army for his relief. To effect this object was, however, by no means easy, unless by the exposure of Saxony to the incursions of Daun's army. Frederick formed the bold design of inducing the Austrian field-marshal, by means of artificial manœuvres, to follow him to Silesia. Similar experiments had been frequently employed by him with success already; in the present instance Daun occupied a strongly entrenched position near Dresden, which Frederick had failed to induce him to relinquish. Several days had passed without any object being attained, when suddenly, on the 25th of June, loud firing in the Austrian camp announced some extraordinary success. From the hostile piquets Frederick received information of Loudon's victory over Fouqué. The latter had kept to his determination. He had been attacked by Loudon on the 23d of June with overwhelming numbers near Landshut, and almost the whole of his corps had perished. Fouqué himself after receiving several wounds, had fallen from his horse, and was only saved by his groom, who had thrown himself over the body of his master, and thus warded off the blows dealt out by the enemy's dragoons: he was taken prisoner, and remained in the enemy's custody until the close of the war. The industrious town of Landshut was severely dealt with by the soldiers of the imperial army. The men got intoxicated, and even Loudon himself could hardly restrain the unbridled license and rapacity of those under his command.

It appears that the intelligence of Fouqué's defeat, instead of exciting consternation in Frederick's mind, but strengthened his desire to execute some extraordinary achievement,—one which, from its novelty and daring, should baffle all the calculations of his enemies, and confound their concerted measures. Nothing seemed better calculated to answer the purposes of a *coup* of this kind, than a direct attempt on Dresden itself. To this end he repeated all his former manœuvres with a view to draw Daun from his stronghold; but in vain. Baffled in this attempt, he finally resolved on making a feint of retiring with his army straight for Silesia. This movement aroused Daun at length from his inactivity. He hastened to anticipate Frederick's motions, and after effecting a junction with Loudon's corps strove to interrupt Frederick's progress : the hostile armies met, and some cavalry regiments, who formed the Prussian van, led on by Frederick in person, became engaged with the rear-guard of the Austrians. Frederick had charged the enemy without waiting to be supported by his infantry. Perceiving, at length, that gallantry unsustained by numerical strength, was insufficient for making any solid impression on the enemy, he was about to fall back upon his infantry, when, at the same instant, clouds of Ulanian horse dashed in amongst his squadrons and put them to flight. His own life was for some time in the most imminent danger, for two Ulanians came charging down on him with their lances in the rests, and nothing but presence of mind, on the part of his page, saved his life. The latter was thrown down, but called out in Polish to the horsemen, "Where the deuce are you rushing?" The page, not wearing any military uniform, was supposed by them to be an Austrian. After pleading as their excuse that their horses had run away with them, they wheeled about and disappeared. A battalion of Prussian grenadiers now arriving, by their well-directed volleys put an end to the contest.

As soon as Daun, according to Frederick's calculation, had advanced sufficiently far from Saxony, Frederick suddenly wheeled round, and moved on Dresden. A corps of the Austrian army, which had been stationed in his rear, now retreated at his approach, crossing the Elbe near Dresden, and, joined by the whole of the army of the empire, which had hitherto remained in complete inactivity, proceeded along the left bank of the Elbe, in the direction of Pirna. No greater obstacles now opposed

Frederick's investment and reduction of the town than such as the garrison presented, the necessary battering ordnance having been rapidly procured from Magdeburg. He calculated on exciting the apprehensions of the King of Poland, and by the threat of laying this splendid capital in ruins, on being able to induce the commandant to consent to a speedy capitulation. The breaching batteries opened on the town on the 14th of July, and it was almost immediately afterwards regularly bombarded. Many of the finest palaces were battered down; whole streets were wrapped in flames, and the position of the wretched inhabitants became frightful. Flying in crowds from the burning city, they left such treasures as they had saved from the flames in the bomb-proof cellars of the houses to be plundered by the licentious soldiers of the garrison. A few guns which stood on the turret of the Church of the Cross, and which were at times fired on festivals, were now employed against the besiegers; the latter considering the church as a battery, directed their mortars against it, and this magnificent pile soon became one sea of flames. Several other churches met the same fate; and the former splendor of this luxurious capital was almost completely annihilated.

But the commandant still held out valiantly, and although the army of the empire did not deem it expedient to stir from its entrenched position, the commandant yet hoped for relief from Daun. The latter also displayed no very remarkable rapidity in his motions, being under the impression that Frederick's movement was a mere stratagem to allure him into some trap. He at length reached Dresden, and the success of Frederick's enterprise became very doubtful, for Daun opened a communication with the besieged, in spite of all Frederick's exertions to prevent it. Many sorties now ensued, giving rise to several petty skirmishes, in which the Prussians were not always successful. One obstinate sortie directed against the trenches forced the Bernburg regiment to retire. Frederick punished this want of resolution, for such he held it, with a degree of ingenious severity wholly unparalleled in the annals of Prussian warfare. The mountings were stript from the officers' shakos, the facings from the men's uniform, and the tambours were forbidden to play the Grenadier march in future. This regiment, which had hitherto felt proud, from the fact of its having been organized under the superintendance of the veteran Prince of Dessau, became now the laughing-stock of the whole army. An opportunity, however, offered shortly after for wiping out this foul stain on its honor.

The result of the siege became from day to day more problematical. A considerable convoy from Magdeburg, intended for the Prussian army, had fallen into the hands of the enemy. A hostile corps was advancing in the rear of the Prussians, and the sad intelligence soon arrived that Glatz had fallen. Frederick was consequently obliged to abandon, after so much vain exertion, the entire enterprise, and raise the siege. On the evening of the 29th of July the Prussian army withdrew from Dresden. Glatz had been besieged by a special corps of Loudon's army, and had surrendered with such disgraceful precipitancy as to fully justify suspicions of treachery. But, notwithstanding this very considerable loss, Frederick did not abandon all hope of saving Silesia. His main object was now, if possible, to prevent a junction between the Austrian army and the Russians, the latter of which was now advancing on Silesia, and with a view to this he put his army immediately in motion. Daun broke up his camp simultaneously, and followed him like his shadow, without, however, interposing any considerable impediments to his march or venturing on a battle.

Loudon had meanwhile moved on Breslau, and was preparing to invest that town. He was at the head of 50,000 men, and the garrison consisted but of 3,000, two-thirds of these being troops on whom but little reliance could be placed. Besides this, there were 9,000 Austrian prisoners confined in the heart of the town, and means had been even resorted to to tamper with the citizens.

The royal lifeguards, consisting of about 1,000 men, who had been stationed in Breslau ever since the battle of Kollin, were the only troops on whom the commandant, General De Tauenzien, could rely ; notwithstanding which, he resolved on making as obstinate a defence as circumstances would permit. Loudon summoned him to surrender, but received a decisive answer in the negative. The bombardment now commenced, and one fourth of the town, including the royal palace, burst into flames. But Tauenzien exhibited equal courage and prudence in meeting every danger external or internal. On receiving a second summons to surrender, which concluded with the threat, that the child in the mother's womb should not be spared, he composedly replied, that neither he nor his men were pregnant. This consummate coolness was soon rewarded by relief from danger. Prince Henry, who had been hitherto engaged in watching the motions of the Russians, now arriving in the neighborhood of the town, Loudon raised the siege ; and the Prince took up a position close to the walls.

The Russians arrived almost immediately afterwards, and Soltikoff was not a little surprised at finding the Prussian army in front of him instead of the Austrian, as he firmly expected. Considering this as an additional ground for suspecting the sincerity of his allies, he felt fully confirmed in his opinion as to the little reliance that could be placed upon them. On receiving intelligence of Frederick's having entered Silesia, and of Loudon's advancing to meet the latter in order to support Daun, he declared in the most decided terms that he should immediately retire, if Frederick were permitted to reach the Oder without the Russian army being strengthened by Loudon's corps.

This solemn declaration induced Daun to relinquish his system of timid hesitation and engage the enemy. Both armies took up a position on the Katzbach, in the neighborhood of Liegnitz. It was the same ground which, from the period of the frightful Mongolian battle,

CAMPAIGN OF 1760. DRESDEN AND LIEGNITZ. 333

in the 13th century, had repeatedly drunk streams of blood. Here, too, Frederick had won one of those splendid victories to which he so often owed his salvation. On this same plain, fifty-three years subsequently, a battle for the salvation of Prussia and Germany was likewise fought. Daun could now gratify his wish for an engagement with the more security, as Frederick's position was in truth very precarious. The Austrian army amounted, since its junction with Loudon, to 95,000 fighting men, whilst the Prussians numbered but 30,000, were short of provisions, and cut off from Breslau. Frederick's endeavors by means of manœuvres to gain a more favorable position proved ineffectual.

Daun strove to repeat the same game which he had played with success at Hochkirch—he intended that Frederick's camp should be stormed on all sides at break of day. His plan was kept perfectly secret; but Frederick could, from several of the enemy's movements, foresee that an attack was meditated. As his position above Liegnitz was not particularly strong, he resolved on drawing his army off to the other side of the town, where the nature of the ground promised to be more favorable; his position here would also render the accomplishment of his design for forcing a passage across the Oder more easy of execution. The night of the 14th was appointed for the execution of this movement. An officer who had deserted from the enemy was brought in during the afternoon, and spoke of important secrets which he had to communicate. He was, however, so intoxicated that it became necessary to have recourse to all possible artificial means to bring him to anything like rational consciousness. His statements confirmed the suspicion of the intended attack, but as he could give no intelligence of the details of the enemy's plans, Frederick did not countermand his previous orders.

The change of position was effected under cover of night. It was now about three o'clock in the morning, and the whole of the troops who had for the most part slept under arms, during the brief interval allotted for repose, awaited the break of day with the utmost impatience. Frederick who had been busy on the left wing, having wrapped himself in his mantle and lain down beside a watch-fire, had just fallen asleep. A general was seated by his side, and stirred the fire. At this moment Major Hundt, of the hussars, who had been patroling to the left of the army, came riding up in full gallop, and inquired for the king. He was told not to disturb him as he was asleep; but Frederick had heard the call, and on inquiring of the major the cause of his haste, was informed that the enemy's columns were in motion, and had already advanced within four hundred paces. Frederick instantly issued orders for the men to get under arms, but supposing that the attack on his position would not be confined to one point, he gave orders for General Zieten to advance with the right wing to meet the enemy, whilst he strove with the left to repulse the coming attack. The troops formed under the enemy's fire, but with precision and speed. Loudon had planned the attack on the Prussian left, but without having any idea that his opponents had shifted their ground. He had also calculated on being able by a sudden attack to get possession of the Prussian baggage, and in order to keep matters secret had purposely dispensed with an advanced guard; his surprise, therefore, at the discovery he now made was extreme. Giving orders to his troops to form with all possible expedition, he put them in order of battle as well as the unfavorable nature of the ground would permit. The thunder of the guns opened the fight. The Austrian cavalry charged the Prussians, but were repulsed. Some regiments of infantry then advanced. But the Prussians valiantly maintained their ground, the Austrians seeming to waver; at the same instant the Prussian cavalry penetrated into the enemy's lines, and made a great number of prisoners. Still Loudon was far superior to the king in numbers, having 35,000 men under his command, whilst the Prussian left wing did not exceed 14,000. Fresh troops kept perpetually arriving to reinforce the Austrians, but the Prussians valiantly repulsed every attack, notwithstanding that their ranks were every moment more and more thinned. Loudon's cavalry once more charged the Prussian infantry, but the latter gallantly withstood the charge. It was on this occasion that the Bernburg regiment regained its lost honors. Charging the Austrian cavalry with fixed bayonets, it flung many of the riders from their horses, and drove the others before them in wild confusion, until at length not a single Austrian regiment retained its position. At six o'clock the Prussians were undisputed victors on that well-fought field.

Frederick now hastened to the right wing of his army, which had been partially attacked. Daun, on arriving at the point where the Prussian camp had stood on the previous evening, and finding the ground deserted, determined on following the fugitives, conceiving that the Prussians must have fled. To effect this, he was obliged to cross the marshy Schwartzwasser, which discharges itself near Liegnitz into the Katzbach, and which sheltered the Prussian position on this side: there was but a single bridge over this river, and Zieten, as soon as just so many of the Austrians had crossed it as he could master with ease, opened a hot fire from the guns upon them; when they fled in all directions, and he took an immense number prisoners. Some attempts of the enemy's artillery were soon silenced by the Prussian guns, as the latter occupied a very favorable position. Daun now paused, undecided how to act. He had received no intelligence from Loudon, and the wind had carried the whole noise of the fight in the contrary direction. At length he heard several rounds of musketry announcing victory, and he soon guessed what it meant. The Prussians had scarcely fired the second round, when the enemy wheeled, crossed the Katzbach, and at break of day departed.

This victory was obtained without any great sacrifices.

The whole losses of the Prussians amounted to 3500 men; the Austrians had, on the other hand, lost 10,000 men, together with 82 guns, and 23 colors and standards. A special mark of distinction was reserved for the Bernburg regiment. As soon as the battle was over, the king ordered the whole army to form in one line; in front of which he rode from one end to the other, to see the gaps which the battle had made. The whole army stood at ease; the Bernburg regiment was stationed at the head of the right wing. As soon as Frederick approached it, he called out gaily to the soldiers, "Children, I thank you; you have done your duty bravely, right bravely; you shall have everything back." The fugleman of the regiment, an old veteran, advanced from the ranks, and addressing the king, said, "I thank your majesty, in the name of my comrades, for giving us back our rights. Your majesty is once more a gracious king." Frederick clapped the soldier on the back, and replied, with tears in his eyes, "Everything is forgiven and everything forgotten except this day." The review now terminated, and Frederick directed that the old fugleman who had just spoken should be made a sergeant: the latter returned thanks, and several soldiers of the regiment crowded round the king, and defended their conduct at Dresden, saying, that the fault was not in them, but in those who led them. Frederick would not grant this, exactly; and the soldiers commenced advocating their views with a degree of warmth, confidence, and familiarity, that so surprised the commander, that he, fearing Frederick's displeasure, ordered them to disperse. This Frederick would not permit, but terminated the dispute by assuring them once more that they were brave fellows, and an honor to the Prussian army. Frederick's influence over the hearts of the soldiers was mainly attributable to the familiarity with which he entered into all their feelings, and often took part in their disputes. The anecdotes told of him are peculiarly rich in details of this kind. The consequence was that his soldiers generally addressed him merely by the name of "Fritz," or the pet name of "old Fritz."

The victory of Liegnitz was the first beam of good fortune which had for a long time shone upon the Prussian arms. But except inspiring the army with moral confidence in itself, little else would have been really gained, had the enemy, taking advantage of their strength, endeavored to oppose Frederick's march anew. Experience should have taught him, that Frederick never did anything by halves; and in the present instance he was equally quick in taking advantage of the enemy's confusion. That very day his army advanced upwards of fifteen miles, and in a short time he effected a junction with Prince Henry at Breslau. Daun retired cautiously to the hills on the Bohemian frontiers. Soltikoff followed the example of his ally, and proceeded with his army to the frontiers of Poland. The great plan for the junction of these two powerful armies had been paralyzed.

CHAPTER XXXIV.

CONCLUSION OF THE CAMPAIGN OF 1760. TORGAU.

NEW plans for effective co-operation were now discussed by the Austrian and Russian leaders, and a new system of warfare finally agreed on between the parties. But these deliberations were considerably protracted both by mutual distrust and the severe illness of the Russian general. It was, at length, after much previous discussion, arranged, that the Russians should make an incursion on Mark Brandenburg, whilst the Austrians took active measures in Silesia; and thus, by dividing the Prussian powers of resistance, easily destroy in detail each individual corps. Daun was strongly in favor of proceeding to an immediate investment of Schweidnitz, and Frederick, not apprehending any very great dispatch on the part of the Russians, resolved on turning his undivided strength against Daun who was, however, almost double his number, and force him to evacuate Silesia. In truth, his manœuvres were directed with such tact, that Daun was obliged, notwithstanding his great numerical superiority, to abandon his enterprise, and confine himself to mere defensive operations. Daun took up, on the other hand, such admirable positions on the heights, that Frederick could not succeed in entirely expelling him from the land, and a considerable period thus elapsed without any decisive result being attained; but as soon as intelligence arrived that the Russians were marching on Berlin, and that a special Austrian corps, under General Lacy, had been likewise dispatched in the same direction, Frederick saw himself obliged to relinquish all opposition to the Austrian main army, and hasten to the relief of his capital. On the 6th of October he set out with his army for Berlin.

His march was not attended with any special circumstances of danger, but many characteristic traits of the peculiarly familiar and friendly intercourse existing between the monarch and his men, elicited during this march, have been preserved to us.

As the army was once halting in front of a morass, on the frontiers of Lusatia, awaiting the erection of a vehicle which was necessary for the transport of the heavy pieces of ordnance, the following incident occurred. It was a cold misty morning in autumn; firewood was quickly collected—fires lighted—and the soldiers lay down in front of them. Beside one of these fires stood Frederick, leaning against a tree. Zieten happened to come to the same fire, sat down on a block of wood, and being overpowered by the march, fell asleep; a grenadier placed a bundle of sticks under the general's head, an act which Frederick observed with pleasure. An officer soon arrived with dispatches for the king, and advancing towards Zieten, was about to awaken him, when the king whispered him softly, "Don't disturb my Zieten, he is tired." One of the soldiers' wives, sometime afterwards, not aware of the king's presence, placed a pot with potatoes on the fire, and kneeling down blew it with such violence that the sparks flew into the king's face. The latter said nothing, but drew his mantle a little in front. A soldier who was passing by recognized the king, and informed the woman of his presence. Upon being made aware of the fact, she seized the cooking apparatus in the utmost horror and ran off in the greatest dismay. Frederick ordered her to be brought back, and to replace the potatoes upon the fire. The soldiers were highly delighted with this considerate condescension of their king.

During the march Frederick frequently called out to his troops, when they happened from weariness or any other cause to relax their military precision, Exact, children, "exact!" They frequently replied, "*Exactly*, Fritz!" Such rejoinders were never taken amiss by the king; but, in return, his troops followed him with the most entire devotion. His invariable morning salutation was, "Good morning, children!" which was invariably responded to with, "Good day, Fritz!"

Towards the close of the march a female hussar, who had taken part in all the campaigns of the army, dismounted, and entering a barn gave birth to a boy. Immediately afterwards she remounted, and advancing to the king presented him with the child, and informed him that she had just given birth to a little Fritz. "Has the child been baptized?" inquired the king. "No," replied the mother, "but he shall be called Fritz!" "Well," replied the king, "take care of him, and as soon as peace comes I'll provide for him."

Frederick was perhaps justified in thinking that the incursion of the Russians would not be executed with extraordinary dispatch or resolution, inasmuch as previous to his departure from Silesia a similar attempt, which had been ushered in with extraordinary preparations, had been defeated with the greatest ease. It was a principal aim with the Russians to obtain a firm footing in Pomerania, and with a view to this a powerful Russian fleet appeared, towards the close of August, in front of Kolberg, and commenced a blockade of the fortress. The garrison of Kolberg was very feeble, but the commandant, Colonel De Heide, succeeded in repulsing every assault and in throwing up such excellent defences, that several weeks passed without the enemy making any considerable progress. A small Swedish fleet also arrived, in order to co-operate with the Russians; but the relief which the harassed besieged had so long desired suddenly appeared: a small Prussian corps marched with such rapidity from Silesia, that they seemed to have sprung out of the earth. The advanced-guard of this corps, consisting of three hundred hussars, flung themselves with such impetuosity

CAMPAIGN OF 1760. TORGAU. 341

on the hostile infantry, that, being mistaken for the main body of the Prussian army, the enemy fled to their ships, leaving a great number of prisoners and slain behind them. The Swedish fleet put to sea at the first onslaught of the Prussian hussars, as if the latter possessed the power of being able to pursue them even by water, On the 23d of September the Russian fleet set sail. The Prussian corps was then dispatched to Swedish Pomerania to hold the enemy in check in that quarter.

But the hopes which Frederick had gathered from this event were illusory. He had scarcely arrived, on the 15th of October, on the frontier of Mark Brandenburg, when he learned that his splendid capital had already fallen into the hands of the enemy. After many deliberations between the Austrians and Russians, the latter had thrown themselves on Mark Brandenburg, and the Russian advanced-guard, under General Tottleben, had reached Berlin on the 3d of October. The feeble garrison had at first offered the most determined resistance, and some of the first generals of the Prussian army, who were stopping there to recover from the effects of their wounds, (Seidlitz especially,) particularly distinguished themselves by their activity and valor. Some Prussian troops were speedily procured from the surrounding districts, and the resistance offered now became considerable. But as the corps under General Tottleben was soon considerably reinforced, and as the Austrian corps under General Lacy had already arrived in front of Berlin, the Prussian troops were obliged to retire, to avoid exposing the town to the dangers of a storm. The court had long since taken up its residence at Magdeburg. The garrison capitulated, and Tottleben entered Berlin on the 9th of October, But the fate which Berlin met was not by any means so hard as was generally the case with such towns as had become exposed to the barbarities of the Russians. The Russian general exacted, no doubt, a very considerable contribution, but the strictest discipline was preserved. The Austrians, whom Tottleben would have gladly excluded altogether from Berlin, were the only persons who committed any considerable excesses. The loss in Prussian ammunition, which was partly carried off and partly destroyed, was very great. The contribution in money amounted to two millions of thalers ; which was subsequently paid off by Frederick out of his private purse, but with the greatest privacy, so that no burthen accrued therefrom to the nation. A worthy citizen of Berlin, Gotzkowsky, a merchant, made himself on this occasion peculiarly conspicuous by his many acts of disinterested kindness. Potsdam, especially Sans-souci, met with very considerate treatment. Prince Esterhazy, the Austrian general in command, paid particular attention to the security of the royal private property, and took away but one picture from the palace, as a memorial of the capture. But the violence and barbarities perpetrated by the enemy in the other towns and villages round Berlin were most atrocious. Charlottenburg, especially, met a sad fate. Everything in the palace of the king was destroyed—the furniture and vases broken to atoms—the hangings torn—the pictures cut and disfigured—the chapel plundered—and the fine organ which stood in it broken. The principal fury of the soldiery seemed directed against the valuable antiques which Frederick had purchased from the heirs of Cardinal Polignac, and which had been employed in the decoration of this palace and garden. The statues and busts were mutilated, and their future repair totally prevented. And these barbarities were not wrought by uncivilized Asiatic hordes, but by the Saxon regiments, who had been made prisoners at Pirna, subsequently deserted to the enemy, and in this unworthy manner gratified their hatred of the Prussian king.

But this hostile occupation of the Prussian capital was but of short duration. News soon arrived that Frederick was approaching to its relief, and the mere announcement—" The king is coming ! " dissipated, like the blast of a whirlwind, the hosts of his enemies. On the 12th a precipitate evacuation ensued ; the Russians repassed the Oder; General Lacy proceeded in the direction of Saxony, and Daun, who had followed Frederick from Silesia, likewise entered the Saxon territories. Frederick received the announcement of the enemy's retreat almost contemporaneously with that of their occupation. He conceived it now unnecessary to advance further at present in Mark Brandenburg, and decided on setting out for Saxony, where his presence became once more imperatively necessary. After having made such fiscal dispositions as would in some measure compensate the inhabitants of Mark for the great losses they had sustained, he set out once more, in the hope of coming to some decisive engagement.

Perhaps the most brilliant proof of his military greatness is to be found in the fact that his mere name was sufficient to scatter the hosts of his enemies. But the danger was as yet by no means over. On the contrary, as matters at present stood, he had reason to apprehend the worst. The whole of Saxony was at this moment in the hands of his enemies. On Frederick's departure from Dresden he had left but a small corps behind him to oppose the motions of the army of the empire. At first this corps had been very successful, but the army of the empire had subsequently made some progress, and the Prussian corps having been called away to the relief of Berlin, the enemy met with no further resistance, and accordingly took military possession of the whole of Saxony. All the fortified towns fell into their hands, and if Daun had succeeded in shutting Frederick up in Saxony, Mark Brandenburg would have been once more exposed to the incursions of the Russians, who only awaited intelligence of this event to march and take up their winter-quarters in Mark. Frederick recognized the greatness of the danger which impended, but the thousand perils through which he had already passed steeled his resolution. He was prepared to meet the worst. In a letter to D'Argens he says " I shall never see the day that will force me to conclude a disastrous peace,

No reasoning, no eloquence shall ever prevail on me to put my name to my own dishonor. I will either be buried beneath the ruins of my native land, or if fate, which persecutes me, deny me this boon, I will put an end to that existence which I am not able any longer to endure. I have always acted in accordance with my own internal convictions, and that honorable feeling shall still guide my steps and be my constant rule of action— my acts have ever been in accordance with my principles. After having sacrificed my youth to my father, and my manhood to my fatherland, I feel entitled to dispose as I please of my old age. I have already told you, and repeat it once more, that my hand shall never sign a disgraceful treaty of peace. I am firmly resolved to attempt the utmost in this campaign; to dare desperate things; to conquer, or meet an honorable death!"

Fortune smiled on his first exertions. Wittenberg and Leipzig were recaptured by the Prussian troops. The army of the empire retired towards Thuringia, without having effected a junction with the Austrians. Daun pitched his camp in the neighborhood of Torgau, and matters seemed likely to come here to a decisive issue.

Daun's army numbered upwards of 64,000 men. The position which he occupied upon the heights of Torgau was almost identical with that of the Russians at Cunnersdorf; his camp was protected in front by a precipitous steep, streams, and marches; its rear fortified by a strong abattis. Frederick's army amounted to 44,000 men. The nature of the ground rendered it desirable for him to deploy his chief forces, so as to be able to attack the enemy in the rear, whilst a special corps, under Zieten's command, was to charge them in front, and as soon as Frederick had engaged them to assail them in the flank and complete their destruction.

On the 3d of November, at early dawn, Frederick put his men in motion. His army penetrated the wood in three columns. An Austrian regiment, which had been stationed as an outpost in the wood, got between the two first columns of the Prussian army, and was almost entirely captured. It became, however, necessary, in order to arrive at the desired point, to proceed to a distance of several miles, and it was already past noon before Frederick reached the outskirts of the wood, and found himself in front of the enemy's position. A cannonade was now heard on the opposite side, which appeared to grow more violent every minute. Zieten had met an advanced post of the Austrian army, which checked his further approach, and he found it necessary to bring up cannon. Frederick taking this as a sign of a general engagement, determined on immediate attack, although his whole army had not yet arrived, and the cavalry was for the most part still in the wood. It was two o'clock before his first regiments advanced against the enemy. Daun, who had been previously informed of Frederick's motions, had taken the necessary measures to defeat them. A raking fire swept down the Prussian grenadiers, who fell in lines. A part of the Prussian army was obliged to march on the skirts of the wood, but the enemy's cannon penetrated even thither. The trees fell shattered on all sides, crushing all beneath them. A huge oak bough gave way immediately above the king's head, killing two men in front of him. The king was obliged to dismount, and lead his troops on foot into the plain. The first attack was fruitless. Two-thirds of the battalions of grenadiers lay prostrated on the ground, and the remainder were obliged to retire. Fresh troops had been in the meantime brought up, and pushed on up the heights. The thunder of the guns, which made the earth quake, pealed out anew, and the dense clouds that hitherto had enwrapt the heavens, seemed driven away by their fire. "Have you ever," said Frederick, turning to an aide-de-camp, "heard a fiercer cannonade? At least, I never have." The Prussians were again swept down in bodies, but the survivors marched undaunted forward, crossed the chevaux-de-frise, gained the heights, and there manfully withstood the most impetuous assaults

of the Austrians, until the lines on both sides were much
thinned, when the Austrian cavalry broke in upon the
Prussians and drove them once more down the steeps.
A third attempt was now made. The Prussian cavalry
had at length reached the scene of action and charged
the Austrian lines with impetuosity: both armies were
now in the centre of a hot fire, success and disaster shifted
from side to side, and Frederick fairly shared all the toils
of his troops. Two horses had been already shot under
him, when a ball struck him in the breast, and he sank to
the earth without a groan. On being supported by his
aide-de-camp who tore the cloth from his breast, he was
relieved by the discovery that the wound was not dangerous, as the ball had been retarded by a fur dress which
the king wore. Recovering his senses, he said, " 'Tis not
serious!" and remounting his horse, gave fresh orders
for the battle; but the Austrian cavalry pressed forward
once more, and the Prussians were again compelled to
retire. Night now came on and put an end to the contest:
the Prussian army withdrew from the field of battle and
took up another position, awaiting the events of the
coming day. Frederick proceeded to a neighboring village; where all the houses being full of the wounded, he
took up his quarters for the night in the church: he here
had his wounds dressed, and distributed the necessary
orders for the disposition of his army. "The enemy," he
remarked, " have not suffered less than we, and as Zieten
is in their rear, they will not venture to remain in their
present position, so that after all the battle is won. But
the officers round him, many of whom were wounded,
could not console themselves so easily, and several hours
passed in painful silence. It was just nine o'clock when
the joyous intelligence arrived, that Zieten had opened
the battle at a late period and had conquered. The awful
silence that had hitherto prevailed was now changed into
loud shouts of joy and thankfulness. Frederick mounting the steps of the altar, penned some dispatches, issued

fresh orders, and laying himself down on the straw litter which had been prepared for him, slept.

Zieten, after pushing in the outposts of the Austrians, had remained inactive, in obedience to the order of the king, till towards evening; when, feeling convinced that Frederick's exertions had proved unsuccessful, he prepared for an attack. In front of him lay a village which was in the hands of the enemy; he stormed it and drove the enemy out, but the latter set the village on fire to prevent the pursuit; this sheet of fire was the torch which lit him to further deeds, as night was approaching: perceiving that the Austrian army on the heights had thronged towards the centre and left the outskirts unguarded, he advanced with his daring troopers, and took up a firm position on the hills, in the teeth of the enemy's fire. A desperate struggle here commenced without leading to any issue. Some regiments that had already taken part in the contest under Frederick's guidance, perceived this renewal of the struggle; hurrying forward to assist at its decision, they were conducted by the blaze of light issuing from the burning village, and succeeded in approaching without being observed: they fell upon the Austrians on the flank, and the fortune of the day was soon decided. The enemy was forced to retire from the field which they already considered as won. Daun, who had been previously wounded, and conveyed to Torgau, now gave orders that his army should immediately evacuate that town, and cross to the other side of the Elbe.

The night was wild and stormy, and numbers of the men of both armies who had been dispersed in bodies, wandered about, ignorant of the result of the battle, in search of their comrades. The flames of the burning village had died away, and the numerous fires, which had been lighted as a preservative against the extreme cold, served but to lead the wanderers astray. The Austrians directed their steps by the murmuring of the Elbe, but whole battalions fell into the hands of the Prussians, detachments of the latter encountered one another, and not being able to recognize their fellow-countrymen, considerable slaughter ensued. The wounded and unwounded of both armies frequently lay in groups round the same fire. Weary of carnage, they had come to a mutual understanding amongst themselves to become reciprocally the captives of whatever side had conquered. Nor were those wild hordes wanting who swarmed round the battle-field, plundering the dead and the dying.

Day dawned at length, and Frederick appeared on the bloody field of battle, to make provision for the wounded and care for their wants. It was a subject of universal joy to his army to find him, whom all thought severely wounded, fresh and unhurt. A grenadier in the last death struggle called out to him as he passed, "Now I die with pleasure, as I see that we have conquered, and my king is alive." On Frederick and Zieten meeting, they clasped each other with much emotion; Frederick wept aloud, and was unequal to the task of returning thanks to his faithful hero.

The loss on both sides had been very considerable. That of the Prussians amounted to between 12,000 and 13,000 men; that of the Austrians to upwards of 16,000; but the latter were still superior in point of numbers; and, had they made but a proper use of their strength, they might have rendered the fruits of the victory of equivocal value to Frederick; but the suddenness of defeat, after the certainty of victory, which they had already sent a courier to announce, robbed them of all resolution, and they withdrew to Dresden, seeking but to retain possession of the capital. Frederick made several endeavors to drive them from thence, and push them back into Bohemia, but the severity of the approaching winter rendered this impossible, and both armies now proceeded to take up winter-quarters. The Russians fell back on Poland, the army of the empire on Franconia. Some attempts made by a special Austrian corps upon Upper Silesia proved likewise abortive. This campaign, like the preceding ones, had been opened by the enemy with over-

CAMPAIGN OF 1760. TORGAU. 349

whelming numbers, and yet, at its close, after all their conquests, Glatz alone remained in their possession.

Between the French army and the allied troops under Duke Ferdinand of Brunswick, several battles had been fought with various success. The French had taken the field with an enormous army, but incompetency and dissension amongst the leaders more than compensated for their numerical superiority; advances were alternately made by one party and the other; but no decisive result was thereby achieved. Towards the beginning of the following year, about the month of February, the duke gained, by a sudden assault, very considerable advantages, but lost them again some months subsequently, and the troops were on both sides drawn off to their previous winter-quarters, without any material change in the relations of the contending parties having taken place.

CHAPTER XXXV.

CAMPAIGN OF 1761. THE CAMP AT BUNZELWITZ.

INEFFECTUAL attempts had been repeatedly made during the course of the winter, by the several European cabinets, to adjust the confused relations in which Europe had so long stood, and by which society was still agitated. The first overtures came from France, which, without having any immediate interest in the struggle, was one of the greatest sufferers by its continuance. The war it had carried on in Westphalia had already swallowed up vast sums, but the losses occasioned by the naval war with England were still more considerable; it was accordingly proposed, that a general European congress should be held at Augsberg, but the same evil passions which had originally led to hostilities were still as active as ever; and though Frederick from his heart desired peace, yet he would not in any way consent to accede to unjust concessions: thus the negotiations, after having been continued for a short period, were soon and abruptly broken off.

The preparations which were on all sides made for a renewal of active hostilities, were now pushed with proportionable vigor; but the strength of all parties gradually began to fail: Frederick was obliged to have recourse to more severe fiscal measures, in order to obtain means for continuing the contest. Poor Saxony, which had already suffered so severely from this unhappy war, was burthened with additional taxes, forced to furnish new contributions, and compelled to submit to a considerable reduction in the value of its currency. Recruits were everywhere enlisted for the Prussian service, agriculture was altogether abandoned wherever the hostile armies appeared and the ploughshare exchanged for the musket. It will be easily imagined what extreme severity of discipline was necessary to give this rabble, collected from every quarter and in every manner, anything like the appearance of a regular army. Austria, on the other hand, possessed in her populous provinces ample nurseries for recruiting her ranks, and it was even easy to observe, that in the same proportion as the Prussian army became depreciated in character and efficiency, the Austrian army improved; but whilst Frederick, by his clever financial operations was always able to meet the demands on his exchequer, the Austrian treasury was wholly drained. All the officers of the staff were obliged to accept of payment in paper-money, which latter was to be exchanged for gold after the termination of the war. Whoever could not conveniently wait for so long and indefinite a period, was obliged to have recourse to a special bank, where the paper was exchanged, but at a very considerable discount. This bank had been opened by the Emperor Francis, the husband of Maria Theresa, whose tastes were decidedly numismatic, and whose activity was exclusively confined to pecuniary speculations.

To meet the deficiencies of his sinking resources, Frederick was obliged to have recourse to severe measures, and the invariable consequences of protracted warfare ensued. He had hitherto conscientiously abstained from touching in any way the royal palaces in Saxony, or the valuable artistic treasures with which they were richly adorned; the only private property which he did not regret to see suffer, was that of Count Brühl, who had always exhibited the most rancorous hatred towards him; but the plundering of the Charlottenburg palace, and the barbarous destruction of the antiquarian remains there treasured up, which had been obtained at immense pecuniary sacrifices, inflamed him to the utmost pitch of frenzy; and as Saxon troops had been chiefly instrumental in this work of destruction, he was determined to retaliate upon Saxony. He waited, notwithstanding, for several months, after having made public complaint of this conduct, and threatened reprisals, without one word of excuse coming from the lips of King Augustus; upon this, Frederick gave orders to plunder the hunting palace, Hubertsburg, which had been called the "heart's-core" of the King of Poland. "The heads of the great," said he, "do not feel the hair torn from the heads of their subjects; we must attack them where they will feel it." But it was somewhat difficult to find in the Prussian army an officer to obey this command. General de Saldern, whom the king first appointed for this service, positively refused, considering it to be contrary to honor, oath, and duty, and for this act was visited with the monarch's displeasure. A free corps under Major Quintus Icilius eventually executed the order.

In the midst of all this, Frederick did not allow the quiet of the winter-quarters, which he had taken up in Leipzig, to pass without some of those enjoyments that had previously constituted his happiness. Leipzig was considered in those days as the centre of German science and poetry, and frequent opportunities offered for his here becoming acquainted with its rich resources, little as he in general valued the exertions of Germans in the intellectual world. He had become acquainted with Gottsched during a former visit, and this poet, to whom Voltaire paid some attention, had made a favorable impression upon him. Frederick dedicated a poem to him, in which he addresses him as the Saxon swan, and closes with the flattering words,—

> "By thy harmonious strains thus addest thou
> Apollo's fairer wreath to that bright crown
> That long since decks the warrior German's brow!"

Gottsched now received a second invitation from the king, but the manners of the poet, which were far from captivating, made no very favorable impression. Frederick took more pleasure in the society of the modest Gellert; he listened with pleasure to the latter whilst reciting his clever fables, and took delight in the flowing metre. "Gellert," said he, "is the most rational of all German scholars, the only one who will descend to posterity." This extravagant eulogium could have only come from a person like Frederick, who formed his estimate of German knowledge from the state in which he found it in the commencement of the century, and who was unacquainted with the names of Klopstock, Lessing, and the other great spirits to whom the German nation looks back with pride. Gellert was, however, but once formally invited to his presence. It is possible that the poet's supplication, which was not very well timed, imploring Frederick to grant Germany peace, to which the latter simply replied, that this did not lie in his power, and perhaps still more, his statement, that he paid more attention to ancient than modern history, may have been in a great measure the cause of Frederick's taking less interest in him.

His evenings, as in times of peace, were enlivened by music, and for this purpose he summoned several members of his orchestra from Berlin, but he took, personally, a less active part in the performance than formally. Playing the flute had already begun to affect his lungs.

The Marquis D'Argens, whose sincere sympathy and respect Frederick prized highly, had likewise come to Leipzig, and Frederick passed his evenings, after the concerts, in conversation with him. On D'Argens entering Frederick's room one evening, he found him seated on the floor with a dish of fricassée before him, from which the royal greyhounds were taking their supper. Frederick held in his hand a small stick, with which he was keeping order amongst his canine favorites, and pushing over the best *morceaux* to his little pet greyhound. The Marquis paused in astonishment and exclaimed, "How much would the five great powers of Europe be surprised to learn how the Margrave of Brandenburg, against whom they had vowed destruction, is at present employed! They probably think that he is laying some deep plan for the approaching campaign, collecting funds, providing magazines for man and horse, or plotting how to divide his enemies and obtain friends. But not one particle of all this. He sits quietly in his room feeding his dogs!"

The campaign of 1761 opened somewhat late, and no event of any importance occurred until the close of the year. Frederick was frequently obliged to oppose a foe immeasurably superior, and in positions which rendered it a matter of the utmost difficulty to supply such losses as were sustained, even when the victory was nominally his. He was reduced to a more strict observance than ever of his system of defence, obliged to await the attacks of his enemies, and watch for such errors as they might make, reserving his strength as much as possible for decisive moments. The prelude to the contest opened towards the close of the winter, when an expedition against the army of the empire was undertaken, and so successfully executed, that the latter was forced to abandon its position with considerable loss, and remain for a long time in a state of inactivity. Silesia next became the seat of war. The chief aim of the enemy was to get possession of this province. An Austrian army, under Loudon, consisting of 75,000 men, together with a Russian army 60,000 strong, under the command of Field-marshal Butturlin, was to be here concentrated. Frederick set out in May for Silesia, in order to prevent this junction, but could only oppose 55,000 men to both these armies. He left Prince Henry behind him for the protection of Saxony.

The three months from the middle of August were passed in different manœuvres, marches, and countermarches. The union of the hostile armies was to have taken place in Upper Silesia; Frederick accordingly proceeded thither, but Loudon's operations were so skilfully directed that no advantage was gained over him. In the meantime, the Russians had advanced into Lower Silesia,

CAMPAIGN OF 1761. CAMP AT BUNZELWITZ.

and crossed the Oder between Glogau and Breslau. Loudon kept moving rapidly from Upper Silesia on Bohemia, occupied the passes of the Riesengebirge, and here effected that junction between the two armies which had been planned for years, and which Frederick was now unable to prevent. Both armies stood in the neighborhood of Striegau; Frederick advanced against them, but seeing himself baffled in his plans, he made an attempt to dissolve their union in another way, and directed his march towards an important post, which the Austrians had abandoned on the approach of the Russians, in order to cut off all supplies from Bohemia, without which the enemy could not retain their position. But here, too, Loudon had displayed his usual foresight, and as Frederick approached the hills, he found them so strongly occupied as to be wholly unassailable.

The immense superiority which the enemy had now obtained in the heart of Silesia seemed to promise a speedy fulfilment of those wishes so long entertained by Frederick's enemies for his total prostration. Unequal to cope with his foes in the open field, he could not even hope to be able to maintain his position for any length of time in the Silesian fortresses. All he could now do was to avoid every unnecessary sacrifice, and wait till the want of provisions compelled the enemy to disperse; in this system he completely succeeded, and gave, in its execution, signal proofs of his military genius. On the 20th of August he encamped near Bunzelwitz, and thus, by covering the neighboring fortress of Schweidnitz, kept up his connection with Breslau, and was completely unshackled in his future measures. Nature had done but little to protect this camp from hostile attack, but several days elapsed before his enemies could agree in their system of operations; and when they subsequently approached, for the purpose of reconnoitring, they no longer found a camp, but a regular fortress, which had grown out of the earth within an incredibly short period. The whole Prussian army had, in fact, unceasingly labored, day and night, in raising these intrenchments; a chain of defences, trenches, and powerful batteries had been drawn round the camp, and the alignments defended by abattis and chevaux-de-frise ; in front, pits had been dug, and the ground regularly undermined. All attacks of the enemy could now be regarded with less apprehension and the foe, on discovering this state of things, found themselves obliged to relinquish their original plans and adopt new measures.

Meanwhile, as the hostile armies stood in the form of a crescent round the camp, and an attack might be momentarily expected, it was necessary to pay the utmost attention to their movements. The troops within the camp were perpetually transposed in order to prevent the enemy from being able to discover the strength of the different regiments, and as the number of the cannon was insufficient for the protection of the whole circuit of the camp, stumps of trees were here and there inserted in the loopholes. Particular care was likewise taken to be provided against a nocturnal assault. The troops rested for the most part during the day and in the evening the tents were struck and the men got under arms. Frederick himself shared all these toils and exertions in common with his soldiers; he always passed his nights in the open air, on the most important battery. He frequently sat down with the men before a watchfire, and would lay himself to rest for a couple of hours, stretched upon a few military cloaks. On such occasions the soldiers were frequently heard to say, "If Fritz sleeps with us here it is better than if 50,000 of us were watching. Now let the enemy come; if we have Fritz with us we do not fear the devil; but the devil must fear him, for God is more powerful than the devil, and the king is wiser than his enemies!" Frederick frequently had a bundle of straw brought into the battery in which he intended to pass the night, and on this he lay down, whilst the crowned heads that planned his destruction were reclining on silken couches.

Several weeks passed in this way. The troops, completely exhausted by their unceasing exertions, began to feel a want of provisions, as the enemy had cut off their communication with the country, and disease and despair were creeping into the camp. Frederick did all in his power to sustain the courage of his men. The sound of his voice and the glance of his eye alone kept up the drooping spirits of the soldiers, and inspired them with something like confidence. The extreme danger of his position was no secret to him, as he was fully aware that his troops could by no possibility, under the circumstances, withstand a determined assault from an enemy so vastly superior. He did not conceal his apprehensions on this subject from his more intimate friends; and to old Zieten, who shared all the toils of the camp, he not unfrequently applied for consolation. Fortune or fate could never break the elasticity of Zieten's fearless heart; he gave utterance to the confident hopes he felt that all would end well. But Frederick, who took a closer survey of his real position, could not abandon himself to any very ardent anticipations. He once asked Zieten, ironically, whether he had a single ally. "No," replied Zieten, "except that old one up there, and he will not abandon us." "Ah," sighed the king, "he works no more miracles." "We don't want them," replied Zieten, "but he fights for us, and does not allow us to sink." But few moons passed, and Zieten's words were verified in a manner little to have been expected.

The bold determination with which Frederick, in the face of his foes, maintained his position, had rendered them doubtful as to the propriety of a joint attack, and the jealousy and want of cordiality existing between the Russians and Austrians proved a further impediment. Butturlin had already felt annoyed at Loudon's not having formed a junction with him sooner, and at his having left him exposed to the danger of being attacked singly by the Prussians; besides which, as the empress was ill, he wished to recommend himself to her successor, by taking no very active steps against Frederick, and it was in vain that Loudon strove to induce him to join in a combined attack on the Prussian camp. The story goes, that once at the dinner-table, when wine had warmed the Russian leader, Loudon succeeded in extracting a promise of consent but as soon as the fumes of the liquor had passed away the orders for the attack were countermanded. The enemy, too, began to feel a scarcity of provisions, and Loudon made repeated attempts to bring his ally to some decided determination. He drew up a plan of attack, assigning the Russians their different posts and duties. This had the effect of wounding Butturlin's pride most seriously; taking advantage of the want of provisions, which afforded him a colorable excuse, on the 10th of September he moved with his army towards the Oder, leaving only a corps of 12,000 men, under the command of General Czernitscheff, behind him with the Austrians. Loudon now took up a new position on the side of some hills, at a further distance from the Prussian camp. The joy that prevailed throughout the latter at so unexpected a deliverance was indeed great, and Frederick, after granting fourteen days' rest, which was much wanted after such toils and privations, broke up the camp.

CHAPTER XXXVI.

CONCLUSION OF THE CAMPAIGN OF 1761.—THE CAMP AT
STREHLEN.

DECEMBER was fast approaching, and the campaign in Silesia had taken a more fortunate turn than could have been at first anticipated. Frederick now laid his measures so as to drive the two hostile armies completely out of the country before they could agree on the adoption of any new plan of operations. With this view he dispatched, immediately after the departure of the Russians, a special corps to Poland to destroy the Russian magazines there; and this corps fortunately succeeded in overtaking an important convoy, destroying and dissipating or taking captive the greater number of its numerous escort; by which means the departure of the Russians from Silesia was considerably accelerated. Frederick sought in person to render Loudon harmless. He desired nothing further than to allure the Austrians from their position by a series of artificial manœuvres, which were intended to appear as if threatening the provinces of Glatz or Moravia, both of which were in the hands of the Austrians. But Loudon did not fall into the snare. He occupied the passes leading to these provinces, and took advantage of the circumstance of Frederick's having separated himself from Schweidnitz, to execute a bold and wholly unexpected measure. On the night of the 30th of September he suddenly appeared, in advance of his army, before Schweidnitz, the garrison of which was not very strong, and the following day carried the fortress by storm.

FREDERICK THE GREAT.

By this bold blow, which gave the enemy firm footing in Silesia, and enabled them both to take up their winter-quarters in the land and commence their operations for the future year with incomparably more energy, Frederick's fate had taken a most unpropitious turn. He did not allow, however, his heart to despair. The sad effect which the dispiriting news of this catastrophe had upon his army was speedily dispelled by an address, in which he appealed to their patriotism and breathed fresh courage into their hearts. He anxiously wished to come to an engagement with Loudon, but as the latter cautiously maintained his position, Frederick resolved on taking up his quarters at Strehlen, from whence he could oppose with equal promptitude any attempts of his enemies either in the direction of Breslau or Schweidnitz. The troops were distributed through the villages round Strehlen, and Loudon's position became valueless for any effective purpose.

The camp of Strehlen was destined to obtain historical notoriety from many circumstances. In the course of the month of October an embassy arrived from the Tartar Cham, Kerim Geray, who, as a decided foe of the Russians, made offers to the Prussian King of furnishing troops at a certain stipulated price. The ambassador, Mustapha Aga, was received with all fitting honor. A treaty was actually concluded, in pursuance of which 16,000 Tartars were to enter Upper Silesia in the following year, whilst a simultaneous incursion on Russia was to be undertaken by the Cham. With the Turkish sultan, too, after several abortive attempts, a treaty of commerce was concluded, and the sultan was collecting at Belgrade a considerable host to oppose Frederick's enemies. Both these treaties were much desired by Frederick, in order to create a diversion, and nothing but the great change in European policy, which took place the following year, prevented their execution.

Another incident which occurred in Strehlen was the treacherous attempt to deliver the king alive or dead into the hands of his enemies. One of Frederick's vassals, Baron Warkotsch, whose possessions lay in the immediate neighborhood of Strehlen, dissatisfied at being checked by the Prussian government in the tyrannical treatment of his serfs, was, in concert with an Austrian officer, Colonel Wallis, the originator of the plot. He had frequently waited upon the king in Strehlen, and made himself acquainted with all his movements. Frederick's temporary residence was outside the town, in the neighboring village of Woiselwitz. The guard in front of his house consisted of but thirteen men, and with the exception of these there were but few troops in the village or in the town itself, as the army had been for the most part dismissed to their winter-quarters. The communications between Warkotsch and Wallis are said to have been kept up through the medium of a clergyman, Francis Schmidt. The letters of the latter and those of Colonel Wallis were conveyed by Mathias Kappel, a servant of the Baron's. This servant had his suspicions awakened from the circumstance of the correspondence being carried on with such secrecy, and from different expressions which had fallen from his master. On the 29th of October, having come with the baron to Strehlen, on receiving directions, in the middle of the night, to convey a letter to Schmidt, which was to be forwarded to Colonel Wallis, his suspicions were confirmed. He opened the letter, and found the whole plot detailed in it. He had the letter copied, without loss of time, by an evangelical clergyman, sent a copy to Schmidt, and hurried with the original to the headquarters of the king. Frederick received the momentous epistle, and addressed the bearer with the words—" You are but an instrument in the hand of a higher power!" Preparations were immediately made to arrest the traitors. The baron and Schmidt were seized, but both found means of escape. The baron, who had been surprised by a Prussian officer in his palace, obtained permission from the latter to change his dress. From his bedchamber he hastened to the stables, and throwing himself upon a horse, got so far in advance as to be out of the reach of his pursuers. The clergyman, who was dining with a nobleman, asked permission to retire for a moment, and taking advantage of this temporary absence of his guards, escaped.

The king was not in reality displeased at the flight of both the traitors. They were, however, sentenced to suffer death. Warkotsch was to be quartered, Schmidt decapitated and then quartered. Frederick was no friend of capital punishments, but could subscribe the sentence with composure, as it was to be executed on their effigies. "Let it be done," said he, "for their portraits will in all probability be of just as much value as themselves." The sentence was executed in May following, on both effigies, upon a scaffold erected for that purpose.

It would appear from all the results of the judicial investigation, that this plot was the work of but a few individuals. From the Austrian leaders it met with the proper abhorrence. The noble family De Wallis publicly declared that this Colonel Wallis was no relation of theirs. The Catholic church had likewise no further share in the plot, than that one of her unworthy servants lent himself to so traitorous a project. Several circumstances are mentioned tending to show that the Catholic clergy of Silesia had frequently acted with hostility towards Frederick, and the conduct of the pope, after the battle of Hochkirch, was calculated to give a color to such suspicion; but all manifestations of this kind are wholly unconnected with the act of Warkotsch, and it seems fully established that this treasonable plot was confined to but few confederates. One of the tales told of the Catholic priests of these times is not without a certain degree of humor, however questionable its historic truth may be. A plot was once, as we are told, laid against the Prussian governors of a Silesian town. They were to be attacked during the night by Austrian troops, and the clergy were to drive the guards from their posts. For the execution of this latter purpose one of them is said to have assumed the character of his Satanic majesty, and sparkling all

CAMPAIGN OF 1761. CAMP AT STREHLEN. 363

over with phosphorus presented himself in the stillness of night before a sentry. The latter, however, sinking the sinner in the soldier, levelled his musket at the arch-fiend, who now deemed it advisable to seek safety in flight. Being overtaken by his sturdy pursuer, he was lodged in the guardhouse, and on the following day conducted along the lines, exposed to the ridicule and mockery of the whole army. From that day forward all similar attempts ceased.

Soon after the danger which impended over the monarch's head had been averted in Strehlen, a second plot was laid, the success of which would have been equally disastrous. Magdeburg, the principal fortress of the Prussian kingdom, the residence of the court, the place of security for the royal treasure, archives, and munitions of war, was to be played into the hands of the enemy. The plan was laid by a man who sat in chains in the dungeons of that fortress, Baron Von Der Trenck, who had been guilty of high-treason and other misdemeanors. He had been already confined in Glatz, but had found means to escape by main force. After having made several unsuccessful attempts in Magdeburg of a similar kind, he was now treated with great rigor, but succeeded, nevertheless, in raising a plot amongst the numerous prisoners confined in the fortress. The hour of destruction was already close at hand, when the conspiracy was discovered, and the severity of Trenck's treatment considerably augmented

Yet, though these threatening dangers had blown over, the king was still destined to meet a blow which, when taken in connection with the loss of Schweidnitz, seemed to augur his speedy fall. The Russian army in Pomerania and a combined fleet of Russians and Swedes had appeared in front of Kolberg. A Prussian corps, under the command of the Prince of Wurtemberg, however, lay intrenched in front of the fortress, and this corps must be conquered before the enemy could proceed to the blockade of Kolberg. The fortress and Prussian camp were now invested by the enemy, but every attack made was valiantly repulsed. A want of provisions began to be experienced, and the situation of the besieged became more distressing on the entrance of the Russian main army into Pomerania, which cut off all means of supply. The Prince of Wurtemberg saw himself eventually reduced to the necessity of forcing a passage through the enemy. In this he succeeded, but his attempts to relieve Kolberg proved ineffectual. After the most valiant defence, the brave commandant of the fortress, who had attained high renown for his chivalrous conduct during the previous year, was forced, from want of provisions, to surrender. The fortress passed, on the 16th of September, into the hands of the Russians, who thereby obtained a firm footing in Pomerania, as the Austrians had already done in Silesia.

But the measure of Frederick's misfortunes was not yet full. It is true some feeble attempts of the Swedes had been as usual repulsed, and Prince Henry had so valiantly defended Saxony against the combined forces of the Austrians, under Daun, and the army of the empire, that the enemy obtained but few advantages there; and further, Frederick's ally, the Duke of Brunswick, had struggled so successfully against the French that little was to be apprehended at present from that quarter. But an ally, whose aid had been hitherto of the utmost importance to Frederick, now deserted him, and he was thereby reduced altogether to a reliance on his own resources, and forced to cope single-handed with his enemies. The death of King George II. of England, and the accession of George III., which events occurred the year before, caused a considerable change to take place in the policy of England. Pitt had been obliged to make way for Lord Bute, the favorite of the new monarch. Loudly as the parliament advocated the cause of Frederick, who had been recognized by it under the names of the Great, and Invincible, yet Lord Bute, anxious that England should enjoy the advantages of peace, succeeded in preventing a renewal of the treaty between England and Prussia, and stopped the payment of all future subsidies.

Thus terminated the year 1761. Prussia Proper and the Westphalian provinces had been from the commencement of the war in the hands of the enemy. Glatz, Schweidnitz, Kolberg, and a great part of Pomerania were now likewise in their hands. A most favorable path to new successes was now open to them. The possessions which Frederick had still left him were waste and desolate. Saxony, which had hitherto furnished such large contingents, was now completely exhausted. The important aid hitherto derived from England, which had been so useful in meeting the current expenses of the war, was now at an end, and England even seemed disposed to conclude peace with France, whereby Frederick would be obliged to oppose the army of this foe also out of his own resources. To counterbalance all this he had nothing beyond the promise of a petty subsidy from the Tartars, and a still more equivocal treaty with the Turks. In truth, that the gigantic foes with whom Frederick struggled had not secured greater advantages during those six years than those we have detailed, is a proof of generalship on his part wholly unparalleled in the annals of history. But Frederick was still destined, although his strength daily melted away, to outlive the storm that threatened to engulf him. His former disasters consisted, comparatively speaking, in mere momentary distresses, which a bold decisive movement might still repair. But now nothing remained, at least within the calculation of human prudence, for him, than to descend in ignominy to such rank as the charity of his enemies might vouchsafe as an alms, or in the alternative meet an honorable death.

There are perhaps few who, on a dispassionate survey of the then state of things, would have arrived at a different conclusion. The enemy exulted; Maria Theresa was so certain of the crowning successes of the next year that she considered it perfectly advisable and safe to disband 20,000 of her army—a step rendered in some measure necessary by the extremely exhausted state of her exchequer. Frederick's convictions were of the same kind, but with the calmness of intrepidity he looked the future in the face, determined on doing nought that might compromise his own dignity. His resolution had been long since taken. He had been too long the intimate companion of death—had too frequently seen destruction in every shape hovering above his head to flinch or feel nervous at coming disasters. Singularly strange were the poems which he wrote in the camp at Strehlen, and in the winter-quarters at Breslau. There was no longer any wild sentimentality, as after the battle of Kollin—no request that his friends should strew his grave with roses and myrtles. No; he no longer wished to escape from life as a burthen; he had so accustomed himself to suffering as to be but strengthened and revived by every blow which fate had dealt him. If he now looked with favor on a voluntary death it was because the continuance of his life appeared to be but the continuance of dishonor. In his calmness and elevated composure he raised his mind above the present, and exalted himself above the petty relations in which he was placed. He commemorated in poetry the heroism of the Emperor Otho, who sacrificed himself to prevent his subjects from being annihilated beneath the sword of the conqueror; he eulogized Cato of Utica, who, as a free Roman citizen, resigned his life rather than submit to be false to himself, and grace in chains the triumphant chariot of a tyrant. With such memorials of the past, he steeled his resolution to wait for the last great decisive moment.

This undaunted heroism was destined to meet with its reward.

CHAPTER XXXVII.

CAMPAIGN OF 1762. BURKERSDORF AND SCHWEIDNITZ. PEACE.

DESTINY, whose throne is above the clouds; she, who overwhelms the mighty and confounds the counsels of the wise, and guides the world unceasingly towards its pre-ordained end, had issued far other decrees than those which short-sighted mortals had read in the past. Her tempest-breath had ere now overwhelmed and sunk in the ocean's deepest abyss the invincible fleet of a monarch on whose realms the sun never set, and the home of freedom escaped destruction. She now numbered to the countless victims whom the angel of death had within the last six years borne away, one victim more, and thus dissipated the haughty councils of the foe; that king, whose powerful mind had opened the way for a new era in the world, was safe!

On the 5th January, 1762, died Elizabeth, Empress of Russia. Her nephew, Peter III., ascended the vacant throne. In proportion as the hostility, which Elizabeth ever evinced towards Frederick, had been uncompromising and deadly, in the same degree was the admiration testified towards him by her successor, the present Emperor, sincere and warm. As heir presumptive, Peter had never appeared in the Russian cabinet when counsels hostile to Frederick were to be taken. He was well acquainted with all the details of the different campaigns, with the operations and relations of the Prussian army; he wore Frederick's likeness in a ring on his finger, and considered him as the great model which he was bound minutely to study. From Frederick to Peter, and from the latter to Frederick, flew ambassadors, bringing congratulations and assurances of friendship. The Prussian prisoners throughout the whole Russian empire were immediately summoned to the capital, and, after meeting an honorable reception there, dismissed to rejoin the army of their country. An armistice was immediately concluded, and this was followed, on the 5th of May, by a formal treaty of peace, by which Peter restored to Frederick all the conquests which had been made under his predecessor, without looking for any compensation whatsoever; the province of Prussia was released from its oath of fealty, and the Russian troops received orders to evacuate Pomerania, New Mark, and Prussia. Czernitscheff's corps, which was still incorporated with the Austrians, and had taken up its winter-quarters in the province of Glatz, was likewise recalled. In fine, the peace was followed by a treaty of alliance, and Czernitscheff, who had been in the meantime sent to Poland, received orders to unite his corps with Frederick's army.

So sudden a change in the political relations caused the world to stand aghast. Europe could not comprehend the strange tidings which every post brought, and which became daily more incredible. Lord Bute, the English minister, who desired nothing but a general peace, and cared little for Frederick's honor, when the amicable relations between the king and the czar were on the point of being concluded, made offers to the latter, in the event of the war being continued as formerly, to secure to him such of Frederick's possessions as he might please to select. Peter was so incensed at this, that he not only rejected the overtures with contempt, but informed Frederick of them, in order to convince him of the treachery of his former ally. Sweden, which appeared most endangered by this new friendship between Russia and Prussia, was the first to recognize its own interest, and the queen, Frederick's sister, was naturally very anxious to open negotiations for peace. On the 20th of May an amicable treaty was concluded with this kingdom, and the international relations replaced on the same footing as that on which they had stood previous to the outbreak of the war. Maria Theresa was more bewildered than any one else, on seeing the brilliant hopes which she conceived herself justified in cherishing at the close of the former year thus vanish into empty air. Through the reduction of her army and the departure of Czernitscheff's corps, her strength now amounted to but 40,000 men, whilst that of Frederick was augmented to the amount of 60,000, thus making a difference of 20,000 in the scales of war. Frederick said that three won battles could not have secured him greater advantages. In addition to this, several contagious cutaneous diseases had broken out and ravaged the Austrian army. The union of Czernitscheff's corps with the Prussians was altogether so incredible to the Austrians, that they considered it as a mere deception, practised by Frederick, and declared that they must be unquestionably Prussian troops equipped in Russian uniforms.

This fortunate turn of events produced in Frederick, his army, and his people the most unbounded, and indescribable joy. Their old confidence in themselves returned, and every one looked forward to a speedy termination of this tedious war. The main strength of the Prussian army was now concentrated in Silesia, in order to recover from the Austrians what they had taken during the preceding year; but the commencement of active operations was through these negotiations with Russia, postponed till summer, and Frederick did not attempt any decisive movement until the arrival of the Russian auxiliary corps. The Austrians felt little inclination, under this change of circumstances, to anticipate the commencement of the war, and sought to employ this interval of rest to the best advantage, in making dispositions for the security of their newly acquired possessions. The fortifications of Schweidnitz were strengthened as much as possible, and the main body of the Austrian army encamped in the neighboring heights for the protection of the fortress. Daun had again succeeded to the command of the army, and the passes of the hills were so strengthened by entrenchments as to be rendered almost unassailable. Frederick made different attempts to seduce the enemy into a less favorable position, in order to be able to commence the siege of Schweidnitz without interruption; but Daun was not to be misled by any manœuvres. Even on Frederick's making an incursion on Bohemia, in Daun's rear, the latter remained without moving from his position. In this expedition the advanced guard of Czernitscheff's corps, consisting of 2000 Cossacks, were employed.

The honor was, however, reserved for Frederick of terminating, without foreign aid, the contest which he had so long maintained single-handed. Few days had elapsed from the junction of Czernitscheff's corps with the Prussian army, when, on the 19th of July, intelligence arrived from St. Petersburg of a nature that threatened to blast all the brilliant prospects that had opened for the Prussians, and bring matters back to their old position. Peter III. had, by a number of ill-advised innovations, rendered himself obnoxious to all classes of his people; he had treated the Empress Catherine, his wife, in such a manner as to warrant the worst fears. A conspiracy against his life had been set on foot, and was speedily followed by a revolution, his dethronement, and subsequent death. Catherine succeeded to the throne. The peace concluded with Prussia was regarded as a national disgrace for Russia, and Czernitscheff received immediate orders to separate from the Prussian army. From Pomerania and Prussia information arrived to the effect, that the Russian troops were everywhere preparing for a renewal of hostilities.

Intelligence so sudden, complicated, and disastrous, came like a thunderbolt from out the serene ether, and seemed likely at first to rob Frederick of his reason. He felt his heart now for the first time sicken—sink within him. He had counted on being able, by the aid of Czernitscheff, to drive Daun from the heights; without this, the siege of Schweidnitz was perfectly impracticable; and he was not alone to be deprived of this aid, but to raise new armies to meet the coming attacks of the Russians too: but the elastic powers of his mind soon recoiled with a force proportionate to their late tension, and his energies, which had been depressed solely by the suddenness of the shock, became again buoyant, and he now rose to combat once more his new difficulties. His resolution was bold and soon taken. Ere the news could have spread, and especially ere the Austrians could receive information of it, he dispatched an aide-de-camp to Czernitscheff, soliciting an immediate interview. Czernitscheff was at that moment engaged in making his soldiers swear allegiance to their new sovereign, and about to send a messenger to Daun, to inform the latter of his intended separation from the Prussians. He promised the aide-de-camp that he would come to the king the following day; but the latter pressed his request so importunately, that Czernitscheff decided on accompanying him. Frederick solicited nothing further of Czernitscheff, than that the latter should postpone the withdrawal of his forces for three days; that his corps should remain for this period quietly in the Prussian camp; and that, on the day of the battle, they should advance merely in appearance, without taking any part in the fight. Czernitscheff was perfectly aware how even this act of disobedience to the commands of the empress might be visited with the most severe consequences; but no one had ever yet been able to withstand the force of Frederick's eloquence and the penetrating glance of his eye. The Russian general was obliged to comply with the king's demand. " Do with me what you will," cried the latter, at the termination of the conversation; " Sire, what I have promised you to do, will probably cost me my life; but I would gladly lose it ten times over, were that possible, to prove to you the strength of my regard!"

The three days which Czernitscheff granted him were employed by Frederick in a masterly manner, in cutting off the enemy from its threatened connection with Schweidnitz. He took all the necessary measures to gain possession of the entrenched posts near Burkersdorf and Leutmannsdorf, which were occupied by the Austrians. His army was, meanwhile, so distributed, that Daun expected an attack on his main body rather than at those difficult points; and in these dispositions the Russians, whom Daun still considered as his enemies, and to whom he opposed a proportionable body of troops, played their part. On the 21st of July the mountain-posts were suddenly surprised and carried by an impetuous assault. A strong battery which had been thrown up during the night in front of the enemy's entrenchments, drove the light troops, which were to have repulsed this assault, by its hot fire to the hills. Then commenced a general storm by the Prussian regiments. Neither the precipitous heights covered with ramparts, pits, palisades, and cannon, nor the fire which issued from forts crowning every precipice, could retard the impetuosity of the assailants. From one mountain-ledge to the other they pushed irresistibly forward, and where the horses could not find a footing, the guns were carried by the men. The Austrians were driven deeper and deeper amongst the hills, until at length the palisades forming the entrenchment of their camp catching fire, they were forced back in wild confusion upon the main army. An immense number of prisoners fell into the hands of the Prussians.

Frederick had gained his object, and could gratefully dismiss the Russian leader. The Russian officers had seen with wonder the desperate plan which the king had formed and the devoted gallantry of his troops, without which its execution had been altogether impossible. Czernitscheff was by the king's side when the latter, towards the end of the battle, met a wounded soldier. The king inquired of him how matters stood. "God be praised!" replied the soldier, "all goes well; the enemy are running and we are winning." "You are wounded, my son," said the king, handing him his pocket-handkerchief; " bind your wound with this." " Now I am no longer surprised," said Czernitscheff, "at the devotion with which your troops serve your majesty, as you act so kindly towards them." On Czernitscheff's receiving a splendid present from Frederick on his departure, he begged of the person bringing it to inform his master that he now had rendered him unserviceable for the whole world, for he should never be able to find any other person to whom he was so heartily and entirely devoted.

The danger which impended from Russia soon disappeared. Catherine, who at first supposed that Peter III. had acted on the advice of Frederick, not only in makiug the many inconsiderate innovations which he had introduced, but also in the hostility which he had evinced towards herself, almost immediately after the declaration of her opposition to Prussia, discovered from the papers of her deceased husband that the contrary was the fact. Frederick had not only recommended to the Czar moderation in reforms, but had implored him to treat his wife, if not with tenderness, at least with respect. All hatred of Frederick was banished by these evidences, which could not deceive; the hostile commands were revoked, the former peace was confirmed in all its conditions with the single exception that the auxiliary corps which had been withdrawn did not return. Thus was Frederick relieved of all the anxieties which had of late harassed him, and he could now once more turn his undivided strength against Austria.

Daun, after the loss of the posts of Burkersdorf and Leutmannsdorf, had penetrated deeper amongst the hills, and was now completely cut off from Schweidnitz. Frederick occupied the passes, and made preparations for the siege. On the 4th of August the fortress was invested, and on the 7th the trenches were opened. Two Prussian armies secured the besiegers against any attempts at relief. One of these was commanded by Frederick in person; the other, which had hitherto stood in Upper Silesia, was under the command of the Duke of Bevern. But Daun was not inclined to leave the Prussians in undisturbed enjoyment of these advantages. He made preparations for a sudden attack on the army of the Duke of Bevern, in the hope of being thereby enabled to effect the relief of Schweidnitz. The greater portion of his army deployed round the mountain passes, which were as speedily occupied by the Prussians, and on the 16th of August he fell, in four columns, upon the far inferior force of the duke, who was stationed at Reichenbach. The Duke of Bevern, although attacked on all sides, boldly maintained his ground, until Frederick hastened to his aid with considerable reinforcements. The Austrians were now obliged to retire with considerable loss, and retreat back to the hills; Daun, giving up all hope of being able to relieve Schweidnitz, drew off his whole army towards the province of Glatz, and remained there, without giving any further signs of life, during the remainder of the campaign.

The siege of Schweidnitz proceeded, however, at a very tardy pace. Within the fortress the defensive operations were conducted by the celebrated engineer Gricauval whilst the offensive operations outside the town were conducted by Le Fevre. Both these officers had distinguished themselves in the science of fortification, and having formerly opposed each other in several controversial works, they were now endeavoring each to justify his respective theory by brilliant achievements. Whilst the guns were day and night sweeping the surface of the earth, a peculiar subterranean way was being carried on underneath. Winding galleries had been sprung according to the rules of art, and each leader strove to surprise or baffle his adversary. They frequently met in these caverns, and contended with fire and smoke for the few inches of ground that separated them. Le Fevre, on the Prussian side, had paid great attention to a newly-discovered species of shell, which was intended to blow up the enemy's mines. Several of these shells had been prepared with considerable care, but their success was defeated by the skilful arrangements of his adversary. In fact, the science of both was so completely equal, that no progress could be made. Le Fevre became desperate, and desired nothing but death, which he courted by exposing himself in the most dangerous places. Frederick at length grew tired of these unsuccessful experiments. He undertook the conduct of the siege himself, and with less artificial arrangements, but more skill, brought matters to a speedy termination. The commandant of the fortress was ready to surrender, provided the garrison was permitted to retire unmolested; but as Frederick would not consent to this, an obstinate resistance was still made.

A few days after Frederick had himself undertaken the conduct of the siege he rode so close to the defences, for the purpose of reconnotring, that the balls fell close by his side. A horse was shot under one of his pages. The latter got up quickly, and was about to fly precipitately from his dangerous position, when Frederick called out to him in a serious tone to take his horse's saddle with him, which the page was obliged to unbuckle beneath a shower of balls. Frederick's nephew, Frederick William, the prince royal, then eighteen years of age, rode by his side, and the king had the pleasure of seeing the intrepid courage which the latter evinced whilst the balls were whizzing round his head. Frederick himself once said, on being besought to leave a dangerous position, emphatically, "The ball which is to strike me will come from above."

The besieged began gradually to feel a want of ammunition, but still every appliance of art was employed to the last. At length a well-aimed Prussian grenade put an end to the siege. It found its way into the powder-magazine of one of the forts which encircled Schweidnitz, and instantly the half of the fort with the whole of its garrison was blown up into the air. The thunder of this frightful explosion was so violent that the neighboring hills rocked to their bases. A passage being thus opened into the fortress for the assailants, the Austrian commandant did not await a storm, but surrendered with the whole of the garrison, on the 9th of October, at discretion, and Schweidnitz was again in the hands of the Prussian troops. Thus terminated the campaign in Silesia. The troops were consigned to their cantonments; one section was dispatched to Saxony, on which a portion of Daun's army had advanced, and Frederick also shortly afterwards proceeded thither.

In Saxony Prince Henry had again made several successful attacks on the Austrians and the troops of the empire, and in many petty skirmishes had obtained victories over the enemy. The army of the empire was forced out of Saxony, and obliged to take an extensive circuit through Bohemia, in order to join the Austrians; upon effecting which they unitedly strove by a decisive movement to drive back the Prussians. Henry accepted battle on the 29th of October, near Freiberg, and again achieved a brilliant victory, to the success of which, as in the former struggles in Saxony, Seidlitz mainly contributed. This was the last battle of the Seven Years' War. The troops of the empire once more evacuated Saxony, and the Austrians concentrated themselves round Dresden. It was not until after this battle that both sides received reinforcements from Silesia, upon which a suspension of hostilities in Saxony and Silesia was agreed on, and both Prussians and Austrians entered their winter-quarters.

Maria Theresa had now but little prospect of success. The plans which she had for years cherished had been so completely frustrated, that she began to entertain much less aversion to the idea of concluding peace than heretofore. She found herself still further necessitated to consent to a termination of hostilities, as France and England both desired peace. The allied army, under Duke Ferdinand of Brunswick, had during the first six months of the year obtained several victories over the French army, although Lord Bute had contributed but little to its reinforcement. In consequence of Bute's inclination for peace negotiations were soon opened; but Duke Ferdinand put a period to the war by one decisive act, thus crowning a series of brilliant military exploits. On the 1st of November he captured Cassel, which the French had until then held. Two days subsequently the preliminaries of peace were signed, Lord Bute consenting to a disgraceful surrender of all the conquests which the English fleet had made in the colonies. The allies on both sides were to be left to their fate.

In the beginning of November Frederick had, through the mediation of the Prince Elector of Saxony, already received overtures of peace from Austria, which he gladly accepted, but resolved, especially as the conditions of the Anglo-French treaty appeared somewhat equivocal as regarded him, by energy, decision, and one bold movement to render the desire for peace general and sincere. As the suspension of hostilities included merely Saxony and Silesia, he prepared a rapid incursion on the possessions of the German empire, which had acted with so much bitterness towards him. A considerable corps penetrated into Franconia, and traversed almost the whole of the empire, collecting considerable contributions, especially from Nuremberg. A general panic was spread by this column. We are told that twenty-five Prussian hussars threatened the free imperial town of Rothenburg, on the Tauber, with storm, and that the latter consented to escape the threatened danger by the payment of a considerable sum of money. The Prussian troops penetrated even close to Ratisbonne, and the members of the imperial diet felt constrained to implore the resident Prussian ambassador, whom they had hitherto persecuted with unmitigated hostility, to grant them his protection, which he accordingly did. Unmolested, and laden with rich spoil, the whole Prussian corps returned soon after to Saxony. The result was exactly such as Frederick had desired. The estates of the empire felt no longer any desire to sacrifice their individual interests for the sake of Austria. They accordingly declared that they would remain neutral, and withdrew their contingents immediately from the army of the empire, in the hope of propitiating Frederick. Mecklenburg also concluded a special treaty of peace with him. A second predatory incursion was planned against the French, who still occupied some of Frederick's dominions on the Rhine. This excursion was likewise attended with so much success that the provinces were speedily evacuated and surrendered to Frederick.

The first predatory incursion had been of most serious consequences to Austria. The cabinet of Vienna had pledged itself most solemnly to the empire, not to terminate the war without remunerating the latter for all exertions and losses which might be thereby occasioned. In consequence of this voluntary retirement of the estates, it conceived itself released from the fulfilment of this promise.

The desire for peace becoming sincere, in consequence of the exhaustion of all parties, it now met with no further impediment. The necessary preliminaries were soon adjusted: three plenipotentiaries representing Austria, Prussia, and Saxony, met at Hubertsburg, and opened the negotiation on the 31st of December. On the 15th of February, 1763, a treaty of peace was concluded on the basis of the former treaties, one condition of which guaranteed the surrender of all possessions acquired by conquest. The Germanic empire was included in the treaty, and Prussia granted the Empress's eldest son, the Archduke Joseph, a vote in the election of Roman kings. Austria had at first proposed some hard conditions, such as that Glatz should remain in its possession; but Frederick insisted strictly on everything being restored exactly to the position in which matters had stood previous to the outbreak of the war; Austria was constrained to consent, especially as the increasing deficiency in its exchequer and the propinquity of the Prussian army left little time for hesitation.

Thus seven years of indescribable toil, bloodshed, and

misery, had led to no other result than the simple perception of the fact, that all these sufferings and miseries might have been spared, had the sovereigns repressed their evil passions. One can hardly refrain from a smile at the vanity of all human plans and calculations; but great, infinitely great, results were attained by this war: at a period when universal torpor prevailed, the power of the human mind, the force of resolution, and unyielding heroism, such as the world had not for centuries seen, was exhibited to the eyes of men. The German people, hitherto without consideration in political relations, and sunk from the heights of intellectual eminence and research, could, in Frederick, and in what Frederick had done for Prussia, clearly perceive what might be attained by patriotic enthusiasm, by boldness, decision, and energy; and how a nation might be elevated from utter prostration to splendor and power. The Thirty Years' War marks, in the annals of the history of Germany, the decay of ancient chivalry, whilst the Seven Years' War marks its resurrection; considered in this way, the countless sacrifices which had been made were not without their value.

But Frederick, although he might fully estimate the importance of the war, could not return home with the same joyous feelings as after the wars of his youth. The seven years of restless anxiety and racking toil which he had undergone had rendered him old; and many of his dearest companions had perished during those years: writing some weeks after his arrival in Berlin to the Marquis D'Argens, he says, "I return an old man to a town in which I can recognize nothing beyond the walls, where I shall meet no old friend, where countless toils await me, and where I shall soon lay my old bones in a grave, which may be, perhaps, soon disturbed by war, confusion, or malice."

On the 30th of May Frederick returned, after a tour through Silesia to Berlin: the citizens had arranged a festive reception for their beloved monarch; but Frederick did not arrive until late in the evening, as he had that day visited the battle-field of Cunnersdorf, and was probably deeply affected by the spectacle there presented, and the memories thereby evoked. He was accompanied in his carriage by the Duke of Brunswick and another of his generals. From earliest dawn till nightfall the citizens had awaited his arrival at the gates and in the streets; and he was now received with a universal shout of "Long live the king!" Countless torches lit his path; but these joyous acclamations accorded not with his gloomy mood; he escaped from the procession as soon as possible, and proceeded to his palace by an unfrequented and circuitous path.

We are told that Frederick, soon after his arrival in Charlottenburg, summoned several musicians and singers, with orders that Graun's Te Deum should be performed in the palace chapel: it was expected that he would appear with the whole court at the celebration, but he entered the chapel unattended, seated himself, and gave the sign to commence. As the voices of the singers poured forth the words of thanksgiving, he leaned his head upon his hand and wept.

CHAPTER XXXVIII.

ORDERING OF INTERNAL RELATIONS DURING PEACE.

FREDERICK had never at any period of the war, not even in its closing years, ceased to labor to be at all times in possession of such funds as should enable him not alone to defray its current expenditure, but also to cover the ordinary charges of at least one year in advance. This was one of the most important characteristics of his system, and one which enabled him to carry on the struggle so long and so successfully against such overwhelming numbers. True to his system, he had made provision, at the close of the year 1762, against every casualty, and had raised sufficient money for another twelve months' warfare; he was, consequently, now that a universal peace had been permanently established, enabled to apply such accumulated treasure to the alleviation of the miseries which the war had entailed. His noble endeavors in this respect were unceasing; and he had the happiness of seeing that his subjects recovered much sooner from the disastrous effects of the war than the greater number of his adversaries. Nay, wishing to give the world proof of his strength, lest any one trusting to such fancied exhaustion, might feel tempted to form new plans against him, he immediately, after the conclusion of the peace, commenced the erection of a splendid edifice, the so-termed new palace of Sans-souci. In the course of six years he had expended many millions on a structure which, to this day, from the expensive materials employed in its construction, and the richness of architectural ornament with which it is embellished, fills the spectator with unqualified admiration and amazement. In the rearing of this edifice he had likewise a second wise object in view, namely, the giving employment to the thousands of idle hands, which the abrupt termination of hostilities and consequent disbanding of large bodies of troops had suddenly stripped of all immediate means of gaining a livelihood; for the labor and materials of the building were almost exclusively drawn from the country itself We may here draw attention to the fact, that this palace presents a peculiar, although little regarded, memorial of the modesty of the great king. He had given orders to Vanloo, the painter, to take for the subject of the picture that was to adorn the colossal marble saloon, which forms one of the principal compartments of the palace, an assembly of gods: the painter conceived the idea of introducing a few of the goddesses of Victory, whose office it was to be the bearers of the initials of Frederick's name heavenward. Frederick, who did not see the painting until completed, was not altogether satisfied with its execution, but on detecting the introduction of his own initials, was so displeased, that he ordered them to be immediately effaced; the expensive scaffolding had to be re-erected, and as the painter could not alter the whole of this gigantic picture, he was obliged to rest satisfied, with veiling the initials beneath a green drapery. The goddesses of Fame bear to this hour this mystery in their hands.

Frederick's sustaining and aiding hand was extended in every direction, and his exertions for the reorganization of trade, which had fallen into decay during the war, were everywhere visible. As the fields lay untilled from a want of seed, cattle, and agricultural laborers, he distributed amongst the different provinces 60,000 bushels of corn and flour from out the military magazines, together with 35,000 cavalry horses. He disbanded about 40,000 of his troops, and sent them back to their respective homes. Immediately after the conclusion of the treaty of peace, very considerable sums of money were paid over to the different provinces, as part indemnity for the losses sustained during the war: Silesia received 3,000,000 of thalers, Pomerania and Newmark, 1,400,000, Prussia, 800,000, Brandenburg, 800,000, Cleves, 100,000; in other places one half of the taxes were remitted. During a series of years, indeed to the very close of his life, his exertions were unremittingly directed to the alleviation of the miseries superinduced by the late horrible conflict, and the diffusion of prosperity and happiness over the whole face of the land. One of his letters, written in the year 1766, and addressed to Voltaire, refers to this subject as follows: " Fanaticism and wild ambition have desolated the most flourishing districts of my kingdom : if you should wish to know the amount of destruction and havoc wrought, I can inform you, that I have been obliged to rebuild 8000 houses in Silesia, and 6500 in Newmark, which gives, according to Newton and D'Alembert, a total of 14,500 : the greater part had been burned down by the Russians. We have not carried on the war with such horrible cruelty ; we destroyed but comparatively few houses, and these in the towns which we besieged ; their number does not exceed in all probability 1000. The bad example that had been set us did not seduce us to an imitation of it ; and my conscience is, on this head, perfectly free from self-reproach."

We have already had occasion to remark, that during the conduct of the war, Frederick had been obliged to have recourse to peculiar financial expedients, in order to meet the heavy expenses incurred. These consisted, in part, of a gradual depreciation of the coin; and, in part, in the payment of the civil functionaries in exchequer notes, which were not convertible into cash until the conclusion of peace. Both these financial arrangements were decidedly disastrous in their effects, and proved the ruin of many families ; but still they enabled Frederick to preserve his kingdom free from the overwhelming burthen of national debt contracted by all the surround-

ing kingdoms during the same period. Every pains was
now taken to alleviate, as much as possible, the injurious
effects of those financial measures, and to replace matters
gradually on their former footing. Modern calculations
have shown, that great as the individual losses unquestionably were, yet the collective injury done was by no means
in the same proportion. The loss sustained in the gold
and silver exchanges amounted to but a few thalers per
cent.; even the coins, which were most depreciated in
value, had been reduced but twenty-two per cent.; and,
by submitting to these comparatively insignificant sacrifices, the people saw the war terminated without the
incubus of a national debt. The Prussians had indeed
good cause to feel satisfied with so small a sacrifice at the
shrine of their country, and had every reason to feel
grateful to a monarch, to whose wisdom they were indebted for so beneficial a result.

The heroes who had distinguished themselves by their
brilliant achievements in the Seven Years' War were now
amply rewarded for their gallant services, and their merits
duly acknowledged by their grateful monarch. Such
generals, officers, and privates as had exhibited either extraordinary courage or devotion, now received in different
ways the meed of valor. Frederick, whose powers of
memory were extraordinary, retained a distinct recollection of such achievements of each as had been communicated to him, and the page of history has preserved numerous memorials of the considerate acts of the monarch
towards the well-deserving, whose services were frequently rewarded when the recipients of the favors least
expected. The monarch's paternal care for the widows
and orphans of the heroes that had fallen was no less
memorable and praiseworthy.

Feeling confident that nothing was more likely to confirm the security of his kingdom, and in a measure preclude the possibility of a war, than due attention to the
military department of his government and the maintenance of a strong disposable force, he omitted no precaution

for the speedy completion of such military arrangements as would leave him a competent and well-disciplined army at immediate command. Indeed, the articles of peace had been hardly signed before renewed exertions were made for completing the levies, as if the war were to be recommenced that very year. The different fortresses were put in a state of repair, and their number increased by the addition of Silberberg in Silesia; the magazines were completely replenished; and cannon, powder, and material of all kinds provided in large quantities. The army was once more raised to its original strength, and as many of the native Prussians had been disbanded, their places were filled up by the numerous foreigners whom the peace had caused to be dismissed from the different European armies. As the discipline had grown very lax towards the latter end of the war, no exertion was now spared in reorganizing the army on its old footing. Nay, the warrior was now raised more than ever to a privileged class in the state, and a predicate of honor especially assigned him. Frederick, in accordance with the military relations of the time, was anxious to retain in his service only such officers as were of noble extraction. The commoners who had been advanced during the war to high military posts were now, somewhat unfairly, dismissed. Noble birth was to be fired to patriotism by the exclusive character of the service, and ambition and the pride of high descent sublimed into heroic devotion for the national safety. A dispute as to precedence happening to arise between a councillor of legation, Count Schwerin, a nephew of the celebrated field-marshal, and an ensign, Schwerin appealed to the king, whose decision was to the effect—that the matter did not admit of dispute: *of course* ensigns took precedence of all councillors of legation. Upon this Schwerin threw up his diplomatic character and—became an ensign!

The strict discipline which Frederick now wished to introduce into his army created very considerable discontent, and several of the new arrangements were, on their first introduction, so unpalatable as to render a considerable degree of severity requisite to their enforcement; but Frederick's personal mediation contributed considerably to lessen a number of these cases. It once so happened that some turbulent members of the Potsdam guards conceived themselves entitled to certain privileges, to which they had really no claim, and resolved on making a demonstration in order to obtain them, without having duly considered the serious consequences to which they thereby exposed themselves according to the Articles of War. They accordingly proceeded to Sans-souci. Frederick, seeing them in the distance, girt on his sword, took up his hat, and advanced out on the terrace of the palace to meet them. Before the ringleader had time to utter a word, Frederick commanded them to halt. The whole body stood suddenly still. "Dress up!" continued Frederick. "Right about face!—march!" This command was punctually obeyed. They marched down the terrace, intimidated by the eye and voice of the monarch, and highly delighted to get off so cheaply. On another occasion Frederick acted with still more lenity. A soldier in a Silesian garrison, who had made considerable spoils during the war, felt dissatisfied with his present slender pay, and betook himself to the expedient of enriching himself as of old. He was shortly afterwards convicted of having stolen several silver offerings from an altar dedicated to the Virgin Mary. He denied the theft pertinaciously, and maintained that the Virgin, to whom he had detailed his misfortunes, had desired him to take one or two of the offerings from her altar. The court-martial found his excuse insufficient, and condemned him to run the gauntlet twelve times. Frederick, on receiving the sentence for signature, considered it advisable to inquire of some Catholic clergymen whether such a case were possible. The clergymen, in accordance with their belief in miracles, found themselves constrained to declare that such a case, however improbable and incredible the statement of the soldier might be, was certainly within the limits of possibility. Upon this Frederick sent directions that the accused should be liberated, but forbade him in the most strict terms to accept in future of any presents either from the Virgin or any other saint whatsoever.

To alleviate the evils generated by the war and execute the numerous projects which the general weal of his kingdom seemed to require; to maintain a numerous standing army, and, more than all, to be provided with resources in the event of a war, was wholly impossible without a greater amount of revenue than Frederick had as yet been able to obtain. He much desired to increase his revenue to the amount of two millions of thalers annually, but finding it the unanimous opinion of the members of the privy council that agriculture was too much exhausted to admit of further taxation, he resolved on introducing certain new fiscal regulations, the results of which he probably had not foreseen, but which were, unfortunately, little calculated to gain him the love or gratitude of his subjects. He had arrived at the conviction that the revenue derivable from the customs was capable of an increase, and should be made much more productive than hitherto; as in other countries the crown obtained a much larger profit from this source. In France particularly the machinery of finance had been screwed to the highest pitch, and the example thus set before Frederick's eyes was so seductive that he could not resist the temptation of making a similar experiment in Prussia. As he felt, however, the want of persons sufficiently experienced in fiscal measures of this nature, he introduced from France some masters in the art of extracting a revenue. The latter were accompanied by a host of followers, who were to fill the subordinate offices. Frederick could not, however, bring himself to adopt the French custom of selling to these aliens the farming of the revenue, and thus completely throwing his own subjects on the mercy of foreigners. A board, constituted under the name of " General Administration of the Royal

Dues," was incorporated as a distinct department of government. The duties imposed were not very high, but being extended to every article of consumption, the most painful of the consequences was the inquisitorial powers necessarily conceded to the officials in order to prevent smuggling; they were invested not only with a right of search at the entrances of the towns, but even in the very houses of the citizens. Notwithstanding this, however, smuggling became daily more general and less disguised. Endless annoyance and dissatisfaction were excited by the litigious prosecutions set on foot, and a general spirit of resistance to constituted authority, and corruption of manners were the speedy results of the new system of taxation. And, after all, these harassing exactions produced nothing like the revenue which Frederick had expected from them, and which might have been readily obtained otherwise, without arousing the ill-will of his subjects.

Besides this increase of universal taxation, Frederick sought to raise a revenue by monopolizing the sale of such articles as were of most general consumption: tobacco and coffee were the most important articles of this royal monopoly. Independent of the fact of this system acting most injuriously on the general consumption, and thus defeating its own ends, its effect on public morality was still more to be deplored.

There was another system, too, which flourished about this period in France, in the advantages of which Frederick was likewise anxious to participate—the *secret police*. The demoralization which had been the necessary result of the war, seemed to render such an institution desirable. With this view he dispatched Philippi, a very experienced man, to Paris, and afterwards appointed him president of police in Berlin. Some years afterwards several crimes were committed, without their authors having been discovered. Frederick took the president of police to task for this seeming negligence. The latter explained, that he had brought all the arrangements to which his majesty had consented into operation, and that he was not authorized to do anything on his own individual responsibility. He entered into full details of a system of secret police, which would infallibly enable him to detect in every case the perpetrator of a crime, but admitted that the moral character of the people would be seriously affected by the system; adding, that its introduction into Berlin must be gradual, as the people of Brandenburg were too sincere and honorable for such a system. These representations had considerable weight with Frederick, who replied, without taking much time to consider the matter, that he would not attempt to displace a lesser evil by a greater, nor disturb the tranquillity or composure of his faithful subjects, and thus the project terminated.

That Frederick—the hero who unceasingly struggled during a seven years' contest, and had sacrificed every pleasure of life to maintain the honor of his kingdom—should have been held in high veneration by his people, is but little surprising; but that, despite those serious innovations, and despite the pertinacity with which he clung to them—that in spite of this he should have still retained the veneration of his subjects, is the best evidence of his real greatness. The people began gradually to submit to what seemed necessity, and every one plainly saw that Frederick's object in raising his revenue was not for the purpose of squandering it in revelry and feasts, or on mistresses and favorites, or from a mere avaricious thirst for gold; but that it returned in the shape of favors back upon the people, and that the monarch himself was as affable, as confidential, as sympathizing as of old, whilst no anxious bolt or bar checked the freedom of discussion, even when the monarch's acts became the subject of animadversion. The soldiers of the Seven Years' War told their tales of their faithful comrade, old Fritz, and whenever Frederick still came in contact with the people his conduct was characterized by the same traits as of old: thus the people retained their affection for their sovereign pure and unalloyed; whilst their exasperation and anger at the new arrangements was reserved for the aliens, who gradually disappeared from their posts, and were succeeded by natives. There are several anecdotes told, which serve to show the place that the king occupied in the hearts of his people, notwithstanding the outbursts of dissatisfaction which the measures we have just alluded to occasionally elicited. One of the principal subjects of irritation was the severity with which the royal monopoly of coffee was insisted upon, and the extraordinary ability displayed by several French agents in detecting the presence of smuggled coffee, obtained for them the sobriquet of "coffee-smellers." Frederick happened to be one day riding up the Jægerstrasse, in Berlin, when his eye was attracted by a considerable crowd assembled in front of the *Fürstenhaus*. He dispatched his only attendant to inquire into the cause of this gathering. "They have posted up something about your majesty," was the answer which the servant brought back. Frederick, who had now arrived quite close to the assemblage, saw himself depicted in a most melancholy frame of mind, seated upon a stool, with a coffee-mill between his legs, which he was in the act of grinding with great assiduity with one hand, whilst with the other he collected every bean that chanced to fall. As soon as the king got a glimpse of the picture, he motioned his hand and called out, "Hang it something lower down, so that a person may not be obliged to strain his neck to get a look at it." He had hardly uttered the words when a universal shout of joy arose; the picture was torn into a thousand pieces, and the king greeted with loud *vivas* as he slowly rode away.

The affability and ease with which he entered into the feelings and met the wishes of those in a subordinate rank, was one of the chief means of winning the hearts of the people, and innumerable stories still extant, bearing the stamp of unadorned truth, acquaint us with the ordinary habits of the king, and exhibit his character in a peculiar and pleasing point of view.

CHAPTER XXXIX.

FRIENDLY RELATIONS WITH RUSSIA AND AUSTRIA. ACQUISITION OF WEST PRUSSIA.

At the time of Frederick's concluding the treaty of Hubertsburg he did not possess a single ally of sufficient influence to sustain Prussia in her proper position, or give weight to her voice in the congress of European nations. England had deserted him in such a manner as to prevent him from ever again placing confidence in its government. His alliance with Russia had been snapped asunder by the sudden overthrow of Peter III. It was only with Tartars and Turks that he could be said to have maintained, during the latter part of the Seven Years' War, anything like a friendly footing. The divan had, towards the end of the autumn of 1763, sent a numerous embassy to Berlin, in full oriental pomp: and, to the great amusement of the citizens of the Prussian capital, this body made their solemn entry into Berlin, on the 9th of November, bringing with them costly robes, arms, and splendid horses as presents for Frederick. It is said that the sultan, through his ambassador, requested of Frederick to send him three of the astrologers by whose aid, as the sultan took for granted, he had been enabled to work such miracles during the Seven Years' War. Frederick is said to have replied, that his three astrologers were his knowledge of diplomacy, his army, and his treasury. The embassy remained in the Prussian capital during the winter, and indemnified the inhabitants of Berlin in some measure for the loss of theatrical and other representations, which had been dissipated during the war. As the Turks were about to return in the following spring, several young damsels had made arrangements to accompany them to Constantinople, and had already taken their places in the Turkish wagons, but the police, having by some chance got information of the circumstance, arrived just in time to seize the fair fugitives. His friendly understanding with the divan was indeed of too romantic a nature to justify Frederick in neglecting to seek a more powerful ally, whose weight should serve in some measure to guarantee the security of his kingdom. An alliance with Russia seemed to offer very considerable advantages, and although steadily opposed by Austria, was not long in being concluded, the political relations of Poland affording a principal means of expediting its completion. King Augustus III. had died in October, 1763, and his son followed him to the grave a few months afterwards. An infant grandson still remained, but it could not, of course, press its claims to so disputed a succession as that of the Polish crown. Russia had always exerted a paramount influence over the affairs of Poland, and had treated it like a dependent province, and the empress was now resolved on maintaining this influence. Polish patriots, alive to the misery in which their native country had been by its own acts plunged, applied to Frederick, and requested him to place his brother, Prince Henry, who had obtained such renown during the Seven Years' War, upon the throne, in order to work out the regeneration of their country. But Frederick saw clearly the dangerous consequences which must have necessarily resulted from such an act, and declined acquiescence in the demand. The Russian empress, finding that Frederick was not altogether opposed to her views respecting Poland, at once concluded an alliance with him, in April, 1764. It was stipulated that Russia and Prussia should reciprocally maintain the present possessions of either kingdom; each to furnish a contingent of 12,000 men, in the case of war breaking out, or a subsidy of 480,000 thalers, and, according to one of the secret articles, recourse was to be had to every means, even force, to maintain the constitution of the Polish republic in its then state, especially the unlimited right of suffrage, which had been the principal cause of the anarchy that had enfeebled and disabled Poland. They at the same time selected Count Stanislaus Augustus Poniatowsky as a candidate for the Polish crown, and he was accordingly, on the 7th of September, proclaimed king, under the protection of the Russian arms.

To this newly-created monarch Frederick sent the following spirited epistle, shortly after his coronation: "Your majesty should recollect that as you have received your crown by election, not birth, the world will scrutinize your acts more severely than those of any other potentate in Europe. And this is but just. In the case of succession by birth, which is more or less a casualty, nothing further is expected, although, indeed, much should be expected, than ordinary abilities; but from the man who has been elevated by his equals from the rank of subject to that of monarch—from him who has been spontaneously elected to rule over those who have elected him—from such a man it is but reasonable to require everything that can deserve and adorn a crown. Gratitude towards his people is the first virtue which such a monarch should possess; for to his people next to Providence, is he indebted for his diadem. A king by birth, if his acts be unworthy of his station, is but a satire on himself; whereas a king by election, if his acts be unworthy of his rank, reflects disgrace upon his subjects. Your majesty will certainly pardon me this warmth; it is the result of sincere respect. The most agreeable part of the picture is not a lecture as to what you should be, but a prophecy of what you will be."

King Stanislaus Augustus was not, however, at liberty to act with sufficient freedom to be able to attend to the wise instructions contained in this communication. Poland was full of internal commotion. Religious fanaticism had created a terrible gulf between the two sections of the population; those not belonging to the Roman Catholic church, and bearing the name of Dissenters, were treated with considerable rigor. The claims of these latter were maintained by the empress, who demanded for them the concession of equal rights. This religious acrimony, and the spirit of retaliation thereby engendered, kept the population in one unending ferment, and in order to put a period to the contest Catherine resolved to have recourse to an act of despotism. The heads of the Catholic party were attacked during the night, seized, and transported in all haste to Siberia. But so tyrannical an act drove the Polish people to desperation. A rebellion broke out in the southern provinces, close to the Turkish frontier, and threatened to overturn the throne of Stanislaus Augustus, and throw off the foreign yoke. But Russian troops entered Poland; the conspirators were dispersed in every direction; the rioters fled to the Turkish territory, and the Russians hastened after them and laid a Turkish town in ashes.

This act of aggression fanned the long smouldering jealousies of the Porte and Russia into flame. The Russian ambassador at Constantinople was without further preface thrown into prison, and the divan published a formal declaration of war with Russia. Frederick, seeing himself dragged, much against his will, into the contest, made every exertion for the maintenance of peace, but his efforts proved fruitless, and he accordingly paid to Russia the stipulated subsidy in money. The acts of the Porte were to the last degree improvident and premature—it was wholly unprepared for war, and Russia obtained several brilliant victories, occupying considerable tracts of the Turkish territory.

It was, however, impossible for Frederick to view the rapid success of his ally without feelings of apprehension; it was to be feared that he might in time be forced to become, from being an ally, the slave of Russia. He was therefore bound to look round for some new confederate to restore the balance of power; and the two states that had so long warred together were soon allied, linked by the ties of identical interests. Austria could as little afford to remain a passive spectator of Russia's successes as Prussia.

Joseph II., born A.D. 1741, succeeded, in the year 1765, to the imperial crown and co-regency of the hereditary provinces of Austria. His mind had been completely dazzled by the splendor of Frederick's career; the hope of equalling, if not surpassing, his rival in ardor for the enfranchisement of the human mind, and thereby transmitting his name to the grateful memory of distant ages, was as fascinating to his imagination as consonant to his feelings. Had he but possessed Frederick's calmness and discrimination of character, and not been prematurely warped from the path he had originally intended to pursue, he would unquestionably have effected much that was great. As early as the year 1766, whilst on a tour through Bohemia and Saxony, which he had entered on with a view to obtain a more intimate knowledge of the localities of the theatre of the great war, he had expressed a wish to Frederick to see him and make his personal acquaintance; he was, however, prevented by Maria Theresa and the Grand Chancellor Kaunitz from the gratification of a desire which, to them, appeared most unseasonable and unseemly; but he wrote to Frederick to assure him that he would, at some future period, take occasion to make amends for the seeming discourtesy of his conduct. This wish of the youthful Emperor could now, in the altered state of things, be gratified, and not alone with the assent of his mother, but with her fullest approbation. As Joseph always travelled under the name of Count Falkenstein, all tedious preliminary ceremonials for such a meeting were dispensed with as unnecessary Niesse, in Upper Silesia, was the place selected for the interview, and Joseph arrived there on the 25th of August, 1769, and proceeded straightway to the palatine's palace, where Frederick had taken up his temporary residence. Frederick hurried forward to meet him, attended by the princes of his suite, but had hardly descended the first few steps of the staircase, when the Emperor flew into his arms. Frederick conducted his august friend into the saloon. "Now," exclaimed Joseph, "my wishes are at length gratified; for I have long desired the honor of standing face to face with the first of kings and ablest of warriors." "I shall ever," replied Frederick, "regard this day as the happiest of my existence; from it I date the union of two houses, which have been but too long at strife, and have need of mutual strength, instead of reciprocally weakening one another." "From henceforward," added the Emperor, "there exists, as regards Austria, no Silesia more." He then gave Frederick to understand, that, though he as yet possessed but little political influence, still neither he nor his mother would ever consent to the Russians remaining in possession of their recent acquisitions in Moldavia and Wallachia. A convention was also drawn up, binding both Frederick and the Emperor to the strictest neutrality, in the event of the war, then anticipated between England and France, breaking out, or any similar commotion. As long as this visit lasted the days were passed in military parade and confidential intercourse: in their walks, the two heads of the Germanic empire were always seen arm-in-arm.

A second and more important interview took place in the September of the following year at Neustadt, in Moravia. Whilst on his way thither Frederick paid a visit to one of his friends of the olden time, (Count Hobitz,) at the estate of the latter in Moravia. Hobitz had obtained a perfectly incredible reputation amongst the friends of artificial gardening in the last century. He contrived, by constant training, to supply the place of statues by living models, and devoted as many of his tenantry and dependents as he possibly could command to this purpose. He now strained every nerve to render the pageantry of his artificial Elysium as enchanting and pleasing to his royal guest as his utmost resources would admit; the meads and dales were filled with Arcadian shepherds and shepherdesses; and in the groves and on the lakes the gods and goddesses of classical antiquity disported at large. The buildings were so constructed as to represent every terrestrial zone; nor was even Gulliver's pigmy city of Lilliput, with its miniature temples and public buildings, forgotten. Theatrical and other exhibitions, fireworks, and, in short, every means of entertaining or amusing the fancy were put in requisition, and the imagination thus precluded from the reverting for an instant to the prosaic realities of ordinary life.

Frederick was highly gratified with his visit to the enchanted gardens of Roswald, and did not reach Neustadt until the 3d of September. On entering the town, he descended from his carriage, in order to meet the Emperor on foot; but the latter had heard of his arrival, and hastened with his suite to meet him. The two monarchs met in the open square of the town. On this occasion Prince Kaunitz formed one of the Emperor's train; and important diplomatic negotiations were now opened. Kaunitz strove to prevail upon Frederick to form a new and intimate alliance with Austria, and represented cordial co-operation between the Prussian and Austrian monarchies, as the only possible means of stemming that torrent which then threatened to burst upon Europe. Frederick was, however, reluctant to break with Russia, but promised to use every means in his power to prevent the Turkish war, then raging, from leading to a general conflagration, and offered to mediate between the contending parties: his conduct was conciliatory in many particulars. As if to test the sincerity of his desires for the maintenance of peace, a courier arrived from Constantinople with a proposition for the mediation of the cabinets of Vienna and Berlin in the affairs of Russia and the Porte, the latter having recently suffered very considerable losses. Joseph and Kaunitz were satisfied with the conduct of the Prussian king, and testified their warmest gratitude.

During this visit to Neustadt, many interesting conversations took place between Frederick and the members of the Austrian suite. Prince De Ligne, who accompanied Joseph, has preserved many of the remarks made by Frederick, and has given a lively sketch of the elegance and tact which always characterized the tone of Frederick's conversation. "Do you know," said Frederick one day, addressing the Prince De Ligne, " that I have served in your army? The first time that I ever drew a sword was in defence of the house of Austria. My heavens! how times passes!" He clasped his hands, says the prince, at the words " My heavens!" and assumed a most thoughtful and serene aspect. "Do you know," continued Frederick, " that I witnessed the last irradiation of the brilliant genius of Prince Eugene?" "Perhaps the genius of your majesty may have caught its first fire from those beams." " Ah!" responded the king, "who could venture to compare himself with Prince Eugene!" " He!" said the prince "who has eclipsed him! He, for instance, who has been victorious in thirteen fights."

With respect to Field-marshal Traun, Frederick remarked, " He was my master; he showed me the errors I committed." " Your majesty," replied the prince, "proved most ungrateful for these instructions. You never, at least in my recollection, allowed yourself to be beaten by him out of gratitude." "I have not been beaten," responded Frederick, " becuse I have not engaged him."

He testified the most especial respect toward Marshal Loudon who was also present at Neustadt. He always addressed him as Field-marshal, although Loudon did not receive this well-merited distinction until eight years subsequently. As all were one day sitting down to dinner, the remark was made that Loudon had not yet arrived. "That is not his general habit," said Frederick; " he is generally on his ground before me." He subsequently bade Loudon sit beside him, as he preferred having him on his side to having him opposite him.

During the whole of this visit Frederick and his entire suite wore the Austrian uniform, white and silver, in order to avoid evoking unpleasant memories but too intimately interwoven with the sight of the Prussian blue, and to make it appear as if he were in the Austrian army, and in the Emperor's train. Being, however, in the habit of taking great quantities of snuff, slight traces of it were sometimes visible on his white uniform. "Gentleman," said Frederick one day, "you see I am not fit— I am not worthy to wear your colors."

Of Joseph, Frederick, shortly after his return from Moravia, spoke in terms of unfeigned admiration, and expressed himself in the following flattering but concise manner in a letter to Voltaire: "I have been in Moravia," he says, "and have seen the Emperor, who is preparing to play an important part on the European stage. Born in the heart of a bigoted court, he is free from superstition; though educated in the midst of ostentation, his manners are simple; though nurtured in the incense of flattery, he is modest; though burning for fame and distinction, he sacrifices his ambition to filial duty, which he is most scrupulous in discharging; he has had pedants for his tutors, and still has sufficient taste to read the works of Voltaire, and appreciate their merits."

The negotiations and mediations between the contending powers were, meanwhile, progressing but slowly. Russia had wrung too many advantages from the Turks to be now inclined to listen to rational overtures; and the Sublime Porte refused to acquiesce in the exorbitant demands of Russia. Austria insisted on warding off Russia from all immediate contiguity with her eastern provinces, and armed to give weight to her remonstrances. The moment became critical, and a general rupture was anticipated. Strong apprehensions were also entertained, that Poland would take advantage of the crisis,—that foreign powers would interfere,—and the torch of universal war be once more enkindled throughout Europe. Frederick's only wish was for the maintenance of peace

and the gradual development of the resources of his
kingdom. On a sudden a new and unexpected solution
of the difficulties, arising from such a chaos of contending
interests, presented itself.

Prince Henry, Frederick's brother, being then on a
visit in St. Petersburg, had already succeeded in obtaining
the full confidence of the Empress Catherine, when intelligence
arrived, that Austria had taken possession of a part
of Poland adjoining its own territories, to which it preferred
some antiquated and long-dormant claims. On receipt
of this intelligence, Catherine, addressing Prince Henry,
made use of this memorable expression: "It would seem
that in Poland one has nothing to do but to stoop to pick
up whatever one pleases : if the cabinet of Vienna intend
to dismember that kingdom, the other cabinets can do the
same with equal justice." This expression was caught
up by Henry; he explained to her how she could in this
way indemnify herself for such concessions as she might
consent to make to Turkey at the instance of the other
powers, and she readily entered into his views; the execution
of the project was rendered easy of accomplishment
from the internal weakness and distracted condition
of Poland. On Frederick's receiving the first intimation
of this proposition, it seemed to him as if he were in a
dream; but when he had convinced himself of its reality,
he felt assured of its being, indeed, the only possible
means of averting a universal war, and lent the project
his full support, as he further hoped to be thereby indemnified
for the pecuniary subsidies which he had been
obliged to advance to Russia. Prussia and Russia were
soon agreed on the measures to be taken, and they now
applied to Austria to join in this singular compact against
Poland. The Austrian cabinet, although it had assumed
the initiative in the whole transaction, now feigned disapprobation
of the entire plan, perhaps out of respect for
Maria Theresa, whose consent it was in reality difficult to
obtain; but as soon as it had promised its assent, it began
to make such exorbitant demands, that the whole project

ACQUISITION OF WEST PRUSSIA.

of partition was well-nigh being abandoned Eventually, after much previous complicated and intricate negotiation, it was mutually agreed, that each of the three contracting powers should take such portion of Poland as immediately adjoined its own territories, and tended to the roundness and compactness of its dominions. This treaty of partition was executed in the autumn of 1772, without Poland being in a condition to offer any opposition to its dismemberment. Frederick exacted the oath of fealty from Pomerelle and the other districts lying between Pomerania and East Prussia, (with the exception of Dantzick and Thorn,) and took immediate and formal possession. Each of the three powers produced proofs of the plausibility of their demands. Frederick's explanation referred chiefly to Pomerelle, which was averred to have originally formed part of the dukedom of Pomerania, and to have been dissevered from the same in the thirteenth century; he, accordingly, based his claims on his right, as Elector of Brandenburg, to the inheritance of Pomerania, and to that which had originally formed part and parcel of the same. Frederick's acquisition was, in point of superficial extent, population, and fertility of soil, inferior to those of his partners; but to him of incalculable importance notwithstanding, as forming the natural connecting link between the straggling members of his kingdom, and giving him, from his possession of the mouth of the Vistula, the entire control of the whole trade of Poland. Being now in possession of all the old Prussian territories, Frederick assumed the style and title of "King *of* Prussia, not "*in* Prussia," as hitherto.

The Polish diet was forced to ratify the partition, though the measure was strenuously resisted to the last by all the patriots in Poland. Thaddeus Reyten, who had taken the most prominent part in defending the integrity of his native land, on seeing all his efforts baffled and abortive, became insane. It was with much difficulty that Maria Theresa was induced to give her consent to the plans of her cabinet. She addressed the following

most extraordinary epistle to Kaunitz on the subject—
the style is as singular as the purport. "When my dominions were on every side assailed, and I really did not
know a single place where I could lie-in with safety, I
still relied on the goodness of my cause and the help
of God. But in this matter, in which not only public
justice cries to heaven against us, but common prudence
and sound sense are violated, I must own I never felt so
uneasy in my life or so ashamed to be seen. Consider
what an example we set the whole world should we, for
the sake of a paltry piece of Poland, or of Moldavia and
Wallachia, fling away our honor and reputation. I see
clearly that I stand alone, and am no longer *en vigueur*,
and therefore allow matters to take their course, but not
without the greatest reluctance." On the draft of the
scheme of partition this high-minded dame wrote with
her own hand the following words: "*Placet*, since so
many great and learned men will have it so; but when
I have been long in my grave it will be seen what
will come of this violation of everything hitherto considered holy and just." The whole world was struck
dumb with sheer astonishment at the occurrence of an
event which had been hitherto without a precedent in the
annals of history. Still none of the other great powers
of Europe interfered; the dawning struggle for independence in America, and the subversion of the order of
Jesuits drew off the attention of the world to other
channels.

If we cannot here forbear paying the tribute of our
sympathy to this, the primal decadence of a people highly
gifted and once great, we are, on the other hand, forced
to seek consolation in what history would teach us to
believe to be a natural law governing the rise and fall of
nations. From her we learn that new, and for the most
part fairer life ever springs from the graves of the fallen.
Poland fell because it lagged behind the general development of its contemporaries—because arbitrary rule and
cringing servitude prevailed throughout the length and

ACQUISITION OF WEST PRUSSIA.

breadth of the land—because no spirit of nationality linked the members of its community together; and Prussia, by wresting from Poland a tract of territory which the latter had originally taken from her, acquired a degree of territorial compactness necessary to its own political development, and that section of Poland thus transferred to the crown of Prussia was speedily elevated from its previous barbarism, and participated in those more exalted goods of life which were then so highly cultivated throughout the other provinces of the Prussian monarchy. If our heart refuse its approbation to the measure which Frederick conceived himself necessitated to adopt, we are still constrained to pay the tribute of our admiration to the zeal with which he devoted himself to the furthering the welfare of his new subjects, and the glorious task of making half a million of human beings happy. He hurried in person, in the summer of 1772, to West Prussia, in order to make the necessary dispositions on the spot. Where confusion and absence of all justice had hitherto reigned, a wise and well-ordered administration of the law was speedily introduced, rendering life and property everywhere secure; a period was put to the degrading bondage of the serf and the barbarities of martial law; numerous schools were founded, in the hope of rousing the people from their moral torpor, and awakening them to a sense of the dignity of human nature; admirable arrangements were made to prevent the propagation of infectious diseases, which had frequently spread the most frightful ravages amongst both the population and their cattle. In fine, no exertion was spared to promote industry and commerce; colonists were settled on the waste lands, and the erection of a post-office for the transmission of correspondence was a new but grand boon.

The good feeling existing between Prussia and Russia, which had been in some degree disturbed by the complicated questions arising out of the partition, as to the relative portions of territory to be had by the respective parties, was soon cemented through the aid of diplomatic agents, and became more and more cordial. Prince Henry of Prussia happening to be on a second visit to St. Petersburg, in 1776, when the youthful wife of the Grand Duke Paul died, his conduct on the occasion was such as to win him the affection and confidence of the whole imperial court, and as the empress was desirous that the Grand Duke Paul should be speedily re-married, he took occasion to propose a princess of Wurtemberg; (her mother was a princess of Brandenburg-Schwedt;) and his selection meeting with the empress's full approbation, arrangements were immediately made for an interview between the grand duke and the princess, to take place in Berlin, in which latter city they were to be formally affianced.

The preparations made by Frederick for the reception of his high guest were on an unusual scale of splendor. A special embassy was dispatched to receive him on the Prussian frontier, and every effort made to give the Prussian capital a gay and festive aspect, and as Frederick's ordinary household was extremely scanty, a number of supernumerary pages and lackeys were engaged for the occasion. The grand duke arrived, and made his brilliant entry into Berlin on the 21st of July; Frederick proceeded from his palace to meet him. "Sire," said Paul Petrowich, addressing the Prussian monarch, "I have come from the depths of the North to these more favored regions for no other purpose than to assure you of the strength of that affection which shall ever form the bond of unity between our respective realms, and to gratify the ardent desire I feel to see that princess who is destined to ascend the throne of the Muscovites. Permit me further to assure you that the fact of my thus receiving her from your hands must endear her still more to me and the nation which she is one day to govern. I have now, at length, an opportunity of gratifying a wish which I have so long and so ardently cherished, of being able to gaze upon him who is at once the greatest hero of his age, the wonder of his time, and will form the envy of pos-

ACQUISITION OF WEST PRUSSIA.

terity." "I but little deserve," replied Frederick, "this flattering eulogium : you see in me nothing but a feeble old man; but of this you may rest assured, that I shall ever regard it as a subject of pride and gratulation to have thus received within these walls the worthy heir of a mighty empire—the son of my best friend, the great Catherine." Then turning to Count Romanzoff, who had won the splendid victories over the Turks, and was in the grand duke's train, he addressed him : " Conqueror of the Ottomans ! I bid you welcome ! I find a strong resemblance between you and my General Winterfeldt." " Sire," replied the Russian field-marshal, " it is but too flattering to me to be held to resemble one who has achieved such distinction in Frederick's service." "Oh !" said Frederick, "you can rest your fame on those brilliant victories, which will immortalize your name to the most distant ages." The ceremonials of betrothal were performed on the second day after the arrival of the grand duke. The visit proved one unbroken round of revelry and feasting.

CHAPTER XL.

FREDERICK'S SOLICITUDE FOR GERMANY.—THE BAVARIAN WAR OF SUCCESSION.—THE PRINCES' LEAGUE.

REALLY anxious for the peace and welfare of his people, he would have thought himself but too fortunate had he been able to devote the whole undivided energies of his mind, during the remainder of his life, to the calm administrative duties of his station. Seeing, however, that sooner or later circumstances, growing out of the then state of things, must arise, highly perilous to that eminence to which he had raised his kingdom, he at once flew to arms, with all the buoyant energy of his youth, resolved to be found prepared in the hour of danger for such conjunctures as might arise.

It had been for centuries suspected that the imperial house of Austria aimed at turning the shadow of power, which the titular distinction of Emperor conferred on the Austrian sovereign, into a realty, and degrading the independent princes of the Germanic empire into tributary vassals, and that it awaited but a favorable opportunity for attempting the realization of its ambitious schemes. Of the correctness of these suspicions Frederick could not entertain a doubt, and the impassioned, aspiring tone of the present youthful emperor's mind was of itself amply sufficient to awaken apprehensions of this nature. Whilst conversing with one of his generals, Frederick remarked, pointing to the Emperor's portrait, which lay before him on a chair in his private chamber, "I have placed this picture right in view; this is a young man

whom I dare not lose sight of. Joseph has head, and
might effect much; it is a pity for his own sake that
he takes his second step before he has taken the first."
These few words contain a perfect solution of the tragic
end which the youthful Emperor subsequently met.

Several opportunities had already occurred for vindicating the rights of the German princes against the aggrandizing spirit of Austria, nor had these been left by Frederick
unemployed. Hitherto, however, nothing beyond remonstrance and negotiation had been resorted to; but on
Austria's attempting to enforce claims, which threatened
to sap the very foundation of the existing imperial confederacy, Frederick saw the necessity of having recourse
to some more energetic measures.

Maximilian Joseph, Prince Elector of Bavaria, died suddenly, on the 30th of December, 1777, and with him the
royal family of Pfalz-Bavaria became extinct. The succession now reverted, of undisputed right, to Charles
Theodore, Prince Elector of Pfalz, to whom, as having no
legitimate issue, Charles, Duke of Pfalz-Zweibrücken,
stood next in succession. Under these circumstances
Austria, which had long coveted the possession of Bavaria,
interfered, advanced some antiquated claims and un-
founded pretensions, and entering Lower Bavaria and
Upper Pfalz with an armed force, terrified Charles Theodore, who was much concerned for the future fate of his
numerous illegitimate progeny, into a compromise, and
the surrender of one half of his inheritance. Prince
Charles of Pfalz-Zweibrücken,' whose consent was altogether essential to the validity of the contract, had not
been consulted, as Austria anticipated no great difficulty
in procuring his subsequent acquiescence.

A proceeding so arbitrary was clearly an infringement
of the fundamental laws of the empire, and if this act
were allowed to pass unchallenged no member of the
Imperial Confederacy would be for a moment safe against
similar aggressions. Frederick decided on becoming the
champion of the rights of the Germanic princes. He dis-

patched a formal declaration to the prince elector, stating that he, as a member of the Germanic empire and a contracting party to the treaty of Hubertsburg, was manifestly wronged and injured in his rights by this dismemberment of a principality. Hereupon Duke Charles, who, from supposing himself too feeble for resistance, had already made up his mind to succumb to the mandates of Austria, now entered, at Frederick's instance, a formal protest, and was assured by Frederick that the claims of himself and those of his family should be maintained to the last against the encroaching and ambitious spirit of Austria. Saxony and Mecklenburg also claimed interests in the matter, and their claims, though subordinate, were unquestionably valid. France and Russia, though not unfavorable to Frederick's cause, could not interfere.

All diplomatic negotiations with the Emperor proved abortive. Austria seemed nowise disposed to release from its grasp any portion of its newly-acquired possessions; on the contrary, troops were concentrated in Bohemia to resist any armed intervention on the part of Prussia. On matters assuming this complexion, Frederick, although in his sixty-seventh year, decided promptly on resisting force with force, as no other alternative was now left him. He accordingly drew his army together, and divided it into two corps, one of which was to advance through Silesia, whilst the other penetrated through Saxony. After holding a general muster of his troops in Berlin, he thus addressed the assembled general officers of his army: "Gentlemen, most of us have served together from our boyhood, and grown gray in the service of our country· we know one another well—we have shared the cares and toils of war together—and I am firmly convinced that you are as unwilling to shed human blood as I am. But my kingdom is in danger: as king, it is my bounden duty to protect my subjects, and adopt the most energetic, decisive, and efficacious means to dispel the storm that threatens to burst above our heads. It is in the execution and carrying out of this great principle that I count upon your alacrity in seconding my views, remembering also that attachment to my own person which you have ever exhibited, and which has never yet been without its great results. Of this you may also rest assured, that I shall ever acknowledge with gratitude such services as you may render to your king and country. I have but one request to make of you, and that is, that you never lose sight of clemency, even though the enemy be completely in your power; and that you insist on the troops under your orders observing the strictest discipline. I am now about to start for the seat of war. I do not, however, intend to travel as a king; expensive and splendid equipages have no charm for me; but as the infirmities of age prevent me from travelling as I was wont when in the vigor of youth, I shall take a postchaise, and you are at liberty to do the same. On the day of battle, however, you shall see me on horseback, and I hope that my generals will imitate my example."

Frederick set out for Breslau on the 5th of April, 1778, to undertake the command of the Silesian army, the other corps having been entrusted to the conduct of Prince Henry. It was Frederick's intention to break in upon Moravia, and had this plan been rapidly executed, the Austrians, who were but half equipped, must have been attacked at a great disadvantage; but negotiations were again opened with Joseph, and, proving as futile as the former, were productive of no other result than giving the Austrians time for a complete organization of their forces. Abandoning his original design on Moravia, Frederick now advanced through the province of Glatz and entered Bohemia. The advance guard of the Prussian army reached the Bohemian frontier on the 13th of July: this incursion produced the utmost consternation in Vienna, as no one had for a moment believed that the old Prussian king was really in earnest in his military operations and demonstrations. Maria Theresa felt but little inclination for a repetition of the disastrous results of the Seven Years' War, and trembling for the life of her son, who really thirsted ardently for military fame, she dispatched, in secret, a second envoy to Frederick to declare, that she felt fully confident that they were both equally unwilling to tear out one another's hair, now grown gray from time; but the terms she proposed were such as Frederick could not accept, and all further negotiations were, after an interval of a few weeks, altogether suspended.

Prince Henry had been, in the meantime, reinforced by a Saxon corps, had penetrated through Saxony into Bohemia, and captured several extensive magazines belonging to the enemy; 400,000 men, well equipped and abundantly supplied with heavy ordnance, now stood face to face on the Bohemian soil. Everything promised a great and decisive engagement, but no one single action of any importance ensued. The name of Frederick had still so terrible a sound in the ears of the Austrians, that they did not dare to pass the lines of the impregnable entrenchments within which they stood, except for some petty skirmish or some foraging fray; and Frederick, feeling himself more than usually feeble and ailing, was unwilling to hazard unnecessarily his well-won laurels in any daring experiment; he therefore confined himself to stripping the Bohemian districts through which he passed, of all means of sustaining an army, and thereby drawing a line of demarkation between Bohemia and Silesia. His personal conduct was, however, signalized by the same spirit of intrepidity as of old; and he exposed himself to the most imminent danger with the same indifference as the youngest officer in his army. As an instance of this, we shall mention an incident, which is quite in character with that coolness and bravery that distinguished him in former days. He had been bled, and on the evening of the same day the enemy opened so heavy a cannonade, that his presence became, as he thought, necessary: mounting his horse, he was proceeding to the point attacked, when the vein began to bleed afresh. He quietly dismounted, and had his arm

bandaged by a field-surgeon who happened to be at hand.
Whilst in the midst of this operation, a cannon-ball came
whizzing past the surgeon's head; Frederick, seeing him
tremble, remarked with a smile to one of the by-standers,
" He cannot have seen many cannon-balls in his life-time."
  A scarcity of provisions began now to be felt in the
Prussian camp. Contagious diseases, want, and consequent desertion were beginning to thin Frederick's lines
more rapidly than the bloodiest encounters; he was,
therefore, left no other alternative, than to retire with
both his armies from Bohemia, and this he did about the
middle of September. The brilliancy of his manœuvring
to effect this retreat shed no little lustre on his name as
a tactician. The Austrian army, without venturing to
oppose his march, merely dispatched single corps to harass his line of route; but these bodies were always repulsed with loss as often as they hazarded an attack.
During this retirade, Frederick William, the heir presumptive to the Prussian throne, distinguished himself
particularly; he conducted the troops entrusted to his
command through the most perilous paths, and valiantly
repulsed the repeated assaults of the enemy's skirmishers.
Frederick listened to the details of his nephew's conduct
with unusual satisfaction; and on their meeting, he addressed him with the greatest cordiality, and said, " From
this day forward I shall cease to consider you any longer
as my nephew; I now regard you as my son You have
done everything that I could have done—everything that
could have been expected from the most experienced
general." He then embraced the prince with much
tenderness. This act of generous affection was the more
gratifying to witness, as it was well known that Frederick and the heir presumptive had not been on the most
friendly footing previously.
  Frederick had taken up his own winter-quarters at
Schatzlar, in Bohemia, the cantonments of his troops
stretching away into Silesia; here he remained until
about the middle of October, and sought to dispel the un-

pleasing recollection of a fruitless and fatiguing campaign by various literary avocations. Voltaire had died in the spring of the previous year, and Frederick, who had long since forgiven him, and had, from the period of the Seven Years' War, maintained an uninterrupted correspondence with him, now composed a discourse in honor of his memory, conceived in all the ardor of youth, and had it read to the members of the Berlin Academy in the month of November following.

From Schatzlar Frederick proceeded to Upper Silesia, and drove back the Austrians, who had begun to annoy his frontiers. After occupying some of the towns in Austrian Silesia, he set out for Breslau, and there passed the winter. The several skirmishes which subsequently took place between the two armies led to no decisive result. But France and Russia now interfered on behalf of the estate of the empire, and remonstrated energetically with the Austrian cabinet; and as the Turks, who had hitherto kept Russia employed, had now concluded peace with that power, Austria became apprehensive of an armed intervention on the part of Russia, and therefore deemed it more prudent to yield at once. An armistice was accordingly concluded in the month of March, 1779, and peace was definitely signed on the 13th of May following. The compromise entered into between Austria and the Prince Elector, Charles Theodore, was annulled; Bavaria, with the exception of a small strip of territory immediately contiguous to the Austrian frontiers, was restored to its lawful claimants, and the interests of Saxony and Mecklenburg duly provided for.

Frederick, who had sacrificed 29,000,000 thalers, besides a vast number of men to the object of the war, sought no compensation whatsoever, as he considered he attained more than an equivalent in having thus given stability to the constitution of the Germanic empire. He did, in reality, derive far greater advantage from his noble conduct, than if he had lent himself to the ambitious projects of the Emperor. His disinterestedness won

for him the entire confidence and friendship of the
other members of the empire; and even such as had
hitherto looked with a jealous eye on the growing power
of Prussia, began now to regard him and the Prussian
state as the palladium of German liberty. He was now
universally honored with the title of the "Great"; nay,
in order to distinguish him from others on whom history
has conferred a similar appellation, he was even styled
"The One." The Bavarians especially honored him as
the founder of their jurisprudence; his picture was
always to be found suspended in the village alehouses
beside that of the holy Corbinian, Bavaria's patron saint;
and the same lamp frequently burned before both
pictures. An Austrian officer, happening to observe this
custom, inquired of the landlord what it meant: "This
one," said the latter in explanation, "is Bavaria's patron
in heaven, and this one here Frederick, the Prussian king,
is Bavaria's patron on earth; both of them are saints,
and we, therefore, as good Catholics, burn lamps in their
honor."

This Bavarian war of succession gave Frederick an opportunity of performing a noble act of generosity. On
his learning, in the spring of 1779, that the inhabitants
of the Bohemian districts, which had been ravaged by his
army in the preceding campaign, were in great distress
from a want of seed wherewith to sow the ground, he
opened his granaries to them, and also gave them the
option of either purchasing the grain at low rates, or
taking such quantities as they happened then to need, on
promise of replacing the same when they should have
gathered in their crops the following harvest.

Thus the closing years of his political career lost
nothing of their former prestige, notwithstanding the
new and manifold moral and political combinations that
had sprung up around him. The world lent an attentive
ear to those wise maxims, to those exhortations to prudence and moderation, which he occasionally addressed
to busy nations; the authority, which his name carried

with it, was such as to be sought for to give weight and sanction to individual resolves. Thus we find Russia, although her interests had again ceased to be identified or to coalesce with those of Prussia, and even although Frederick had no fleet at his command, soliciting his adhesion to a treaty of armed maritime neutrality, merely with a view to obtain the sanction of his name: to this treaty he became a party in 1781. In the troubles which arose in Holland between the viceroy (the husband of his niece) and the so-called patriots, he sought to allay the asperities on both sides, without, however, presuming to interfere further in the internal affairs of a foreign kingdom, than by the tender of his advice. He recommended the viceroy to assure himself above all things of the confidence and respect of the nation. " With these," he added, " you will, like your great ancestors, from whom I also esteem it an honor to be descended, command influence and power in abundance." He received a most flattering recognition of his greatness from the United States of America, which entered, in 1783, into the class of independent nations. Being desirous of extending as much as possible their commercial relations with Europe, they solicited Frederick to join in a treaty of neutrality, " as the monarch best calculated to set an example to the other powers of Europe." To this request Frederick assented without hesitation; and Franklin, Jefferson, and Adams concluded a treaty with the Prussian ambassador at the Hague, in 1785, the terms and stipulations of which, based, as they are, on considerations of the purest philanthropy, form one of the most honorable memorials of which history can boast.

In the same year Frederick established the *Fürstenbund*, or Princes' League, and thus accomplished the object he had in view when he undertook the Bavarian war of succession. Joseph, now sole sovereign of Austria, his mother having died in 1780, still continued to awaken the suspicion, that he had not yet abandoned his designs for subverting the institutions of the empire. These apprehensions were much strengthened by the discovery that he had not yet relinquished all hopes of gaining possession of Bavaria, notwithstanding the recent treaty, though his object was now to be carried not by force of arms, but by the aid of Russia and France. Charles Theodore, the Prince Elector of Pfalz-Bavaria, was required to exchange his hereditary possessions for the Austrian Netherlands, which, with the exception of Luxembourg, together with a sum of three millions of thalers, he was to receive in lieu thereof. The measure was communicated to the Duke of Zweibrücken in January, 1785, through a Russian delegate, who at the same time gave him to understand, that as Russia and France approved of the exchange, any resistance on his part would not avail. The matter created a great sensation, not so much from the circumstance of the terms of the exchange being so monstrously disadvantageous to Bavaria, as from this being regarded as the first step on the part of Austria to future aggrandizements. It was rumored that a similar offer had been made to the Duke of Wurtemberg, to exchange his possessions for Modena; and the mind readily pictured to itself the gradual merging of all the small principalities of Southern Germany in the overwhelming sovereignty of Austria. The Duke of Zweibrücken protested, and again had recourse to Frederick, who immediately remonstrated loudly with the Russian cabinet on the illegality of Joseph's conduct; and the Empress Catherine was thereby induced to declare that her sanction had been obtained solely on the assumption that the exchange of territory was to be the free act of both parties. France published a declaration to the same effect; and Joseph himself was constrained not only to abandon the project, but even to declare likewise, that he had never, from the first, for a moment contemplated anything more than a purely voluntary exchange.

This equivocal conduct on the part of Austria made a deep impression; and although this last attempt had been so easily baffled, yet it seemed a matter of prudence that some effective measures should be taken to prevent the recurrence of similar efforts, curb this spirit of encroachment, and protect the subordinate princes of the empire from aggression. This subject had long engaged Frederick's most serious thoughts, and he had even submitted, twelve months previously, for the approval of his counsellors, the draft of a plan for leaguing together the several members of the Germanic empire for one common end, similar in its spirit and provisions to the many confederacies that had subsisted centuries before. The Bavarian dispute induced him to mature his deliberations and to bring them into speedy operation. Saxony and Hanover were the first solicited to join the league. They gave in their adhesion on the 23d of July, and the greater number of the other regents throughout Germany soon after joined the confederacy unsolicited.

Thus had Frederick, shortly previous to the termination of his lengthened career, bequeathed to his kingdom, and to his whole native land, a noble bequest, the *Fürstenbund*, a guarantee of international strength and lasting peace; at least, as far as human foresight could control the fate of nations. Who could have then dreamed that a new era was about to open with his death—a new chapter in the history of states; that a few years would suffice to bring forth the most awful convulsions; and that from thenceforward the policy of nations was about to assume a completely different aspect! Frederick brought his period of political activity to a worthy termination: he could now close his eyes in the unruffled composure of a noble self-satisfaction.

But before referring to his last moments, we must pause to bestow a few passing words on his internal administration;—on those remedies which he applied to heal the wounds inflicted by protracted warfare on the social relations of his people.

CHAPTER XLI.

FREDERICK'S INTERNAL ADMINISTRATION FROM THE PERIOD OF THE SEVEN YEARS' WAR.

DEVOTING the utmost energies of his mind to the internal government of his kingdom, from the moment of his so gloriously terminating the Seven Years' War, Frederick had recourse to his old partition of time amongst his several avocations, and allotted to the hours of each day their respective and stated objects, including both the official engagements of his high calling, and the intellectual enjoyments of the philosopher. He would at one time guide the machine of state from his rural retreat in Potsdam, at another examine with his own eyes into the working of each law, and take personal cognizance of each act. It was his master-mind that up to the hour of his death infused life and vigor into the organization of his many-membered state—it was his hand that held all the reins of government, and gave every force its due direction.

But before casting a retrospective glance at the administrative activity of the Great King, it is absolutely necessary that we disengage our minds from their present impressions—that we abstain from taking the present standard of intelligence and experience as the criterion by which to judge of the soundness of his political views. Frederick stood on the threshold of a new era. He conceded a larger amount of intellectual liberty than had ever been previously granted, and he accorded to all his subjects perfect equality before the judicial bench. But it is only in such generalities that we find him paving the way for the new era; he carefully abstained from removing those barriers which he had found erected; and his conservative tendency was even so decided as to render him desirous of confining the activity of his subjects within certain narrowly prescribed limits. It is very possible that he may have been induced to adopt this course from the circumstance of his having inherited from his father such perfect state-mechanism as it would have been difficult to supersede with advantage, and which was eminently calculated to give full play and ample scope to the preponderance of his own genius. He was thereby enabled to exercise unlimited power in a greater degree than history informs us of having elsewhere existed. In the latter years of his life, as is always the case, this unlimited authority became more obtrusive. But though the political development of his people was, unquestionably, thereby retarded, still the pure and active regard for their welfare which he ever evinced—the aiding hand which he always held extended—and the untiring zeal with which he labored for the completion of his great task—largely neutralized the noxious influences of the spirit of political tutelage which he labored to organize.

It is thus, and thus alone, that we can at all comprehend or explain the strict lines of demarkation he so sedulously strove to perpetuate between the different classes of society, and the pains he bestowed on propping up distinctions which had begun to be levelled towards the latter end of his reign. Nobles, citizens, and peasants, each in their prescribed sphere, were to labor severally for the common weal: neither was to infringe upon the prerogatives of the other. The nobles were to maintain their position as the first class in the state; the highest posts in the government and the most distinguished rank in the army were to belong exclusively to this order: in accordance with this high calling, the noble was not to degrade his mind by mercantile speculation; his rank was to be maintained by the possession of large landed property. As, however, many of the

FREDERICK'S INTERNAL ADMINISTRATION. 419

nobles had begun to prefer commercial opulence to aristocratic poverty, every possible provision was made to prevent them from parting with their estates. The sale of knights' holdings to commoners was first impeded and subsequently interdicted altogether. Large sums of money were freely advanced by the king, to be laid out in improving the estates of the nobles. Their sunken credit was also raised by the subsequent introduction of a system, according to which the money raised on estates in any particular province could be levied upon the whole district. Several other institutions, such as Military Colleges and Knights' Academies, were likewise introduced, with a view to sustain the influence of the noble order.

Entertaining such views as these, it is easy to understand how zealously he labored for the advancement of agriculture; but these labors brought him into immediate connection with the third estate—the peasants—to whose interests he paid particular attention, as he considered the distance of this order from the throne rendered the monarch's personal interference in their behalf a matter of necessity. He did not, however, venture, though he would not tolerate anything like feudal servitude within his realm, to interfere with the relations then existing between the peasant and his lord, as he feared the effects of every curtailment of prerogative belonging to an order which he desired to see privileged. Of course his endeavors to raise agriculture to anything like its proper elevation proved altogether abortive in consequence. But he made this deficiency in a manner good by introducing a vast number of immigrants from abroad, amongst whom he parcelled out the waste lands, and to whom he lent every assistance in his power. Nothing, indeed, afforded a higher gratification to his heart than to gaze upon what had once been a wilderness, now converted by his agency into a garden. The sums of money which he devoted to these and kindred purposes were incalculable. Previous to the outbreak of the Seven Years' War he had drained several morasses and swamps, and he now extended the blessings of drainage and irrigation to all the provinces of his kingdom. He raised dams to prevent inundations, strengthened the sand-barriers, and rendered them capable of supporting vegetable life. He interested himself in the minutest details pertaining to these subjects, and many of the conversations he held with the provincial authorities during his tours have been rescued from oblivion, and are frequently of unusual interest. Some of those smiling meadows that now gladden the eye and produce rich harvests to their owners are indebted to him for their existence.

Having thus circumscribed the spheres of action of the nobility and peasantry, he revived the mediæval restrictions of guilds and corporations to control the rights of citizenship. But even in the changes that he himself attempted to introduce he was swayed and fettered by his regard for existing institutions. He lent much of his influence, however, to nurse manufacturing industry; and he both advanced large sums of money, and imposed high protective duties to attain this object. The manufacture of porcelain enjoyed his special patronage, and this branch of industry was soon, under his fostering care, able to compete with the productions of Saxony. He displayed, indeed, a particular *penchant* for porcelain, and in order to encourage its manufacture he ordered a grand dinner-service for his own use, and employed porcelain largely in making presents. Formerly, as often as he visited the carnival in Berlin he used to bring with him a large number of snuff-boxes, for presents, which were borne in two chests on the back of a dromedary that had been presented to him by General Czernitscheff, during the Seven Years' War. With a view to the promotion of commerce and trade within his dominions he paid much attention to internal navigation, and amongst other works which remain to the present day to attest the important benefits he conferred on his country, we shall only mention the Bromberg Canal, connecting the rivers Oder and Vistula.

FREDERICK'S INTERNAL ADMINISTRATION.

Though now gradually sinking beneath the weight of years, his ardor for the welfare of his subjects does not seem to have in any degree abated, and we find him as busy as ever in relieving the distresses and administering to the wants of the needy and afflicted of all classes. He provided in seasons of plenty against seasons of scarcity, so that his people might not suffer from their own improvidence. Thus, in the year 1770, the crops proving extraordinarily abundant, so much so that the peasants were in some instances obliged to allow the corn to rot in the ground from want of buildings to store it up, Frederick filled all his vast magazines, and was thus enabled in 1771, which proved a year of unusual scarcity, to retail at low prices, and distribute amongst the poor the corn he had so treasured up. Many thousands died of famine during that year in the adjoining kingdoms, whilst, so far from any one perishing of want in Prussia, whole hosts of foreigners, who sought refuge there, had their wants liberally and promptly relieved.

On the occasion of a disastrous fire desolating the town of Greiffenberg, in Silesia, Frederick immediately placed very considerable funds at the disposal of the magistracy, to assist them in rebuilding the town. The following year, as he was proceeding on a tour of inspection through Silesia, the corporation of Greiffenberg sent a deputation to wait on him in Hirschberg, and express their gratitude. Frederick happened to be seated at a table, with the Prince of Prussia and two aides-de-camp, when the deputation entered. The spokesman of the delegates thus addressed him: " We render unto your majesty, in the name of the inhabitants of Greiffenberg, our humble thanks for the most gracious gift which your majesty deigned to bestow in aid, and to assist us in rebuilding our homes. The gratitude of such dust as we are is, as we are aware, of no moment or value. We shall, however, implore of God to grant your majesty his divine favors in return for this your royal bounty." At these words the tears started in Frederick's eyes, and he uttered the memorable words : " You have no occasion to return me any thanks. I am bound to aid my distressed subjects—it is for that I am here."

By the erection of numerous buildings he continued not only to beautify his capital, but also to give employment to numbers. To the list of noble edifices raised by him in his latter days belong the Library and the huge Gens-d'arm Towers in Berlin. One of these towers, raised in 1780, fell down the following year, but was speedily restored, and the whole vast work completed in 1785.

The improvements introduced by Frederick in the system of popular education were few and unimportant; and this is probably the best-founded objection that can be raised to his government. But, although it be impossible to avoid acknowledging the justice of this reproach, we must not forget that the many restraints which he removed from the thoughts and consciences of his subjects paved the way for that enlightenment amongst all classes, and that spirit of scientific investigation which so strongly characterize the then dawning era. He never to the last lost sight of those principles of religious toleration of which he had been in earlier years the advocate. However free his own individual opinions may have been, he in no case interfered with the religious convictions of others. Persons of all persuasions—and some of the strictest religious principles—were to be found amongst his most intimate friends; he could but envy them the strength of their convictions. He threw no impediments in the way, nor even sought to check religious enthusiasm, as long as it did not overstep the bounds of toleration. The Catholics of West Prussia and those of Silesia were treated with the same paternal lenity and kindness. Nay, out of regard for the beneficial influence exercised by the order of Jesuits on the education of the Catholic priesthood, he tolerated the continuance of that order within his states, even after it had been dissolved by the pope. The severity of the censorship was during his reign much relaxed; he showed himself particularly tolerant of all satires on his own person. The good people of Vienna were on one occasion very much offended at an almanac, published in Berlin, in which several illustrations, taken from Don Quixote, were prefixed and appended to a likeness of the Emperor Joseph. Frederick ordered that he should be the subject of the next year's satire, and his wish was complied with accordingly; the subjects were in his case taken from Orlando Furioso.

The due and impartial administration of justice was of all subjects that which engrossed the greatest share of his attention in the evening of his life. Alluding to its all paramount importance, he uses the following expressions in a letter addressed to D'Alembert, in 1780: "Kings were originally the judges in their respective states; multiplicity of business has since forced them to delegate this office to others. But still they must not wholly neglect this branch of the royal prerogative, and should take especial care that the authority so delegated and exercised in their name is not abused and perverted to evil ends. It is this consideration that compels me to watch narrowly over the administration of justice; for an unjust judge is worse than a highway robber. It is the clear duty of every one presiding over any society of men to secure the rights and property of every member, and endeavor to render each as happy as is consistent with the nature of man. This duty I endeavor to discharge to the utmost of my ability. To what end have I studied Plato, Aristotle, and the Institutes of Solon? True philosophy consists in carrying into practice the wise precepts of the philosophers." Frederick was the more sedulous in his attention to this matter, as the previous sweeping reform had been carried through with too much rapidity to allow of its having been perfected in its details. It had consequently given rise to many incongruities and manifest wrongs. Frederick was also very unwilling that distinctions should be made in the judicial as in the political administration of his people: before the tribunal of justice there should be no orders or castes. Indeed, so far from this, he generally became the champion of the poor against the rich, and in this spirit conferred on the meanest of his subjects the right of applying personally to himself as the appellate tribunal in the last resort. This last measure, whilst it secured him the confidence of the humbler classes of the people, was the means of bringing under his notice some of the most glaring defects of the law. If many of the complaints subsequently poured in upon him were frivolous and groundless, they still, from their number, sufficed to fill him with suspicion, and create strong doubts in his mind as to the impartiality of the judges by whom the laws were administered. Detection in individual instances called forth bursts of such violent indignation as to color the medium through which he viewed the great bulk of the decisions. The following incident which we are about to detail will exemplify the latter part of our statement, and whatever may be the opinions as to the merits of the particular case, it had at least the incidental advantage of having led to the most comprehensive and beneficial judicial reforms.

A miller, of the name of Arnold, held a mill in Neumark from Count Schmettau, for which he paid an annual rent. He fell into arrear, and alleged that a pond, formed immediately above his mill by a neighboring landed proprietor, Justice Gersdorff cut off the supply of water necessary for the working on his mill. Count Schmettau sued the miller for the arrears of rent, and the mill was sold by order of the court. The miller laid several appeals, but his suit was invariably dismissed, as being, under the special circumstances, groundless. He therefore repeatedly applied to the king in person, who at length deputed an officer, whom he considered perfectly impartial, to investigate the circumstances of the case. The report of the latter, who may not have inquired narrowly into the merits, was strongly in favor of the miller. Fresh legal investigations were now, at the king's instance, set on

FREDERICK'S INTERNAL ADMINISTRATION. 425

foot, but led to no other result than the confirmation of the former decision. Prejudiced by the representations of the officers, and indignant at justice, as he conceived, being so long denied the poor man, Frederick referred the matter to the Court Chamber in Berlin, with orders that the matter be brought to a speedy issue. The Court Chamber felt bound to confirm the former decisions. Frederick now began to think that the scales of justice were influenced by the rank of the respective parties, and that the law tribunals were but bent on vindicating their proverbial independence, as opposed to him; he therefore resolved on interfering with a strong hand, and thus afford a warning to all unconscientious judges in future. The circumstances alluded to occurred in the year 1779. The grand chancellor and three justices of the Court Chamber received orders to appear in his presence. They found him in his chamber, laboring under gout in the hand. On their entrance he upbraided them in strong terms with their conduct: "Know ye," said he, "that the pettiest peasant and meanest beggar in my realms is as much a man as the king. A bench of justices that acts unconscientiously is more dangerous than a band of robbers: against the one a person may protect himself, but against villains who employ the mantle of justice to no other purpose than for the attainment of their own dishonest ends and for the gratification of their own passions, no one can be safe. Such persons are the greatest rascals in the world, and deserve double punishment." He dismissed the grand chancellor with a harsh reproof, and at the same time intimated to him that he should not want his services any further; that his place was already filled up. The three justices were committed to prison. A suit was then instituted before the criminal senate of the Court Chamber, against the different tribunals that had previously decided in the matter: the senate acquitted them all and severally. But Frederick, by virtue of his unlimited authority, reversed their decree, sentenced the justices of the Court Chamber to dismissal, to be immured, with several others, for a year in a fortress, and further, to indemnify the miller for his losses and expenses.

The whole transaction, but especially the royal decision, created the most unusual excitement. The king's uncompromising sense of justice formed the theme of praise in distant lands; and his determination, so singularly evinced, to uphold the rights of the meanest of his subjects, was universally and deservedly applauded. At a less distance, however, his conduct produced a strong sensation, and the unhappy objects of royal displeasure were sincerely commiserated, though the benevolent intentions of the monarch were not for a moment questioned. So complete was the confidence reposed in the purity of his intentions, that no one disguised or dissembled his opinion of their merit. Every one hurried to condole with the grand chancellor, so unceremoniously dismissed, and the carriages of the visitants were so drawn up as to be within full view of the palace-windows. A new Austrian ambassador had arrived from Vienna but a few days before, and his hotel being immediately contiguous to the residence of the degraded chancellor, he was altogether at a loss how to explain the conduct of the immense crowd of visitants. "In other countries," said he, "people hurry to pay their respects to the minister who has just received his appointment, but here, as it seems, to the minister who has just been dismissed in disgrace." Universal sympathy was likewise testified towards the unfortunate justices condemned to incarceration, and many expedients were resorted to for the purpose of lightening their sufferings; with these Frederick in no wise interfered. His conduct in this respect was as humane and generous as his intentions were unquestionably pure and paternal.

In the room of the late chancellor Frederick appointed De Carmer, who had been previously minister of justice in Silesia. De Carmer he looked upon as the man of all others best qualified to effect a thorough reform in the legal department, and accordingly commissioned him to prepare the draft of a code of laws and forms of procedure consistent with the spirit and intelligence of the age, and the ameliorated condition of the middle classes in Prussia. De Carmer set about his task with vigor, summoned the ablest lawyers of Prussia to his aid, proposed rewards for the best solution of certain legal difficulties, and thereby eventually succeeded in drawing up a code of laws superior to anything previously known to modern Europe. Frederick did not live to see this work completed, but he is fully entitled to lay claim to its merits and excellencies, notwithstanding, as it was at his instance and under his auspices that the task was undertaken.

CHAPTER XLII.

FREDERICK'S DOMESTIC LIFE IN OLD AGE.

VERY different from that scene of gaiety and life which had once flung its bright but fleeting gladness round the leisure moments of the monarch had the domestic circle of Sans-Souci now become. Many of those bright stars, whose lustrous light had shed a brilliancy on that scene, had long since sunk and set forever, behind the carnage-covered fields of the Seven Years' War. Most of Frederick's joys had long since ceased to have any other existence than in memory's waste;—they had vanished one by one ere he returned from the storms of war to the silence of his solitary asylum. Still his mind loved to pause on those happier days, and he would fondly watch each ray as it fell back, reflected from that sunnier period on his now lone and cheerless path. To perpetuate the memory of his departed sister, the much-loved Margravine of Baireuth, he erected a singular monument, of which he speaks as follows, in a letter addressed to Voltaire, in 1773: "Be it weakness—be it excessive admiration—enough—I have executed that for my sister which Cicero contemplated for his Tullia; I have erected a Temple of Friendship in her honor. It stands in a *bosquet*, and I often go thither to ponder on the many losses I have sustained, and reflect on the many blessings I once enjoyed." The elegance of this marble temple, and the beauty of the landscapes with which it is adorned, possess to this day an indescribable and characteristic charm.

To the memories of the many gallant heroes who had

fallen under his command in defence of their country he now erected marble monuments. A statue of Schwerin, which had been commenced under his orders during the Seven Years' War, was subsequently completed and erected, in the year 1769, in the *Wilhelmplatz*, in Berlin. Others of Seidlitz, Keith, (who had fallen at Hochkirch,) and Winterfeldt were subsequently raised on the place. Zieten, who died but a few months before Frederick, received this mark of honor from Frederick's successor ; and to these five a sixth statue was at a later period added, in honor of the victor of Kesselsdorff, Prince Leopold of Anhalt-Dessau.

Down to the period of the Bavarian war of succession there had still remained to Frederick a few of his more intimate friends, with whom he could talk over the past, and cull such flowers as shot forth in the autumn of his life. The Marquis D'Argens, who had remained so faithful to Frederick during the Seven Years' War, and had written so powerfully in his defence, found, as he advanced in years, the climate of Prussia too rude and cold, and began to long for the genial warmth of his native land—the lovely Provence. Frederick was constrained to grant him leave of absence, and the marquis retired thither in 1764, but as his stay was becoming too protracted, Frederick was necessitated to have recourse to a peculiar artifice to hasten his return. With this view he accordingly issued a pastoral letter, in the name of the Archbishop of Aix, denouncing all Free-thinkers in general and the marquis in particular, and transmitted several copies to persons of D'Argens' acquaintance. This *ruse* had the desired effect; the marquis found it impossible to remain any longer in his native land, and hurried back to Frederick. Some years later he again began to feel a yearning for home, and requested permission to retire thither. This request, however, Frederick peremptorily refused, and the marquis conceiving his detention to be mainly in consequence of his having several of Frederick's confidential letters in his possession, folded them up and returned them, with a further entreaty for permission to retire. Frederick was deeply affected, and granted the request, but sent the letters in the packet unopened, as he had received them, back to the marquis, who, however, left them behind him when he again set out, in 1769, for home, where he died shortly after his arrival.

Two others, Fouqué and Lord-Marshal Keith, remained faithfully by the monarch's side to the last, and enjoyed all those comforts which Frederick, who himself began to feel the weight of years, took care to provide for them. Fouqué, after returning from Austria, where he had been made prisoner, withdrew from the army, feeling himself unequal to the discharge of its duties, and was appointed Provost of Brandenburg, where he accordingly took up his residence. He used to pay frequent visits to Sans-Souci, and when he became too old to travel he was visited by Frederick in his retirement. Frederick was in the habit of sending him everything that could sweeten the enjoyment of life, such as wines a hundred years old, and the choicest delicacies of the table that the royal gardens afforded. To enjoy the pleasure of his conversation in his walks, when Fouqué's legs refused any longer to support his weight, Frederick had a chair made, in which he used to have him drawn along the avenues of Sans-Souci, whilst he himself walked at his side. When the old man's powers of hearing and articulation began to fail him, Frederick contrived a species of voice-conductor, and an instrument by means of which the other could express, mechanically, whatever syllables he found difficult of utterance. Fouqué died in the year 1774.

The intimacy that subsisted between Frederick and Lord Keith, who had been entrusted with several most important diplomatic missions during the Seven Years' War, was of a still more friendly character. He, too, had felt a yearning for home after the close of the war, but being then in his seventieth year, on his arrival in Scotland he felt so isolated and lonely that he returned to Sans-Souci in 1764. Frederick had a house built and fitted up for him immediately beside his own in Sans-Souci, and Keith had the following inscription engraved over the porch: "*Fredericus II., nobis hæc otia fecit.*" The most easy and unrestrained intercourse was thus effected, and Keith professed himself highly satisfied with the life he led in the "Monastery," as Sans-Souci was often jocosely termed. "Our father abbot," he would say, "is one of the jolliest men in the world. But," he would add, "still, if I were in Spain, I should consider myself bound in conscience to denounce him to the Inquisition as a magician, for certainly nothing short of magic can keep me here, where I only see the picture of the sun, whereas I could live and die in Valencia." Keith had formerly passed many happy days in the latter place, and had, as he said, "many excellent friends there —particularly the sun." He remained to the last devotedly attached to Frederick, and was generally known simply by the appellation of "the King's Friend." He died during the Bavarian war, in his eighty-eighth year.

The monarch's special regard was also extended to the aged Zieten, who resided in Berlin, where the king always visited him on his coming to the capital. Zieten fell asleep one day at the royal table, and some person present was about to awaken him, when Frederick interposed, saying, "Let him sleep; he watched long enough over us." In 1784 Frederick went to Berlin, to the carnival, and Zieten, then in his eighty-fifth year, made his appearance in the reception-chamber of the palace. On recognizing him, Frederick advanced to meet him, and, after welcoming him heartily, assured him that he felt exceedingly distressed at his having taken the trouble to mount so many flights of steps. Had he known of his presence, he would have gladly gone down to him. He then inquired after his state of health. "Right good, your majesty," replied the veteran; "I can still relish both meat and drink; but I feel my strength gradually decaying." "I am glad," said Frederick, "to hear the first part of your statement; but you must be tired standing;" and he ordered a chair to be brought. On Zieten refusing to be seated, "Sit down, old father," said Frederick, "otherwise I shall go away, as I do not wish to prove in any way burthensome to you." Zieten was at length seated, and Frederick stood for a long time conversing with him.

With such friends as resided at a distance he still maintained an uninterrupted correspondence and interchange of thought on the most important subjects. His correspondence with Voltaire and D'Alembert is particularly interesting. But the hand of death created new chasms here also. Voltaire died, as we have already stated, during the Bavarian war, about the same time as Lord Keith. The correspondence with D'Alembert comes down as late as the year 1783.

Frederick's domestic life had, after the close of the Seven Years' War, known brief periods of gaiety, in consequence of the festivities attendant on the intermarriage, in 1765, of the Prince of Prussia with the charming Princess Elizabeth of Brunswick. Several guests were daily invited to Sans-Souci; where dancing, music and theatrical representations served to entertain this select circle of friends. The king used to enter with spirit into all these amusements. But the marriage proving unfortunate, it was found necessary a few years afterwards to have it dissolved, and to banish the princess from court. Solitude and gloom soon supplied the place of gaiety and mirth. This Princess Elizabeth, who died on the 18th of February, 1840, in Stettin, at a very advanced age, was the last of those who could speak from actual knowledge of the glories of Sans-Souci.

The outbreak of the Bavarian war determines the period up to which musical entertainments, which had so materially contributed to invigorate Frederick's mind, continued to afford him pleasure. Till then concerts were, as of old, regularly held every evening in the king's apartment. One of these concerts, which took place in the month of September, 1770, on the occasion of Frederick's receiving a visit from the Dowager Electoral Princess of Saxony, is deserving of being noticed here. The princess sang, and played the pianoforte ; Frederick, accompanied by Quanz, led on the flute ; the Hereditary Prince of Brunswick played the first fiddle ; and the Prince of Prussia the violoncello. Quanz died in 1773. The loss of his front teeth prevented Frederick from playing the flute, and once constrained to desist from taking a personal part in the concerts they soon ceased to afford him any pleasure.

We have now seen the royal chamber grow gradually more and more lonely. The very members of the king's own family, and some even in the bloom of youth, dropped off one by one. He was particularly affected by the death of Prince Henry, a younger brother of the Prince of Prussia, a nephew whom he had loved tenderly, and in whom he had placed great hopes. The Prince died in 1767, in the twentieth year of his age. Frederick composed a monologue on his death, in which he gives full vent to the anguish of his feelings. Indeed, his estrangement from his family increased daily. The queen lived in the most complete retirement, devoting her days to the benevolent discharge of every Christian duty, and without having once seen Sans-Souci. She was sometimes honored with Frederick's company at dinner, in the palace at Berlin, during the winter, but no conversation passed between them on such occasions. No public demonstration of any kind took place in honor of the fiftieth anniversary of their marriage, which occurred in 1783. But Frederick took care that every attention and courtsey due to his royal consort as queen should be scrupulously paid. She outlived him eleven years.

Between Frederick and the heir apparent there existed also but little cordiality, for which various reasons have been assigned ; still he testified no ordinary degree of satisfaction at the birth of a grand-nephew, issue of the prince's second marriage, which took place on the 3d of August, 1770. Alluding to the birth of this infant prince, who afterwards became king, under the title of Frederick William III., Frederick, in a letter to Voltaire, speaks as follows:—"I trust that this child will possess those qualities which it should possess; and that instead of its proving a scourge of mankind, it will prove its benefactor." Writing on the same subject to another friend, he says, "An event has occurred of the deepest moment to me and my whole house; and my joy is the more heartfelt as it is shared by my whole kingdom. Could the latter but share with me the gratification of one day seeing this infant prince treading in the glorious paths of his ancestors!" We are not in possession of any details respecting the infant's baptism; but a comparison of the dazzling ceremonials observed under Frederick I., with a description which has come down to us, of the ceremonies observed on the occasion of the baptism of the Prince of Prussia's youngest son, would indeed lead us to think that a mighty revolution must have taken place in this respect in the habits and manners of the age. This latter baptism was appointed for the 10th of July, 1783. The commanding officers of the guard assembled in front of the palace of the Prince of Prussia, in Potsdam, and there awaited the arrival of the king. Frederick came, attended by the Duke of Brunswick, and was immediately ushered by the Prince of Prussia into a saloon, into which the officers followed him. Here, in front of the princess's chamber, stood the young princes, to welcome their grand-uncle; in this room stood also a table, and on it a silver font, and at one side a cradle in which the infant lay; a court-chaplain, the nurse, and ladies-in-waiting were also in attendance. Having passed a few moments in this room, Frederick entered the chamber of the princess, and after a brief congratulation, returned. The infant was now placed in his arms by one of the ladies, and the clergyman dismissed the ceremony in a few words, contenting himself with giving expression to the hope, that the prince might in time prove an ornament and honor to that high lineage from whence he came. This done, the king returned to take leave of the princess. Before quitting the apartment the young princess kissed his hand, and the younger one, Louis, (who died in 1796,) then in his tenth year, kept looking earnestly at his grand-uncle with an uneasy stare. "What is the matter?" asked the king. "Is it that his coat does not suit him any longer? Well! let him put on a soldier's coat, like his brother." The little prince, highly delighted with this permission, returned his thanks; and Frederick departed, attended by the Prince of Prussia. He then mounted his horse, having devoted just seven minutes to the ceremonies we have above detailed.

There was now little to break the placid current of Frederick's existence, except the casual visits of such distinguished strangers as came to see the great man of the age. Many names memorable in the history of nations are to be found amongst his visitants. We shall particularize but two; La Fayette and Mirabeau. The latter was presented to him on the 25th of January, 1785. Thus we find the old and the new era linked together.

Frederick's household consisted of but few persons; his manners were simple and his wants few. The anecdotes told of his treatment of his domestics, exhibit him in the light of a very rigid, but, at the same time, very considerate master. The following incident is so characteristic, that we cannot refrain from mentioning it here. Frederick rang the bell in his chamber; no one came; opening the chamber-door, he found the page-in-waiting asleep in his chair: he went up to him, and was about to awaken him, when he espied a paper protruding from the page's pocket that excited his curiosity. He drew it out and read its contents. It was a letter from the youth's mother, pretty much to the following effect. She thanked her son for the assistance he had lent her out of his savings: God would assuredly reward him for it; and if he served Him with the same zeal and fidelity as he did the king, he would never be in want of blessings. The king went noiselessly back to his chamber, took a roll of ducats, and inserted them with the letter into the page's pocket. He shortly afterwards rang the bell so violently that the page awoke. "Hast thou slept?" inquired the king. The page stammered out a half excuse and half admission, and then thrusting his hand into his pocket, found the roll of ducats. He drew it out, turned pale, and with tears in his eyes looked at the king without being able to utter a word. "What ails thee?" asked Frederick. "Oh, your majesty," replied the page, falling on his knees, "some one wants to ruin me! I know nothing of this money!" "Ho!" said Frederick, "what God gives, He gives in sleep. Send it to thy mother, and tell her I shall take care of her and you."

We now come to speak of the canine companions of royalty, those exquisitely formed greyhounds, whose grace and agility afforded him so much amusement in former days, and in which he continued to take delight up to the hour of his death. Three or four of these animals were constantly about his person, one being the favorite, and the others intended to bear it company. The favorite always lay at its master's side on a chair, which was covered with a cushion in winter, and slept at night in the royal couch. These dogs were permitted to take every liberty, and select the most expensive coverlets for their resting-places. Leathern-balls were placed on the floors of the different chambers for their recreation, and whenever Frederick visited the picture-gallery of Sans-Souci, or strolled about the gardens, they were his constant companions. They even accompanied him to the carnival in Berlin; and on such occasions they rode in a coach drawn by six horses, and were attended by a groom-in-waiting. It is said that this groom used to sit with his back to the horses rather than disturb his canine charge, and that his conversational tone, when addressing them, was scrupulously free from anything like an approach of familiarity. Beside the statue of Flora in Sans-Souci, the spot designed by

FREDERICK'S DOMESTIC LIFE IN OLD AGE. 437

Frederick for his own grave, his favorite dogs lie buried; marble slabs, inscribed with their respective names still mark their graves. Frederick displayed likewise a particular regard for his favorite chargers. He took great care that they should be well treated, and assigned them, according to their respective characters and capabilities, the names of distinguished contemporaries. Thus Brühl, Choiseul, Kaunitz, Pitt, were amongst the number of his favorite steeds. One bearing the title of Lord Bute was obliged to atone for the faults of his namesake; and when England broke from Prussia in 1762 and joined France, Lord Bute was condemned to every species of drudgery, and sent to keep company with mules, and assist them in all their servile duties. Cæsar, a dapple-gray, was a special favorite, and treated with the most distinguished consideration: when old, he was permitted to range at large through the pleasure-grounds of Potsdam Palace, and out of gratitude for this gracious treatment, he always exhibited to the last the greatest delight whenever Frederick came from Sans-Souci to Potsdam to review his troops. It not unfrequently happened on such occasions, that the guard going on parade were obliged to wheel to the right or left to avoid interfering with Cæsar, when he stood in the way. But the most exalted place in the monarch's esteem was occupied by his charger Condé, whose symmetry of limb, fine temper, and great capabilities fully justified this preference. Frederick had two splendid sets of housings of blue velvet, inwrought with silver tissue, specially made for him, and never employed Condé except in short rides for pleasure. He used to have him brought to him daily, and was in the habit of feeding him with sugar, melons, and figs. Condé soon came to know the person of his patron so well, that when let loose, he always came cantering up to Frederick in search of his accustomed dainties, and would sometimes follow the king into the chambers, and even into the saloon of the palace of Sans-Souci.

A solemn stillness seems creeping over Sans-Souci. All mirthful converse, gaiety, wit, have long since died away within its walls. No flute—no chord—are touched within its lonely precincts! One thing alone has not departed, and this it is that still enables the unbroken spirit to bear up against the multiplied infirmities and pains of old age and disease—this talisman of more than magic properties was Frederick's devotion to science; and he seemed to imbibe fresh strength and vigor with the copious draughts he drew from this hygeian fount. The productions of the demi-gods of Greece and Rome, together with the fascinating speculations of the great French school still supplied a fund of entertainment and delight to the aged monarch. Nor does his own intellectual activity decrease. Very many of the productions of his pen are assignable to the latter years of his life—even long subsequent to the Seven Years' War. Indeed, this war was hardly concluded when he became its historian. The partition of Poland and the Bavarian war likewise employed his pen, so that he has left us an almost complete chronicle of all the leading events subsequent to the Silesian war, besides a historical view of many of the most interesting circumstances connected with the government of his predecessors; the whole forming a series of historical records more interesting, perhaps, than any other of the same kind in existence. In his writings we find the strictest impartiality observed in the criticism of his own acts and times. As none of these works were intended for publication during his life-time, his judgment was not warped either by prejudice or favor. His labors were undertaken solely for the benefit of posterity. He also composed several treatises on ethical and political subjects, many of which, as, for instance, his "Treatise on the Forms of Government and the Duties of Rulers," written in the year 1777, and his "Letters on the Love of One's Native Land," are singularly consistent in the advocacy of doctrines, perfectly accordant with the opinions professed by him in his earliest production, "Machiavelli."

Even his latest poetical effusions are pregnant with the same aspirations after eternal truth, and in his elegant "*Unde? Ubi? Quo?*" composed shortly before his death, he seeks to solve those mysterious doubts—to dispel those hovering clouds that darken the soul of man, and preclude the vision of that eternal light as it breaks upon us from beyond the grave.

In connection with literary and scientific labors, a reflection of a most painful nature obtrudes itself upon our memory, and renders us truly sad. Frederick had devoted a long laborious life to the most patriotic and chivalrous service of his country; he had proved himself at once the most uncompromising and successful champion of the interests of his kingdom; he even had the satisfaction of seeing, in the evening of his life, his country honored, respected, flourishing, and rich; his heroism and sagacity had lent a prestige to the whole German name; and Germany had far and wide received enlightenment and renown from his individual talents and exertions. This was indeed the best reward for his labors; but to render it complete—to convince him how entirely he had attained all for which he had ever struggled—he should have been able to see those fruits—the sole, unerring indices of the high moral culture of the tree—those palpable exponents of permanent intellectual elevation. His estimation of mental greatness must have rendered him peculiarly desirous of seeing his people amongst the foremost in the paths of science and intellectual refinement. It is the bitter thought that he might have enjoyed this, which must have been to him the most ardent of his aspirations, and that he did not, that gives us pain. No sooner, in fact, had he restored to the German people their pristine dignity, than there arose a host of gifted spirits, endowed with the noblest attributes of German genius, and songs re-echoed through the length and the breadth of the land, not unworthy of the most glorious days of the Minnesingers. The names of Klopstock and Lessing gave place to those of Winkelmann, Herder, Wieland, Goethe, and others, whose productions are second to none, be their age or clime what they may. But of this Frederick was not aware, and what is still more afflicting to think, betrayed no inclination to comprehend their language. He, who would have given the whole of Homer's Iliad for a single thought in Voltaire's Henriade, could not free himself from the court-etiquette of French poetry. So little did he dream of the nature of that soil in which the poetry of Germany is rooted, that on Professor Myller of Berlin drawing his attention to a splendid collection of the relics of Teutonic minstrelsy, culled from the middle ages, he pronounced them "not worth a charge of powder." He was thus condemned to poverty in the midst of profusion, and failed to derive that pride and satisfaction from the talents and genius of his subjects and countrymen, which he must have otherwise done, had he not perversely and wilfully alienated his mind from his country's literature. And yet, although believing his people still immersed in the rudeness and barbarism prevailing at the period of his youth, he entertained the cheering conviction that Germany was destined, at some future and not very distant period, to burst forth in splendor, and enforce its claims to a proud pre-eminence amongst nations. In 1780 he wrote a lengthened dissertation "On German Literature; its Faults, the Objections generally raised, and the Means of remedying them." This treatise is so imperfect as to be completely worthless, as his acquaintance was limited to the insignificant productions popular in his youth. But the spirit in which the treatise is composed more than compensates for its glaring deficiencies and defects, as evincing the truth and fidelity with which the old king clung to his country to the last. His concluding words contain aspirations, if prophetic, certainly conceived in the most sanguine spirit of prophecy, and are as follows: "We too shall have our classical authors: every one will read them with delight; our neighbors will learn the German language, and it will be spoken with pleasure throughout Europe: it is possible that, when cultivated and improved, it may become the great European language. Those glorious days for our literature are not yet come, but they are approaching. I tell you they will come. I shall not live to see them—my advanced age does not allow me to indulge such a hope. Like Moses I see the land of promise from afar off, though I shall never enter it."

CHAPTER XLIII.

FREDERICK'S DEATH.

REVERED by the generation which had sprung up around him, Frederick, now past his seventieth year, never abated in his solicitude for their welfare, and cordially reciprocated the attachment of a people who felt his glory inseparably intertwined with their existence, and paid him more than filial homage. In truth whenever he appeared amongst his subjects he was received like a father amongst so many children. Reposing the amplest confidence in the love and attachment of his people, his palace, unlike those of most other sovereigns of Europe, required neither cannon nor hireling guards for its defence. The perfectly defenceless state of the royal residence is thus graphically portrayed by a contemporary: "I ascended this hill (Sans-Souci) for the first time in the dusk of a winter evening. On coming in view of that small, memorable house, I found I was already close by his room. I saw a light, but no guard before the house-door: not a soul to ask me who I was or what I wanted. I could see nothing of the kind, and strolled about free and unconcerned in front of this little tranquil abode." Another person describes his having come one evening, accompanied by a page, to Sans-Souci, and on entering an inner chamber, through a half-open door, having found Frederick slumbering on a sofa, the only attendant being a valet, who was fast asleep.

Whenever Frederick rode into town it was quite an

event for the lower orders. The citizens would step in front of their houses and make their obeisances to him as he passed, which he always returned by taking off his hat. Many would walk by his side, so as to be able to take a satisfactory survey of the personal appearance of the great king. He was generally escorted by a troop of youthful urchins, who kept continually shouting, flinging up their caps in the air, wiping the dust off his boots, or giving way to other demonstrations of satisfaction and general approval. With these ebullitions of juvenile loyalty Frederick did not in general interfere; at times, however, he found it necessary to repress the sportive propensities of the more gamesome, especially when they included startling his horse in their pastime; to curb this superabundant buoyancy of feeling Frederick had recourse to a volley of annihilating threats, backed by a brandishing of his staff: it does not appear, however, that the effect was more than very temporary, and it is even on record that on one occasion, when the royal indignation and wrath was vented with more than ordinary energy, and accompanied by the mandate, that they should be off at once, and go to school, the juveniles rallied the monarch with "Ho, ho! he pretends to be a king, and does not even know that Wednesday afternoon is always a half holiday!"

There was an equal degree of anxiety evinced by the upper classes to catch a glimpse of him whenever he went to the opera. "How the heart beat," say an eye-witness, "when a flourish of trumpets and drums announces his arrival, and every one strains to get a view of him. The eyes of the old warriors in the pit are never taken off his."

The respect and admiration paid him in distant lands was quite equal to that enjoyed by him in his own. In the year 1780 a captain of a ship, of the name of Klock, a native of Amsterdam, who had become a citizen of Emden, lost his ship in a storm on the coast of Morocco. Both himself and his crew were carried off in the most horrible captivity to Magadore. As soon, however, as the Emperor Muley Ismael learned that they and their flag belonged to the great king, he had them conveyed to Morocco, and there questioned them about Frederick. "Such strange things," said he, "have come to my ears respecting your king, that my breast is filled with love and admiration of him. The world can boast no greater man than he : as friend and brother I have locked him in my heart. It is, therefore, not my wish that you, who belong to him, should be regarded as prisoners in my realm; and it is my intention accordingly to send you home frank and free to your native land. I have further given orders to my cruisers to respect and protect the Prussian flag wherever they meet it!" Klock and his crew were provided with new suits of clothes, well treated, and received a free passage to Lisbon.

Frederick had entered the world with a feeble frame; many apprehensions for his life had been awakened by its delicacy in his youth. In addition to this, a complication of cares and toils had made many inroads on his constitution. But his body had been so completely case-hardened by fatigue, and his strength so surprisingly developed by exertion, that he bore up with fortitude against the numerous diseases with which he was periodically afflicted. His carriage was no longer erect, but his spirit was as unbroken as ever. His personal appearance is thus described by an eye-witness, a few months previous to his death. " I gazed with feelings of no ordinary interest on this man, whose genius is so grand and person so small, bowed down, as if bending under the weight of his laurels and toils. His blue coat, almost as worn as his body, his high boots, reaching above his knees, his waistcoat covered with snuff—all forming a singular but striking *ensemble*. In the fire of his eye one saw that he had not yet grown old. Though his gait was that of an invalid, one could see that he would still fight like the youngest soldier in his army."

FREDERICK'S DEATH.

But repeated attacks of illness, which became more violent as he advanced in years, were gradually undermining his constitution. "As regards my health," (these are his own words in 1780,) "you will not, of course, be surprised to hear that at the advanced age of sixty-eight I feel the feebleness of years. I am at one time attacked by gout in the hand, at another time by gout in the hip, or ague, and these afflictions, whilst they gradually wear away my life, prepare me for casting off this worn-out covering of the soul." But still he discharged the most onerous of his royal functions with the same punctuality as ever. There was no suspension either of the daily business of his cabinet, or of the daily parade; even the tours through the provinces and the reviews were still continued. As late as August, 1785, we find him sitting for five hours on horseback at a review in Silesia, in the midst of a torrent of rain, bidding defiance to all the inclemency of the elements. A slight indisposition was the only consequence of this rash act.

Towards the autumn of this year a more alarming phase of disease set in; dangerous symptoms of dropsy were soon recognizable. But in the midst of his torturing and harassing sufferings his activity as ruler never abated. All his cabinet business was transacted with the same diligence as in the days of his most robust health. The latter years of his life were marked by the realization of the *Fürstenbund*, a memorable treaty with North America, and several acts of internal administration. Being anxious to deliver his charge faithfully and well into the hands of his successor, he hurried all pending plans and projects to a speedy close, and appropriated not less than three millions of thalers to public uses. The low lands on the Baltic had suffered considerably from inundations; measures were therefore immediately taken to repair the dams, and half a million of thalers were distributed amongst the sufferers. He also took the necessary precautions to provide against the evil consequences of the failure of that year's crops.

Zieten died on the 26th of January, 1786. On learning his death Frederick became very much affected, but composed. Some general officers afterwards came in, but studiously avoided all allusion to the topic, until he himself broached it by saying, "Well, our old Zieten has shown himself a good general even in death. In the wars he always commanded the advanced-guard—he has taken the lead now too. I used to bring up the main body—I'll follow him."

April came, with its warm, genial weather, and Frederick hoped, though his disease was now in a very advanced stage, that he should also participate in the general revival of nature. The beams of the sun and the perfumed breath of spring were grateful to his senses, and in order to enjoy their genial influence he was in the habit of having a chair placed on the steps in front of the Potsdam Palace, where he had passed the winter; he would here sit for hours inhaling the fresh air. Whilst so seated, he one day observed that the sentinels in front were standing with grounded arms, afraid of disturbing him. Beckoning to one of them to advance, he said in a kind tone. "Keep walking up and down, ye cannot stand so long as I can sit."

As early as April he returned to his dearly-loved summer retreat and here made several attempts to ride about on his favorite, Condé; but his strength failed him. His physicians now declared him beyond all medical aid, and even the celebrated Hanoverian doctor, Zimmermann, though his brilliant conversation amused, could afford him no relief. About the beginning of summer dropsy had formally set in, and Frederick's sufferings became indescribably acute. He could no longer endure a recumbent posture of any kind, and was constrained to sit night and day in his arm-chair. Still his manner was free from all peevishness and irritation, and gave no external indication whatsoever of his internal sufferings; not a single murmur or complaint escaped his lips. When seized in the night by a painful fit of coughing, he would call out in an under-tone, so as to avoid disturbing the other attendants, to one of the servants to come and hold him in an upright posture in the couch. The Duke of Courland happened to pay him a visit about this period, and was asked by him whether he was in want of a good watchman, "because," added Frederick, "I am a famous hand at keeping awake all night." All this did not, however, interfere with the business of government. The cabinet councillors, who had been hitherto admitted to his presence between six and seven o'clock in the morning, were now regularly summoned at the somewhat inconvenient hours of four and five. "My state of health," said he, "compels me to put you to this inconvenience, but it will not be of long continuance. My life is at its lowest ebb. I am bound to make the most of such time as is still left me. It does not belong to me, it belongs to the state."

If the afternoon were fine, he would have himself carried out in his chair, and sit in front of the palace, basking in the sun. On one occasion he was overheard to exclaim, as he gazed upon the orb of day, "I shall soon come nearer to thee!"

About the middle of August his disease came to a crisis that seemed to forebode a speedy dissolution. On the 15th he slept until eleven o'clock, with him a most unusual circumstance, and then in a feeble tone of voice, but with his faculties as clear and collected as at any period of his life, transacted his ordinary cabinet business. He dictated the same day several despatches, which for comprehensive clearness would have done honor to the coolest head. He also communicated to the commandant of Potsdam, Lieutenant-general De Rohdich, the necessary dispositions for a manœuvre of the Potsdam garrison, which was to take place the day following, and his arrangements were not only perfectly correct in a strategetic point of view, but admirably adapted to the peculiar nature of the terrain.

On the following morning he became much worse; his

utterance failed him, and he seemed almost lost to consciousness. The cabinet councillors remained unsummoned. De Rohdich entered, and advancing to the monarch's couch, saw him evidently making one grand struggle to summon up all his strength for the performance of his favorite duty. But the sunken eyelids remained closed—the parting lips speechless. He turned his head, with a plaintive look, that seemed to say, "I can do it no longer," and sank back exhausted. De Rohdich left the room in tears.

This day passed likewise without the physical dissolution that had already set in being able to overcome the strong vital principle within him. Night came on; it struck eleven. The king inquired the hour in a distinct voice, and on being told it, replied, "I shall get up at four." A fit of coughing now seized him, and his breathing became violently oppressed. One of the attendants knelt down, and placing his arms round the king's shoulders, sustained him for a while in an upright posture. By degrees the features began to change; the eye became sunken and hollow; convulsions ceased to agitate his frame; the breath of life had fled. Frederick expired a few hours after midnight in the arms of his attendant. Two other domestics and the surgeon were the only witnesses of his end. His death occurred on the 17th of August, 1786.

The new monarch, Frederick William II., arrived the following morning, and paid the last sad tribute of affection to the departed. Clad in the uniform of the first battalion of the Guards, Frederick lay extended on a camp-bedstead. The officers of the garrison were then admitted to pay their respects to the remains of their idolized monarch. The scene was truly affecting. There were not a few moist eyes amongst those present.

At eight o'clock the same evening the body was placed in its coffin by twelve non-commissioned officers of the Guards, and conveyed in a hearse drawn by eight horses to the palace in the town. The adjutant of the Guards rode in front; the twelve non-commissioned officers walked at either side of the hearse; three carriages brought up the rear. As the procession moved mournfully along towards the Brandenburg Gate in Potsdam it was joined by many officers, who took part in the mournful ceremony. The streets of Potsdam were filled with vast crowds, but a death-like stillness rested on all; nought reached the ear but the ill-suppressed sob, or the plaintive sigh for "the poor, good king!" At the entrance of the palace the coffin was received by four colonels, and laid out beneath a canopy in state. His body was to be seen here the whole day, attired in his ordinary simple dress-suit, his gray locks slightly powdered and tastefully arranged. The expression of the face was that of seriousness and repose. His staff, sword, and sash lay beside him. Thousands hurried from Berlin and the small towns in the neighborhood to cast a last look on the father of his country.

The vault in the terrace of Sans-Souci which Frederick had marked out for his own grave seemed to his successor unworthy to become the resting-place of so great a king. The new ruler decided on the vault under the chancel of the garrison church, which contained the ashes of Frederick William I., as the more fitting place of interment. Thither, on the evening of the 18th of August, the procession moved, attended by the officers of the army, the magistracy, and the members of the household. Two clergymen preceded the coffin, and accompanied it to the entrance of the vault. The muffled tones of the organ breathed, "We are thine, O God, unto eternity." The text of the sermon preached throughout the land in memory of the departed was everywhere taken from the First Book of Chronicles: "And I have made thee a name like the name of the great that are in the earth." The solemn obsequies were performed on the 8th of September in the garrison church of Potsdam.

It would be indeed difficult to convey an idea of the universal sorrow felt throughout the world at the blank created by Frederick's death. He whom the world had so emphatically styled the Great—the One—was now no more. Perhaps no better index to popular feeling at the time can be found, than the exclamation of a simple Swabian peasant: "Who is now to govern the world?"

FREDERICK'S LAST WILL AND TESTAMENT.

FREDERICK's dispositions were, in the most important particulars, as follow:

"Our life is a fleeting passage from the moment of our birth to that of our death. Man's destination within that brief period is to labor for the welfare of the society of which he is a member. From the time of my succeeding to the administration of the affairs of state, I have labored with such strength as nature bestowed upon me, and to the utmost of my small abilities, to render the community over which I had the honor to preside prosperous and flourishing. I have upheld law and justice; I have introduced order and punctuality in the management of the finances; I have introduced a degree of discipline into the army that has enabled it to cope with and transcend the armies of the rest of Europe. Having thus discharged my duty to the state, I should reproach myself were I to neglect the affairs of my own family. To preclude, then, all possible dissension or dispute amongst the more immediate members thereof in respect of my property, I declare, by virtue of this solemn record, my last will to be as follows:—

"I give and bequeath, freely and without reluctance, this breath of life that animates me to the same beneficent Nature that lent it to me, and my body to the elements of which it is composed. I have lived as a philosopher, and as such I desire to be buried—without ostentation, show, or pomp. I do not wish that my body should be either opened or embalmed. Let me be placed in the vault I have had prepared in the terrace of Sans-Souci. Should

I die in battle, or whilst travelling, then let me be buried in the nearest spot, and afterwards transferred in winter-time to Sans-Souci.

"I bequeath unto my dear nephew, Frederick William, as unto my immediate successor, the kingdom of Prussia, the provinces, towns, palaces, forts, fortresses, all ammunition and arsenals, all lands, mine by inheritance or right of conquest, the crown-jewels, gold and silver services of plate in Berlin, my country-houses, collections of coins, picture-galleries, gardens, and so forth. I also specially bequeath unto him the treasury, in such condition as it may be in on the day of my death, on trust, as belonging of right to the people, and only to be applied to their protection and support.

"Should it appear that at the time of my decease I have left any small debts unsatisfied, the payment of which had been prevented by my death, such are to be paid by my successor. This is my will.

"To the queen, my consort, I bequeath, in addition to the revenues of which she is at present in receipt, the annual sum of ten thousand thalers, two casks of wine yearly, together with firing, and game for her table free of all charge. In consideration of the above the queen has promised to appoint my nephews her heirs. As there is no fitting place of residence to make over to her, let it be Stettin, nominally. But I hereby require of my nephew to provide her with suitable apartments in the palace at Berlin free of all charge: he is to pay her that respect she is entitled to as his uncle's wife, and one who never forsook the paths of virtue.

"As to my personal property. I have never been either covetous or rich, and have consequently not much property to dispose of. I have ever looked upon the treasury as the ark of the covenant, which no profane hand should touch. I have in no instance applied the revenue to my own private uses. My annual expenditure has in no instance exceeded two hundred and twenty thousand thalers. My management of the treasury leaves my conscience free from all reproach, and I should not object to going into a full account of my trusteeship.

"I appoint my nephew, Frederick William, my sole heir."

After enumerating certain provisions to be made and legacies to be paid by his successor, he proceeds as follows:

"I recommend with all affection and attachment unto my successor, the officers who have served under my command in the wars. I particularly beg that he provide for such as served on my personal staff; that he do not dismiss any of them, nor permit them in sickness or old age to perish of want. He will find them intelligent soldiers—men who have given proofs of their abilities, courage, devotion, and valor."

He recommends in a similar manner his private secretaries and household. After certain other dispositions, he closes with these words:

"I further recommend unto my successor to honor his family in the persons of his uncles, aunts, and other relatives. Chance, which presides over the destiny of man, determines primogeniture, and one is not more worthy because of his being king. I recommend all my relations to live in amity, and not to forget to sacrifice their individual interests for the general good.

"My most fervent aspirations, when breathing my last, shall be for the prosperity of my kingdom. May its government be ever conducted with justice, wisdom, and decision. May the mildness of its laws render it the happiest, and the due administration of its finances the most prosperous of states! May its army, mindful of nought but honor and renown, render it the most valiantly defended of kingdoms! Oh, may it continue in the enjoyment of the most perfect prosperity to the end of time!"

THE END.

www.ingramcontent.com/pod-product-compliance
Lightning Source LLC
Chambersburg PA
CBHW031306150426
43191CB00005B/92